Motion Picture Photography

# Motion Picture Photography

## A History, 1891–1960

H. Mario Raimondo-Souto

McFarland & Company, Inc., Publishers
*Jefferson, North Carolina, and London*

Manuscript translated from the Spanish by Herbert M. Grierson

LIBRARY OF CONGRESS CATALOGUING-IN-PUBLICATION DATA

Raimondo Souto, H. Mario.
Motion picture photography : a history,
1891–1960 / H. Mario Raimondo-Souto
    p.    cm.
Includes bibliographical references and index.

ISBN-13: 0-978-7864-2784-0
ISBN-10: 0-7864-2784-1
(softcover : 50# alkaline paper) ∞

1. Cinematography—History—20th century.
2. Cinematography—History—19th century.   I. Title.
TR848.R35  2007       778.5'30904—dc22      2006027781

British Library cataloguing data are available

Cover image ©2007 Comstock

Manufactured in the United States of America

McFarland & Company, Inc., Publishers
Box 611, Jefferson, North Carolina 28640
www.mcfarlandpub.com

# Table of Contents

# Preface

Here is a book designed for those who are researching, studying or working on any of the main aspects of the profession of recording moving images. This is a trade that has long involved and still involves many people in the field of cinematography. This art was born together with motion pictures and has a vast heritage we must know and appreciate to better value its possibilities.

More than a century has passed since the birth of the film medium, sometimes called the seventh art, and this discipline maintains its fascination. Those who practice it, the cameramen, must constantly keep up to date with technology in preserving the moving image day by day. But it is also necessary, at times, to look back to realize the achievements made, so as to make sure one is on the right track towards the best aesthetic and practical performance of this task.

This book intends to give an accurate picture of how this craft came about, who its pioneers were, how the techniques and means were developed decade after decade, and what resources were used during those early golden years so full of meaning. It also intends to show certain details of changes in the motion picture camera and varied allied equipment built in many different parts of the world.

It also tries to show the life, the hard work and the challenges experienced by technical crews and performers in the half century when cinematography was taking its present shape: the director of photography and his assistants in the studio, the special photographic effects expert, and the newsreel, the documentary, and the war cameraman.

The author also wants the present generation to get to know the cinematography of the past in all its varieties, so as to understand the love and devotion of its practitioners to their profession, how they advanced in it, and their foremost achievements.

He also wants to show the progress made by companies, researchers, investigators and technicians in the advance of cinematography, the design of cameras and their complementary equipment, wide screen and 3-D processes, color systems, special effects, lighting and metering equipment, the manufacturing of raw stock, and complex equipment for processing and printing.

The second home of the cameraman was on many occasions the motion picture studio, where the "magic" of this profession is elaborated. The author also wants to show how these installations came about in different parts of the world, what facilities and peculiarities they had, the atmosphere in them, and how they were sometimes affected by international affairs.

The most representative creations of cinematography during the golden years are discussed in this book to give the reader an idea of how they came about, in what circumstances many films were made and who the artists were who created those images.

Unfortunately the whole theme is too vast. It seems that too many names, too many stories and too many feats had to be summarized to write this book. So the most important accomplishments were selected in the period through 1960, which covers the richest and most effervescent years, when beautiful black-and-white images alternate with richly colored pictures and with the spectacular effect of the wide screen and 3-D, and when the contribution of craftsmanship had not been constrained by new technology substituting for the human factor.

This work also intends to report how things were done in the past, and what means were then devised by human ingenuity, as background for a cultivated cinematographer, whether he now records images with photochemical or electronic means.

The author hopes that the discerning researcher would analyze the notable films listed in view of the easy access to DVD and videotaped copies to better appreciate the concepts expounded in the text. He also hopes that new and old active cameramen should, in these pages, re-encounter well known colleagues, old practices, and equipment used in some countries but not others, and that searchers of vintage instruments should have here another source with data on little known equipment.

The author wishes to recognize the generous contribution of his late and dear friend Daniel Arijon, who helped greatly in this book. He also wishes to express special thanks to his colleague César Seoane Cabral for his continued encouragement with this project. Thanks are also due to the American Society of Cinematographers for the use of reference material in the *American Cinematographer* and the Society of Motion Picture and Television Engineers of reference material in *SMPTE Journal*. Special thanks are also given to Arnold & Richter Cine Technik, Munich; Juan José Mugni and Alfredo Castro, who kindly provided photographs for this work.

Moreover, the author wishes to thank his friend Alfredo Baldi from the Scuola Nazionale del Cinema, Rome, for the valuable material supplied, as well as for that from Associazione Italiana Autori della Fotografia Cinematografica, Rome; Larry Roberts, Hollywood; Vaclav Simek, of National Technical Museum, Prague; Vladimir Opela, director and curator of Film Archiv, Prague; Javier Soto, Madrid; Oscar Mendoza and Musitelli Ciné, Montevideo; Francisco Tastàs Moreno, Buenos Aires; and Michael Rogge of Cinematographica, Amsterdam.

Finally the author would like to express his gratitude for the patient and careful work made by Herbert M. Grierson, who translated the text and supervised the language of the English version of the book, supplying useful suggestions.

H. Mario Raimondo-Souto

# PART I
# THE BEGINNINGS

## 1. Chronology of an Invention

The complex knowledge that brought about motion picture photography in itself and as a profession evolved over a very period; however, a compilation is needed of the facts that contributed through the years to the gradual appearance of photography first, and then the moving image.

In Egypt of the Ptolemies (347 BC) image production was discovered. An outside image could be obtained in a black covered body: making a very small aperture on a side, a projection of light rays on the opposite inner surface was obtained making up an inverted image of the lighted external surrounding.

In the Middle Ages the English Franciscan monk and scientist Roger Bacon rediscovered this physical principle toward 1260, though at the risk of his life as he was accused of witchcraft, but was saved by Pope Clement IV. During the Renaissance this principle was called by the Latin name of *Camera Obscura*, used by illusionists, conjurers and painters using devices which were made to this purpose. Leonardo da Vinci used and described it in his writings. Benvenuto Cellini also appreciated its possibilities and worked on its development. In the year 1544 the astronomer Frisius used this method when studying a solar eclipse. Towards the end of the sixteenth century Giambattista della Porta worked to perfect this principle, making a portable unit adequate to a painter's requirements by adding a lens to the small aperture and a mirror which produced a radical improvement in the image quality and luminosity. Later on, the famous Venetian painter Canaletto, an expert in perspective, overcame difficulties with such an instrument to make perfect paintings of his city's canals and views. During the seventeenth century and onwards this device was used also to project drawings on a glass by means of an oil lamp and a lens condenser. Athanasius Kircher, a German Jesuit, in 1654 described this apparatus, called a magic lantern, which was later used by conjurers.[1]

In the following years this "black chamber" continued to be improved with optical lenses by William Hyde Wollaston and others, being intensely adopted by conjurers and portrait painters. The use of sensitive material placed in this camera allowed the creation of photography toward the second decade of the nineteenth century by Nicéphore Niepce, Mandé Daguerre and Fox Talbot. After this the invention of the moving photographic image was now close. It became possible after experimenting and applying the physical property of live beings: the persistence of vision.

The Greek philosopher and mathematician Ptolemy in A.D. 130 wrote some books about optics which explained the physical persistence of vision by exposing how a disk colored on one surface was totally discolored when it was rotated rapidly. Many centuries later this physical property was used for effects created by the Abbé Jean-Antoine Nollet in about 1765 with moving artifacts.

Towards 1824 Dr. Mark Roger made experiments with figures on cards that changed their size and shape when rotated. In those years some toys appeared. One, called a Thaumatrope, was conceived by Dr. W.A. Fitton; two separate drawings, a bird and a cage on each face of a disc, appeared as one when the disc was rotated. These toys or instruments continued being conceived with complex names, such as the Phénakistiscope of the Belgian Plateau in 1832, the Zootrope or wheel of life of William George Horner in 1834 and the Praxinoscope of Émile Reynaud in 1877, which incorporated a central mirrored prism to send images to the viewer. Reynaud improved this device considerably in 1892 to produce the "optical theatre" where a long strip with drawings was projected in a fifteen minute show.[2]

In the last two decades of the nineteenth century, the basic elements that allowed the production of the moving image reached the required level. These elements were: the photographic image, derived from the camera obscura and the evolution of sensible emulsions; the photographic image projection; the progress of the primitive magic lantern incorporating strong light sources; and the knowledge of the fundamentals of image persistence that allowed breaking up the movement of figures. The only missing link was to create an effective device to produce successive photographic images of a body in motion.

In 1878, to win a $25,000 bet, the English photographer Eadweard J. Muybridge made, in the U.S.A., one of the most successful records of movement synthesis using twelve and later twenty-four photographic cameras to register horse foot movements during a trot.[3] In 1882 the French doctor Étienne-Jules Marey conceived a "photographic rifle" based on a device built four years later by an astronomer named Jules Janssen, who recorded Venus' transit of the Sun. Marey's "rifle" used twelve light-sensitive plates to record animal and human movements. Later he developed a camera to obtain exposures of the different positions of animals or a human body in a single light-sensitive strip.

In 1887–88 Marey built an apparatus named the Chronophotographe with a design very similar to the later classic motion picture camera, with a lens, a special shutter, a gate, an intermittent mechanism, and sensitized Kodak paper film, including loops, two reels, and a hand crank. During the 1889 Paris Exhibition, Marey presented this camera to Thomas Alva Edison.[4]

Marey's assistant, Georges Demény, improved Marey's device in 1891 and took a close-up of himself talking to this camera. Later he included such images in an apparatus he called a Phonoscope with a glass disc with the images combined with a shutter. The result was striking. It was the first motion picture close-up effect ever obtained and projected. Thomas A. Edison was also impressed by it and made comments about it in 1894.[5]

After Marey's and Demény's experiments, two inventors who worked in this field made interesting improvements in motion picture recording. One was a Frenchman, Louis-Edmée-Auguste Leprince, a producer of diorama shows who first built a complex camera with several lenses and redesigned it in 1890, leaving only one lens and using sprocket holes in the light-sensitive strip. The other was an English photographer named W. Friese Green who in 1888 built a motion picture camera with perforated light-sensitive paper. In 1890 the paper was substituted with perforated celluloid which was moved vertically and had six round holes at each side of the image. The film speed of the camera was approximately four frames per second.[6]

During the eighties and nineties several well known manufacturers of light-sensitive materials were founded: around 1867, Agfa in Berlin, Germany; in 1879, Ilford Photographic Company, by Alfred Hugh Harman, in Ilford, Essex, England; in 1880, Eastman Dry Plate and Film Company, by George Eastman in Rochester, N.Y. (later named Eastman Kodak Film Company); in 1892 Perutz A.G. by Otto Perutz, in Munich, Germany; and in 1894 Gevaert & Cie, by Lieven Gevaert in Antwerp, Belgium.

In 1888, in the United States, the Scotsman William Dickson obtained a long requested employment with Thomas A. Edison's firm and was in charge of developing a motion picture apparatus. That same year, after long research, Henry N. Reichenbach, an engineer at Eastman Kodak, produced a satisfactory transparent celluloid film, and the next year it was produced with photographic emulsion in rolls 200 ft. long by 1.377 in. wide. In 1891 Dickson developed the Kinetograph, a motion picture camera to be used with celluloid film bought from Eastman Kodak, which was cut the same size and with rectangular perforations on both sides. This was the first effective instrument conceived to obtain motion picture photography, made by a big enterprise, which had been developed for practical use.[7]

In the Kinetograph camera the film traveled horizontally by means of two sprockets. It was driven by an electric motor and the working speed was 46 frames per second. The film gate covered four film perforations at each side. The film was wound in fifty foot capacity reels forming a double magazine unit on a side of which was the film gate opposite the film lens. In front of the lens was a large shutter. The camera was considerably heavy and required a large base. The motor had to be connected to the main electric supply. The instrument was designed to be coupled to a phonograph to take shots synchronized with sound.

In 1893 Edison put the Kinetoscope on the market. It was an individual viewing machine, designed by Dickson, which allowed viewing the images taken with the Kinetograph. The Kinetoscope, a huge apparatus, worked by inserting a coin to allow viewing by one person at a time. A 56 ft. film band passed behind a magnifying unit, driven by a continuous movement. The mechanism included a rotating shutter which produced an intermittent movement over a light source as each frame came up. The film circulated inside in long loops. The machine was driven by means of an electrical motor. This was the first commercialization of motion pictures, which was very successful in its first exhibition and was an important incentive to other inventors. However Edison did not consider the Kinetoscope had a commercial future and did not patent it outside the United States to save about $150. In 1895, after producing some films for the Kinetoscope, Dickson left the Edison organization. Kinetoscope sales dropped and in 1896 Edison manufactured the Vitascope, a motion picture projector which included film loops, and designed by C. Francis Jenkins and Thomas Armat around 1895.[8]

In the United Kingdom, Birt Acres, an American born scientist experimenting in the field of photography and moving picture appliances, joined forces in 1895 with Robert William Paul, an English scientific instrument maker. Paul had been dealing with this kind of apparatus when he was requested to build several units similar to the Kinetoscope, since this equipment had not been patented in England; Paul made several units, some of which went to France.

Paul was also requested to produce films for this apparatus to cover Britain and France. With the help of Acres he undertook the enterprise of producing a movie camera, which was patented March 29, 1885, a month and half after the Cinématographe of the Lumière brothers. Paul's camera was very portable; it had two film compartments, one on top of the other, and a large shutter behind the lens. It used an intermittent mechanism based on a double Maltese Cross of seven blades. It had a side viewfinder and was driven by means of a large crank wheel. With this camera Paul filmed the 1895 Derby and the opening of the Kiel Canal.

The association of Acres and Paul broke up that year, and Paul subsequently constructed a motion picture projector, patented in 1896. Primarily known as the Theatrograph this projector was renamed the Animatographe and installed in the Olympia Theater and later in the Alhambra Theater in Leicester Square, London, where Paul exhibited films with great success for some time. Later Paul continued with the construction of an important number of cameras and projectors for the British and overseas markets after entering the field of film production.[9]

Another European forerunner of cinematography was the Italian Filoteo Alberini who in December 1895 patented "a motion picture camera for taking, printing and projecting a film." After making other inventions as a panoramic wide film camera he founded an important studio and producing company in Rome called "Cines." In 1897 two other Italians built their own motion picture camera. One was Luigi Sciutto in Turin and the other was Oreste Pasquarelli in the town of Alessandria.[10]

In Germany, Dr. Ottomar Anschütz made several experiments. Later on, Max Skladanowsky patented in 1895 an apparatus named the Bioskop using perforated celluloid film in two linked projectors that operated at eight frames per second with a dissolving mechanism to combine both units. Skladanowsky was followed in 1896 by Oskar Messter who manufactured projectors, the Thaumatograph camera, slow motion cameras, film perforators, printers, developing apparatus and amateur film equipment and was also an important film producer in that country.[11]

The name that together with Edison and Dickson deserves to be listed among the fathers of motion picture photography is undoubtedly that of the Lumière brothers. Louis and August Lumière, under the direction of Antonie, their father (who was a painter and photographer), founded around 1981, a photographic factory in Lyon, manufacturing photographic plates. The plant flourished thanks to the talents of Louis, who developed an improved photographic emulsion. In the mid–1890s, the plant was considerably important; it produced 50,000 dry plates a year and 4,000 meters of photographic paper, with a labor force of 300 workers. About 1894 the Lumières already knew of Marey's and Demeny's experiments and Antonie had seen the Kinetoscope show in Paris. There is information that he even bought one Kinetoscope unit. They had been in the photographic trade for years and had their own ideas of how to handle motion picture photography.[12]

They found that the Edison Kinetoscope had faults: specifically that the pictures had to be shown on a screen, and that a reliable intermittent system was necessary, capable of producing steady and clear large-size images. They began to design a portable instrument ideal for taking motion pictures. One night in 1884, August went to his brother's room; Louis was in bed but awake. August told Louis that on trying to sleep he found a solution to the intermittent mechanism they were searching for. It was by placing an eccentric cam inside a frame, as in the sewing machines. They immediately began working with the firm's chief mechanic, Eugène Moisson, on the prototype of this camera based on the principle of the portable photographic still cameras, the vertical displacement of a perforated film strip, an intermittent mechanism actuated by an eccentric cam and a hand cranking drive. The initial speed was 10 and later 16 frames per second.[13]

During the building period they used strips of paper that Moisson perforated with a special punch he had made. Later they imported celluloid from the New York Celluloid Company, to which they applied emulsion, and stripped and perforated it. In September

1894 they made the definitive test of the camera, shooting the famous film *La Sortie des Usines*, which was developed, printed and then projected in their plant for their collaborators and friends.

The camera conceived by the Lumière brothers was different in many aspects from the one designed by Dickson and Edison. The unit was small and light with a wooden body, following the concepts then used in still cameras. The rotary shutter was behind the lens. The supply magazine was of 50 ft. capacity, the same as the Kodak film supply of Edison. The film was also 35 mm wide but with one round perforation at each side of the frame. The camera included a film channel and an exposure gate. The film drive was by means of a hand crank. The drive speed was sixteen frames per second. The film moved vertically from up to down.

The first patent was obtained on February 13, 1895, and improvements were patented later: in the design of the intermittent eccentric cam, the interchangeable shutter for film projection, and the inclusion of the name of the instrument, the Cinematographe. The first public show of their first film was March 22, 1895, organized by the Société d'encouragement à l'industrie nationel. Several other private exhibitions were made afterwards prior to the successful show for the general public in the cellar of the Gran Café in Paris, on December 28, 1895, and with paid access.[14]

The Lumière brothers made an arrangement with Jules Carpentier, an excellent scientific instrument constructor, to manufacture a very complete instrument of good design and finish which was capable of working as camera, printer and projector, abilities not found in any other similar device. The Lumières later undertook the sale of their instrument, the production of negative film using celluloid provided by Victor Planchon's firm and the production of motion pictures taken by operators he organized and sent to several parts of the world. Thus the long search of a practical media for filming and exhibiting motion picture images was completed, establishing the fundamental principles that still are maintained today.

# 2. The First Cameramen

When the first motion picture cameras appeared, very few of their inventors realized the importance and consequences of the instruments they had devised. A new medium and a new industry had been born, which in the near future would require diverse specialized activities. The most immediate was the job of operating the machine. Many of the several creators of movie cameras, like William K.L. Dickson, Louis and August Lumière, Robert Paul, Birt Acres, Filoteo Alberini and others, were the first cameramen that came about, and many of them had a close relationship to their instrument, shooting several films with it.

For some time, Dickson worked with Edison's Kinematograph, shooting a large number of brief films destined for that company's catalog of shows to be viewed with the Kinetoscope, which by 1894 reached nearly sixty titles shot in a small studio named Black Maria. They mainly showed dancers, conjurers, cowboy skills and boxing matches against a black background. After leaving the Edison firm, Dickson continued working in his own business as inventor and cameraman. His next work was for the American Mutoscope and Biograph Company using a large Mutoscope camera he had invented, with a complex design to avoid Edison's patents. As cameraman and supplier of films to the Biograph Company, he covered a large number of events in Europe, e.g. Queen Victoria's Diamond Jubilee in 1897, the first motion picture taken of Pope Leo XIII at the Vatican in 1898 and the Boer War, 1899–1900 in South Africa.

It could be said that the new profession of cameraman, which Louis Lumière named "operateur," came after the invention of his "child," the Cinematographe. After creating their camera, the Lumière brothers quickly planned to exploit this invention in their new business undertaking. They understood that it would be more attractive to show the films on the screen. Their profit would not be selling the new instrument, but producing and exhibiting films for the new and exciting show medium. They had the machine invention rights, they could produce the raw stock and they were ready to form an important staff to produce and project their films (that they called "panoramas") the world over in order to prepare the future market. Soon after the first private exhibition, Louis began to shoot films himself of the most varied subjects, so as to have interesting material for the premiere and to start his film catalog.

Louis Lumière had a natural instinct for organization. He had been a photographer; he knew well how to select and contrive the most attractive subjects and his main interest was to show real life under the sun. He and his brother were educated men with a scientific inclination. Louis once saved the company when he invented an improved photographic emulsion known as Ettiquette Bleu, placing his company advantageously in the world's photo industry. This rational approach inspired him from the start and was often applied.[1]

When he and his mechanic Moisson developed the prototype of the camera, several problems had to be overcome. First was manufacturing long strips of photographic paper to test the new invention; this required building a perforating machine to produce regular round holes on both sides of the paper, as noted above. They made several tests to obtain the proper results. A working method had to be conceived to develop and print such unusually long strips. The tests with celluloid also required similar research which had never before been done. This was the experience they gained before the final stage of shooting with the prototype film.

Perhaps the practical sense of Louis was applied when they decided to shoot a natural scene for the final celluloid test, selecting a very simple subject with human interest, close by, and connected to their working shop, where the new camera had been born. Perhaps he foresaw that this first film, made in March 1895, *La Sortie des usines* (*Workers Leaving the Lumière Factory*), could also be an excellent piece of publicity for their company, showing the factory where their invention had been designed, and the considerable number of employees working in it. Some said that this was the first commercial film ever made.

But if his first film was very effective on the viewers, the impression he prepared for the selected audience of his colleagues of the French Photographic Societies seems to have been more calculated. There he projected for them in June 1895, twenty-four hours after shooting, the *Dèbarquement du congrès de photographie* (*Arrival of the Conventioners*) showing themselves on the screen, landing from a ferry in the Saône, including Jules Janssen discussing with his friend Lagrange. This was a tour de force that astonished his audience and produced continuous applause from the qualified audience.

Excited by the results obtained in the preliminary free exhibitions, Louis Lumière started his production plans. At that early time, he personally shot, as cameraman, more than thirty films on the most diverse subjects. He also began the training project to teach new "operateurs" to carry on this job in different spots of the globe, shooting attractive aspects of other countries, their people and different types of events. They had to be not only cameraman but also mentally enterprising representatives of his firm. They must shoot kings, czars, emperors, presidents and important military ceremonies. They must not only project the films made in Lyon, but also include subjects of local interest to attract their audiences. They had to send the newly obtained material to Lyon to be incorporated into the firm's archive and included as new titles in its catalog. That was to be the headquarters of processing and printing copies to be distributed to their correspondents the world over.[2]

During his cameramen's training Louis emphasized the need to keep the technical characteristics of his camera secret, to make no comments on it, nor allow anyone to see it, not even kings nor pretty women. They must be very careful in keeping their instrument in a safe place and if they were invited to eat after work, they must keep the camera between their legs.

The new "operateurs" were taught to develop a considerable skill in their new profession. They learned how to thread the camera when shooting, framing and focusing through the gate (the camera had no viewfinder). The lens used gave them good image quality and a depth of field from three feet to infinity. They learned how to expose and select their position in relation to the sun. They learned how to print with the same camera, select the printing light and the correct distance from it.

Finally they also were taught how to use the camera as a projector, controlling the arc light, the Molteny projection lantern and the use of ether lanterns if there was no electric supply. The dangers of this operation had also to be borne in mind. General recommendations were given also on how to organize shows, the use of hotel facilities for them, and how to select the program. They were also taught methods to send negative material to Lyon.

Louis Lumière selected those most accomplished for this kind of work from among his collaborators. One was André Carré, who traveled with Lumière's representative, Louis Jannin, to Constantinople. Carre installed his headquarters in the Srpska Kruna Hotel in Serbia. He formed a working team with A. Valhora and Jules Gérin and organized several film shows. In Belgrade he made more film shows in the presence of King Obrenovitch and Queen Nathalie. After this, he moved to Romania and, following instructions, he used several important hotels in that country. He also took films of his travels, including a journey on the Danube.

Another well known cameraman of Lumière was Francis Doublier, who was the young man in the film *Workers Leaving the Factory* who mounts his bicycle and leaves. Louis felt Doublier had the required personality and trained him in this profession. He was sent first to Belgium, and then to Germany, Poland and Spain, where he shot some bullfights. Lumière decided to cover the coronation of Czar Nicolas II and sent Moisson to Russia to head the operation with Doublier. There, trouble occurred on May 28, 1896, when around 5000 people died when the police charged on the crowd during an act of delivering presents. They covered it with about 400 ft. of film, but the authorities seized the film and the camera, and no footage of this disaster was seen.[3]

Moisson returned to France and Doublier made a new trip to Germany, then returned to Russia, established himself in Moscow and opened a film theater. In 1899 Doublier traveled to Odessa, Constantinople, Cairo, Bombay, Shanghai and Peking. In 1900 Doublier returned to France and afterwards went to the United States where, in 1902, he opened an American branch of Maison Lumière in Burlington, Vermont.

Constant Girel was sent to Germany in 1896 where he filmed several events, such as the dedication of the monument to Emperor William I in Breslau and shot without permission German warship maneuvers in Görlitz. He also filmed some interesting coverage of the Rhine River. After returning to France he filmed the arrival of Czar Nicholas II at Cherbourg. Later on he went to Italy where he found his colleagues Charles Moisson, Alexandre Promio and Marius Chapuis. In 1897 Girel went to Saigon and followed on to Japan, taking shots of Tokyo and Kyoto.[4] The same as in the Far East, Édouard Porta, M. Tax and Gabriel A. Veyre covered the capitals of some South and Central American countries such as Chile, Colombia, Cuba and Mexico. Porta later went to the United States, working in New York and San Francisco.[5]

Another well known cameramen taught by Louis Lumière was Félix Mesguich, a young Algerian, who, after his military service, joined the Lumière cameramen and projectionist crew. First he worked in France projecting films and then went to the United States, where he make an important showing of Lumière's films in the B.F. Keith Music Hall in New York. Later on he went to Canada and Russia, returning finally to France. His book *Tours de Manivelle* (*Turning the Crank-handle*) was an interesting account of his work in this field. Another cameraman was Marius Sestier who shot films in far overseas countries, such as India and Australia; he organized many film shows in Australian cities and took shots of that country.[6]

Alexander Promio was one of the most prolific correspondents of the Maison Lumière.

He made films in Spain, Belgium and Italy, where he shot his famous Grand Canal coverage from a Venetian gondola, the first travelling film ever made, an idea inspired by the appeal of passing images on a gondola trip. Its effect was so successful that later on he made similar traveling shots from a train, an elevator and a ship on the Nile River. Other Lumière cameramen also used this technique, filming from a train. Later on Promio visited many countries. In the United States he took shots in Boston, Washington and New York. About 1897 he traveled to Egypt, Turkey and Sweden; there he filmed the Stockholm exhibition. There also he met and taught his profession to Ernest Florman, son of the Swedish court photographer, who became the first Swedish cameraman. In June 1897 he covered the Jubilee of Queen Victoria and in 1901 returned to England to film her funeral. Promio contributed a long list of films to the Lumière film catalog.[7]

The cameramen taught in Lyon by Louis Lumière with the help of professor Maurice Perrigot, visited most of the cities of the world. They improved their profession with continuous practice. The results obtained were scrupulously checked at Lyon. Some of the material was analyzed and the authors received the examiners' comments. Many of them learned the techniques of making camera tricks. Some astonished their audiences by projecting the film backwards.

The growing number of cameramen meant that the initial order of 25 units of the Cinématographe that Lumière placed early in 1895 with Carpentier was increased in less than a year to 200 more units to cover world demand. By 1897 the Cinematographe was well known in the most important cities of the world. The seed had been sown and the orders for buying this camera and the films continued coming from everywhere on the globe.

The number of films received and incorporated in the Lumière catalog was considerable and varied. It included different sections such as General Views, Comic Views and Travel Views to be used in all kinds of shows. But the expenses of travelling and producing and exhibiting films abroad were considerable. The competition of other cameras and projectors began to increase. At the end of 1897 the Maison Lumière announced a change in their policy. The sale of the Cinematographe would now be open to all those interested. The firm would now sell raw stock also and the films of their catalog. The firm's international film show and a great part of the film production would now end, but some material would still be made by their cameramen.

The difficulties in obtaining a Lumière camera had induced many enthusiasts to build their own. One of them was the Spaniard Fructuoso Gelabert who, in 1897, after finishing his camera, filmed one of the first series of films made in this country, becoming one of the pioneers of the Spanish film industry. Another Spanish pioneer was Eduardo Jimeno who bought one of the first units of the Cinematograph sold and filmed many of the first Spanish films and continued later in the film theater business. During this period the later celebrated Segundo de Chomon began working mainly in Barcelona, Paris and Rome.[8]

The orders for the Lumière cameras came from many different countries, from enthusiastic photographers who saw new possibilities of covering government ceremonies, military parades and private events, as well businessmen who wanted to open film theaters and show the large numbers of films available. This was the beginning of a new profession for many, varying from the man who shot and made the film, to the one who went into film exhibition as a business.

In Hungary, Eugène Dupont, a Lumière representative, gave the first show in Budapest in 1896. Two years later, the two owners of the Café Mercur, named Mor Ungerleider and Jóseph Neumann, converted it into a movie theater. The café's headwaiter, Jóseph Bèczi, began a new career as the first Hungarian cameraman. The new firm continued producing great numbers of short features and news films. Later they began the first newsreel in that country.

In Argentina the first exhibition of Lumière films was done in Buenos Aires in 1896, sponsored by Enrique Lepage, the Belgian owner of a photographic shop. Several Lumière films were shown. Soon Lepage imported a Gaumont-Demeny camera model 1897 and a projector from France, and his collaborator Eugenio Py was the first cameraman of this country when he filmed 70 ft. of the Argentinean flag. In 1901 the first feature film was photographed and directed by Eugenio Cardini, and this was followed later on by experiments with the Gaumont sound recording system.[9]

In the nearby Uruguay, the first film show was on July 25, 1896, in Montevideo, with Lumière films. In 1898 Felix Oliver, a Spanish trader, went to France, bought a Lumière camera and started shooting films of several local subjects: street scenes, public events, bicycle races, celebrations and even an advertising film of his own shop. One year later, Oliver returned to Paris, visited Méliès and learned the techniques of making camera tricks and applied them in his productions.[10]

In Brazil, Alfonso Segreto was the first Brazilian to turn the crank handle for his new motion picture on June 19, 1898, when returning from France, his ship entered the famous Guanabara Bay, in Rio de Janeiro. He had been sent by his brother to buy films for his show theater. With them, he also bought a camera with which he began his activity in this field. Very soon film theaters expanded in that city and news cameramen appeared. In 1906 the cameraman Antonio Leal photographed the first long feature film.[11]

In the remaining years of the last decade in the nineteenth century and early in the twentieth century, the film industry grew and important film enterprises started in Paris, London and New York. In Paris, mechanic Henry Joly made a camera and filmed material for Charles Pathè who in a few years created a big organization for manufacturing raw stock, film cameras, film projectors, and built studios and laboratories for his film production. Léon Gaumont was another inventor who had conceived with Georges Demeny a motion picture camera using 60 mm wide film. Soon this firm received Swiss financial support and expanded greatly, manufacturing cameras and projectors; he also built a large film studio called Cité Elgé, and there he produced his own films, entered in the film business and made experiments in color and sound films. Toward the end of the nineteenth century he created an important branch in Great Britain.[12]

In 1895, Antoine Lumière refused to sell a Cinematographe to Georges Méliès, the creative wizard. Though limited in funds, he built his own camera, then worked as an expert cameraman and with the profits of his films built the first glasshouse studio where he filmed the long and famous series of fantastic and imaginative productions that were extensively distributed, but also suffered many counterfeits. France had become the leading European film production center with four important enterprises and vast installations, and had conquered an international market including its several colonies.

Great Britain was head of an empire too, and its production had perspectives of their own. Several firms started manufacturing film equipment there such as cameras, projectors, film printers and raw stock giving rise to its film industry. Several firms like Charles Urban's Trading Company, Gaumont-British Company, Hepworth Company, R.W. Paul, Warwick Trading Company and Smith & Williamsons of Brighton reached a production of more than 500 short films per year, which demanded building several glasshouse studios and employing a considerable number of cameramen.

After Europe, the United States was the most important center in those years. After Dickson left it, the Edison company continued producing films, making several titles inside the Black Maria, but they also took their heavy camera outdoors to shoot films copying Lumière subjects such *Wash Day Trouble* (1896–97) filmed by Edmund Kuhn and *The Black Diamond Express* (1897). The hits of the Edison Company's film production were *The Life of an American Fireman* (1902) and *The Great Train Robbery* (1903), both directed by Edwin S. Porter, two of the best films of a series of features he made for this firm.

The American film industry in those years was based in New York, Chicago and Philadelphia. Several producing firms were established there which contested the Edison monopoly. After Edison, the most important were the American Mutoscope and Biograph Company, the Vitagraph Company, the Selig Polyscope Company based in Chicago, Siegmund Lubin, Kalem, Essany, Pathé and others. Some, such as Mutoscope, had a camera that did not infringe Edison's patents. Others, like Lubin, made their own cameras, but had to continuously evade Edison's inspectors while shooting their productions outdoors, since the camera design was based on the perforated film principle and used sprockets. The standard productions were short subjects of one reel of about 300 to 500 ft. made in a day, and which were sold by the foot. Some firms had their own film studios and laboratories, as in the case of Mutoscope, conceived by the inventive Dickson. Vitagraph had constructed its first studio in 1897 on the roof of a building in the center of New York. Essany had its installations in Chicago.

Edison's prosecution of patent infringement brought about that all producers had to evade the inspectors when shooting outdoors. In 1904 the Motion Picture Patents Company was established in which producers like Lubin, Vitagraph, Kalem, Seiling, Pathé, Essany, Kleine, Méliès, and later Biograph, agreed to pay royalties to Edison. Eastman Kodak reached agreements with the members of the trust. The famous MPPC set out on a war against independents outside the trust, including arrests and seizure of equipment. This monopoly limited the possibilities for motion picture equipment manufacturers in America, and led independent producers to move to Los Angeles, California, in search of more freedom and facilities in which to operate.

The independent producers united and created the General Film Company to contend with the monopoly and after a long trial the trust was finally dissolved in 1917. Thus Hollywood began to be the most important film production center in the United States and many European producers found a good market in this country to sell their films and motion picture equipment. That was why cameramen that cropped up in the beginning of the American film industry worked mostly with European cameras, mainly from France and England.

In those years the first generations of cameramen were generally learned laboratory procedures well and worked mainly covering news events. Sometimes they came from different activities such us portrait photography, mechanics, electricity, or engineering. Most of them began in the profession in various kinds of shorts before joining firms producing feature films. Some, after working as cameramen, became directors and producers.

Edwin S. Porter started working with the Edison Company due to his mechanical abilities. He began as projectionist, became a cameraman later, shooting diverse kinds of events, then he learned the techniques of camera tricks seen in the Georges Méliès films. When he was allowed to shoot features he incorporated trick photography in his films to add production value. In *The Great Train Robbery* he used a double exposure twice to incorporate background through a window and a door. After passing from cameraman to director Porter took his final step to producer and later on formed his own company. John Arnold, who worked with Edison and Biograph as a cameraman, had an engineering background which was important for his future career, later becoming the head of the MGM camera department.

Albert E. Smith, before becoming the head of the important Vitagraph Company, was a news cameraman who filmed boxing matches, faked the *Maine* explosion in Havana Harbor, filmed other faked news on the Spanish-American War, covered the Boer War in South Africa, and finally ended his career producing feature films. Fred Balshofer was a news cameraman and cinematographer who afterwards moved to the production field, heading the New York Motion Picture Company, and was later a member of the Keystone Film Company and Universal Film Manufacturing Company in Hollywood.

Famous cameraman Billy Bitzer started as an electrician to become a news cameraman in 1890 for Biograph, where he covered important events such as William McKinley's presidential campaign, the Jeffries-Sharkey boxing match and the Boer War before entering the field of shooting films for Biograph, where he met D.W. Griffith, then an actor. When Griffith became a film director, Bitzer was his first cameraman and his right hand in his productions during sixty years, being called in Hollywood "the best cameraman in the industry." Bitzer was an example of experience, imagination, good taste and know-how on using light to enhance the artistic value of an image. Bitzer introduced the use of backlight, the lighting touch, and it is said that the lens hood he used to produce a better contrast in the image suggested the idea of applying the iris in front of the lens, as a framing control to attract attention. The result, the iris effect, was an effective means to produce a transition of themes when cutting. The Griffith-Bitzer team produced the best films in the early years of American filmmaking.[13]

Towards the second half of the teens a new generation cropped up in the United States; they were people trained in laboratories, portrait studios or coming from the news film field. Charles Rosher, an Englishman known in his country as a portrait photographer of the royal family, made newsreels for Pathé and filmed Pancho Villa's Mexican revolution for Mutual. Later on he worked in the Nestor studio and afterwards as cinematographer in Mary Pickford's films for Famous Players (later Paramount). Arthur Edeson a former portrait photographer, joined Éclair Studios in Fort Lee, N.Y., in 1917 and stepped up as cinematographer and worked later with Douglas Fairbanks. Arthur Miller came from laboratory work and afterwards took different kind of films including news and feature films for Pathé. Harry Stradling, another cinematographer who came from England, gained a reputation with his refined close-up lighting, and was also another of Mary Pickford's preferred cinematographers.

Victor Milner started as a projectionist, became a news cameraman for Pathé and later on went into Hollywood film studios as an expert in studio lighting. Al Gandolfi was Cecil B. DeMille's first cameraman when he went into the movies, associated with Jesse L. Lasky, and formed the Feature Play Company, filming in the Edison Studio in the Bronx. Dan Clark became the cinematographer of Tom Mix's western comedies. Alvin Wyckoff was Gandolfi's successor with DeMille and his excellent lighting was called "Lasky light" or "Rembrandt light." Other DeMille cinematographers were Oscar Apfeld, Fred Kley and Peverell Marley, who some years later and with a large camera staff filmed important De Mille productions like *The Ten Commandments* (1923) and *King of Kings* (1927). Marley later went to Fox Studio.

In the field of comedies five cinematographers become well known for their long-term work with famous comedians. William Foster and Frank D. Williams were the first cameramen of Chaplin's early films about 1916, followed by Rolan Totheroth who worked with Essanay Studios and later with Chaplin. Elgyn Lessley was the usual cinematographer for Buster Keaton. Both had the difficult task of working with two of the most perfectionist Hollywood film directors, and carried out very complex camera tricks to make their gags possible, maintaining a clear and effective photography. Another cinematographer who specialized in this type of comedies was Walter Lunding who worked with and was responsible for the camera tricks of Harold Lloyd's films.

The list of Hollywood cameramen coming up during those years is long and includes: Virgil E. Miller, Philip E. Rosen, Gilbert Warrenton, Clyde De Vinna, Jackson J. Rose, and many others. The credits they obtained sometimes overshadow the names of many experts in the newsreel field like Ariel Varges, Al Gold, J.A. Dubray, Faxon Dean, Enrique Vallejo, George Doran, Carl Von Hoffman or Jack Painter among many others who worked in anonymity in several newsreel firms in the United States in the silent days.[14]

In the United Kingdom there was a steady production of films and several producers during the teens. There were very active film producers like Cecil Hepworth, who was an expert cameraman himself, using numerous camera tricks, and maintaining his practice of using natural lighting whenever possible. Alternately, he worked also with cinematographers like Geoffrey Faithfull, Tom White, Gaston Queribet and Charles Sanders, who maintained Hepworth's aesthetic pictorial style.

A reputed cameraman of the time was Alfonso Frenguelli who worked for the Neptune Film Company shooting films such as *The Harbour Lights* (1914), and *In the Ranks* (1914), and also for the London Film Company. The Swede Gustave Pauli obtained a good reputation working for the London Film Company, where his work in *King Outcast* (1915) won repute. Other cinematographers at that time were: Silvano Barbone, George Pearson, Barry Salt, Frederick Burlingham, Emil Lauste, Walter Buckstone, Elwin Neame, Ernest Palmer, Hedry Edwards and Roland Hill.[15]

Some cameramen specialized in topical films, such as Herbert Ponting, an excellent professional who covered Scott's Antarctic expedition (1910–13), and Hubert Wilkins, who in 1913 filmed Shackleton's Antarctic expedition. Cherry Kearton was a noted cameraman and a prolific producer of wildlife films in Africa, India, the United States and Canada. Kearton was also owner of the Clapham Studios in Crammer Court and edited the newsreel *Whirlpool of War*.

Several cameramen, e.g. W.E. Davies, Harold Jeapes, E.G. Tong, G. Taylor and H. Raymond, participated in the First World War, but two of the best known in this field in the British film industry were Geoffrey Malins and J. B. McDowell. Both were official war cinematographers during the First World War and together made the famous feature film *The Battle of Somme* (1916), followed by *The Battle of Arras* (1917), remarkable for their photographic quality. In 1927 Gaumont produced again the film *The Somme* in which a later famous British cinematographer acted as second cameraman. Malins was the author of the book *How I Filmed the War* and produced, directed and wrote the films *Girl from Downing Street* (1918) and later *Peep Behind the Scene* (1918). McDowell specialized in topical films and was head of the British and Colonial Kinematograph Co. Ltd.[16]

In France from the last years of the nineteenth century and in the beginning of the teens, the principal producing companies were Pathè, Gaumont, Éclair, Eclipse and Film D'Art. Pathé had cameramen like Caussade, Segundo de Chomón, Louis Forestier, Alfred Guichard and Paul Castenet. At Gaumont the cameramen were Guèrin, Sorgius and Klausse, who filmed with the well-known director Louis Feuillade. The later-renowned Georges Spetch was cameraman for Leònce Perret between 1912 and 1916 and the later well-known director Jacques Feyder. Gaumont also engaged Victor Morin, Paul Pargel and Jean Letort, who filmed with two future famous directors: Marcel L'Herbier and Léon Poirier. Lucien Adriot worked in the Société Éclair created in 1907, photographed films with the director Maurice Tourneur and in 1914 both went to the United States. Other cameramen with this firm were Raymond Agnel and Ravet. This firm had also the newsreel "The Eclair Journal" and studios in Fort Lee, New Jersey. Le Film D'Art was another French firm which began in 1908 and was created by its directors, Charles Delac and Marcel Vandal, for producing selected feature films based on books by famous writers; among the cameramen who worked in those films was Léonce Henry Burel, who afterwards obtained a reputation in France and continued his work with filmmakers such as Abel Gance, Guèrin, Louis Chaix and Alphonse Gibory. Many other cinematographers worked in France during those years, e.g. George Lucas, Renee Guissard, Maurice Forster, Victor Armenise, Georges Millon and René Batton. Three cameramen, Fedor Buourgassov, Joseph Mundviller and Nicolas Toporkov, were cinematographers of productions made in Paris with the Russian colony exiled in France after the 1917 revolution.[17]

In Russia, the best-known cameramen at the beginning of the century were Joseph Mundviller, Alexander Drankov, Nikolai Kozlovsky, V. Silversen, Alphonse Winkler, Louis Forestier, A. Bulla, Ivan Frolov and Alexander Rillo, among others.[18]

The development of film production in Germany in those years was more limited. After the work of the German film pioneer Oscar Eduard Messter, who made the first motion picture camera in that country and later on shot several films, the film industry was small, and the presence of filmmakers such as Urban Gad and the influence of the Danish firm Nordisk Film was important. The most representative feature films began early in the second decade. Messter produced *Im Schatten des Meeres* (*The Shadow of the Sea*) (1912) and *Der Andere* (*The Other*) (1913) was produced by Vitascope. However the film *Der Student von Prag* (*The Prague Student*) (1913) produced by the Deutche Bioscop firm was excellently made and showed the high quality of Guido Seeber's cinematography.

Seeber, born in Chemnitz in 1879, was the son of a portrait photographer. Attracted by the rise of motion pictures in Germany he began working as cameraman and made some original inventions: the Seeberphono and the Seeberographo. In the first decade the production firm Deutch Bioscop started building the first glasshouse film studio in Berlin in 1909 and hired Seeber as a director. In 1914 he left this position and began as cinematographer working with Asta Nielsen; soon he was recognized as the best German cameraman, making several hundred films from shorts to long features. Later on he wrote three books about his profession: *Der Trickfilm* (*Camera Tricks*), *Der Pracktishe Kameramann* (*The Practical Cameraman*) and *Kurble* (*Shoot*).

Seeber was a symbol in German cinematography and the profession's pioneer in his country. He was followed by other excellent cameramen like Ernst Kron, Carl Hoffman, Alfred Hansen, Axel Graatkjar, Kurt Richter, Theodor Sparkuhl, Willy Hameister, Emil Schunemann and Karl Freund, before the beginning of the twenties and the creation of UFA. The German lighting style later developed great prestige in international film centers. Guido Seeber was, years later, the creator of the first German cameramen club.

The Italian film industry was the third film industry in Europe. It increased its development after 1904 from the beginning of Filoteo Alberini in Turin, the first film center in that country. The most important film producer was Arturo Ambrosio of Maniffatura Ambrosio but many other producers cropped up, like Celio Film, Italia Film, Savoia Films, Corona Films, Milano Film, Cines, Italica Ars, Morgana Films, Caesar Films, Tiber Film and others. Ambrosio was one of the first and it was the most active and best organized film producer with a large film studio which built its own motion picture cameras and with an ample staff of cameramen.

The remarkable lighting of the Italian film *Cabiria* was made by four cinematographers (courtesy Unitalia Film).

The pioneer cameraman in Italy was Giovani Vitriotti, born in Turin in 1882. After studying painting when young he was attracted by photography and earned several awards. From photography he moved on to cinematography and was hired by Arturo Ambrosio. With this firm, Vitriotti made a very large number of documentary and feature films and traveled to many European countries; he made a co-production with Russia, where he received an award from the czar for his contribution to the Russian cinema. He made several films in that country and later went on to Africa and other distant countries, covering many subjects. The quality of his work was an excellent contribution to his profession. He left Ambrosio to form his own company; he worked in German productions and large colossal films in Italy such us *Teodora* (1922) and *Quo Vadis?* (1913) directed by Gabriellino D'Annunzio, and continued actively working until 1964.[19]

There were a considerable number of other cameramen in Italy during the teens. Natale Chiusano must be mentioned, who worked with Italia Film; Angelo Scalenghe, also a member of the Ambrosio staff; Massucco, who filmed for Corona films; and A. Bona, who worked with the important Roman Cines studio. Others were Augusto Navone, cameraman for Savoia Film; and A.G. Carta, one of the cinematographers who photographed great film stars such as Francesca Bertini for Caesar Films during 1918. Foreign cameramen of international reputation also came to Italy and stayed there some years like the Spaniard Segundo de Chomon, an expert in special effects who was hired by Itala Film and shot famous films like *Cabiria* (1914) with the well-known director Giovanne Pastrone. Carlo Montuori was another well-known Italian cinematographer of that time, who was called the "Master of Masters" by his colleagues. He started in 1913 with a film directed by Augusto Genina and continued with another film directed by the famous Carmine Gallone. Montuori's career was outstanding and very prolific. Finally, other cinematographers of prestige in the Italian film industry in the immediately following years must include Ubaldo Arata, Anchise Brizzi and Arturo Gallea.

## Outstanding Cinematography of the Teens

| Year | Title | Country | Cinematographer | Director |
|------|-------|---------|-----------------|----------|
| 1912 | Quo Vadis | Italy | Giovanni Vitriotti | Enrico Guazzoni |
| 1913 | The Student of Prague | Germany | Guido Seeber | Stellan Rye |
| 1914 | Cabiria | Italy | Segundo de Chomón<br>Giovanni Tomatis<br>Augusto Battagliotti<br>Natale Chiusano | Giovanni Pastrone |
| 1915 | The Birth of a Nation | USA | Billy Bitzer | David W. Griffith |
| 1916 | Intolerance | USA | Billy Bitzer | David W. Griffith |

# 3. Motion Picture Cameras and Lenses

## French cameras

After the cameras developed by the pioneers, the next batch manufactured in Europe (mainly France and Britain) followed the same principles of many other similar instruments made at that time. The mechanical parts were generally made in bronze and were separated from the body, built of polished wood (being a light material) and tending to look like small furniture. The same concept had been adopted for photograph cameras and some scientific instruments. When Jules Carpentier's mechanical workshop manufactured Lumiere's Cinematographe the body was made by the joiners who made all the bodies for all the scientific instruments they produced. All other camera makers proceeded in the same way.

The camera of the Lumière brothers was probably the most compact instrument built for that end; many others were built at that time, but none was so compact, no doubt due to their effort to achieve dimensions similar to those of the typical photo cameras of the time. Soon after the Lumière brothers stopped making their famous cameras due to a fire in the workshop near the end of the 19th century, Charles Pathé ordered the Etablisements Cotinsounza to design and build one of their first cameras which sold very well.

### THE FIRST PATHÉ CAMERA

The body of this first camera was built of wood covered with Moroccan pigskin (which was also used in the next models). The unit enclosed two wooden 400 ft. magazines are placed on top of the other. Two other spare magazines could be installed beside them. All magazines were fastened with milled head bronze screws worked from the outside. The mechanical unit comprised a series of gears driven by a crank handle, and was placed at the front side.

The mechanism included two sprocket wheels, one at the top and the other at the bottom of the film channel. The intermittent drive was a shuttle with claws, travelling on a straight plane. The shutter had a fixed opening. The camera was provided with an adjustable f./4.5 Voigtländer lens. A side viewfinder reproduced the frame field through an auxiliary lens, casting a bright image on a ground glass in the camera body. The meter counter was placed below the viewfinder. On the front of the camera there was a door giving access to the mechanism. The main door had two safety locks and allowed exchanging the magazines and threading the film on the sprockets and film gate.

## PATHÉ PROFESSIONNEL PORTATIF

This was the next model this firm ordered, with a new design but with the same compact, parallelepiped shaped body. Among the new features was the internally placed, metal, 400 ft. magazines, parallel to each other, to make film loading easy. The camera's rear face could be opened upwards. The front of the camera with the mechanism, the lens and the crank handle could also be opened sidewards. The film meter was placed above the crank. The focus was adjusted by opening the front and placing a ground glass on the film gate.

## PATHÉ PROFESSIONNEL

This was the best-known camera produced by this firm, it was used in professional film making the world over, as well as by the most important newsreel firms. It came out in about 1908 and its production went on until after World War I. In Hollywood it was the classical instrument adopted by most of the studios for their feature productions, and in Europe it competed in many production centers with Debrie's Parvo.

The body of Pathé Professionnel was a vertical parallelepiped 4¾ × 8 × 12 in. without magazines and it weighed 22 pounds. The front of the camera allowed access to the mechanism and to adjust the lens focus. The design of the intermittent system was excellent based on the harmonic cam producing a very steady image. The film channel was long so as to render good film stability, and was provided with steel strips on each side of the film gate. The shutter was of the variable opening type, made up of two adjustable blades rotating very close to the emulsion side of the film. The 400 ft. magazines were installed on top of the camera body. A crank handle, with its axis parallel to the axis of the lens was placed at the rear, for

*Top:* **The first Pathé camera, which included spare magazines inside the body (***courtesy Archivo Nacional de la Imagen, Sodre***). Bottom: Pathé Professionnel Portatif camera (***courtesy Archivo Nacional de la Imagen, Sodre***).**

Pathé Professionnel studio camera (courtesy Archivo Nacional de la Imagen, Sodre).

normal drive, single frame or reverse. A film punch marked the film separating the takes. The camera was provided with interchangeable lenses of the Heliar series made by Voigtländer; the 51 mm focal length model had an aperture of f/4.5.[1]

The camera had direct viewing through the film, and a viewfinder on the left hand side with a projected image. It was also provided with meter counters; by pressing a button on top of the camera, an internal device effected dissolves and also automatic fades over a film length of four ft. The firm's service was very efficient: they had perfectly numbered spares of all mechanical parts of the camera; therefore, other makers afterwards used the same parts to provide a wide scope for their units. This camera became very well known for the many adaptations added to it, especially devices in front of the lens, and others for warming its inside to avoid static discharging on the film surface as was done by Billy Bitzer.

## CHROMO-GAUMONT CAMERA

Another camera appeared in France at that time, built by the Etablissement Gaumont, an improvement of the previous model IIB based on the Demeny movement. It was not so widely accepted as the Pathé, but it was extensively used by Gaumont in their many feature film productions in several parts of the world. Its mechanism was noted for its simple design, and for using a single central sprocket forming two loops, above and below the film channel.

The intermittent mechanism of the Gaumont was made up of a two claw shuttle, based on a design producing very steady images. The 400 ft. film magazines were installed one on top of the other. A projected image viewfinder was also installed on top. The adjustable opening shutter was placed in a special housing in the camera front, which also had interchangeable lenses, which could be slid vertically. The camera had two crank handles: one for frame-by-frame takes and another for normal drive. Two counters showed the exposed footage and the number of exposed frames for special effects.

## THE DEBRIE PARVO

Joseph Debrie, a specialist in perforating sheet metal, while building his own plant in 1900 expanded his plans to make equipment for the recently born cinematography industry when he took on an order for a device to punch notches in celluloid film. He quickly produced a film punch which was adopted by raw stock manufacturers the world over, notably Thomas A. Edison himself.[2]

After designing a complex professional printer in 1905, Debrie and his son André conceived a camera of unusual design which they called the Parvo, a Latin word meaning small. After many trials, this instrument was launched onto the market in 1908, to compete with Pathé's Professionnel. It had been carefully designed to make the cinematographer's work easier, and to provide him with a reliable camera, quick and easy to handle, and free of mechanical trouble. Among its many advantages was that its portability exceeded all other equipment on the market at the time, resulting from the original disposition of its internal mechanism.

During more than a decade the first Parvo cameras were supplied with a body built of five ply walnut, small in size: 11 × 8 × 6 in. (27 × 30 × 13 cm.) and weighing 17 pounds. It was the result of André Debrie's creative efforts and it soon drew the attention of film makers in France, and then abroad, achieving recognition in a few years. It's internal mechanism,

The first Debrie's Parvo camera (*courtesy Archivo Nacional de la Imagen, Sodre*).

built of bronze and steel, was noted for its fine craftsmanship and the accurate finish of its parts, as well as the absence of drive belts and flexible shafts. The mechanism was entirely independent of the body so that the camera would not be affected when used in different climates.

The innovation in this camera was the arrangement of its two 400 ft. metal magazines placed side by side, and with a positive clutch for takeup. This meant that the film would travel in three planes: one in the feed magazine chamber, then another one going through the film gate and a third plane when being taken up by the corresponding magazine chamber. The mechanism could run forward drive and reverse. The intermittent mechanism was very efficient and rendered a very steady image. Access to the inside was through two lids at the side and a section at the front which opened upwards to give access to the film gate and for threading the film, as well as checking and cleaning the plates. The shutter was housed behind the lens. The manufacturers afterwards included, optionally, an ingenious automatic dissolving system.

Direct focusing was made easy by a direct viewfinder through the film, rendering a magnified upright image, provided with an automatic closing eyecup, placed at the rear of the camera. Also at the rear there were a film counter, a speedometer and the film punch. A direct iconographic finder of the folding type with range correction was placed on the left hand side. The operator, in this framing position behind the camera, could adjust the lens focus and diaphragm by means of the corresponding rod sliding on a plate with graduations adjustable according to the lens being used. The crank handle on a side drove the mechanism smoothly and without effort. Lenses could be easily interchanged on the Parvo camera as they were bayonet seated. Some time later they added an appliance acting as a sunshade and filter holder. As a complement to the Parvo, Debrie manufactured an elaborate tripod with crank operated head, affording widely varied operations for both slow and fast pans.

An instrument of such characteristics appearing in the early years of cinematography drew the attention of camera operators and film makers, and soon was widely accepted in the industry. Some time after, foreign camera makers reached agreements with Debrie and many of his original concepts were adopted in Germany and Italy. But Debrie kept always in the lead, not only because of their advanced design and high quality make and finish, earning this firm worldwide prestige, but also because they had adopted standardized production, ensuring them a competitive price.

## British cameras

Varied cameras were produced in Great Britain to cover demand in the United Kingdom. After the instrument made by Robert Paul, the earliest was the Prestwich Moto Photograph, built in 1897 by the Prestwich Manufacturing Co. of London, which included important innovations like the variable shutter. This firm continued building other models, such as the N/44, provided with a main sprocket wheel and increasing its film capacity with internal 75 ft. magazines plus external 500 ft. ones.

In 1889 the Urban Bioscope company experimented by building a camera with unusually (then) larger magazines of 1.500 ft. capacity, for filming the Boer War, allowing takes up to 30 minutes without reloading. These were some of the advances in an embryonic industry.

The construction design generally applied in Britain in making cameras was based on a body of treated and polished mahogany, with brass corners and elaborate bronze hinges which were expanded over the doors of the instrument in order to reinforce them, while smaller ones were used on the magazines. A long leather belt was attached on the top, instead of the shorter one used on the Debrie Parvo, which was maintained during the latter's long life.

But a fundamental difference in the design of British cameras was their shape. Most British camera makers adopted the single plane travel and with the 400 ft. magazines inside the unit, that meant they had to be placed one on top of the other, thus increasing the size of the body. Consequently most British cameras were of a vertical parallelepiped shape, contrasting with the similar, but horizontal and much more compact shape of Debrie's design, later on adopted by other camera makers on the continent. Another difference was that British makers used rectangular wood magazines, while on one model Pathé experimented making them in metal, while Debrie, striving to reduce dimensions, adopted metal.

With these general trends, British cameras looked much like each other, and there was also an interchange of parts of their mechanisms. A well-known British camera maker, Darling Bros., also made movement and mechanical parts which were afterwards used on other cameras, such as the Urban Bioscop Studio and the Williamson. Another noted firm of two engineers, Ernest F. Moy and Percy H. Bastie, specializing in making electrical and precision equipment for the Royal Navy, had developed their original intermittent mechanism known as the Drunken Screw.

A look into the mechanism of one of the cameras appearing late in the first decade of that century shows it interconnected by means of a chain. Their mesh mechanisms were generally made in bronze and then varnished, and were easily accessible through the lid. The Moy-Omnia made models with 200, 350 and 400 ft. film capacity, and their last models included devices for fades (in and out). The Cinechrome Instrument Ltd. firm conceived their Cinchro camera with more compact dimensions, with many controls placed at the rear, and other features which were absent in other British made instruments.

The typical arrangement of most British cameras was the use of a sprocket roller above and below the film channel, the claw system at one side of the roller, below the aperture,

Moy & Bastie British camera (*courtesy Archivo Nacional de la Imagen, Sodre*).

and two square wooden magazines at the rear of the body. The viewfinder, generally of the iconographic type, was mounted on top of the body. In some cameras, critical viewing and focusing was effected through the film itself by means of a prism. Some cameras, e.g. the Prestwich, had a projected image side viewfinder. The controls, normally the footage counter and the speedometer, were near the drive crank handle. A film punch was generally included, making either a notch on the film edge or a hole in the centre of a frame. The taking lens with its typical bronze mount stood out in front, but the camera makers rarely included a sunshade and filter holder, which was often added on by the cameramen, among the many adaptations they made, sometimes applying spares obtained from Pathé. In some equipment the lens focus was adjusted with a lever acting on the focusing ring.

Other British manufacturers, such as Alfred Newman and W. Vinten, participated in making motion picture cameras and introduced important innovations like the pilot pin (conceived by a mechanic of Alfred Newman named Woodhead) or showing the way to making metal bodies. Moy & Bastie made special equipment for filming from the air with a metal body, electric motor and gyroscopic system for steadiness. However, although there were very qualified camera makers in Britain, the film studios there tended to prefer French equipment, such as Pathé Professionel and Debrie's Parvo, which were increasingly used, until they were gradually displaced (at least in the best equipped firms) by the introduction of the Bell & Howell Standard from the USA.

Finally, we must not overlook the important contribution to this field of a Polish engineer, Kazimierz Prószyński, of the OKO cinematographic equipment factory of Poland. In the U.K. Proszynsky developed the Aeroscope, a hand held camera driven by compressed air inside several cylinders to run 600 ft. of film. The camera included an internal gyroscope to dampen vibrations. The air cylinders were recharged by a device acted upon by a pedal. This camera, built by Newman & Sinclair, was extensively used by British newsreels, and it was later improved and used in World War I.[3]

## Other European cameras

Though camera production in other European countries was limited as compared to France and Britain, some makers cannot be disregarded. Among them, there was the above mentioned Maniffatura Ambrosio in Italy, owned by Arturo Ambrosio of Turin, who produced models similar in some aspects to British equipment, partially influenced by Pathé designs, and including innovations of his own such as an extremely narrow wooden body and a chain drive outside the body. Other noteworthy cameras from Italy were those from Ernest Zollinger, models A and B, excellently finished, with bodies of polished wood and internal side to side magazines. Furthermore, near the end of the twenties there were those by Attilio Prevost in France, who must not be confused with Lucien Prévost, who also constructed motion picture cameras and laboratory equipment.

In Germany Oskar Messter made motion picture cameras and later on the manufacture by other firms was very intensive but only for domestic use. At that time the Ernermann company in Dresden was actively producing cameras with some design aspects similar to the André Debrie Parvo.

## American cameras

We have seen above that most of the film productions in the USA, initially on the East Coast and then in Hollywood, were made with imported cameras, first from Britain and then from France, especially the Pathé Professionel. In some isolated cases the pioneers used locally made cameras. Of course the patents war influenced this situation, but not for long.

In 1907 Donald J. Bell, a projectionist and mechanic, and Albert S. Howell, an engineer, formed a small company in Chicago (the name combined both surnames) for the purpose of manufacturing, hiring and jobbing equipment for the motion picture industry. This firm's previous first steps were repairing and adjusting cameras. The first instrument they built was a projector they called Kinochrome with the outstanding feature of being one of the first (if not the first) to have a Geneva cross unit rotating to adjust the framing. In 1909, the new firm manufactured its first motion picture camera; like most of the cameras of the time, its body was wooden (covered with leather), but its movement included the novelty of a fixed pilot pin. Only a few units of this model were sold, but it was a valuable experience for the near future.[4]

They continued building equipment in 1910, first a film perforator which made history since it set a standard as to dimensions of perforations adopted by the whole industry. The machine effected eight perforations simultaneously per frame, with a pitch of .1870 in., its efficiency widely improving upon all similar equipment. It made perforations on negatives and positives with different characteristics in sizes, all of which proved to be extremely efficient.

The third instrument designed and built by this firm appeared in 1911 and it continued their standards of high precision and ingenuity. It was a film printer working on the continuous printing method by means of a special sprocket, where the negative and the positive met emulsion side-to-emulsion side in front of an aperture adjustable to modify the light intensity. The item was followed by their model D which became a classic the world over.

## The Bell & Howell Standard Camera

In 1911–12 The Bell & Howell Co. completed this series of revolutionary equipment with and exceptional motion picture camera which radically changed the building concepts for this kind of equipment. Its design discarded the handcrafted concept adopted until then and opted for stoutness and precision of the components. Wood was substituted by metal and ball bearings were applied in most parts. A new fast way was found for focusing and precision framing through the taking lens. Finally and most important, an extremely precise intermittent mechanism was included which was considered one of the best in the industry in producing a steady image.

They decided to adopt single plane film travel using a double chamber (compartment) metal magazines with screw-on compartment lids installed on top of the camera body. A four-lens turret was mounted on the camera front, which facilitated the cameraman's work and was necessary for the new focussing and framing system. The mechanism was a high precision one, with a 32-tooth sprocket wheel for supplying raw stock and taking exposed film, using its surface at the top and at the bottom to achieve the required two-turns per second rotation.

The camera body was aluminum alloy carefully machined after castings, so that the parts should fit with great precision. The outside was finished in black enamel making it very attractive. Its size was $7 \times 14\frac{3}{4} \times 15$ in. including lenses. The weight, including magazines and lenses, was 27 pounds, but without them it was only 16 pounds. The shutter was of the variable angle with a maximum opening of 170 degrees, of which one of the blades could be opened or closed by moving a lever. Also built into the camera was an automatic dissolve operating from 0 to 170 degrees over a length of 64 frames, equivalent to four feet.

The intermittent mechanism system, the heart of the unit, was based on a two-cam high precision system and thus ideal for multiple exposures, but it was quite noisy though this did not matter much at that time. It could operate forward or reverse, and the complete unit could be drawn out for cleaning and lubrication.

The viewing and framing system required sliding the camera sideward by means of a sliding base arrangement and rotating the turret 180 degrees so that the taking lens would be placed before a focusing magnifying glass rendering an amplified image. The front part of the camera also carried a matte box and filter holder. To start taking, the camera

displacement and the turret rotation had to be reverted and the matte box repositioned in front of the lens. This camera system was accurate and reliable, relatively simple to operate and fast to make ready, and was one of the most efficient at that time. Complementary viewing while operating the camera was through a spyglass type side viewfinder, later replaced by a projected image viewfinder with mattes adequate to the lenses.

The controls were placed on one of the sides of the camera, including the footage counter; a Veeder counter was attached to the rear or directly on the crank-

*Top:* The Bell & Howell camera 2709 with accessories (*courtesy Bell & Howell*). *Bottom:* Bell & Howell 2709 camera inside view with removable movement and sprocket roller (*courtesy Bell & Howell*).

shaft. The viewfinder eyepiece was close to the camera controls, as well as the shutter control and the crank handle. The latter was mounted on ball bearings and it ran very smoothly.

An electric motor was added in 1919. With all these features this camera soon became very well accepted in the industry. Beginning in 1912 prominent Hollywood producers started acquiring one or more of these instruments for their studios and the more outstanding cinematographers for themselves.

This company kept in their files the numbers of the first cameras they had sold, starting the numbering from no. 9, which followed after the eight units of the first wooden body model they had put out in 1909. After some time, the Bell & Howell Standard was known as Design 2709; additional letters and numbers (e.g. B1, B2, B3, C1, C2, C3) indicated modifications to their technical features. The price of this camera was, at that time, high, about $1,000 because of the high precision and finish it was made with. One thousand units were manufactured from its debut till the beginning of the thirties.[5]

## THE AKELEY CAMERA

Karl E. Akeley, an American, was an exceptional character who, by accident, became a camera maker. He was a man of many arts: a naturalist, taxidermist, lecturer, sculptor and inventor. Working as curator in the New York Natural History Museum he had to travel to Africa to film the wildlife in that continent. For this purpose he took various motion picture cameras which were popular at that time, but due to special working conditions there they required quick readying of the equipment and fast follow-up of the subjects, and he failed to record them adequately. Back home, he took up the task of designing an instrument to overcome the deficiencies he had experienced. The resulting product broke all the concepts followed by all camera makers at that time and introduced innovations to follow fast movements.

This instrument soon became a classic in the world of newsreels, as well as with explorers and scientists. It appeared about 1915 and was intensely used in World War I. It was ideal for shooting from aircraft and for smoothly following the flight of an aircraft from the ground, for horse races, and for any fast moving subject. When well-known explorers, among others Mr. and Mrs. Martin Johnson, went to Africa to shoot ethnographic films, then a novelty, or when shooting feature productions in Africa, like *Trader Horn* (1932), the Akeley camera was there, overcoming the difficulties that led to its creation.[6]

The fundamental feature of this camera was its all-metal, cylinder-shaped body of 9 × 14½ × 15½ in. outside. The previously prepared, 200 ft. capacity magazine, included a master sprocket wheel and formed a loop, which was easily threaded into the aperture plate. The shutter was of the focal plane type, with a slit in it, and it rotated around the inside of the camera body. Three types of shutter could be provided: one with a fixed opening, one with an adjustable opening and a special one for making dissolves; the fixed type had an opening of 180 degrees while in the others the opening was 220 degrees and effected through a threefold magnification viewfinder installed on the camera door, and adjustable to the operator's height. It was combined with a plate, which included a viewing lens identical to the tanking lens; focusing was achieved by means of a thumb screw acting on both lenses, a unique device which allowed for fast focus changes during a take and in the middle of a pan. The camera was provided with a very compact sunshade.

The intermittent mechanism of very simple design acted on one side of the film, achieving very steady images. The camera was crank-handle driven, either forward or reverse and included high speed without affecting the film. The footage counter was inside the lid. The camera body was mounted onto the tripod so that pan or tilt could be made in any direction and simultaneously at any gyration speed with one handle. The tripod head could be instantly

The Akeley camera, ideal for newsreel and wildlife cine-matography (*courtesy Archivo Nacional de la Imagen, Sodre*).

levelled by means of a ball-and-socket attachment which included a patented split-gear system to eliminate any form of backlash in pans or tilts.[7]

The design of this camera was revolutionary, and its advantages were well accepted in the markets all over the world. It became standard for most newsreel companies of that time and was also acquired by many studios for special needs. Afterwards this firm continued making other equipment such as a sound-on-film camera and later an editing table.

## OTHER AMERICAN CAMERAS

Some other cameras appeared in the USA in the years just after the First World War, for shooting topical films, newsreels or home films. Some of the makers tried, vainly, to sell their equipment to the studios. Many began making them with wooden bodies, but later changed to metal. The box shape, the crank handle drive and focusing through the film were standard features of most of them. Among the best known makes were Universal, Wilart, Box, Photo Cine Press and Russell. But none was adopted by Hollywood studios, where after the Pathé, the Bell & Howell became standard, as well the Akeley for special shooting.

## Camera lenses

The birth of photography towards 1840 and the rapid growth of Daguerreotypes brought about the wide use of photo cameras and the need to manufacture lenses for this purpose. Until then firms in the optics field were concerned with making lenses for spectacles, microscopes, binoculars, and optical instruments for surveying and for the armed forces. Thus, they had no experts in designing lenses for photography. The few available items rendered poor image quality and their effective aperture was below f/8.

The first one to face this problem scientifically was Joseph Max Petzval, a higher mathematics professor at Vienna University which encouraged him to submit a proposal in a contest by a French institution. Petzval designed two lenses: one for portraits with a large aperture and another with a wide angle to cover landscapes adequately. To construct both lenses he engaged P.W.F. Voigtländer, an optician, but who only built the one for portraits in 1840, with an aperture of f/3.6, an extraordinary achievement for that time, unequalled by any other design for many years.[8]

Photographic lens makers started retaining mathematicians to design their lenses and they created specialized departments for that purpose. Among the most noted experts were E. Abbe, Paul Rudolph and Ernst Wanderleb of Zeiss, the well known German firm; Ludwig Jakob Bertele of the Ernemann firm of Dresden, also in Germany; Harold Dennis Taylor and Horace William Lee, of Taylor, Taylor and Hobson in Leicester, England; and John Henry Dallmeyer and Thomas Rudolph Dallmeyer of J. H. Dalmeyers Ltd., in London, England.

In the following years the work of these experts fructified and lenses were designed which were landmarks of progress in this field. Some become famous, e.g. the Anastigmat designed in 1890 by Paul Rudolph for Zeiss; the Cooke Triplet designed in 1893 by Dennis Taylor and made by Taylor, Taylor & Hobson (unrelated); the series of lenses designed by Paul Rudolph in 1896 for Zeiss and named Planar and Unar and in 1899 the renowned Tessar, which was extraordinarily accepted to the world over and its rights sold to the most important makers in Europe and America.

In this series of designs, aberrations were considerably reduced by using new, specially conceived optical glass, but without appreciable progress regarding the aperture; e.g. Anastigmat lenses for portrait, values of f/4.5 were reached near the end of that century. Progress on apertures was made in the first decade of the 20th century but the longest stride came in the USA in 1916 and the twenties, especially for motion pictures.

# 4. The First Studios

## The Black Maria

The basic working area of the new motion picture photographer was, as in photography and painting ateliers, the studio. The first motion picture studio was built soon after the creation of the first motion picture camera by Dickson. In 1893, in an area adjacent to the Edison Laboratories in New Orange, N.Y., Dickson designed and erected a wooden building covered with tar paper called Black Maria due to its resemblance to the American police paddy wagon. It is said that its cost was $637.67. The presumed size of this strange, black structure, was 48' × 10' × 14' × 18'.[1]

The central part of the roof could be opened to allow sunlight into the set. The building was mounted on a rotary base with a graphite pivot, to be swung to follow the sun's transit, so that the subjects on the set would always be lighted by the sun. Inside this studio there was a black background against which the players acted as they were filmed by the camera. It is said that Dickson claimed he sometimes used four parabolic magnesium lamps or several arcs to complement the natural light. The Kinetograph camera was large in size, with the mechanism inside a big wooden box, and it was heavy, so the base rolled on rails installed on the floor to allow the camera to be moved close to or far from the stage. Sound films were experimented with, combining the camera with a phonograph. The first ten of several short films were shot in this studio with very limited space. Afterwards they were produced for the inauguration of the Kinetoscope, in the Department of Physics of the Brooklyn Institute of Arts and Sciences, on May 9, 1893.

## The Méliès studio

In 1897 Georges Méliès built the world's second film studio, when he urgently needed an appropriate covered space to shoot his films, since the famous singer Paulus refused to be filmed outdoors. His father, a shoemaker, had a property in Montreuil sous Bois, near the Paris gates. There, Méliès built a series of glass houses at the cost of twenty-five thousand gold francs. This studio became his headquarters and during fourteen years he made about four thousand short films there.

The initial studio was small in size, about 60 ft. long by 20 ft., and had been conceived using stage techniques. In 1902 the studio space was enlarged. The camera was situated in a special small building adjacent to the stage and in front of the camera was a complete stage with space behind the floor and a pit with machinery and counterweight devices. The whole stage machinery was completed in the ceiling with a rail system. The space for the sceneries was behind the stage area. Years later, H. Claudel, Jacques Colas and P. Lecointe among others participated in painting sceneries for this stage.[2]

Méliès painted his sets mainly on canvas with forced perspective, well combined with furniture and he enhanced the depth of field with painted highlights. The camera was installed in a fixed position to allow the use of multiple exposures. In this studio Méliès was in charge of great part of the work but he had several collaborators; he was the cameraman who produced the excellent trick work with his heavy camera and then processed the film in the studio. Later on the laboratory work was done in the installations at his Robert-Houdine Theater with improved equipment. The Méliès studio was the first building to be conceived by an independent artisan to carry out his own work with the required facilities when he changed from being a conjurer to the new film media. When his finances declined, Méliès sold his studio to investors who thought they would obtain very high prices if the French government would offer to buy the building. The sale fell through, as did a plan including American buyers, and finally the owners demolished this historic installation during the First World War.

## OTHER FRENCH STUDIOS

Pathé and Gaumont built very large studios in France during the early days of the new century. First Pathé started their production in 1901 in a small studio in Rue du Bois, Vincennes, in a three-floor building with glass walls and roof, and in 1904 another at Montreuil, with a metal structure entirely paneled with glass on walls and roof with two very large doors to allow the entrance of large settings. Complementary constructions were made near the big set. Pathé built other studios later on at Joinville, Paris, and Nice. This firm also built other studios in foreign locations like London, New Jersey, Saint Petersburg and Barcelona.[3]

Thus they became the world's most complete organization in the motion picture business. They manufactured raw stock, motion picture cameras, processing equipment, and projection equipment; they produced films in their studios in France and overseas, processed them in their laboratories, they had their own method of coloring the prints as well as a very organized newsreel firm with stringers overseas, and an organization to distribute, sell and exhibit the films in all markets. All the fields of the film industry were covered under the name of Pathé Frères during those years.

Léon Gaumont, the other great French film enterprise, also covered several fields following the expanding lines of Pathé, manufacturing film equipment and production of features and newsreels. About 1905, this powerful organization erected in Paris a large glass house studio in Rue des Alouettes, in the zone of Buttes Chaumond, Paris, with a large stage of 150 ft. × 70 ft. × 112 ft. high. The Gaumont-British society also built in London years later, one of the most important studios of the United Kingdom, in Lime Grove, Shepherds Bush, London, with an entirely glass house stage of 90 ft. × 40 ft. × 20 ft. high including a 30 ft. high end section.

## British studios

A large number of British film studios (more than thirty) were built in England. The Ealing studio was the one with more space with 3 daylight stages, the larger one 80 ft. × 30

Pathé studio in Montreuil, France (*courtesy Archivo Nacional de la Imagen, Sodre*).

ft., on a first floor with workshops beneath. Most of the other studios had only one glasshouse stage the biggest of which was at Twickenham studios in The Barons St. Margarets, operated by the London Film Company, which had a size of 165 ft. × 40 ft. This glass-house stage was blacked out during the First World War. The standard size of the glass stages of the studios was about 70 ft. × 30 ft. Among others, the studios at Alexandra Palace, Walton-on-Thames, was operated by the well known producing firm Hepworth Film Manufacturing Co, Ltd.; it had two all glass stages, one of 50 ft. × 25 ft, and another of 35 ft. × 25 ft, on a half acre ground. This firm's facilities included workshops and a laboratory underneath.

Many of the studios had reduced grounds, the largest of which was the Ilesworth Studios in Worton Hall, Worton Road, with about 5 acres of well wooded grounds and lawns. The space of other studios ranged from ¼ to 3 acres. Some studios were converted old theaters or were large mansions in which the ballroom or the boat shed were adopted as stages. The Hakney studio in Tuilleries Street was converted from a gas plant. The Walthamstow studio was built from an old skating rink. In 1914 Elstree was selected to erect the Neptune Studios by Percy Nash and John East. Later on, it became the first specially conceived "dark stage" of the Boreham Wood Elstree Studio, operated by well-known English producers such as Ideal Films and the first British Lion Films. Most of the British studios used commercial power and only five had their own gas fired power generator.[4]

## German studios

Neubabelsberg Studios was probably the best-known film center of the German motion picture industry before World War I. This studio was built in 1911 by the producer Erich

Zeiske, in Strandorfer Strasse in Neubabelsberg, near Berlin. Neubabelsberg Studios comprised a stage of about 50 ft. × 20 ft. × 20 ft. high, built of glass, beside a concrete production building, in a large lot. The stage was later transformed into a black studio and the adjacent offices rebuilt in a spacious building. This studio was the beginning of the Deutschen-Bioskop-AG production company under the control of Erich Pommer, an organization that included sixty film theaters. In 1921 the Neubabelsberg Studios was the base where the famous UFA studio was built, the most important in Germany, and one of Europe's best. Later on other well known German film studios were Saturn-Film Atelier, Bioskop, Weissensee, Joffa-Atelier, Cserépy-Atelier, Geiselgasteig Atelier, etc.[5]

## Italian studios

In Italy films were produced in several cities. During the teens this production was based on spectacular historic films, exported the world over, which required adequate organization and facilities. Initially the film production center was in the city of Turin where the Ambrosio studio was erected with a large stage of about 120 ft. × 70 ft. with glass roof and one wall of glass and a ceiling structure at about 20 ft. from the floor. This studio complemented the firm's camera factory and services.

About 1913 the Societa Anonima Milano Films had a two-story "dark studio" in the city of Milan. The shooting facilities of the firm Partescope Film Company were in the city of Naples. In Rome, Cines Film, the first big glass-house studio, was erected in 1906 in Via Veio, near Porta San Giovanni, with a large glass house behind the production building and complementary shops, which later were rebuilt into a dark studio with three modern stages and services. This important studio was destroyed by fire three decades later. Another of several Italian studios was Celio Film, built in the second decade of the last century, with an all-glass medium-size stage two stories high, annexed to the main building. Later on, several new studios were built in other Italian cities.

## American studios

In the United States, the first film studios were built on the East Coast, in New York. and New Jersey. The Edison Studios was one of the first to be built at a cost of $100,000, a large glass-house stage at a side of a four story building on Decatur Avenue, Bronx. There, several films were filmed simultaneously, arc lighting equipment was used and cameras were on rolling pedestals.[6] Some film companies began shooting in New York, e. g. Vitagraph in 1897, on the roof of the Morse Building, and in 1903 they built their first studio in the second story at the back of their building in Flatbush, Long Island, where two glass houses were made to be later converted into a large one. The studio included dressing rooms and production offices. Later on, in 1910, this firm made one of the largest studios of the East Coast, in Brooklyn, N.Y., with five all-glass large stages, a long three story building for laboratories, workshops and several complementary services. The stages now covered ten times as much space as the studio they started with in Long Island. Foreign companies like Pathé also installed studios in Jersey City Heights, New Jersey, with two glass-house stages and a water tank, 30' × 30' × 8' deep.

Towards the end of the decade film production companies began to explore new possibilities on the West Coast in search of attractive landscapes, better climate, more sun hours, inexpensive land to extend their premises and to elude patent trust detectives. In 1907 Col. William Selig, a Chicago film producer, erected the first set in Los Angeles on a rooftop. One year later he returned and in 1908 erected permanent facilities in that area. In 1910 Fred Balshofer, a New York producer, installed his new Bison company in Los Angeles using adobe buildings. Soon, important East Coast producers visited that city and decided to settle there. One was the important Biograph Company, which first sent D.W. Griffith in 1911 to make a careful study of the place.[7]

The first Hollywood studios were very elementary, with dispersed buildings and open air stages covered with muslin diffusers hanging from wires fastened to telephone poles near the corners. The harshness of the sun was the only inconvenience. A common practice was to build indoor-outdoor stages formed with three set walls and several framed diffusing screens overhead. The attraction of western subjects was shooting outdoors to improve production values.

Although provisional studios were built first, a few years later, new well-made studios were built with all-glass stages or concrete walls with glass roofs. Some of them were the Triangle/Fine Arts in Sunset and Hollywood Boulevards; the Triangle Company of Thomas Ince, which was sold later to Samuel Goldwyn; the Paralta studios; the William Fox Studio; the United Studio at Melrose Avenue; and many others. All those studios differed from the eastern buildings in the large lots available, the bungalow type buildings and their ornamented colonial Spanish style front entrances, for example, the Selig-Zoo Studio in Mission Road and the William Fox Studio.

## Facilities and working methods

The early glass-house studios suffered from the inconvenience of high temperatures in the summer and cold in the winter, especially in harsh weather zones as on the American East Coast and in some European countries. Frosted, morocco or Murano type glass sheets were used, to reduce the effects of the sun. Large numbers of openings were made in the walls to facilitate ventilation. Light control was by means of awnings, blinds and calico for diffusing and large black flats to create dark areas. Reflecting screens and large mirrors were commonly used for light touches.

The stage was the main working area and behind it were the scene dock and the sheds with the flats. Large studios had appropriate buildings for these work aids and to store props. In many studios the production buildings were at the front and the stages behind; the dressing rooms were close to the stage. But in many of the early Hollywood studios the distribution of premises was unorganized. However, there were well-organized studios with special technical departments. One of these was the Selig studios, which toward 1911 organized an efficient camera department to maintain their different cameras, where the magazines were prepared for next day's work and after work each camera unit was carefully inspected, oiled and stored. The magazines were carefully labeled and installed on special shelves. The standardization of one camera brand was considered important by many firms, to unify the replacement of spare parts and accessories and to use uniform raw stock with perforation size.

In the small European studios the limited space available was carefully studied and many had their developing plant underneath the stage. In early small studios very few had facilities in the ceiling to install lighting units or scaffold planks for electricians to move in that area; these came later when artificial light began to be used. In some English studios many glass-house stages had large double sliding doors so that when an indoor setting had windows, the background of the studio surrounding area with trees could be seen through such windows when totally opened. The constant inconvenience of many British studios was the loss of time waiting for sunshine and the presence of the famous London fog which caused the installation of many studios far from the London area.

In medium and large size stages several films were filmed simultaneously and the sets formed by light flats separated each production. The noise and confusion was intense and the use of the megaphone was in consequence a necessary tool for directors to overcome the din. Generally the directors worked sitting down and the cameramen stood behind the tripod, operating the camera and the tripod crank handles while the players waited their turn.

Artificial lighting units began to be used on cloudy or rainy days, especially in some European studios and on the eastern coast of the United States. In British studios individual Westminster arc units were used hanging from the ceiling.[8] The use of similar light implements was classical in some New York studios like Edison's. In the French Gaumont Studios, lighting was based on large arc spot units installed on top of a high rolling metal trestle. Large banks with six arc lamps were also adopted. In 1905 the Biograph Studio in New York was provided with the newly developed Cooper-Hewitt mercury-vapor lamp giving highly actinic floodlight, which was very comfortable for players and workers. This kind of implement and other types of lighting units that cropped up later were increasingly used after the end of the second decade when the glass house studios were converted into dark studios.

The cameras used by the different studios varied in each country. The preference of each studio was influenced by the availability, the prestige of each camera maker and the recognized good design of each instrument. In France, the Gaumont studio used Gaumont cameras, the Pathé studios used Pathè cameras and Éclair used their own cameras. In Britain, Prestwitch, Moy or Williamson English-made cameras were first used. Soon however, foreign cameras of excellent design like Debrie and Pathé were standard in England and Germany. In Italy the Ambrosio was first used and later on the Prevost, but soon the compact Debrie and the Pathé gained acceptance. In the United States the patents war induced the adoption of several camera makes such us the Mutograph 35, used by that firm, the Shuctek used by Selig, the Lubin, the Moy-Omnia, Williamson, and the Darling or Éclair, used by the Éclair Film Company in Fort Lee, N. J. Carl Laemmle introduced the French Prévost with its top placed side-to-side external magazines in Hollywood's Universal Studio. However the camera that was standard on the East Coast and in Hollywood studios before World War I was the Pathé Studio, that had gained reputation in many important studios in Europe and the United States.

In Europe the Debrie Parvo was a preferred camera in many countries but in the United States, although it was often used, it did not displace the Pathé from the studios. The new American all metal Bell & Howell camera was the one, which achieved that change. In the field of newsreels the new all-metal Akeley newsreel camera produced a similar effect over the Debrie Parvo.

The first film studios began to change when production methods were altered after the war, and the use of lighting equipment was developed. The new controlled lighting affected film shooting organization and procedures and production indoors did not depend anymore on natural light indoors. The transition took some years to adapt glass houses to the more effective black stage method. In many studios with glass roofs the change was easily made by painting the stage roofs. But soon other developments required changes in these new shooting facilities.

# 5. Film Processing

The first attempts in film processing were possible due to research during more than fifty years which brought about continuous progress in many aspects of still photography. Such progress had produced improved photographic emulsions, the elaboration of chemical solutions to facilitate the processes of developing, fixing, and several other complementary treatments of the exposed image. The basic difference that appeared in motion picture processing was the new techniques to be applied to a different kind of film support in relation with the small, light-sensitive photographic plate.

It seems that the first strips of film shot by the pioneers were processed by the simple method of submerging the film in a large tank with the developing bath, then washing and fixing baths, and its careful handling (avoiding touching the emulsion with the fingertips), with the emulsion side up and controlling the even action of the bath along the strip. The instructions that Lumière and his experts gave their operators for processing their material were based on the photographic experience of the Lumières, and the results obtained from their early experiments, first with the long strips of photographic paper and then with celluloid film.[1]

The second step in this early processing was the printing stage, which Lumière and his operateurs made with the same camera. In this operation they must have found the difficulties of combining the slightly altered size perforations of the processed negative with an unprocessed positive raw stock in a step-by-step printing method. The classic photographic method of making several initial experiments, as used during the developing process, must have been the method adopted, especially when selecting the adequate printing light. The old practice of learning by trial and error must have been once more the basic rule. The camera used as a printer required the use of a special double capacity magazine for the negative and the positive films, as well as withdrawing the camera lens, and using an adequate adjustable light source near the instrument.

Very soon after the first films made by the Lumière brothers, manufacturers appeared making equipment for motion picture film processing according to the basic creativeness of many who improved the initial working method. Consequently some classic basic design procedures were set. One was similar to traditional still photography processing. The principle was based on a pin frame, a cross made generally of close grained wood like maple, with diagonal rows of pegs about 1½ in high. The film loop was wound spirally round the pins with the emulsion side inwards. This method was very effective for short strips of film. Another system was with a rotating drum on which the film was wound and afterwards submerged in a half cylinder tank and driven by hand; this was used in Georges Méliès laboratory.[2]

The classic bath vessel was a flat stoneware trough or an upright tank when having to process simultaneously more than one pin frames. The combination of the pin frame and the stoneware developing trough was an effective method adopted when film production was limited to short lengths of about 50 ft. Special units were made to include 100 ft. lengths.

When the film length to be processed was of the order of 200 ft, the developing frame was the standard method. The film frame was the classical system adopted by professionals when working with cameras allowing large capacity magazines. This frame was generally made of teak with a row of projecting brass pegs on top and bottom to avoid overlapping film. This frame was seated on metal supports screwed to the floor or on a rolling device when the frame was taken to the drying sector after the processing. The frame was made of selected wood according to design specifications. The sides were thicker than the ends, which had a rounded surface on top and sloped inwards to prevent the film from touching. The nails were brass with a well-smoothed surface nailed to project out about ¼ in. and 1½ in. apart. A 200 ft. capacity developing frame had a size of about 67 sq. in.

The film was wound with the emulsion side out with its end secured with a drawing pin. The operation had to be made under a safe red light, of course. While placing the film on the frame, the operator revolved the frame slowly onto its support so that the film was seated between the pegs, rather tightly wound but taking care not to strain it, because when wet, the film expanded. The other end of the film had to be secured by another drawing pin.

The need to process long negatives without cuts produced the design of a double frame. This allowed a small frame inside it to take the additional film length. This was a great advantage for very long shots, such as those of races, etc., which could not admit cuts.

When the developing frames were ready they were taken to the developing room where they were placed near the developing tanks. These were made of different materials, none of which should be affected by the solutions. Several types of materials were used for these tanks: wood, paraffin treated wood, enameled steel, glass, porcelain, asphalt-coated metals, lacquered metals, rubber, nitro-cellulose and alloys. With time, experience proved that some metals, such as brass, were affected by chemical solutions and could fog the emulsion severely. Also, the fragility of glass proved to be inconvenient for large tanks.

In the late teens, R.O. Stineman of Los Angeles, California, conceived a very compact and useful developing outfit, entirely made of corrosion resistant metal, to develop from eighty to two hundred feet of film, and based on a special developing reel with a spiral inside in order to insert film into round tanks with the corresponding baths. The film was threaded onto the reel from the center where it was held by a stationary pin and at the outer end by an ordinary paper clip. The center of the reel was made to form the handle by which it should be held. The film was guided into the reel only on the edge. This outfit was ideal for practical work away from large laboratories and included a practical motorized printing machine and a drying rack as complementary items.

The developing tanks conceived for the use of flat frames admitted about four units. The frames were submerged in the solutions in the tanks after having made several tests to determine the immersion time. The operator had to stir the frames gently a couple of times to produce an even effect of the solution on the emulsion and avoid bubbles. The use of orthochromatic emulsion allowed the expert, called the developer, to check the process visually. The developing baths were of the Glycin formula type, preferred by many because their oxidation in the alkaline medium was limited and they produced a fine grain image; other formulas were based on Pyro-soda or Metol and Hydroquinone. The preferred negatives were called "strong," "robust" or "plucky" according to experts of that time.[3]

Developing frame ready to be submerged in the tank (*courtesy Archivo Nacional de la Imagen, Sodre*).

Washing tanks with plain water were used before the fixing bath step. There, the frames remained for some time to remove creaminess and obtain transparent images. A long washing process was next in a special washing tank, provided with a running water siphon for about one hour for total elimination of residues of fixing chemical components. In some laboratories, before the drying process and according to the characteristics of the support, the film received a final treatment with a solution of glycerin and water to obtain a soft and pliable condition after the drying process.

The drying process required transporting the flat frames holding the washed film to the drying room, which had to be dust free and well ventilated. There, the film was transferred, emulsion-side out, from the rolling support of the flat frames to a big drying drum formed by two wooden discs with a large number of thin, springy laths with a narrow separation between them. Generally the drum was rotated by means of a motor but in the early days some were hand turned and the action of the warm air on the film emulsion and support produced the drying effect. After drying, the celluloid support was carefully cleaned of smudges or finger marks by means of a soft rag slightly dampened with a solution of methylated spirit.[4]

The chemical procedures to correct underexposed or underdeveloped film were well known from long practice in still photography, using techniques such as intensification. The use of reducers with ammonium persulphate was one of the methods applied and intensifiers based in mercury iodide were also adopted. Over-exposures were remedied with ferricyanide and hyposulphite.

Several formulas were adopted for developing positive film, including the following chemicals: sodium sulphite, sodium carbonate, potassium metabisulphite, hydroquinone and potassium bromide. The exhibitors demanded that the prints have plenty of contrasts and sharp details, and the laboratory selected the best suited laboratory formulas.

Very few attempts to build continuous developing machines were made at the beginning of the 20th century. In 1905, Gaumont developed drying cabinets with forced air and later the same year, they built a developing machine using tubes for positive developing which after several tests was converted into a negative developing machine. Toward 1913 six of this kind of machine were used in the Gaumont laboratories. Important French firms such as Pathé and Éclair also built similar equipment. In England the well known company Hepworth and Barker was the pioneer in this field.

The printing stage was another important laboratory process. Pathé was one of the first to build a printing machine similar to a camera, with a wooden body and a magazine on top of the unit to include two rolls of about 80 feet of developed negative and positive raw stock. The two films were threaded through a film channel and the gate was faced to an external light source. A film bag at the bottom received the exposed film; the printer was hand crank driven. The table printer manufactured by Charles Urban around 1908 was also hand driven.

Pathé also built a professional printer during the teens. The basic printing unit was similar in design to the first model, but the unit incorporated several improvements: a top mounted double magazine with 400 ft. capacity for both negative and positive film; it was mounted on a large wooden light-tight body to receive exposed positive film; its design allowed framing regulation; and the light source was a Nerst lamp connected to the printer, which allowed adjusting its distance to the printing gate by an outside regulating button. However, the main facility of this professional unit was its motor drive that produced even printing exposures all along the film.

Lucien Prévost of France also produced a printer of very similar design, and with the same facilities in which the lighting unit was metal and the rest was entirely of wood.[5] The British Williamson firm was one of the first to design an entirely metal motor driven printer without magazines, using external plates to install the film stock with rewinding facilities for the negative and the positive, two sprocket wheels, loops and a handle for adjusting the intensity of light on the printing gate. These types of printers were conceived consistent with the practice at the end of the first decade, in which the negative shots were first divided according to their density and classified in groups as standard, transparent, weak, hard or opaque. Afterwards the shots were spliced in groups of similar density and printed with the required light.

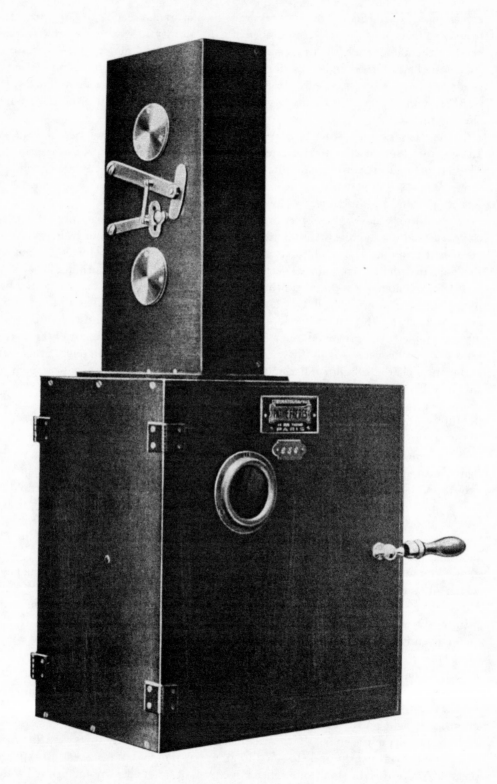

Pathé hand printer (courtesy Archivo Nacional de la Imagen, Sodre).

Pathé professional printer (courtesy *Archivo Nacional de la Imagen, Sodre*).

*Left:* **Dr. August Arnold** (*courtesy Arnold & Richter Cine Technik*). *Right:* **Dr. Robert Richter** (*courtesy Arnold & Richter Cine Technik*).

Very soon other professional printers appeared, such as the Gaumont; these were continuous printers with adjusting devices for light control by resistors, and a voltmeter. In 1911 in the United States, Bell & Howell manufactured the later-renowned continuous contact printer which soon became the Design 5205 Model D, of very advanced design and sturdy construction; it allowed easy adjusting of printing light during the operation, based on a previous check of negative requirements. The Bell & Howell was a fast action printer induced by its special continuous sprocket with an adjustable slit and a handle to regulate the size of the slit and consequently the amount of light. It soon became the classical instrument in most American film laboratories.[6]

In Germany, the well known film equipment manufacturing pioneers August Arnold & Robert Richter produced in Munich, during 1916 and 1918 several hand and motorized Arri printers.

André Debrie in France first built a complex printer and afterwards the Matipo, working by means of a perforated strip of film prepared before checking the negative. After World War I, laboratory equipment reached an adequate level to meet the requirements of mass film production.

An important and complementary improvement of prints made during the silent days was the process of toning or tinting selected scenes in each production. The addition of color was conceived as a way to create an effective atmosphere in certain sequences to produce in the audiences an sensation of intimacy with the subject and sometimes was

Bell & Howell Model D continuous contact printer (*courtesy Bell & Howell*).

carefully determined. The practice began when this method was used on the projecting still photography lantern slides.

Toning was a complex method of coloring an image by which the color affected the shadows and halftones, so a varied degree of color was given, while the highlights remained white or clear. The technique used was to replace the silver with a colored metallic compound, usually a ferrocyanide of a metal. The iron (ferric) ferrocyanide produced the blue. The silver sulphide ferrocyanide produced a warm brown. The copper ferrocyanide produced a bright red. The vanadium ferrocyanide produced a greenish yellow. Finally the reddish brown was obtained by means of uranium ferrocyanide. Two methods were conceived to produce this toning process, but the one preferred was a two-solution bath method, which included a bleaching bath and the action of a metallic salt, usually in the presence of an acid.

The tinting method was very simple and consisted of immersing the film in a solution with an aniline dye and leaving the film in the bath the sufficient time to obtain the required amount of color. If the color was too saturated the aniline dyes could be washed with plain cold water. This method proved to be very useful, and cheaper but with different results in image appearance in relation with the toning process, because the highlights were also tinted.[7]

A complementary work to film processing in the laboratories was making the titles. In the early days white enamel letters were used. To obtain contrast, positive films was used as negative. Special contrast formulas were also adopted to process the title negative. A standard system was the use of a typographic press and shooting with positive. Special methods were conceived to shoot the titles using positive raw stock through the support. Later on a technique was conceived, printing the titles with black ink on transparent sheets and shooting by transparency. Titles from lantern dry-plates were also obtained by reduction. Ornamented titles required the work of an artist. An ornamented fancy border with a cut in the center was very common for using with different titles.

# 6. Color and Film Formats

## Color cinematography: beginnings

The process for color cinematography, like many other processes in this field, arose from research carried out for still photography. Among several investigators taking part in these trials we should remember the French inventor Louis Ducos du Hauron, whose works were published in 1897, and those of Charles Cross, an Englishman, on mixing three images with three basic colors, using additive process for projection and even considering methods like the mosaic screen process and subtractive systems.

### HAND PAINTING AND STENCIL PROCESS

Experiments to apply color to motion pictures started about 1894, by Thomas A. Edison in the USA and Robert Paul in Britain, the latter carrying out his trials for a hand stencil process. Paul used this method to make the color version of his film *The Miracle*, coloring 112,000 frames, corresponding to 12 reels. Georges Méliès used a similar process to turn out seven color productions from 1898 to 1912. In 1900, Charles Pathé improved this system to an industrial mass process using complex equipment and up to 500 workers (mostly women) who methodically operated a machine provided with a magnifying glass enlarging the view of each frame in an 8 × 10 ratio; also a 10:1 reduction pantograph applied the tint by a vibratory system. Such color was applied by a different worker at the first stage, which was followed by the next stage, completing the operation automatically. The system was highly effective and afforded excellent color registration. In 1901, Léon Gaumont also used a similar process in several of his firm's productions.

### KINEMACOLOR

In 1908, the Charles Urban firm in Britain patented the Kinemacolor process developed by C. Albert Smith, then forming the new Natural Colour Kinematograph Co. They adopted a two-color additive process, which soon evidenced its quality and was well accepted in its inaugural show in 1909 at the Palace Theatre of Varieties in London. However, it was not successful in the USA.

Kinemacolor used a camera with a single film running at 32 f.p.s. The shutter in this camera completed a revolution every two frames, exposing them through green and orange filters. The resulting material was processed in black and white. It was then shown by means of a special projector which restored the system applied in the take, incorporating similar filters. With this system they shot *The Story of Napoleon* (1909), *The Durbar of Delhi* (1911), *Robin Hood* (1913) and several other films.

## CINECHROME

Also in Britain the Cinechrome system was developed in 1912, created by William Friese-Greene and Colin Bennet, also based on a two-color additive method using a red filter and a green one, on the camera and on the projector. The camera had been made by the Darling Company. They continued experimenting for a decade until they adopted a beam-splitter prism to obtain two frames on a single film.

## GAUMONTCOLOR

In 1913, Léon Gaumont designed a color system known as Gaumontcolor based on shooting with a camera with three vertical superposed lenses. The films taken by this method were shown that same year, but there was no other show until July 14, 1919, with a film called *Défilé de la Victoire*, in a panoramic gauge frame with three perforations. The projector required a similar optical system with several adjustments for the images and included filters and electric remote control in for image registration.[1]

## KODACHROME

In 1914 J.G. Captaff, in the Kodak Research Laboratory of the Eastman Kodak Co., developed a color system that they named Kodachrome. It was a two-color subtractive method requiring a camera with a beam-splitter, which recorded the two images on the same film. The printing was a quite complex process, requiring a set of master positives obtained from the original by means of a projection printer to produce a double-coated positive.

## TECHNICOLOR # 1

The Technicolor Motion Picture Corp., which afterwards became famous, was formed in 1915 by Dr. Herbert Kalmus, Daniel Frost Comstock, both graduates of the Massachusetts Institute of Technology, and W.B. Wescot, an industry and finance entrepreneur. The firm's name was in honor of their M.I.T. origin. Their first installations were in a covered railway wagon and they endeavored to create a two-color additive system based on work by Kalmus' two partners. The method required a special camera with a beam splitter prism which printed the frames alternately. Projection also required a projector with a specially designed lens and a registration device.

The first film shot with this system was *The Gulf Between* (1917). This first experience showed that the additive system had limitations and was inadequate for industrial mass production, which was their goal, so they leaned decidedly towards the subtractive method. Time would show they were on the right track.[2]

## Film formats

Various and varied were the film gauges, types of perforations and film bases used late in the 19th and early in the 20th centuries. Without pretending to be complete here is a list of the items used by the motion picture pioneers and those conceived for home filming.[3]

| Year | Format | Origin | Description |
|------|--------|--------|-------------|
| 1888 | 35mm | USA | Rectangular perforations on one edge only. First raw stock ordered by Edison from Eastman Kodak. |
| 1889 | 35mm | USA | Rectangular perforation on both edges of the film; four on each side of the frame. Ordered by Edison from Kodak Co. |
| 1895 | 35mm | France | Four rectangular perforations on both sides of each frame. Chronophotographe by Demeny. |
| 1895 | 35mm | France | Round perforations. One on each side of each frame. Lumiere's Cinematographe. |
| 1895 | 2.7/8in | G. Britain | Two vertical perforations each side on the frame line. American Mutoscope and Biograph Co. |
| 1895 | 62mm | USA | Four rectangular perforations on each side of each frame. Modified version by American Mutoscope and Biograph Co. |
| 1897 | 63mm | USA | Five rectangular perforations on both sides of each frame. Material used for shooting the famous Corbett vs. Fitzsimmons boxing match. |
| 1899 | 2.3/8in | G. Britain | Four rectangular perforations on both sides of each frame. Material used by Burton Holmes for Prestwich. |
| 1899 | 50mm | Germany | One round perforation both sides of each frame. System used by Skladowsky in this Graphonoscope for sound projection. |
| 1899 | 17½mm | G. Britain | Rectangular perforations at center of frame line. Used by Robert Paul and Birt Acres. |
| 1900 | 15mm | France | Rectangular perforations extended at center for amateur use, gauge devised by Gaumont-Démeny. |
| 1910 | 35mm | Unknown | Two rectangular perforations on the edge and a long thin one in the middle. |
| 1910 | 30mm | France | Five perforations of different sizes on the frame line. |
| 1912 | 22mm | USA | Three strips of 4 × 6mm frames separated by two strips of perforations. Edison's Home Kinetoscope. |
| 1914 | 28mm | Unknown | Four round perforations on one side and one large round perforation on the opposite side of the frame line. Nitrate film base. |

| Year | Format | Origin | Description |
|------|--------|--------|-------------|
| 1915 | 8mm | USA | One perforation on one edge of the film at the frame line. |
| 1916 | 11mm | USA | One long perforation at the frame line. |
| 1918 | 28mm | USA | Four round perforations per frame on one edge of safety film base by Eastman. |

# 7. First Conflicts and Wars

The 20th century was born in the midst of an important armed conflict, the Boer War (1898–1902). Before that, the filming of warfare had been partially faked, as occurred in the American-Spanish War in Cuba (1898), where the sinking in Cuban waters of the Spanish warship *Admiral Pascual Cervera* was re-created by Albert Smith with scale models. Georges Méliès also recreated this event.[1] It is believed that the Spanish government was interested in buying part of this material they considered of strategic importance, ignoring that it was a fake.

The Boer War was filmed by Albert Smith for Vitagraph with two cameras. It was also covered by an unconventional camera which broke from the standards of that time: the Biograph, made by the American Mutoscope & Biograph Co. It was the largest camera then, weighing about 200 lbs.; it printed images at a speed of 30 frames per second; it was provided with a special mechanism designed to avoid infringing the Edison Trust patents and thus avoid their lawsuits.

The camera used an unperforated sensitive film; as it was exposed, the film was punched at the line dividing two frames. Thus the camera had the characteristics of leaving a "blaze" wherever it was installed, a heap of celluloid perforation clipping falling between the tripod legs. The operators of this camera, Billy Bitzer, who afterwards became famous, and W.K. Dickson, formerly a Thomas A. Edison assistant, had to organize actual safaris to take their equipment, including its special rolling tripod, to the front line.[2]

The First World War (1914–1918) was an event which shook the world and led many to believe that it would be intensively covered by motion pictures. However, the actual coverage fell short of expectations because in all the countries involved military authorities greatly distrusted that new medium, and consequently restricted the appearance of newsreel cameramen to record military action on the fronts. Moreover the passage of film cameras or other film material through customs was strictly forbidden. Some limitations were lifted in 1917, and the belligerent nations adjusted their film coverage services accordingly.

The ground for military distrust of filming military action was that they looked on it as a new form of a war medium that had always existed: espionage. Therefore, takes filmed at the front without special permits could be considered spying, for which the penalty was death. Moreover, in trench warfare, positions changed suddenly, and sometimes, a camera operator could find himself alone in no-man's land or, even worse, in enemy territory, with an incriminating instrument.

Furthermore, it was difficult to film from the trenches; they were narrow and impeded setting up the tripod, without which it was impossible to turn the crank handle; besides officers would not allow a tripod in a trench, obstructing the free passage of men; also a camera on a tripod, seen from afar, could be mistaken for a machine gun and would be a preferred target.

On the roads, camera operators would climb up telegraph poles to cover extended views, troops movements or long lines of refugees. The most commonly used lens was the 50 mm, and wide angle lenses were seldom seen. Telephoto lenses were very valuable items for shooting action of special interest; Dallmeyer, the British makers, supplied many units of their latest perfected model. Nearly all cameras were crank handle driven. Military personnel assigned to film warfare had to carry, apart from their usual impedimenta, a load of trade equipment, including a camera, weighing in all, over one hundred pounds.

Film taken from the trenches often mean forming a protective nest with sandbags, leaving a loophole for the camera lens. When using the automatic Aeroscope camera, a remote control could start the instrument from a safer position, overseeing the scene with field glasses. The most common cameras were the Debrie Parvo, the Pathé, the Gaumont and Aeroscope in the French forces. The British used the Moy Bastie, the Darling, the Newman Sinclair, and the Williamson, as well as a special camera designed by Darling and Vinten for takes at sea from high up in a balloon. When the U.S. Signal Corps entered the war, their forces brought their cameras with them, mostly in metal bodies: the Universal Liberty War model, the Bell & Howell Standard and the Akeley, the latter being ideal for installing on aircraft to shoot aerial warfare.

The Aeroscope gradually become the favorite for taking warfare action, as it was the only one with automatic drive: compressed air. A single air load allowed shooting several hundred feet. It took ten minutes to reload the five compressed air cylinders (fitted inside the camera) with a pedal pump. The camera was provided with a gyroscopic device which kept it always level on whatever surface it was based upon. After the battle of Verdun one of these cameras was found on a cameraman's lap, a Frenchman named Dupré, who had died in action; apparently he was killed while he was filming, but the camera went on running by itself and remained level, recording the scene in which the courageous operator gave his life and where an enemy patrol is seen approaching.[3]

The European belligerent best organized officially in covering war events was Germany. A German War Ministry ordinance created the Koningliche Bild und Film- Amt (BUFA) (Royal Picture and Film Bureau), employing a personnel force of about one hundred, and with the task of filming warfare actions, producing instructional films, and organizing internal and foreign distribution of filmed material carried out by a private enterprise. In their first year they already had more than 300 titles available.

Great Britain had based its war coverage initially with newsreel camera operators, who were given special permits. At the beginning of the war, the newsreels demanded material taken directly in action, but they had to make do with takes from archives of maneuvers, troop movements and armaments, but material from actual warfare was scant. Finally, a cinematography committee was set up to span the gap, and camera operators were sent to all the fronts and a newsreel was produced called War Office Topical Budget and Pictorial News, but eventually only the last two words were kept in the title; it came out weekly or biweekly in about 1917.[4]

Among the filmmakers who organized such productions as well as training films, the following were outstanding: Geoffrey Malins, J.B. Mac Dowell, E.G. Tong, F. Bassil, Harold Heaps, and the already renowned director and producer C. M. Hepworth. Allied authorities realized how effective German was propaganda films were in neutral countries, so they strove to counter them with productions with the same purpose but opposite intention.

In France there were many private newsreel firms, and the government issued permits to cameramen of Pathé, Gaumont, Éclair and Eclipse to cover warfare from the beginning. Later on, they also organized official film productions. It is believed that more than one thousand camera operators participated in that war, of which about 300 were French.

At the beginning of the war, American newsreel companies were desperate as they were not allowed to film at the fronts, and the material available to them was scant. When the USA declared war, combat was covered by about 600 cameramen of the U.S. Army Signal Corps, which, after a strict censorship passed the material to private firms for exhibition; but there was an important amount of filmed material that was never seen by the public. As there was very little experience in this field at that time, the material obtained was of a poor quality, and private newsreels had a limited access to it, as there was no experience of how to handle this new medium.

Many scenes of very varied kinds were filmed in World War I which were used in intensive propaganda campaigns carried out by most of the belligerent countries: the USA, Germany, Britain, France, Austria, Russia and Italy. They show the disasters of a different and fierce war, with shocking views of gassed or maimed soldiers, ruined towns and villages, and long lines of refugees carrying the most varied sorts of belongings. Many scenes were taken of aerial and naval warfare, the latter showing warships sailing stormy seas.

The most efficient takes in naval warfare were made by the German navy, which assigned cameramen aboard some of their feared U-boats. The best known of these records was carried out by U-35, commanded by Kapitanleutenent von Arnauld de la Perrier, which sank 54 enemy ships with only 4 torpedoes and 900 shells in the 1917 campaign. Ironically, von Arnauld de la Perier was the son of a French officer made prisoner in the Franco-Prussian war. Most of these sinkings of cargo and passenger steamers, as well as sailings ships, were filmed in full detail by a cameraman aboard named Loeser. The shots covered the warning to abandon ship, this action by the captured ship's crew, its shelling, the presence of prisoners abroad the U-boat and the arrival of the U-boat at an Austrian port. This effective naval war document let the German government to produce the film *Magische Gürtel* (*The Enchanted Circle*) (1917) which became famous and was shown in many neutral countries as propaganda of Germany's war power at sea.[5]

However the most dramatic takes filmed during all the war were probably those of the torpedoing of the Austrian warship *St. Stephen* in the Adriatic by the Italian navy, on June 10, 1918. The scenes of the sinking are heart wrenching. The ship is shown capsized on its starboard side while hundreds of survivors scattered on the waters swimming desperately to get away from the ship's suction as it sinks. Finally the ship overturns with many terrified seamen appearing on its hull, slipping or diving into the water, until it sinks, drawing down the unlucky men on or near it. Whoever saw these scenes on a screen will never forget them, so much so, that years later this material was used by the U.S. Navy as a training film showing the perils at sea and survival practice in such situations.[6]

# PART II
# THE TWENTIES

# 8. Cameras

The third decade of the 20th century was called "The Golden Twenties" for many reasons. The tragic World War I left behind a sequel of depression in all countries involved, which required a slow and painful recovery affecting most people. The following decade encouraged hopes and created a search for evasion and breaking through the hard rules and conventions of an extremely rigid world. Everybody in those years was looking for a freer, more pleasant life, the pleasure of good moments, removed from ties of old schemes and experiencing intense emotions and stirring situations.

The conflict had painfully affected Europe and the recently born film industry also suffered the shock, especially in France, which had been the leader in this field, both in film production and in building film equipment. World markets that for years had been provided with diverse French films and well known makes of cameras, projectors and laboratory equipment turned now to Hollywood productions with pleasant themes and sceneries, fluid film language techniques and also film equipment from the United States was appreciated. When Europe returned again with their products, they had to fight hard to recover part of the lost markets, especially in film production. During the war years, moviegoers had developed a taste for Hollywood films, with attractive characteristics and striking backgrounds, lacking in European films.

In America, besides the classical feature films, many producers of newsreels and short films also appeared. In Hollywood the number of film studios grew from twenty in 1910 to more than forty towards the end of that decade. Many newsreels, apart from their official cameramen, also had a large number of stringers who worked as free-lancers; there was one of them in each of the most important American cities. Some were professionals, others semi-professionals and some only amateurs; but all had to have a camera for this work. Many supposed that several thousands cameras were needed to cover this specific field. This was the local market, to which American camera manufacturers responded with a variety of products. Home motion pictures, now extended to the high and middle classes and growing year after year, still used the 35mm format. In Europe also, the old camera manufacturers returned to the work; among them, Germany was the most prolific. At the beginning of this decade, motion picture camera makers had a promising panorama in this field of the film industry.

## American cameras

### THE MITCHELL

An important event in American motion picture camera making began in October 1920, when the first Mitchell professional camera made its appearance. It was an instrument designed to fulfill the most exacting requirements of the film studios and compete with the widely accepted Bell & Howell Standard, afterwards known as 2709.

The initial manufacturing firm was first known as National Motion Picture Repair Company and started in 1919. Their first jobs were repairing and adapting the most utilized cameras of Hollywood, such as the Bell & Howell, the Pathé and the Debrie Parvo, for studios and cameramen. Henry Boger and George A. Mitchell, two outstanding employees of this firm, were promoted to head the firm which was renamed Mitchell Camera Corporation. They had the rights of some patents of John E. Leonard, an ingenuous cameraman who had developed three camera prototypes with important improvements in 1914.

George Albert Mitchell was an optics expert and mechanic born in Nebraska in 1889. He was trained in the U.S. Army Signal Corps and later in the camera maintenance shop of Universal Pictures. There he became acquainted with many cameramen in the industry whose technical problems he resolved and also produced accessories according to their requirements, thus acquiring an invaluable experience in this field. Later on he learned the mysteries of this profession when an opportunity arose to work as cameraman in that studio's newsreel department and later as second operator for the shooting of a film series.[1]

The new Mitchell firm decided to build a new camera incorporating some basic concepts of the then popular Bell & Howell Standard, but improved with Leonard's new rackover device and other refinements. In 1920 the new camera came to life. The first proof of its operating capabilities was when shooting the United Artists production *The Love Light* (1921). The result was better than expected and soon important Hollywood cinematographers like Charles Rosher, Arthur Miller and Tony Gaudio bought their first units.[2]

The new camera created by Mitchell, which was afterwards referred to as Model A, had several advantages over the others in the studios, such as John E. Leonard's instrument, boasting almost instantaneous focusing and framing through the taking lens; thanks to that, with only ¼ turn of a handle, a finder was placed behind the lens to check on a magnified image the characteristics of the image to be taken. Reversing the movement of the handle, the film in its gate inside the camera box returned exactly to the previous position to start shooting. This method proved to be easier and more practical than that adopted by the Bell & Howell camera, where it was necessary to rotate the lens turret, shift the sunshade filter holder ahead, move the camera box to a side, and afterwards reverse all the operations.

Three eccentrics made up the new intermittent movement of the Mitchell: one for the double film claws, another for the two mobile pilot pins and the third for the gate pressure plate. Towards 1925 the third eccentric was eliminated and the new movement was based on gears and the resulting instrument was known as Model B, with the ability to operate at up to 128 frames per second which gave it the name of "High Speed." The Model A and later the Model B were identical in their other improvements such as: built-in matte disc of stock mattes; built-in four way mattes; adjustable inside iris; rising and falling front; automatic shutter, independent of focusing aperture; shutter speeds in two, four or eight feet, automatic and controlled from outside; built-in hand dissolve lever; four lens turret; frictionless light trap for magazines; small spools in magazines and high speed take-up; built-in Veeder footage counter; sunshade arm as part of the camera, not attached to tripod. All these were improvements of great importance in comparison with other cameras.

The Mitchell camera kept the Bell & Howell design of single plane film travel including one main 32-tooth large sprocket with pressure rollers above and below. The shaft of this sprocket was directly connected to the camera handle. This was the basic mechanical design, as used in America, that differed from that usually adopted by many European firms. The Mitchell, like the Bell & Howell, also included a double compartment magazine installed on top of the camera box, with 400 ft. capacity during the silent days. The complementary viewing system was a spyglass viewfinder with inverted image. Later, during those years, a projected (but also inverted) image monitoring viewfinder was included with masks, like the one used by the Bell & Howell Standard camera. Finally, the development of this camera was completed by a new refined monitoring viewfinder with upright image by means of a prism, conceived by Tony Gaudio and engineered by Bausch and Lomb.

**Mitchell Standard Camera with high speed movement (*courtesy Mitchell Camera Corp.*).**

**Detail of the Mitchell Standard four way mattes and iris mechanism (*courtesy Mitchell Camera Corp.*).**

## THE BELL & HOWELL EYEMO

In 1925 Bell & Howell continued with the production of 35mm professional cameras, introducing the Eyemo Standard Automatic Camera Design 71 A. The Eyemo was the professional version of the Filmo, a domestic 16mm camera that this firm successfully put on the market in 1923. The Eyemo was the first 35mm hand camera created from a design originally conceived for a small format and was its proportionally enlarged version. For this reason it was called "Filmo's big brother."

Like the Filmo, the Eyemo was the result of a brilliant mechanical conception to unify an excellent intermittent movement, two 100 ft. film spools in a very compact body that set the body's shape, and a strong 50 ft. drive spring motor. The Eyemo was one of the first truly portable 35mm cameras conceived for handheld use and ideally suited to the needs of the newsreel stringers and to ease the work of the cameraman who had depended before on the camera crank handle and the tripod. Three models of this camera were made, one for eight and sixteen frames per second, another for twelve, sixteen and twenty f.p.s. and a third for high speed work at sixty-four f.p.s. The speed control was placed on the camera front, near the lens, and was part of an excellent and ingenious intermittent movement. The camera finder fixed on the door allowed detecting the marks of the lens focus ring from the shooting position. An easy to grasp camera grip with wrist strap was of great advantage for holding the unit easily.

## THE DEVRY "A"

In the same year when the Bell & Howell Eyemo appeared, another well known American manufacturer of film projectors introduced a new 35mm automatic camera to the market. It was the DeVry Corporation, whose owner, Herman A. DeVry, was an inventive genius and a perfectionist. The first silent 35mm portable projector he had developed was so well accepted that 30,000 units were sold the world over. His dedication to the quality of products with his name made him a great success in world markets. In 1919 he decided to sell his firm, QRS-DeVry, for a million and half dollars. After some time he learned that the new enterprise gradually lowered the quality of its products. He did not doubt and immediately repurchased the firm, paying in cash, to

Improved version of the Bell & Howell Eyemo Model K camera with the basic design and a new viewfinder turret and filter holder (*courtesy Bell & Howell*).

maintain the excellence of the products and the good name of the brand.[3]

The first model of the DeVry camera, called "A," was conceived as a very handy camera for shorts and newsreel work. It was a low price unit in a rectangular box shaped with rounded corners, had one interchangeable lens, internal 100 ft. film spools, and a leather covered body. The spring motor was vibration free as it was made up of two springs installed so as to eliminate uneven torsion. The drive allowed 55 ft. per winding. The camera was provided with three types of finder: direct through the film, Newtonian on top of the camera, or by a brilliant reflecting mirror device for low camera handholding. The DeVry and the Bell & Howell Eyemo were soon the two most popular hand cameras used by stringers in the news field. Some units were also available in the film studios for special requirements like very low level shots or risky set-ups.[4]

## THE WILART MODEL "A"

Wilart Camera Corporation was a small American firm born in the early days of the movies. They built several cameras for amateurs and semi-professionals, but were practically never used in the film studios. These cameras competed with other well known wooden-box instruments of those years, such as the Universal, Box and other European makes like the Debrie Parvo, Askania or Ernemann that remained from the previous decade. During the early twenties Wilart made a special unit with the name of Wilart Model "A" with a radical change in the classic shape of the standard cameras. The body followed the round shape of the 400 ft. inside film rolls. The classical hand crank and the shutter control lever were

DeVry automatic camera (*courtesy Archivo Nacional de la Imagen, Sodre*).

installed on a side. The camera was provided with two identical lenses: the film lens and the finder lens. This camera allowed the use of automatic dissolve and was provided with a Veeder counter and the classic film punch.[5]

## THE INSTITUTE STANDARD

The Wilart Camera Corporation was a specialized mechanical shop that also produced cameras to order. One of these orders came from a distinguished American institution on the East Coast: the New York Institute of Photography. This organization had been created early in the first decade of the century with the purpose of teaching this new craft. The fascination of motion pictures was so great that soon they added to their regular professional photography course, both on their premises and by mail, a motion picture course intended for news, commercial and industrial films; this course was a pioneer in America.

The expanding possibilities of film production at that time opened a new and exciting career in the fast growing film industry. The leaders of this educational enterprise were two well known professionals: Herbert C. MacKay, A.R.P.S, director of the institute, technical writer and expert in photography; and Carl Louis Gregory, F.R.P.S., a highly reputed cinematographer, expert in underwater cinematography, technical writer and former chief instructor in the Signal Corps Photographic School. MacKay, Gregory and William Nelson designed a new camera for the students of this course that was unique in its design. Its name was the Institute Standard. They wanted to create a very low cost basic instrument, with excellent workmanship and the possibility of starting it as a basic unit to which other elements could be attached, to turn it into a complete camera for news cinematographers, travelers, scientists, educators as well for all kinds of films. The film student could buy this basic camera with only one lens and a 200 ft. exterior obliquely top-mounted magazine. Later he would be able to incorporate several accessories which would be attached by the owners

Institut Standard camera (*courtesy Archivo Nacional de la Imagen, Sodre*).

such as: four lens turret, horizontally top mounted 400 ft. magazine, range finder and dissolving shutter, special hooded finder and direct on film focusing devise.

The basic body of the Institute Standard included a Newtonian finder and a movement based on the Wilart harmonic cam, which could be used for running normal or reverse. Following the American design concept, the arrangement of the mechanism inside the camera box was for single plane film travel with a 32-tooth large sprocket, with pressure rollers above and below the sprocket shaft, which was the same as the camera crank handle. The Institute Standard was a camera adopted not only by many film students of this institute, but also by several film branches of many industrial firms (e.g. the United States Line).[6]

## European cameras

The production of 35mm cameras in Europe returned in full after World War I and Germany was one of the most prolific producers in the early twenties, with different models built either of wood or metal. Other important camera manufacturers were in France, England, Austria, Italy, Switzerland, and the new Czechoslovakia. The 35mm standard film format was then in common use in the home market and the manufacturers provided all kinds of equipment for different requirements. The tendency was growing towards compact, all metal, automatic cameras. The introduction of home film format towards 1923 sponsored in France by Pathé with the 9.5mm, and the United States with Kodak's 16mm, with the advantages of the economic and non-flammable small gauge, defined the options. Many manufacturers chose the more limited market of the professional film industry. Others selected the wider and very competitive field of home cameras which required an up-to-date competitive design and mass production.

Some established firms remained for some years in the professional market: Newman & Sinclair, Darling, Cinechrome, Moy-Omnia, Butcher or Vinten in Britain; Ernemann, Askania, Ertel, Lytax, Zeitlinguer, Bamberg, Amigo, or Maurer & Waschke in Germany; André Debrie, Bourdereau, Éclair, and L. Maurice in France; Prevost, Micro, Zollinger, Fotovita, and Serra in Italy and Slechta in Czechoslovakia. Other firms like Pathé in France and Zeiss Ikon and Arnold & Richter of Germany started camera production in the 16mm format. Finally, there was a large number of firms coming up in Germany, France, and later in other countries, created to manufacture portable automatic home cameras either in 9.5 or 16mm.

## French cameras

### THE DEBRIE PARVO

During the twenties the Etablissements André Debrie, with their varied motion picture equipment, gained great renown. They issued about fifty new patents including for the several instruments they had designed. The firm started mass production of their Parvo cameras, by mechanical procedures while maintaining the precision of each item, so as to achieve competitive prices. In 1921, André Debrie developed an automatic dissolve device using the camera shutter. One year later he introduced the Parvo Interview, a light model, which

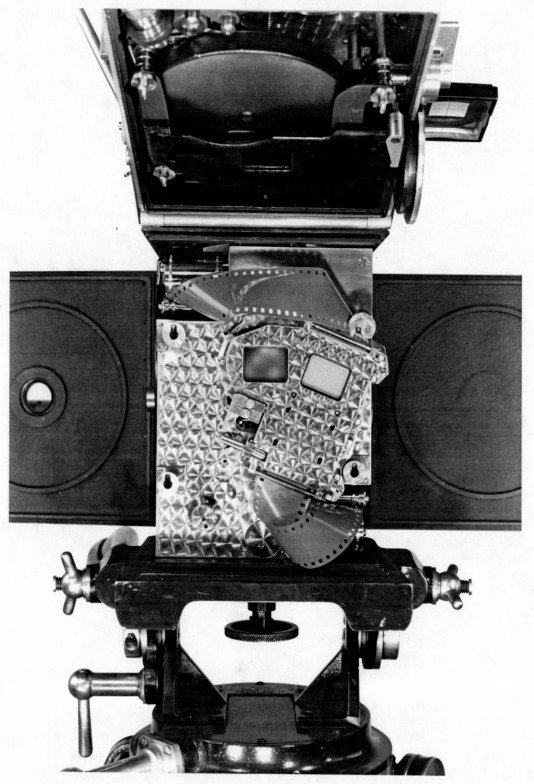

Debrie's Parvo viewing system (courtesy André Debrie Matériel Cinématographique).

included a "sport finder" on top of the unit conceived for newsreel work. In that year, the model JK also appeared, the first model entirely made of aluminum. The mechanical design was completely revised including a new film counter incorporated in the camera body.

In 1924 the Etablissements André Debrie celebrated the sale of their Parvo number 3,000, a record never reached yet by any other professional camera manufacturer the world over. In that year, Debrie incorporated the electric motor into the Parvo. Finally, in 1926 this firm developed the Parvo Model L, the most sophisticated version of this compact camera. This model included the ingenious method of moving the film with the channel and gate to a side to include a ground glass for precise and clear framing and focusing through of the taking lens. With this system, Debrie offered two alternatives to European camera operators: those who preferred viewing through the film and those who want a clear image similar to the rack-over or shift-over method adopted by Mitchell and Bell & Howell.

With this device that set aside a checking magnifier introduced in the gate in the JK model, the new Parvo L was soon the preferred camera of a large number of European cinematographers who had become accustomed to working with this compact unit. As we will see below, this camera was expanding its sales in other markets, but other French manufacturers were waiting for their chances in this field.

## THE CAMERAÉCLAIR

The Etablissements Éclair also followed the technical evolution of the professional cameras very closely. During the early twenties the mechanical designer of the firm, J. Méry, developed a very refined design camera known as the Cameraéclair, that was conceived to have all sorts of devices attached in order to effect camera tricks while shooting. This camera was introduced in 1923 and was built with an all-metal body of about 8 × 11 × 5 in. It had two internal side-to-side 400 ft. magazines, a four-lens turret, only one camera door and many controls on the right hand side and the back of the unit. The focusing unit through the film used an amplified viewer at a right angle and an iconography finder on the side. In 1926 the original design of its framing and focusing methods was improved including a six lens turret, three of them for a complementary viewing system, changing the position of the Newtonian finder to the top of the instrument and adopting a sophisticated double bellows sun-shade and filter holder. This new model was adopted by the French film industry during the thirties for trick shooting.[7]

## THE GILLON-MAURICE CAMERA

During the twenties, other interesting but little known professional cameras were developed. One of them was the Gillon, a product conceived by the Société Cinéma-Tirage L. Maurice, which in 1925 introduced this entirely aluminum model. This new unit included three lenses placed vertically, an automatic dissolve system, and an ingenious device which enabled focusing the taking lens through a ground glass when the camera was in stop position. When the first turn of the crank handle was activated the ground glass automatically went out of position allowing viewing and focusing on the film. The camera was of parallelepiped shape; it was provided with interior side to side a 400 ft. magazines, and a bellows sunshade and filter holder adjusted from above. Few units of the Gillon were sold in France and one was exported to the Kinefon studios of Barcelona, Spain.

The French Cameraéclair was ideal for trick cinematography (*courtesy Éclair International Diffusion*).

## THE BOURDEREAU CINEX CAMERA

The Etablissements Alfonse Bourdereau was another well known French constructor of motion picture equipment with a plant in the center of Paris. Its different types of movie machines included scientific instruments, automatic movie film developers, domestic film projectors and a small 35mm camera conceived for newsreel work. The Cinex camera was introduced in the mid-twenties with a very small body of about $7 \times 5 \times 6$ inches. Two 60 ft. spools were included inside. The finder was of the Newtonian type on top of the unit. The camera allowed installing compact 200 to 400 ft. capacity magazines on the back of its body. The Cinex was devised to produce fades, stop motion, included only one lens and was hand crank driven. It was one of the most compact cameras used in France.[8] Many feature film productions adopted this instrument in difficult set-ups. When sound films appeared, an electric motor with two handles was added in the front for covering news. Some expeditions and well known French sport films of those years, e.g., *La Croisière noir* (1927–29) by Léon Poirier, used this special camera in the most difficult conditions, such as in the Sahara Desert.

## DE BRAYER CAMERA

In 1924 the French engineer A. de Brayer developed a camera with a new mechanical shutter design. Instead of the normally accepted rotary shutter, he conceived a focal curtain shutter as the used in still cameras. The new shutter was a steel ribbon which passed at ¹⁄₁₀ mm from the film emulsion. This device had several advantages: it worked at a maximum shutter high speed of ¹⁄₂₀₀₀ or ¹⁄₃₀₀₀, at 16 f.p.s., necessary in trick or scientific cinematography; the mechanism allowed the change of direction of this curtain shutter from left to right or right to left, according to image requirements; and it allowed obtaining better image quality of moving subjects and the possibility of taking shots in very low light by regulating this special shutter. This camera was patented in several countries, but in those years important camera manufacturers were not interested in this proposal.[9]

Other interesting cameras produced in France during this period were the Sept, a small instrument of only 21 ft. capacity, built by André Debrie for the home movie market, and the Debrie H.V. (High Speed), designed by M. Labrely, a compact unit destined for shooting at speeds up to 250 f.p.s. with a top mounted 400 ft. double compartment magazine.

## German cameras

In Germany, important production firms used the Parvo cameras as standard during the early twenties. Great German films such as *Nosferatu* (1921), made in the Jofa-Atelier Johannistal studios of Berlin, *Phanthom* (1922) and *The Last Laugh* (1924), filmed in the famous UFA studio in Neubabelsberg, used the Debrie Parvo camera, complemented with a Stachow camera. For *Tartüff* (1925), filmed in the Tempelhof UFA Studios of Berlin, two

De Brayer camera: left: external view; right: inside view showing the curtain shutter (*author's collection*).

French cameras were used: a Debrie Parvo and a Pathé. In 1926 the UFA studios acquired the new Debrie Model L and the first Cameraeclair of four lenses with which they filmed another great film by F.W. Murnau: *Faust* (1926). By the end of the decade the Mitchell finally arrived at the UFA studio of Berlin.

It seems hard to understand why the German film industry, having developed more than 100 varied types of cameras, depended on equipment made in foreign countries for their important productions. Germany produced several professional cameras during this period, first the Geyer, based on the design of the Pathé B, and later based on the Debrie Parvo as: Ernemann, Askania, Lytax, Bamberg and Maurer & Waschke. Two were sold in Europe and overseas countries and even in the United States: they were the Ernemann, and the Askania.[10]

The Ernemann was a cheaper camera with a wooden body but with an excellent mechanism and binocular finder and used in low budget productions and shorts. Askania was an excellently built all-metal camera: metal shields protected the inside mechanism from dust. The optical finder included a range adjustment, its front sunshade and filter holder was very complete and it had a full assortment of accessories. It was a perfect studio camera for the standards of those days, but the manufacturer had to wait some years to obtain the recognition in German studios for his Model Z which it earned in other markets. Lytax Apparatebau of Freiburg constructed several 35mm cameras of professional design in those years. In their 1925 model the unit had an all-metal body with inside 400 ft. magazine and compact sunshade and filter-holder. Its ingenious crank handle drive system was remarkable: it could be operated by a flexible cable by another operator, independent of the cameraman who handled the unit. This system was specially conceived for news coverage with a 400 ft. film load.

The firm Carl Bamberg of Fridenau, Berlin, specialized in the construction of equipment

Ernemann, a popular German camera (*courtesy Archivo Nacional de la Imagen, Sodre*).

for astronomy and geodesy. They also built during those years a very robust professional camera with a refined finder system that was an advance over the Debrie Parvo JK in its system of framing and focusing with the taking lens, using the film or a ground glass. The Stachow camera, used in *The Last Laugh*, was built in Berlin in the mid-twenties, and was the only German instrument currently used as a "B" camera in the UFA studios during those years. The design of this camera was up to date, with double chamber 400 ft. back mounted external magazine, three lens turret, adjustable sunshade and filter holder and electric film drive. In 1923–24, Arnold & Richer produced the Kinarri 35 and Kinarri II and also models for 16mm home cinematography.

## Czech cameras

### SLECHTA AND CINEPHON CAMERAS

In the new Czechoslovakian Republic born after World War I, the construction of professional movie cameras began with the work of two pioneers in this field: Josef Slechta and Vaclav Rysan. Slechta was born in Prague in 1893 and from 1908 to 1912 studied and graduated as locksmith. In 1918 he founded a locksmith workshop where he also constructed improved theater projectors. At the suggestion of friends and clients, in 1922 he founded the Slechta firm for the purpose of building motion picture cameras. In 1923 he produced the first compact Slechta camera.

During 1925, Slechta built a very complete unit, which was outstanding for its modern

**First Arnold & Richter cameras (*courtesy Arnold & Richter Cine Technik*).**

design and excellent construction. It was an all-metal camera with a molded aluminum body with top mounted double compartment 400 ft. magazines designed for single plane film travel through the mechanism. This differed from the typical European arrangements, and followed the principle used in America by Mitchell and Bell & Howell. Slechta introduced a special concept in this camera to rotate and adjust the four lens turret. The several controls of the unit and a large hand crank to provide smooth operation were on the right hand side of the camera. Other facilities included shutter opening control and framing and focusing through the film by means of a prism and a binocular finder eyepiece.

Vaclav Rysan was another well-known entrepreneur of the Czech Republic. He had studied chemistry and headed an electric workshop. In 1925 he created the firm Cinephon, which later was widely know as Cinephon Camera Corp., Praha. In 1928 Slechta and Cinephon joined forces and produced a series of cameras based on the above Slechta design we saw. Cinephon cameras were soon well accepted by the local film industry and

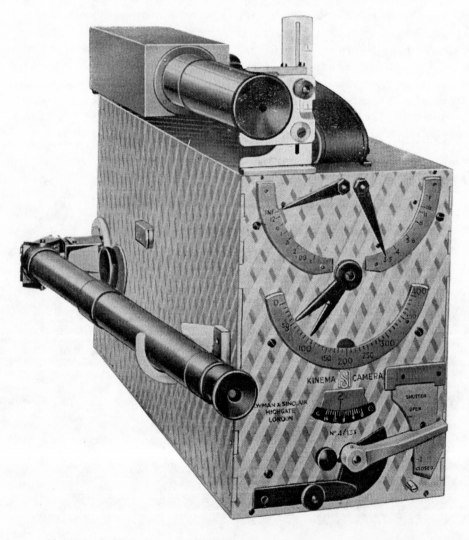

Newman & Sinclair studio 400 ft. camera (*courtesy Newman & Sinclair Ltd.*).

producers and studios of other countries. Both firms continued this partnership to the next decade.[11]

## British cameras

During the twenties, the British film industry used few British cameras such as Williamson, Moy, or Darling in feature films. The preferred cameras in the studios were the Debrie Parvo, the Pathé, and later on the Bell & Howell Standard. The Debrie was the standard one as it was in German studios. The British made cameras were used only in productions known as topical films. One was well known in this area: the Newman Sinclair, an all-metal camera with a duralumin plate body, sturdy construction and adaptable to all kind of climates. It had a long rectangular format with a 400 ft. inside magazine with controls in the back and suitable for exploratory missions. Its intermittent movement included a pilot pin. Captain J.B.L. Noel filmed the expedition to Mount Everest in 1924, at 23,000 feet, with this camera using a twenty-inch telephoto lens specially designed by Taylor and Hobson. Newman Sinclair produced also a small 200 ft. model destined for the same purpose without the inconvenient bulk and weight of the 400 ft. model. No other British camera obtained such appreciable acceptance during this period.

## Italian cameras

### The Prevost Camera

Just as in Germany and Britain and other European countries, in Italy the presence of French cameras was standard in Italian film studios. The Pathé first and afterwards the Debrie were mostly used. But the influence of Hollywood productions after World War I also made Italian technicians aware of the American way and their preferred instruments like the Akeley, the Bell & Howell Standard and later the Mitchell, first used in 1924 while shooting *Ben-Hur* (1926). But Italy also built its own cameras. The Officine Meccaniche di Precisione Attilio Prevost of Milan were well known as instrument makers when, in 1919, they started working on a movie camera, to become afterwards the most important camera maker in Italy. The instrument produced by this firm produced in 1921–22 was totally professional and based on the principles of André Debrie's Parvo. However the Prevost boasted several improvements in shape and mechanical design.

The lenses and lens mounts had been designed for quick change and furthermore allowed shifting the lens along the optical axis. A diaphragm and iris system was provided for special photographic effects. A variable shutter opening produced fade-ins and fade-outs. Critical viewing was achieved through the taking lens with the loss of only one frame. The film load was carried in separately mounted 400 ft. magazines. The camera had an all-metal body, which could be opened upwards from the back. in order to allow very easy threading and checking the film gate. The unit included the possibility of reversing. The camera controls included a meter counter, frame counter and film seconds counter. In the front the Prevost was provided with an elaborate sunshade with mattes and filter holder. Though this camera was very competitive, Debrie and Eclair cameras were used in the Italian film studios.[12]

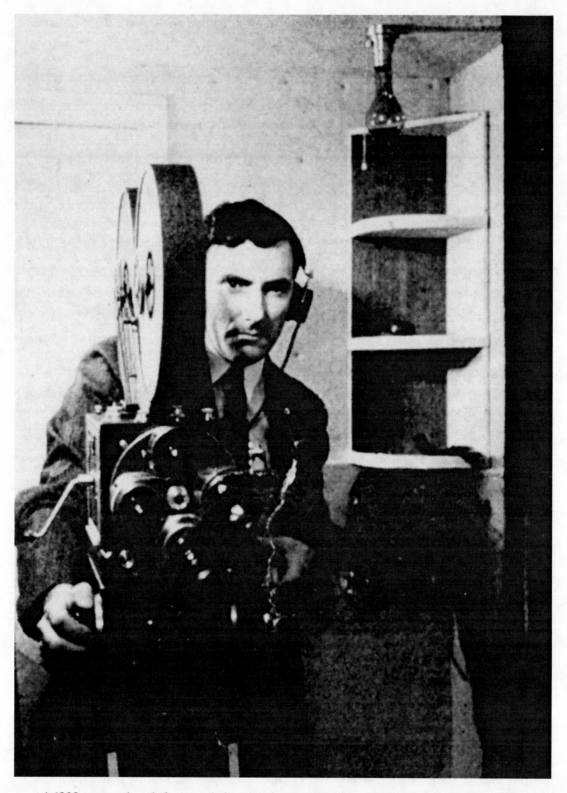

A 1929 camera booth for sound shooting (*courtesy Archivo Nacional de la Imagen, Sodre*).

## The coming of sound

The arrival of sound in 1927 greatly altered the activities of cameramen, as well as their main tool. We shall see different aspects of film technology and film business structure in the next chapter. Effects on cameras were radical: the first requirement was to change the old established film speed of two turns of the crank handle per second, the mastery of which was one of their professional prides. The electric motor had been incorporated in many cameras during the silent days but many cameramen still used the crank handle. They felt it a means to control the speed of the player's action while shooting, and to provide fluidity during certain action shots. This was of great importance in films such as westerns, where the player did not always have good training to mount a horse quickly, as well as in some comedies with gags. Cameramen constantly used their experience in adjusting the camera speed while shooting and simultaneously changing the shutter angle during the action to keep constant exposure. This was a specialized task they felt was a basic ability of their job. Now everything changed in a short period, sometimes from one production to another, and they had to be able to accept this new work method.

The new shooting film speed of 24 f.p.s required that it should remain constant to synchronize image with sound. The three turns of the handle instead of the old two turns was not feasible for this purpose, because the camera had to be synchronized with the sound recorders when sound shooting. At the beginning sound shooting was a big headache for technicians on the set and for the cinematographer, since the old standard rules were drastically changed.

Shooting with sound was very different from the techniques used during the silent days. The available cameras were too noisy for sound recording, so it was necessary to enclose the unit with the operator in a soundproof camera booth. This practice was used in Hollywood and in some film centers in Europe. Sound shooting required many camera set-ups, so there must be several camera booths on the set which therefore had to be numbered. Many studios had two types of camera booth: for indoor and for outdoor shooting. The latter had wheels for easy displacement. Camera booths had a large front window with double glass or only single glass ¼ in. thick. A black cover was laid over the window to avoid reflections, and a soundproof door behind. Certain camera booths for indoor shooting had other conveniences such as a small light, an electric fan, a bracket to put film magazines or camera accessories and a connection for the sound recorders to the camera drive motor. In some cases a stroboscopic disc with a neon light allowed synchronization between the camera and the sound recorders. Generally, a cameraman and an assistant worked inside the booth. Between takes they had to renew the air of the booth, and very frequently there was a sign on the booth's door asking: "Please don't smoke near this door." Also, on the booth's large front window another similar sign prevented smoking in the camera's range.

The use of those camera booths imposed many limitations: they reduced the action and the view of the camera crew; the cinematographer's work changed because he was now far from his instrument; he depended on other camera operators, had to control the proper lighting in many set ups and communications with his several crews were complex. During this period he felt that his old duties changed. His responsibility was now based in the lighting of the scene, the determination of the proper exposure of each camera and the coordination of the several working units under his charge.

Working with camera booths was complex also for the photographic quality of the images. The double or single but thicker glass affected image definition. The use of multiple set-ups to cover the action from several angles was a difficulty for scene lighting, motivating the return to the old general diffused lighting design. At that time film editors didn't know how to cut on the sound film, it was necessary that all cameras must cover the same scene simultaneously from different angles. Sometimes the set-ups required twelve cameras filming continuously. At the end of the day the exposed film was frequently about 30,000 ft, a length never reached before. This affected production costs considerably and was one of the motives for a revision of shooting methods and camera crew organization.

Another inconvenience with camera booths was the considerable space they required on the set. The floor space was so limited that the lighting units sometimes had to be installed practically on the tops of such booths. This implied organizing the set lighting from above and reducing floor lighting units. The big step towards elimination of the camera booths was the search to eliminate camera noise at the source.

The Bell & Howell 2709 camera which had a running noise similar to a sewing machine was closely studied by the makers. At the end of the decade the firm produced the model 2709-C1, which included a new intermittent movement with a limited stroke of shuttle and the use of fiber gears; the camera box and the shutter housing were lined with felt. The internal surfaces of the magazines included rubber lining; alterations were made also to the take-up belt and the belt tensioner. Mitchell too changed parts of their camera, creating the High Speed model with a silenced mechanism based on a modification of their sleeve-bearing AC movement.

In France, André Debrie produced first the Parvo Model T, similar to the basic Model L., with the internal size for the two new 1000 ft. magazines. Below the body, the camera motor was included in a special unit, seated on the tripod base by means of a Cardan mounting.

The modified American and European cameras reduced but did not eliminate all the noise. The solution then was the use of camera blimps thus eradicating the camera booth. In Hollywood, each studio conceived its own unit making tests with the most diverse types of materials. Some were cumbersome, others more compact. The Fox Studios made experiments with horse blankets, giving their cameras a ghost-like appearance. In Europe, Debrie in about 1929 provided a well-designed blimp to the Parvo Model T with an ingenious device to open it completely by turning a handle.

The development of film cameras during this third decade ended with making units conceived to new wide film systems such as the Fox Grandeur. Mitchell designed a 70mm version of its well known camera also adaptable to the 35mm format, changing the mechanism and the lenses but keeping the enlarged body. During those years a new firm, Fearless Camera Company of Hollywood, introduced a new 65mm camera designed by Mr. Fear, adaptable also to the 35mm format. This camera had basic concepts similar to the design of the Mitchell and incorporated facilities for sound recording on the film; one particular feature was that its mechanism was enclosed in an oil-proof box in order to work in an oil bath, consequently operating very noiselessly.

In the field of wide format film cameras, we must mention the 65mm compact camera that André Debrie built for Paramount Famous Lasky in October 1929. This camera had a square front body with only one lens, it included a 230 degrees aperture shutter, a direct focusing tube, the "orthoviseur" (the Debrie's monitoring viewfinder) on the left hand side, and a 400 ft. double compartment magazine seated behind the unit.[12]

The coming of sound also induced camera manufacturers to produce a sound-on-film camera to cover the demands of newsreels. Akeley Camera Company fulfilled this requirement first with the Akeley Sound Camera, which we will examine below, as it was extensively used by newsreels during the thirties.

# 9. Shooting Implements and Systems

## Camera supports

During great part of the twenties the classic camera support, the tripod, keep its basic characteristics, developed during the last days of the 19th century. The tripod head was driven by means of two hand cranks, one for panning and another for tilting. The mechanism of this type of head varied according to each manufacturer to obtain a better performance. One improvement was the possibility of adjusting the mesh of the gears thus reducing play. Another variation was enclosing the mechanism in a body to stop dust and sand from getting into the mechanics. With the years the size of the crank handles were reduced and a thumbscrew was included to be easily inserted in a hole at the camera base, to secure it firmly to the tripod head plate. The tripod legs were still wooden, usually treated beech or maple, because of their strength, light weight and low flexibility. Each leg was tipped with aluminum shoes provided with a spur and steel point to avoid sliding. Some manufacturers provided different methods to obtain rigid and firm tripod legs to prevent slipping.

One of the tripods including considerable improvements in its design was known as the Precision ball-bearing tripod. Its stability was based on its good design and metal reinforced legs. The tripod head was provided with ball bearings that produced fluid panning and tilting. Each handle was inserted into a hollow shaft so the unit had no projecting pieces. The pan and tilt movements were graduated on scales.

The tripod produced by Mitchell for their camera also included innovations such as an amply adjustable aluminum alloy head, mounted by means of standard Keuffel and Esser instrument thread. The head steadiness did not depend on the worm gear, but had two discs on bearings, pressed together with spiral springs. The panning device was of a different type: the worm wheel, with bronze bushing in the center, fitted on a steel spindle threaded at its lower end. Another interesting tripod of that time was developed by Fearless camera; this included a large bowl in between the legs for quickly leveling the camera and was controlled without cranks, by a handle.

Carl L. Akeley primarily used the bowl concept with his Akeley pancake camera, which was commented on above. Toward 1929 he complemented the design of a new tripod, with the revolutionary gyro head panning that was outstanding for its characteristics, though it did not use a real gyroscope. This tripod was extremely sturdy so as to support a heavy camera: the new Akeley Sound. The head included a ball bearing mechanism with a flywheel that was put in action by means of gears when the handle was actuated. The inertia of the flywheel and its intensive impulse was fundamental to obtaining fluid panning and to

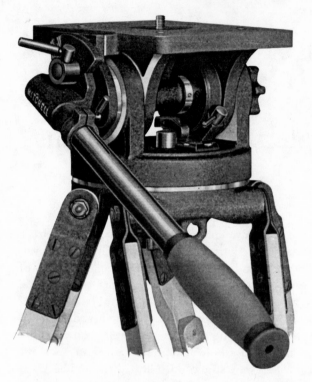

Mitchell tripod head (*courtesy Mitchell Camera Corp.*).

avoiding uneven starts and stops. The mechanism had quick releases for movement in any direction. The unit was conceived to produce three different pan speeds, very useful for sports assignments. An automatic device produced camera balance on the tripod, preventing accidental up and down tilts. The bowl method was very useful to level the camera quickly, whatever the position of the tripod legs. However, the Akeley tripod was remarkable also for its heavy weight, too much to be carried personally: the tripod head alone weighed forty pounds.

In Europe, the tripod built by André Debrie used separate enclosed worm gear drives, which operated at two speeds by means of crank handles; it was the classical unit adopted in many studios. Debrie also conceived an ingenious special tripod with very long and sturdy legs which could be transformed into a large camera platform 7 ft. high, capable of supporting two cameramen. Éclair and Bourdereau in France, and Vinten and Cinechrome Instruments Ltd. in England, also produced new types of tripod heads, some of them with panning handles. The panning handle was a step forward for freeing camera movements and producing quick pans. The use of panning handles showed their practical possibilities but they worked better with friction heads. The gear heads were heavy and demanded long practice to combine the rotation of the crank handles when panning and tilting, or both in opposite directions. That was why unskilled cameramen frequently made zigzag pans and tilts.

Working with the panning handle required well-designed friction heads. Some good friction heads were later provided with several perforated fiber discs to disperse the grease evenly; this produced and effective damping effect. One of the best camera heads was Hollywood-made by Fred Hoefner under the name Trueball. Two units were used successfully by Clyde De Vinna in Africa with motor driven Bell & Howell cameras during the difficult filming of wildlife in the film *Trader Horn* (1931).[1] Other wildlife shots for this production were obtained with the old Akeley pancake camera, with its unique tripod head often used in Hollywood studios; this tripod head was the favorite of the then well-known cameraman Fred Parrish.

Another variation of camera head was the geared head conceived for heavy blimped studio cameras, to provide accurate and fine panning and tilting movements. This head used racks and gears and was controlled by hand-operated wheels; it was considerably bulky, heavy and was generally installed in an all metal rolling tripod to move the camera on the set. Mole & Richardson was one of the first firms to provide this kind of unit in Hollywood.[2]

In Europe, André Debrie worked during the late twenties on a refined, very compact electric driven pedestal for its blimped Debrie "T" camera. The pedestal was aluminum made with a maximum width of about 30 inches. The unit had three motor driven rubber wheels that moved in all directions controlled by a single handle. The speed was changed by rotating the handle. It allowed all kinds of movements. Its central column was telescopic and its height was adjustable from 3 ft. to nearly 10 ft. with an attachment in the camera support line. This firm afterwards built its classic rolling column, used over many years.[3]

## Camera lenses and optical devices

After the above mentioned achievements, optics were considerably developed during the twenties for cinematography as consequence of a new and different market with special preferences. In still photography, the limitations of the low sensitivity of photographic emulsions could be overcome by stopping the subject's movements and adjusting the exposure time. But in motion pictures this was not possible, and the minimum exposure time was only $\frac{1}{30}$ of a second with the standard 16 f.p.s. The growing tendency to film indoors with artificial light required that film studios should do research for new fast aperture lenses at a time when the camera lenses had a standard aperture of f/3.5.

In 1916 Charles Minor of Chicago had adopted the crown elements with a Taylor developed formula to obtain the aperture of f/1.9.[4] The lens was manufactured by Gundlach. However, in 1920 several camera manufacturers such as Debrie, Zeiss, Ertel, Bourdereau, Ernemann, Universal, Box, etc., had their different equipment on the market with a standard lens of 50mm with the classic aperture of f/3.5. But about the middle of that year Horace Lee, lens designer of Taylor, Taylor & Hobson, developed a lens with an f/2 aperture, which was very well accepted and altered the classic speed of such type of lenses.[5] This was followed in 1922 by the Ernostar f/2 lens designed by Ludwig J. Bertele of Ernemann. Also that year Bausch & Lomb of Rochester produced the Rapid Anastigmatic lens with an aperture of f/2.7, developing a triplet to obtain a satisfactory quality lens, with 70 percent more aperture.[6] In 1924 Ernemann produced another Ernostar lens from another Taylor formula, with an aperture of f/1.8. This lens was the father of the afterwards famous Sonnar f/1.5 of Zeiss, designed by Paul Rudolph, and from its design the Tachonar f/1 of the German firm Astro was born later.

During 1925 the race between different American and European optical firms in this specific field ran on and cinematographers achieved what they wanted. Afterwards, W.F. Bielicke, an optic designer, patented an adaptation of Cook's formula in the United States to achieve to an aperture of f/2.3 and even of f/1.8. This patent was soon sold to Astro. In 1929 Bausch & Lomb took another step forward with the f/2.3 Raytar lens, reaching a product competitive with the famous European firms. Some time after, Zeiss produced a good quality cine lens with an aperture of f/1.4, using the double Gauss formula. The desired target in motion picture lenses was finally obtained during this decade.

The lenses available for professional cinematography at that time were of the following focal distances: 32mm, 40mm, 50mm, 75mm, 180mm, 240mm and 270mm. The wide-angle lenses of lower values than 32mm did not cover the image adequately, and many telephoto lenses had poor definition at their maximum aperture, that was of f/3.5 for 75mm and f/4.5, and f/6. for long focal lenses. Many of the early lens mounts were bronze and the optical unit was heavy. Goerz made one of the best-developed lens mounts in those years, which was built in two models—A and B—to be adjusted to different optical units.

Professional camera lenses were anastigmatic. Available lenses did not provide adequate contrast in certain strong backlight situations, due to internal reflections of the glass components. However one must recall the good image results obtained in the photography of many films.

The best-known optical firms in this specific field were: Carl Zeiss of Jena, Hugo Meyer & Co. of Goerlitz, Jos. Schneider & Co. of Kreuznach and Astro Gesellschaft of Berlin, in Germany; J. H. Dallmeyer Ltd., of London, Taylor, Taylor & Hobson of Leicester and Ross Ltd. of London, in the United Kingdom; and Etablissements Ermagis and Optis of Paris, France. In the United States were the well-known Bausch & Lomb of Rochester, Wollensack Optical Co. of Rochester and C.P. Goerz American Optical Co. of New York. Later on, other makes entered the field of home movie lenses for 9.5 and 16mm film formats.

Other important changes produced during those years were connected with the lens aperture and the use of new materials in the lens mount. During this period the classic wooden camera body was disappearing and was substituted by all metal units. This produced a greater precision in image reproduction. New camera optical devices were improved like the magnified image focusing tubes, upright image viewfinders by means of a prism and adequate ground glass with reticle to facilitate framing and focusing.

We must remember that fundamental changes appeared during the twenties, influencing the photogenic qualities of the players, whereby optical firms helped the cinematographer's artistic research. The well-known soft focus touch of feminine close-ups, or in landscape shots, was obtained using the cinematographer's personal gadgets but also by means of special lenses such as the Verito Soft Focus lens of 50 and 75mm developed by Wollensack, to produce idealistic effects in some shots.

Also, image alteration with cuts in it, or changes in its size, were effects used as sequence transitions and obtained by special devices produced by firms like Goertz, to be installed in front of a standard lens. During the last years of the decade some optical devices were conceived to change the image geometry and alter the focal values of some lenses. So, in France, the firm Optis, well known for its lenses and focusing finders for the Debrie Parvo, conceived the Brachyscope, that "produced effects of advancing or backing the image without moving the subject or the camera"; this concept was an introduction to the future arrival of the zoom lens.

In 1922 the Hollywood cinematographer Joseph Walker, experimenting with camera lenses, discovered that an important variation in the size of an image was produced if the inside glass negative element was moved. His research continued and several years later, Walker patented a lens with the name of Travelling Telephoto, having the capacity to change the focal distance during the take. The practical use of this new lens was developed later and was the starting point of a radical advance in lens performance during that fruitful period known as "the crazy years."[7]

## Film stock

Towards 1927 the standard motion picture negative used in world wide film production centers was the orthochromatic emulsion which had been born with still photography. This photographic emulsion had a sensitivity of about 12 to 20 of today's A.S.A. ratings.

The Eastman Kodak Co. first, and Dupont Pathé Film Mfg. afterwards, who started their raw stock film products in 1923, made the standard negatives used in the United States. French negatives manufactured by Pathé Vincennes were also well appreciated and used in America. Other manufacturers elsewhere in the world were Gevaert, in Belgium with a slower negative; the British produced raw stock with imported film base at Kodak, Criterion, Brifco and Austin Edwards factories in Harrow, Birmingham, Ashford and Warwick; and in Germany the best known negative was Agfa but that was difficult to find in the States.

The Eastman orthochromatic negative had two types of emulsion: the standard one and the X back, for very cold climates, with a specially treated celluloid base to avoid static effects by the friction of the support with the film gate channel. Many of the emulsions were anti halo treated. The classic length of the rolls was 200 and 400 ft. Kodak also produced unperforated negative film rolls of 2000 ft. to be perforated by the users. This was usual in big production centers in order to unify film perforation according to the type of cameras each studio used, and afterwards they cut the wanted roll lengths. The negative image was usually printed in black and white or tinted positive stocks. In the early twenties, Kodak had lavender, red, blue, green, light amber, yellow, orange and pink. In Europe, Agfa provided the same tinted positive colors. Agfa continued improving their orthocromatic film and introduced the Agfa Super Speed, with excellent results for very low light conditions.

In 1922 Kodak launched the Eastman panchromatic emulsion on the market. The first American film that adopted it entirely was *The Headless Horseman* that same year. But this new film emulsion had some limitations yet. It was only in 1927 that cinematographers approved its qualities and its limitations were laid aside. The panchromatic had been born in America in 1913 as a consequence of scientific experiments researching for a cinematographic color system. But the film industry took some time to adopt this type of raw stock as it was very unstable a short time after it was manufactured. Dupont introduced its panchromatic emulsion, which was particularly superior in its red sensitivity. The Agfa Pankine had very good response to the yellows and oranges and a higher contrast than Kodak's and Dupont's emulsions. Radical technical changes demanded the panchromatic for shooting, but especially for processing. But it also had advantages especially in the field of the player's makeup. When good results were obtained, cinematographers found that this new emulsion also produced more realistic images and natural reproduction of the gray tones in outdoor shots.

The components of natural landscapes made with panchromatic negative were now more realistic and with better modeling effects. The image obtained showed different contrast values, and the natural scenes had a better response. For the first time the sky, controlled by filters, could show the clouds. The use of filters by cinematographers acquired then a special relevance and the filter was now considered a very important tool to be included with the camera gadgets. In Germany the first use of the cine panchromatic negative was in 1925 in the film *Tartuffe the Hypocryte* directed by F.W. Murnau with a partial use of the Agfa Pankine. In the United States the film that earned a reputation for the photographic quality of its outdoor images made with Kodak's panchromatic film was Robert Flaherty's *Moana* (1923–1925). The first Hollywood feature film that gained special reputation for its use of the Kodak Panchromatic Cine Film was *Sunrise, a Song of Two Humans* (1927), which merited the first Academy photography award.

Shooting inside the studio continued using orthocromatic film, because many thought the old emulsion was faster and produced a better image. The use of panchromatic film inside required new lighting practices, new makeup treatment, and many old methods changed drastically. The blue light of the Cooper-Hewitt mercury vapor tubes was no longer necessary. The use of arc lighting was limited since tungsten lamps proved to be extremely effective with this kind of film, reducing costs, and it was more adaptable to different filming situations. This produced an important variation in shooting procedures and in the kind of lighting units used.

During the twenties these were important improvements in the production of a sub-standard safety film conceived for the home movie market in the sizes of 9.5, 16 and 17½mm. These came from the introduction of the acetate safety film obtained by Kodak in 1910. In 1925 Pathé produced a 35mm safety positive film to release prints, but its limited resistance to intense circulation in the film theatres brought about its withdrawal.

In 1923 Kodak produced the matrix stock for the Two Color Technicolor system. In 1928 Kodak introduced the new Type II and Type III panchromatic emulsions. This firm also continued with its contribution to color cinematography for the domestic market introducing the 16mm Kodacolor lenticular additive film. For the first time a special duplicating film was introduced by Kodak, which was in high demand for different types of duplicates. Another great step forward was the achievement of a super panchromatic film by Kodak and Dupont that merited an Oscar award for both firms.

## Film formats

During this period, the attempts to introduce new film formats grew considerably in relation to previous decades. This was the consequence of many factors. First, the film industry was in a state of expansion and was searching for more possibilities for motion pictures in many fields besides entertainment. The growing demand was becoming evident for films to cover science, training, industry, advertising and several other fields. Soon the limitations of the standard 35mm format were serious drawbacks to these ends, due to their excessive volume and weight, when storing or for transport, as well as their demand of bulky projection equipment, and especially, the risky inflammable film base used. Consequently, other smaller and safer gauges had to be adapted and standardized.

On the other hand the entertainment industry also considered that the use of a wider format for the large screen would attract larger audiences to film theaters bringing new and good business opportunities. In the first place there were big manufacturers of home equipment and raw film who knew the possibilities of the big market in that field. There were also some big film studios and imaginative filmmakers who wanted to change the way of making films with a tendency towards the big show. The arrival of sound was an important incentive to develop this new kind of show. Let's look at the basic options one by one.

| Year | Format | Origin | Description |
|------|--------|--------|-------------|
| 1920 | 13mm | French | Ozaphane. Film support manufactured of nonflammable cellophane, with 5 centesimal silver bromide emulsion. This film support had ⅔ of the weight of the nitrate and had no perforations. The Société Cinelux of Paris manufactured this film. The film was developed using ammonia steams. A 1,100 ft. of nitrate film has the same size as a 5,000 ft. roll of Ozaphane. The projection was by means of a continuous sprocketless prism. |

| Year | Format | Origin | Description |
|------|--------|--------|-------------|
| 1920 | 17mm | French | Proposed by Pathé. Two square perforations placed at each side of the film frame line. |
| 1920 | 22mm | French | Four open perforations, each one at the edge of the film, in the end of the frame line. The image had no side edges. |
| 1920 | Twin 16 | French | Kodak support with rectangular sprocket holes. 1920 16mm French Agfa safety film support with rectangular sprocket holes at the end of the frame line. |
| 1922 | 9.5mm | French | Introduced by Pathé. Safety support. One perforation in the center of the frame line. Was conceived for printing this firm's film productions. |
| 1923 | 9.5mm | French | Safety film support, which included reversal emulsion for home use. |
| 1923 | 16mm | American | Safety film support, with four rectangular perforations in the film line. Used reversal emulsion. Introduced by Eastman Kodak. |
| 1924 | 24mm | French | Safety film support. Four perforations out of the frame line. Proposed by the Société d'Explotations Cinematographiques. |
| 1924 | 35mm | American | Used a silent frame of eight B&H perforations in the negative. Corrugated positive for 3-D effects. |
| 1925 | 24mm | French | Four square perforations outside the frame line in safety film support. |
| 1925 | 18mm | Soviet Union | Four square perforations out of frame line. |
| 1925 | 13mm | French | Four rectangular perforations inside the frame line. |
| 1926 | 63.5mm | American | Silent. Developed by the R.K.O. Hollywood Studios with the name of Natural Vision for production of spectacular show films. |
| 1929 | 56mm | American | Had five perforations on each side of the frame. Developed by Fox Studios of Hollywood for great spectacular films. |
| 1929 | 70mm | American | Developed by Mr. Earl Sponable for Fox Studios with the name of Fox Grandeur. The image was 48 × 22.5mm. Four perforations on each side of the image with a wide space for optical sound track. |
| 1930 | 17mm | French | Included only one perforation on the side of the frame line. Had a space for an optical variable density sound track. |
| 1930 | 17.5mm | American | Three perforations per frame on one side. Used optical sound track. Developed by Fox Studios for distribution of their newsreels in South America. |
| 1930 | 17.5mm | German | Adopted double edge perforation in the frame line, with space for optical sound track. |
| 1930 | 65mm | American | Developed by Paramount Famous Lasky Corporation of Hollywood. Image size: 46 × 23mm. Five double edge perforations. |
| 1930 | 62mm | American | Frame size: 45 × 25mm. Five rectangular perforations on both edges and 6mm space for the sound track. 1930 70mm American Developed by Metro Goldwyn Mayer for the Realife wide screen system. |
| 1930 | 65mm | American | Developed by Warner Bros. Studio for the Vitascope wide screen system. |

## Color systems

Color cinematography was another technical achievement that obtained considerable attention during the twenties. The number of methods adopted during this decade was similar to those conceived during the 25 years elapsed since the birth of cinematography, but the researchers and promoters of each were mostly from a new batch. The origin of many systems was due to the enthusiasm and dedication of experts or the plans of some enterprises in which several American, British and French researchers participated. From all the systems proposed, half of them opted for the subtractive method and the other half for the additive system. Here is a summary of the more representative characteristics of each method.

COLORCRAFT. It is estimated that it appeared in the USA in about 1929, but some believe that it was earlier. Its promoter was W.H. Peck, based possibly on the 1905 printing techniques patents of A. Traube. The system adopted the subtractive bichromate method with a camera with a beam-splitter or a bipack system. The printing raw stock was tinted by iodide mordants. Very little is known of its other characteristics, but it did not prevail in the industry.

DUFAYCOLOR. This color method was conceived by Louis Dufay and developed later by the British firm Dufay-Chromex Limited around 1925. This system made feasible the use of the principles conceived by Dufay, a French still photographer, for his color photographic plates named Dioptochrome, in 1910. Adapted to motion pictures, the method used the additive color principle with a mosaic made up of a web of very thin colored lines (red, green and magenta) that crossed each other at right angles forming a reticule. A panchromatic emulsion of about 10 on today's ASA rating covered this mosaic. Exposure had to be made with the film support towards the camera lens, and the positive print demanded a very complex treatment. We will see efforts were made in the next decade to impose this system.

FOX COLOR. A system developed by Eastman Kodak around 1928 in the United States. It was based on the subtractive two-color method, which adopted the techniques applied with the first Kodachrome color film.

FRIESE-GREENE. This British color system appeared in 1923. It was developed by Claude Friese-Greene, a cameraman, using his father's patent. It made use of an improved two-color process. The camera used a disc so that one image was obtained through a red filter, but the next image was exposed without a filter. The positive raw stock was alternately tinted in blue-green and red. The film projection was made at a normal speed and with a shutter without filters, as the color was on the print. In 1925 this system was exhibited in London but it was found that this singular method produced eye fatigue.

HERAULT TRICROME PROCESS. This was a French process created in 1925 and based on an additive three color system. The projection print was obtained by contact, and a continuous drive system was used for the projection. The color was obtained by tinting the print in red, green and blue in the corresponding film frames. The projection speed was 24 f.p.s.

KELLER AND DORIAN PROCESS. The American firm Keller-Dorian Color Film Corporation experimented with this process. It adopted a lenticular process on the film and consequently was an additive color method. In 1925 the 16mm rights were acquired by Eastman Kodak to be marketed in 1928 under the name of Kodacolor. Some time before, experiments were made in England and France where this lenticular method was known as Keller-Dorian-Berthon. An exhibition was made in Paris in 1923 with a test production.

KELLY COLOR. It was developed in the U.S.A. around 1923 by the prolific expert Van Doren Kelly, inventor of the well-known Prizma Color with other systems. It was a two-color subtractive method. It required a camera running at 32 f.p.s. with a shutter provided with two filters. The printing process included the use of a double-coated positive stock where two images were formed. One was first printed, developed and tinted. A second image was later printed on the unexposed silver halide and then also developed and tinted.

KODACOLOR was a tricolor additive method based on the Keller & Dorian patent which later on was developed by Eastman Kodak. The principle was based on the use of a lenticular film with microscopic cylinder lenses in the film support. For shooting and projecting the film, a special three-color filter had to be installed in front of the camera and another in front of the projector. This system was adopted only in the 16mm format for some years. This name was used many years later for this firm's other color system.

MULTICOLOR appeared in the United States in 1928 based on the improvement of the Prizma Color System and the participation of W.T. Crespinel, who researched the bipack system. This color method used two negatives in the camera film gate, which had to be adapted, as well as a bipack magazine. In Mitchell cameras a pressure plate with four rollers was used. The focus plane of the ground glass also had to be adjusted to the film emulsion position. During daylight shooting an 86-wratten filter was used. The two negatives were printed simultaneously in a step printer that used two light units. Each printing gate light acted on each of the two emulsioned sides of the positive film, which were toned to blue and magenta respectively. In those years the double bipack negative required for this system was called Rainbow negative.

PHOTOCOLOR was created in the United States in 1930 by the Photocolor Corporation and was a two-color subtractive method. It needed a special camera with a beam-splitter prism. The printing method was very similar to the English Polychromide process that we will see immediately below.

POLYCHROMIDE PROCESS was conceived by the American photographer and chemist Aaron Hamburger. This color system appeared in England in 1922 and was afterwards improved. It worked with two negatives: one with an orthochromatic emulsion and the other with a panchromatic emulsion. Both negatives were printed simultaneously during the shooting in a camera with a beam splitter with two gates at right angles. A. Hamburger and W.E.L. Day had previously developed this camera, and patented it in 1918. The positive raw stock had emulsion in both sides of the support independently treated with special products. The emulsion side printed from the orthochromatic negative obtained a color radiation from red to yellow. The other side printed from the panchromatic negative had tones from green to blue. This way a four-color system was obtained. Later the system was changed, eliminating the beam-splitter prism and adopting a bipack system with a Debrie Parvo camera specially developed to these requirements. The Polychromide process was used in London for several years.

SENNETT COLOR was created in the Hollywood studios of Mack Sennett between 1928 and 1930. It was a bipack subtractive system and consequently required a camera conceived for it. The printing process was made on positive stock with emulsion on the two support sides. One side was toned red-orange by means of uranium bath and the other was toned with an iron bath.

TECHNICOLOR # 2. This Technicolor process appeared in 1921, and was the result of the great variation made by Herbert Kalmus when he replaced the additive by the subtractive process. This step was the result of the complex limitations he found in developing a practical additive method. The new Technicolor, later known as # 2, required a beam-splitter camera (an adapted Bell & Howell Standard) and a special intermittent mechanism with pilot pins and a shuttle that pulled down the film so as to obtain two frames instead of one. Only one panchromatic negative was used. On it, two images were produced from the lens by means of the prism. One image was filtered through a green filter and the other through a red filter. The length of this negative was twice that of the standard since the registered scene was simultaneously printed twice in the camera. The two images were identical, but with the variations in the density of the silver, according to each filter effect. Both images were also exposed in the camera with an inverted position to each other. The printing process of this system was very complex and both images were unified in two printed films that were cemented back to back with registration of the images. A printing process by imbibition was finally made by means of colorants on the two faces of the film support. Some Hollywood films were made with this color process, e.g. *The Black Pirate* (1926). But this Technicolor method had several drawbacks concerning print damage, when the emulsion side passed through the projection gate or when the heat of the aperture tended to buckle the print with the inherent loss of focus. Technicolor moved then toward new research made by their expert, Leonard Troland, who achieved another improved process.

ZOECHROME. T.A. Mills, using a three-color additive process, invented this color system in the United States in about 1920. It was based in the use of three small secondary lenses behind the primary lens of the camera. This method allowed having three small images inside the main camera image, which later were filtered with red, green and blue filters. Panchromatic negative was used. During the complex printing process, each one of the three small images was enlarged and superimposed using a recoated method to print each color. This system had a short life and no information was found about an effective solution to the inherent parallax of such images.

## Lighting implements

Some time elapsed in the early twenties before the design of lighting units changed radically. During those years the principle of the dark studio against the studio with plenty of natural light, coming through the glass walls and roof, was the basic dominant concept. Lighting equipment maintained the classic characteristics of the previous decade: the arc light, the mercury vapor light and the diffusing light screen. But in the late twenties incandescent bulbs appeared.

The voltaic light units were manufactured according to several models, some of them derived from public lighting units. Westminster Co. of London conceived other arc lamps, to be hung from the top and with vertical carbons enveloped in crystal housings. American manufacturers of this kind of equipment, like the Kliegl Brothers of New York, had long experience in theater stages (begun in 1896), and produced several types of arc lamps with pedestals or to be hung, in single and double models with horizontal positioning of the carbons, automatic operation, taking up 35 amperes at 110 or 250 volts.

The latter firm produced also small lightweight units. One of them, known as Lilliput, used two vertical arcs in series but with a reduced current of 15 amps. Some models were arc lamps conceived for special effects. One was enclosed in an oil lamp or to simulate a lantern. They also built a very small size arc lamp to be held in the hand to simulate a lighted match.

Another important American arc light units manufacturer was The Chicago Stage Lighting Company, which made also motion picture stage light equipment as well. Some of these units used carbons in horizontal positions or at an angle of 90 degrees to provide more efficiency; these lamps drew 35 amps at 110 volts. This firm also produced heavy duty 35, 50 and 75 amp spot lamps for studio work. This firm's arc spot lamps were well known in the Hollywood industry. Another well known firm in this field was M.J. Wohl & Co. Inc. of New York, who produced portable lighting units with 18,000 candlepower illumination on 20 ampere current, in a portable carrying case, weighing 36 pounds, ideal for newsreels and shorts films.

In a listing of white flame lamps used in the motion picture studios for the Society of

Westminster studio arc lamp (courtesy Archivo Nacional de la Imagen, Sodre).

Motion Picture Engineers, Mr. William Roy Mott, of the research laboratory of the National Carbon Company, stated that in the early twenties, the film industry had 18 models of flame lamps available with an amperage that varied from 15 to 150 amps, diversity in the number and position of the carbons from four arcs vertical, to twin vertical, right angled or single vertical or adjustable carbons, from 15 different manufacturers. This specific lighting field was well covered in those years.[8]

The arc lights used by the motion picture industry during the twenties were improved instruments. The bodies allowed placing a reflector behind and a support in front to use special diffusion glasses. The heavy models included a rolling column and a crank handle system to raise or lower the lighting lamp. The spot line had a 10-inch plane convex lens and drew from 70 to 200 amperes at 125 volts.

One of the most used arc lamps in some Hollywood studios was the Sunlight with the searchlight characteristic developed at the end of the previous decade. Its current was 120 to 150 amperes. It used ⅝ × 12 inch upper white flame and ½ × 7 inch lower white flame carbon trims with a punctual and close to daylight response. Thirty and 60 amps broadsides were also used, which included four vertical carbons and provided a great amount of light to obtain an adequate foundation in large sets.

Arc lights were adopted in motion pictures according to different procedures. One was hanging several units from the stage ceiling so that all the sources were filtered by means a large tracing cloth to produce a special kind of diffusion over the set area. Some studios conceived stages with aluminum painted walls and ceiling which reflected the light of high intensity arcs directed to the ceiling. The classic lighting touches in the windows, open doors, and sunrays or in the hair of the players were obtained by means of arc spots with the classic plane convex lens. No light control of the beam was then available, as barn doors, or flags, but black cloths were hung in some studios.

The continuous use of arc light in the stages was very hard for the players and the technical staff. Many operators used glasses with a dark yellow filter for protection from violet radiation emitted by these units during a twelve hour day's work. Certain powerful arc spots were so strong that if the protection glass cover was broken, the lamp had to be switched off, immediately, because otherwise it would burn the face, skin or the hands, besides causing eye damage. Conjunctivitis was a very common disease among players and the technical staff, and carelessness in eye protection was sometimes paid with sore eyes for four or five days. Arc lamps were also used in European studios, where the best known was the Jupiter, made in Germany with a characteristic half cylinder protecting device. In Britain the classic arc lamp used was the above mentioned Westminster. France built the Lebarden, a huge lamp with several arcs and a frosted glass in its front. This arc was afterwards improved and converted into a most suitable spot lamp.

Other important lighting sources in those years were the Cooper-Hewitt lamps devised early in the century. They were a series of long tubes with a small quantity of mercury. When the mercury came in contact with one of its supply poles, it was vaporized all along the tube. The light emitted had strong actinic qualities and was extremely soft. This condition was very valuable for the orthocromatic emulsion then used. It also favored the lighting techniques to provide a fill light source or as a basic exposure foundation, and it was a very comfortable light to work with.

The manufacturers of this type of lighting unit produced them in banks of several models, according to the number and size of the tubes. Some banks of this type were conceived to be installed above, hanging from the ceiling. Important studios like Metro installed the banks on complex cranes to be moved along the length of the stage. One stage had 20 banks installed above. Rolling banks also covered both sides of the stage. The stage then had 32 banks available, totaling 226 mercury vapor tubes, which produced an enormous amount of light but without excessive heat. The most used units were floor banks, heavy rolling platforms to bring out an effect of a large lighting wall. The large banks had 8 vapor tubes each. Small mercury vapor tubes were made with four or only two units for close-ups, especially in short film productions. In Europe the Cooper Hewitt mercury-vapor lamps were also used in the U.K. and France. Other units were the Sperry Giroscopic lamps. Many studios in London also used Boardman Northlight lamps and Winfield-Kerner and Digby equipment.

In 1927 important changes came about in studio lighting techniques when the new panchromatic emulsion was adopted. The characteristic blue light of mercury vapor tubes was not suitable for this new raw stock. The immediate possible light source was arc lamps but these items were noisier and thus unsuitable for the new sound shooting. The solution was consequently tungsten lamps that were growing in consideration with many cinematographers, because they were very easy to use though not very efficient with the old orthochromatic emulsion. The total displacement of the old raw stock was produced when Kodak lowered the cost of the panchromatic film considerably and most Hollywood studios adopted the incandescent lighting that year.

The Mazda lights as they were called in the studios (because it was the General

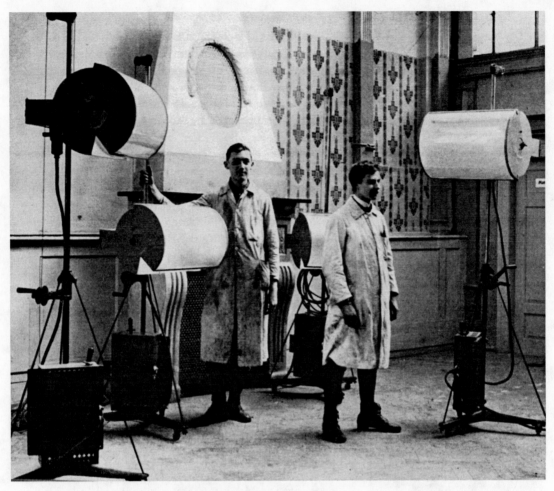

German Jupiter arc lamps (*courtesy Arnold & Richter Cine Technik*).

Electric Co. trade name for them) were attractive because of their economy. The basic considerations experienced by cinematographers, who used these lamps primarily, and later on, in 1928, in a very organized industry test, showed the following conclusions: a) they were absolutely silent for the new sound motion pictures; b) they were lighter than other kinds of lights; c) they used half the electric energy required by other light sources; d) they allowed unobtainable lighting effects including dimming, and e) required one-third the labor of electricians. Thus, the urgent economic requirements of the studios were combined with technical advantages in motion picture photography. In a few months, after more than a quarter of a century, two established lighting sources were ousted from studio stages in the new sound films: the old arc lamps and the classic mercury vapor lighting banks.[9]

The ground was ready now to produce new fruits. In 1927 two experts in electrical engineering with experience in this field, working for the Creco Lamp Company, quickly saw the absence of a specialized firm in this field and decided to open their own enterprise. They were Peter Mole and Elmer Richardson. The new firm, with a definite concern for research, soon contacted the main suppliers of the basic elements: General Electric Co., producer of electric bulbs; Corning Glass, manufacturer of parabolic mirrors; and National

Carbon Company, supplier of the carbons for the future arc lamps. With film technicians and the film studios, they also studied the specific requirements and the new lighting methods to be adopted. The task was not easy, because the film people had no uniform technical concepts and the scientific solutions sometimes clashed with the artistic practice of some cinematographers or the economic concern of the studios. However, the accepted solutions arrived.[10]

Based on the above investigation the new firm, Mole & Richardson, soon designed ten new lighting units specifically conceived for the motion picture industry, and not brought from the theater stage. The new equipment appeared on the market with a definite exclusive functional design. Thus, the "Sun Spots" were compact incandescent lamps of 24-inch or 36-inch front opening, conceived to obtain the best combination between the bulb used and the reflecting surface. The pedestal included new telescopic extensions; heavy units were rubber-tired and some had folding legs. An easy to use mechanical system was developed to adjust the lamp body.

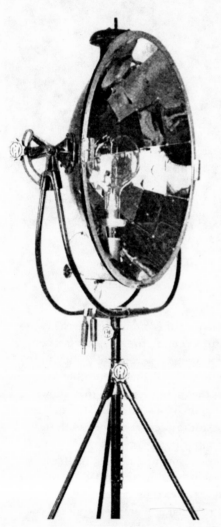

Mole & Richardson broad with incandescent Mazda lamp and faceted mirrors (courtesy *Archivo Nacional de la Imagen, Sodre*).

The revision of each item included also a new type of electric connector, which later on were developed into classic safety plugs.

The soft light lamps provided were called Bell Flood, with nine incandescent units, or bowl or broads and strip lights. The first spot was a 2000-watt unit with a plane convex lens. But the firm also produced other necessary items such as dimmer banks, camera dollies and microphone booms. The Hollywood film studios favored the lighting units of Mole & Richardson and soon this firm was the main supplier of the motion picture industry with its classic M&R trademark seal. One year after its appearance the firm expanded its production and moved to new premises. The Hollywood market was big however and later on other firms such as Bardwell & McAlister entered this expanding field.

In the United Kingdom, General Electric of London was an important provider of well designed tungsten spots, like the 10,000-Watt Inky with a compact rolling base, a 3000-watt studio lamp with a light rolling pedestal and easily interchangeable parabolic mirror or the new compact size bank of inkies. This firm also developed a new type of tungsten bulb, which did not require abrasive powder inside, to clean the blackening. Said bulbs were designed with radical changes in the small wire supports of the tungsten filament that produced a very important advance in this area and was exported to several countries.[11] Finally, around 1924 Germany produced a new line of tungsten lamps with faceted parabolic mirrors with excellent and modern design, built by the growing Arnold and Richter Filmfabrik of Munich.

# 10. Studios of the Twenties

During that decade, production firms continuously grew, as we saw above. The new studios were built to conform to the new shooting techniques and to the economic boom of the industry. Year after year the rickety installations of the old glass buildings kept vanishing, replaced by new construction concepts, using solid materials like brick and concrete. Film stages were built taller and larger with arched or sloped roofs. The glass walls and roofs of old studios were painted black or dark blue, and later on lined with asbestos cement sheeting. The companies gradually reorganized their changing work, adding other buildings to house new departments as they were needed.

## USA

As a consequence of the risky, unstable characteristics of this industry, many firms collapsed, other merged and changed their names, and some were taken over by more successful competitors. The best-organized studios extended their activity as much as their available space allowed. But there was not enough space available to meet the requirements of all, and some studios moved to the outskirts of Hollywood endeavoring to unify all their requirements in a single place; this was the case of Warner Brothers and Fox Studios. In the early twenties very few people could imagine that no further large studios would be built during a period of almost seventy years.

At that time, the best qualified technicians in these motion picture "factories" were the cinematographers who were considered persons with a hard to acquire skill and craft. Their base of operations was the camera department, which therefore gradually grew as its facilities increased.

There, filming equipment was adequately stored as well as maintained in its best working condition for the next day's production program, there were several darkrooms available for camera assistants to load and unload magazines, and desks for noting down the takes made that day and the raw stock used, which was packed to be sent to the laboratory. Several workshops were created to meet the studio's needs with these concerns, e.g. camera maintenance, adapting them to special shooting requirements, camera supports, etc. Such workshops became a must when sound films appeared. Warner Bros. and Metro Goldwyn Mayer were two of the large studios which first developed very organized camera departments to comply with what was wanted for several films being produced.[1]

Camera departments were also the first place where photo tricks were tried and tested.

Some studios set apart adequate space for that purpose. These small processing rooms for trials were the starting point that years later led some studios to install their own laboratories. This ensued when film production reached levels where it paid to cover this operation in order to ensure an adequate control of the quality and cleanliness of the images on the prints. This was the beginning of a process of change that was fulfilled later in that decade.

But the cinematographer's natural working place was the film stage, except when the production required filming outdoors. The evolution of incandescent lamp lighting equipment when filming with panchromatic raw stock allowed recreating many locations on the stage in order to reduce production costs, to be free from weather conditions, and to comply with sound recording requirements. Shooting methods began changing when mercury vapor lamps were replaced by incandescent lighting equipment; another factor was when the use of Klieg lights was limited as their noise interfered with sound recording.

Tungsten lights units were first spread over the stage floor, but soon they were plentifully installed above the set, a first step in leaving the floor free for décor. Heat radiating from tungsten lamps reduced comfort in studio stages. Camera booths were another factor changing standard shooting methods as they reduced shooting area for players to move in, but they did not last long and were replaced by camera blimps. Sound recording brought about a new implement called black sound, consisting of a body of absorbent compound, about ten ft. high and three ft. thick, placed on both sides of the microphone to produce a net sound effect; but it was also short-lived.

Sound on films had a strong influence on the construction of the new stages the studios were needing. Big mistakes were made at the beginning, as there was very little experience in this field. In 1928 MGM decided to build two large sound stages to overcome the heavy traffic noise from the avenues on two sides of the triangle area where their premises were placed. The firm searched for experts in acoustics and engaged one from the University of California. The acoustician determined that in order to neutralize vibrations the stages should be built on foundations 22 ft. deep and the walls had to be made of concrete and bricks. After the stages were built, the sound recording experts found that the required soundproofing had not been achieved. The stages became the most resistant warehouses in the studio, but were unable to be used as sound stages. For MGM these two buildings became the silent physical evidence of the difficulties in the sound film era.[2]

Other building variations were lining walls with Cellotex, a material made from sugarcane fiber, or Arkie, a conglomeration of sea-weed, or Insulite, which was cork sheeting. These linings improved sound wave bouncing, but they were not a final solution to the intense noise of heavy traffic. Many studios, like the MGM one in Culver City, were very close to heavy traffic areas; others ruefully saw it increase in their previously calm surroundings. First, some studios started shooting at night when there was much less traffic; but finally other remedies appeared based on the principle of erecting a building inside another, with independent foundations and sometimes leaving a narrow passage all around the perimeter. Later on stage doors were redesigned, with large soundproof sliding doors to allow access for large pieces of décor and large items of equipment, and much smaller soundproof doors for personnel.

Signaling systems were also introduced at that time as well as communication between sound cabins away from the stage. Pits below ground level were planned on building the new stages, in order to seemingly elevate the height of the sets, to simulate elevator outlets as well as the bottom ends of staircases, to be used for underwater shots or as swimming pools, etc., adjusting the required temperature and lighting conditions. Air conditioning

**Studio stages with external sound insulation** (*courtesy Archivo Nacional de la Imagen, Sodre*).

was also brought to the studios in the thirties. All these facilities were conceived during this period but the Depression after the 1929 stock exchange crash delayed the application of many of these developments.

## Europe

In Europe, studios evolved similarly, but the organizations behind them and their facilities were not as large as those in Hollywood, nor had they as many stages nor enough grounds for outdoor shooting. In Britain there were 33 film studios, but they were all small, the largest of them with no more than four acres, and with only one, two or at the most, three small stages. One of the best known was the British & Dominions Studios at Elstree, built in 1929–30 and destined to produce the then new Quota Quickies, a system created by the British government to increase the production of low-cost, locally made films. The B&D Studios also appeared then, with three air-conditioned sound stages, and having applied the best, at that time, soundproofing techniques and having created a very well organized camera department with Mitchell, Bell & Howell and Vinten equipment, as well as sound recording equipment imported from the USA. However, it was very short lived, only six years; in 1936 a fire destroyed all the installations and the insurance money was invested into the large Rank enterprise studios at Pinewood. The thirties was the era of the large British studios away from the London fogs.

The Pathé-Cinéma Studio was one of the most important in France. It was located in the Joinville area, 8 km from Paris, and connected to it by train, bus and tramway. It included seven stages of different sizes, the largest of which was approximately 130 × 65 ft. and could be subdivided into two. Each stage was 37 ft. high with a metal structure above on which to install lighting equipment, mainly long tungsten lamp appliances called plafoniers, and spots on the décor. The electric power plant comprised four 24 kA. turbines. The studio facilities allowed shooting three films simultaneously.

The Pathé-Cinéma studios were improved each year, including warm-air heating, compressed air-conditioned stages, a 200 seat restaurant, and 5,000 sq. m. outdoor space. The studio included a camera department with several darkrooms, a laboratory for sensitometric tests, a mechanical workshop for maintenance and another for building special equipment. The available cameras were Debrie Parvo L and T with blimp and Cameraeclair. The studio grouped 20 buildings of different sizes, which covered all requirements for its purposes which included a large and very complete laboratory. The organization and the ownership of this studio were modified during the thirties.[3]

There were other important studios in different production centers in Europe. The best known of these was the UFA studio in Germany, in Neubabelsberg, twenty minutes from the center of Berlin. It had been erected in 1911 by the German producer Zeiske in a classic early motion pictures glass construction in Strandorferstrasse. In 1921 it had been transferred to the Universal A.G. (UFA) organization. There with a 25 millon mark investment, a German government endorsement and the support of powerful capitalists in Germany (such as Krupp, Stinnes and private banks), this organization boomed considerably. UFA studios soon became the most important film production center in Europe, with an infrastructure to produce a large series of world renowned films which greatly influenced German cinematography.

UFA studios were well-known for their excellently made productions, as well as for their complete installations and efficient organization, following Hollywood standards adapted to their circumstances. Near the end of that decade they erected stages, with a sound cabin inside having a special window in order to record sound synchronized with shooting. Sophisticated systems communicated the sound cabin with the stages, either by an internal telephone or by a seven-color teleoptia system indicating cues such as "silence," "ready," "louder" and others to the sound recorder. UFA was the first studio to adopt remote control to move lights on a grid over the décor. Halfway through that decade many large arc-spots were used in this studio, and later on efficient tungsten spots. The cranes and vertical sliding platforms in this studio were very useful for difficult shots and for simulating elevator effect. Its special effects department was well known for having applied the Schüfftan process in several films. The large, 82 ft. high stage in UFA's Tempelhof site was a feat never achieved by any other studio; it had been the hangar for the Zeppelin dirigible airships.

The pride of the techniques applied by UFA were the quality craftsmanship of their décor and miniatures. Films like *The Nibelungen I and II* (1923–24), *The Last Laugh* (1924) and *Metropolis* (1926) were examples of their high level work. Like many other important studios, UFA had its own advanced technology laboratory, including the excellent German optical-register Klangfilm sound system.

The best known European directors converged in UFA studios to carry out many coproductions in the twenties and thirties. There they were struck by the excellent technical media available, the prevailing efficiency, and the remarkable organization. They were able to appreciate the high level of German cinematographers, whose workmanship was admired worldwide by motion picture industries. This was one of the reasons why many cinematographers who worked in this famous studio found it easy to obtain positions in Hollywood and in other European studios when the Nazi regime took over the UFA premises.

# 11. The Work of the Studio Cameraman

During the era of silent motion pictures there was a gradual, slow transition in the work of the man behind the camera. In the early years cameramen received only this title. Sometimes they were called with disdain "crank turners." But after some time in this activity they were given the more fitting name of cinematographer. It was after the coming of sound, and the organization of a complete camera crew under their charge, that their designation was changed to director of photography. It was a long and slow transition in a hard and difficult activity that concentrated in only one person a series of qualifications, such as a very good technical knowledge of the trade, handicraft abilities, good taste and a defined artistic sense.

In many Hollywood studios and in other production centers, it was common that the cameraman brought his own equipment to work, which was kept and maintained in the camera shop of the studio. Many cameramen had preferred some camera makes, because they were accustomed to them and they appreciated the characteristics of the chosen equipment. The most popular cameras varied with the years and after the preference of the Pathé during the teens, the Bell & Howell and the Mitchell were later the selected cameras of many cinematographers. Some cameras like the Akeley were complementary units for specific works. In European studios the preferred instrument was the Debrie Parvo and the Bell & Howell. The Mitchell took some time to be introduced in the U.K. and in Germany.

The Bell & Howell Standard was for many years the most preferred equipment in Hollywood, due to its all-metallic construction. All shafts turned on ball bearings, which was extremely effective for hand cranking. But also it was selected for its extremely stable image, ideal for making multiple exposures. Moreover, the movement was easily removed to be cleaned. In its moment it was appreciated also for its viewing system that amplified six times the image produced by the lens, and the sturdy and precise construction among other features. This type of camera was made to order, taking some time to be available to buyers. With the required lenses and accessories they could cost close to the value of a house. The personal purchase of this equipment was accessible only to reputed cinematographers who could afford this kind of investment in order to work with the best equipment of the market.

In those years the cameraman was a jack of all trades in his field. He made about twelve stills of the film per day, which were taken on 8 (10 in. glass plates. Later on, this was one of the first duties he passed on to his assistant. With the help of the chief electrician and his crew, he organized the lighting of the set and the actors. He threaded the camera, checked the focus, established the exposure, framed the shot, operated the crank handle of the camera, actuated on the shutter lever if required by the weather and speed of the action, and personally produced the numerous camera tricks demanded by the director. After the end of the journey the cameraman went to the laboratory to define the kind of developing need by the exposure and controlled the test. The assistant appointed by the studio took some time to be assigned to responsible duties.

The work of the cameraman was not only complex, but frequently of extreme responsibility. The laboratories were then unable to make any kind of tricks and transitions effects; they were made in the camera, while shooting. The camera tricks that the cinematographer was personally required to make during the take in many instances greatly endangered the previously made shot, still undeveloped.

While effecting a dissolve, he had to shoot a new take over the previous shot, and combine both with fades. If the operation was wrong, he ruined the previous shot, and if it was complex and with many players, it signified an important production loss. On some occasions during the shooting, imaginative directors asked the cameraman to make multiple and successive dissolves that involved the risk of several days' shooting work.

In his book *The Parade's Gone by...* the film historian Kevin Brownlow described the difficult circumstances undergone by the cinematographer of the Hollywood director Allan Dwan. He was requested to make twenty-five continuous dissolves of costly scenes of the film *Paths of Glory*, all linked in the camera; this operation took several days and almost broke the cameraman's nerves to combine all the shots inside the camera.[1]

The cinematographer of the twenties (courtesy *Archivo Nacional de la Imagen, Sodre*).

This kind or work required a highly methodical procedure, a clear mind, ability, good memory and mastery of the craft. But the appropriate camera was a must, especially with some requisites as frame indicators, dissolving shutter and other refinements. The surge of the Mitchell camera in 1922 with its built-in variable mattes, iris, filter disc and the effective rack over device was a big advance to facilitate this kind of work. In Europe, the Cameraeclair was another instrument specially conceived for this purpose that also filled this gap, before the arrival of the duplicating film that shifted many of these camera tricks to the safe hands of the laboratory. After this, both cameras were the preferred instruments also of the lab services in the United States and Europe.

In the earlier five years of this period, the cameraman was the only one that carried the weight of his responsibilities, because the assistant was only assigned to elementary jobs such as moving the bulks, holding the sun reflectors, the slate and on some occasions rotate the hand cranks of the tripod head, to make a short panoramic. Some time was needed before this assistant received the duties that first camera assistant has today.

The workday in the studio was long and hard. It began at seven in the morning and nobody was sure when it finished. Sometimes it could last until to 11 P.M., depending on the shooting circumstances. No working rules had been established at the time and the work conditions of this job were abusive. It was usual to pause only for twenty minutes to eat a sandwich and drink a cup of coffee or cocoa. This was the only rest period of the day as recalled by Arthur Miller ASC. It was frequent to work on Saturday nights "for production reasons," and without extra pay. After sound films came out, such unfair work conditions led to the formation of trade unions which prompted discussions and subsequent agreements with production heads, who were always striving to increase their profits.[2]

When the cameraman arrived early at the studio, he received the raw film for the day's work in 2,000 ft. rolls. In the early days the film had to be perforated by the studio to control image stability; the cameraman himself loaded the magazines. He also installed the camera on the tripod with its legs wide open. One leg was always pointed towards the subject so as to allow adequate space behind the cameraman to operate the hand crank. An immediate operation was to check and mark the field covered by the lens, because this was the working area in which the players would act, making their entrances and exits. During the shooting some takes required telescoping the tripod legs to a maximum, and the only solution for the cameraman to reach the level of the instrument was to stand on the camera case. Apple boxes weren't then standard accessories, and the sturdily built camera cases made by Bell & Howell or Mitchell were the most effective solution.

Panoramic takes were kept to a minimum. When it was necessary to follow a player, the movement was short, either pan or tilt, and sometimes the assistant helped the cinematographer. But many cinematographers refused this help because they had the ability to work with both hands, the right on the camera crank handle and the left on the hand cranks of the tripod. This was another professional ability they took pride in.

More than one original negative was required in many productions to cover distribution plans and foreign markets sales. Before 1928 it was impossible to produce adequate duplicate negatives, so it was then common to use more than one camera in some films. This produced changes in the old work routine of the cinematographer assigned to the film. Now he was beginning to work with colleagues, and he had to take the responsibility to define the photographic lines to be followed. In big productions many complementary cameras were also used to cover different set-ups and he was responsible for them. In the film *The Four Horsemen of Apocalypse* (1921) thirteen cameras were used to shoot numerous set ups. The cinematographer John Seitz was in charge and had the responsibility of the takes and he gave the orders to the personnel assigned to him. In the film *Wings* (1927), directed by William Welman, a very large number of cameras were used, and Harry Perry the cinematographer had the difficult task to coordinate the many specialists in aerial shots and photographic effects. Those variations in the cinematographer's work methods in those years were the prelude to changes that sound soon would bring about to camera crews.[3]

During the long day's work in the silent film days, the cameraman worked on foot, save the brief pause to rest and eat. This was because he personally did the hand cranking, a duty that he did not want to resign. The electric motor was then available, but very few used them. Their pride was to propel the camera and thus control the speed of the action he was shooting. The cranking had its technique with two requisites: one was to keep the correct speed; the second was a uniform turning. The standard silent speed was of two turns of the handle per second, in cameras that used 32 sprocket wheels displacing eight frames per turn.

The most accepted method to obtain a constant speed was by turning the crank handle so that the wrist was a prolongation of the crank axis. The other method that others adopted was a pumping action on the crank, moving the elbow and the whole arm, but it could produce uneven exposures in four of the eight frames per turn. Many who used this second method knew a trick to avoid this flaw. To keep the pace, many used different methods: one was counting "one thousand and one." To cancel inertia, the crank handle had to be turned some time before starting the action to be taken. For this reason the director's orders, "camera ... action," was later changed to, "camera ... speed, action" with the use of motors, because their inertia must also be considered.

The coming of sound imposed the use of a constant motor speed at 24 f.p.s., a combination speed derived from a search made on the minimum requirements of sound recording and the average speed of the projectors in film theaters in the U.S.A. With the arrival of sound, the mark of identification of the take was made by means of a slate. The sound recorder also needed a sound identification mark. This was made by means of two long boards that were clapped in front of the camera. This procedure was considered of great importance, and for some time it was made by the film director himself who spoke out the number of the take after the clap. Soon it was realized that this was not so important and was demoted to an assistant. Some time later somebody inventive combined the boards with the slate arriving at today's clapper board.

The change of set-up at the beginning was a job that the cameraman himself did using either of two methods. One was moving to the selected area while holding the camera and tripod on the shoulder. The other was to hold the camera and tripod with two of its legs on the back and the third on the chest. When the tripod was installed, the classic ditty bag was always hanging between the legs. These were the classic devices the cameraman used, but different methods were also used. When sound came, the weight of the electric motor and the 1000 ft. magazine brought about that an assistant carried the camera whenever necessary.

The cinematographer determined the exposure based on his personal experience. When in doubt, he made tests and developed them with the implements he had available. He rarely used the exposure meters accessible in those years such as the Harvey, conceived for outdoor work and based on tables; the Watkin's, an actiometer that used sensitive paper which darkened when exposed to light; or more sophisticated devices like the Cinophot. This one was an instrument manufactured in Germany by Dr. E. Mayer, similar to a small pocket telescope

**Debrie director finder with blue viewing glass** (*courtesy Museo de la Fotografía y el Cine Oscar Mendoza*).

with a finder with two rings which when rotated allowed the user to check the brightness of the image, according to a gray scale, following the extinction method.[4] The cameraman's work methods did not include these resources. His pride was based on his capacity of defining the correct stop value at the blink of the eye, because this way he defended his profession. As a complementary defense he worked close to the labs, checking the processing and the printing. In order to control the efficiency of his work he systematized it in all cases to overcome the many difficulties of his trade. Each step of work was previously planned, checked and rechecked. By repeating an operation identically many times, a sense of safety based on experience was achieved. That is why important films made in those years were so perfect in spite of the technical limitations of the time.

For many years, Hollywood cinematographers depended on the spyglass finder and later on the monitoring viewfinders. The early viewfinders had to be parallax corrected and produced an inverted image. This would not be acceptable today, but then, the automatic checking and rechecking method with the direct upright image produced good results. In Europe the use of cameras which were framed and focused through the film, like Parvo, produced very low light-level images during the take, due to the diaphragm effect. This was why cinematographers used a black cloth for outdoors takes to avoid being dazzled by sunlight. The big difference between the Hollywood and the European methods was that in Europe cinematographers wanted to control the amount of light that reached the negative during the shooting and developed the practice of appreciating it as a control.

The formalism of habits was another interesting aspect as to how they worked in those days. The careful way of dressing was for many years a way to show the personality and the rank in the job. In the teens and twenties the typical dress of many cinematographers was a suit with tie and in some cases a hat or cap. For some time, many cameramen began to use a kind of work uniform, composed of long sleeve shirts, silk tie, trousers with puttees and a cap worn backwards. The silk tie was used to clean the camera lens; the cap with the backwards peak made it easy to look through the finder, and the puttees were an effective support for the long day's work. This "uniform" was used by some Hollywood cameramen and was adopted as a trade symbol by the American Society of Cinematographers. It was also traditional with some newsreel cameramen. In Europe, the Scandinavian, Italian and German cinematographers generally dressed in a long white or dark tunic.

# 12. The Mobile Camera

The mobile camera was used since the dawn of movies. One of the first of such takes was in 1886 when one was installed on a Venetian gondola. In 1913 the Italian filmmaker Giovanne Pastrone made a mobile camera take during the shooting of *Cabiria* and shortly afterwards David Wark Griffith used this resource in *Home Sweet Home* (1914). During the zenith of the crazy comedy, many gags and pursuits required mounting the camera on moving vehicles. At that time this was done in different countries by installing the camera on cars, trains, tramways, boats, ships, sledges, hammocks, lifts, on horseback, on a camel or an elephant, sliding on a toboggan, and on any kind of moving object. No idea was too crazy to be discarded if it could follow a moving subject or obtain the attractive images of passing by rapidly.

The most usual method to cover a chase was to install a platform in front of or behind a car for mounting a camera there and with room for the operator. Sometimes a travelling car was installed on the platform of a truck, so as to displace the camera laterally. In Buster Keaton's film *The General* (1926) the subject train was followed from a travelling car on which the camera was installed pulled by another locomotive running on a parallel track. Some takes were also shot along from a vehicle moving alongside that allowed the camera to go forward and back.

Newsreels also used the system of installing a camera in the front of a car on top of the vehicle. It was common to see a camera and the operators on the roofs of cars to obtain a better coverage of an event. Many plots of the crazy comedies, with many very effective tricks, were based on the car and how it was changing American society. The takes of that time with a moving camera were outstanding for their stability, even when made by crank handle at slow speed. Towards the end of those years some devices were conceived to facilitate this work, e.g. a pedestal built by Frank Cotner with tubes installed on a car's running-board, and from the seat the operator could easily run the camera.[1]

The monitoring viewfinders installed in the Pathé, Bell & Howell or Mitchell cameras had an inverted projected image but were adequate for these situations, because they allowed framing without the operator's body making contact with the camera and thus transmitting his vibrations. Another essential factor was that the driver should be able to match the speed of his car with that of the moving subject. But it was also fundamental that the cameraman should be highly skilled in turning the camera crank handle the right way and at constant speed, while turning the tripod cranks with the other hand at another speed in a different direction.

The first advance in the technical evolution of the mobile camera was the construction

All kinds of animals were always used for film shooting (*courtesy Éclair International Diffusion*).

of a rolling platform to be used in studio shots. This platform, where the camera was seated with the tripod and the operator, used car or motorcycle wheels and was placed along the studio floor. When this floor was irregular, wooden rails were installed. This solution was also effective outdoors. Also, light tricycles were made with tubes, to move the camera and change its path. Many of the travelling cars used by the studios were made by the camera departments themselves and varied in their design and the size of the wheels. Over the years some devices were incorporated such as a brake or a back bar to push the unit. For shooting outdoors, several men with ropes were needed to move these travelling cars on uneven ground. A mechanic named Madigan made one of the first sophisticated mobile camera mounts in 1927. It was used by the Paramount Studio in the film *The Rough Riders*, 1927, and allowed mounting two cameras on a boom.

In Europe, the mobile camera had a wide application during this period. Swedish and Danish film productions used this resource many times with great efficiency. But we find in Germany the most outstanding use of these aids in narrative film language especially in several films of the remarkable director F.W. Murnau. The film in which this intensive application was relevant was *The Last Laugh*, 1924. There, Murnau made intensive use of this technique in several takes from which arose the legend of the "Die Entfesselte Kamera" ("the unchained camera") as a revolutionary innovation in movies. It is said that the idea came from the screenwriter Carl Mayer, who in a previous film, *Silvester* (*A New Year's Eve*, 1923), had a complex device built to move the shooting cameras very smoothly. This equipment was built by the cameraman Guido Seeber and the director of that film, Lupu Pick, and it consisted of a central rolling platform with rubber tires; two sections made up of tubes emerged from the platform where two electrically operated cameras covered the scene simultaneously while the whole unit was being displaced.[2]

The success of this appliance led Carl Mayer to conceive more scenes using the mobile camera in his next film. Thus, in *The Last Laugh*, Murnau and Karl Freund, the cinematographer involved, made visual effects never before obtained, such as the famous scene where the actor Emil Jannings blows the trumpet, and the camera, imitating the expansion of the sound, is moved backwards and up. The scene was shot with the camera installed in a trapeze platform pulled by a rope. Also in this film effective takes were made with a mobile camera like the one following smoke from a cigar held by a millionaire standing on a great staircase, using a long fireman's crane at the top of which was Carl Freund with the camera. Another memorable moving shot in this film starts inside a descending lift and continues without cuts through the wide hall of the Atlantic Hotel towards the main gate of the building. Varied resources were used for shooting this series of mobile camera takes, such us the use of a bicycle or when the operator held a portable camera in his hands.[3]

Other European filmmakers followed the remarkable precedents obtained by Murnau with this innovative use of the camera. Abel Gance, who had experimented with non-conventional film language in *La Rue*) (1922) and used a mobile camera in a small rolling triangle, applied this technique again in the most varied forms in *Napoleon* (1926), mounting the Parvo on many different vehicles. This was possible with the assistance obtained from the French studios of Billancourt. Some time later, another great French director, Marcel L'Herbier, made use of the "unchained camera" using the Parvo to obtain long mobile camera shots with hand held shooting or spectacular travellings from a cable suspended platform crossing inside the set over a large ballroom in the German-French co-production *L'Argent* (1928).

The "unchained camera" had multiple enthusiasts in Europe, who searched for a new form of shooting films. One experiment in France used a cameraman with a harness suspended from a rail on top of a set holding a Parvo camera to take an aerial travelling shot. Simon Feldman, the expert mechanic designer of Paris Cinéma Studios, built a 21 ft. long crane on a rolling base. It included a high platform in the middle, for taking long travelling shots. In the UFA studios in Germany high camera lift devices were made, which were very appreciated by Charles Rosher, the Hollywood cinematographer.

Around 1929 one of the biggest camera cranes ever developed was built in Hollywood to shoot the Universal Studios film *Broadway*. It had been conceived by the director Paul Fedjos, an inventive expert in many fields (he also was a biologist), who worked on its design with the cinematographer Al Mohr. The crane was built by Llewelling Iron Works at a cost of $ 50,000; it had a boom 45 feet long and weighed 28 tons.

This new unusual instrument, known as "The Broadway crane," provided unknown possibilities to make all kind of shots and could reach heights above the stage ceilings. Its wide platform could rotate 360 degrees in both directions and stop at the required place. The boom could make any desired displacement and both sections were able to work simultaneously. The whole unit was electrically operated and needed a trailer with a generator. The tramway type controls were placed on the platform and could allow the installation of another camera. The trench scenes of *All Quiet on the Western Front* (1929) and later *The King of Jazz* (1930) were filmed with this elaborate piece of equipment. The effective capacity of the long boom on the Broadway crane induced Universal Studios later on to build a new very high stage, known as stage 12, to make use of the unusual features of this crane. The use of very large cranes and their weight required that about ten men were needed to push it.[4]

The development of mobile cameras during this period was of great consequence to film language in future years. The experiments in this field by pioneers in Italy were the initial steps toward further applications in America and Europe. Some Swedish films like *Herr Arne's Treasure* (1919) by Mauritz Stiller ignited the spark that influenced Murnau. *The Last Laugh* provided the catalyst for this storytelling method that also affected other directors. The technical evolution of film media in those years helped develop the early improvisations of camera moving facilities to more sophisticated equipment.

# 13. Lighting Techniques

The lighting techniques used in this silent period had a tendency to follow the practices in use after World War I, both in Hollywood and Europe. But they were influenced by the new concepts of the black studio, whereby the artificial light was controlled, preferably inside the stage. The Hollywood practice that won general acceptance was the adoption of a base light which allowed the emulsion exposure to obtain the necessary diaphragm aperture in order to produce a good sharp image. It was also considered important to have an adequate depth of field in the background to produce a good reproduction of the settings. The stop value was about f/5.6 when the arc light was used, and f/3.5 f.4 or f/4.5 when the mercury vapor lights were adopted.

The arc lights installed on top were one of the basic lights from above used during the two first decades of the century: they perfectly covered the requirements of the ortho emulsion, but their hardness had to be attenuated by means of diffusing screens installed in front of the units. The arc lights were also arranged to produce a general soft light effect directing them towards aluminum painted walls. In several studios a large length of veil material was placed before several arc lights to diffuse light rays. Reflecting screens were also often used at that time with the sun and later on with arc lights.

In many studios mercury vapor lamps also provided the basic light source because they were economical and did not require continuous attention; moreover, they produced a comfortable working temperature, contrasting with the heat produced by arcs lights. Over the years, cinematographers learned how to calculate the number of light units required to cover a specific stage with flame arc units working with a given aperture of f/5.6. So, for a large stage, the average was between 20 and 32 arc units, that demanded 100 kW. Half of these units were needed in a medium size stage and needed 50-kilowatt. A small stage could be covered with 4 to 6 flame arc lamps, with a 20-kilowatt load. The intense use of flame arc lamps achieved intense illumination which in certain circumstances reached values of more than 10,000 candles per square foot. In the film *The Hunchback of Notre Dame* (1923), produced by Universal Studios, 52 arc lights were used plus, 51 high intensity incandescent spots and about 300 complementary lighting units requiring the power supply from ten generator wagons.[1]

Cinematographers used a blue viewing filter to determine the response of ortho emulsion to light. Some directors used a small finder like the one Debrie built later on, including a blue filter to see how the lighting came out on the film. Day after day work produced a good understanding between the cinematographer and the art director in order to combine efforts correctly. This, in many cases, defined the criteria in the selection of the gray tones used in painting the sets, the inclusion of apertures for the camera set-ups and determination of spaces for installing the floor lighting units.

The progress reached in lighting motion pictures was the result of pioneering work by famous cinematographers of the previous decade, like Billy Bitzer in Hollywood, and the excellent use of light and shadows adopted by many European cinematographers. The lighting techniques of the twenties combined practical methods to solve classic situations, like the technique known as Hill, which combined flood lighting from both sides of the camera and a series of spots from the back and above. But in many circumstances the lighting pattern was designed to suit dramatic situations that required highly elaborate image conceptions. Cinematographers consequently had the incentive to develop the fundamentals of the chiaroscuro lighting technique that they learned basically by studying the pictures of the classic great painters. Maybe, that was the reason why Rembrandt, the great Dutch painter, was well known in the film medium in the mid teens, and his name was used by Cecil DeMille to promote *The Warrens of Virginia* series (1915), photographed by Alvin Wyckoff taking advantage of having used his "northern lighting technique." The cinematographers knew that the chiaroscuro of the image added effective dramatic value to the film, but it required the courage of that film director to sell this artistic concept to the reluctant studio bosses.[2]

In those years the basic requisite of a Hollywood cinematographer was his ability to produce the best pictorial value of the principal studio investment: the film star. The star

The lighting of the players was the principal concern of the cinematographers (*courtesy Unitalia Film*).

system was the essence of this business and the first target was to obtain the best visual appeal from this player, male or female. The studios ruled that the stars were the most relevant players on the set and the supporting actors were relegated to a lesser lighting consideration. The stars were carefully considered in the lighting pattern adopted, in order that it should not reduce their attractiveness, sex appeal or glamour. The cinematographer was forced to subdue the lights directed to these players near the stars in order to draw audience attention to the star, to the detriment of the supporting players. The lighting of the stars was so important during part of this period that it impaired the realism of a scene.[3] A dark shadow on the face of a star during a dramatic scene could be anathema that might mar the cinematographer's reputation.

Extreme care was taken to enhance the stars' looks in the medium shots as well as in the close-ups. In the former their costumes were also included which demanded using special lighting on them. In the close-ups several techniques were created to magnify their photogenic qualities. Many cinematographers specialized in lighting female faces with the most varied resources to obtain the wanted results. Those experts carefully studied several aspects of the star's face: its regularity, the characteristics of the cheekbone, the shape of the jaw and the nose, the color of the hair and the eyes and details of their expressions. Each aspect was considered from different angles to obtain the adequate lighting formula in each situation and to define the best side of the face and the one to avoid.

Blonde hair was considered undesirable for the ortho emulsion, if it was not expertly lighted to enhance it. Clear eyes did not register well on this emulsion and required that the crystalline lens of the eyes should reflect a black flag or a black screen close to the camera to obtain a good response. The classic method of using soft focus lenses that came from the teens was maintained for many years. The soft focus concept was also used for long shots of rural scenes. In the case of the close-ups diverse kind of lenses were used. The 75mm or 100mm was an often-used focal length in those situations because it avoided image distortions, reduced the depth of field and enhanced the figure. Other techniques were also conceived for such image control.[4]

Some of them involved the use of gauzes in front of the lens, mattes, vapor fumes, the independent low-contrast developing of the take, the use of veils behind the figure, or the wide-open aperture of the diaphragm to reduce the sharpness of the image. Other camera tricks were adopted by many cinematographers such as two crossed threads in front of the lens, a glass with Vaseline, a glass plate with scratches on one face, gauze with a small opening in the center, and special filter devices. The Hollywood cinematographer Hendrik Sartor developed a special device two feet long with six different gauzes inside, to be installed in front of the lens. Anything was effective if it allowed reducing image details and diffusing the highlights effectively.

The tendency in this search of close-up image control led to the use of special lenses designed by several lens makers and by cinematographers. Several of them were built including spherical or chromatic aberrations like the Verito of Wollensack, the Kalostat, the portrait lenses of Dallmeyer, the Pictorial conceived by Carl Struss, the 100mm Effligior from Optis and Rosher's Kino Portrait developed by Astro about 1926. Many cinematographers, such as Joseph Walker, used special still portrait lenses as a result of their experiments.

However the key to photogenic control was in the lighting methods adopted and the characteristics of the light used. Cross light from a hard source was common to light male faces, but the opposite was the rule for female close-ups. The light had to be filtered and bounced, carefully angled in such a way that the nose shadow should fall so as to reach a point near the lips. The use of the make-up to control the size of the mouth was very important, and also by this means and with lighting, the prominence of the cheekbones and the jaw. But the eyes were the most important part of the face and several practices were developed to light them, making them bright, with strategic small, single or multiple, light sources.

Hollywood masters in this field, like Joseph Walker, used the most varied devices. Sometimes they used mirrors to produce small light touches on a selected point of the face to complement the lighting pattern adopted. The hair light was always a necessary complement that finished the most attractive effect of a moving face. At this time the ability to obtain the best looks in the stars' close-ups created the fame of many cinematographers. This was a guarantee that their good looks and sex appeal were enhanced.

Over the years, the arbitrary nature of the star system was reduced in those aspects when the leading roles affected the proper lighting of the supporting players or when the lighting of the star was against the natural and dramatic values of the scene. This change came about by the persistence of cinematographers, art directors and film directors defying film producers and studio heads. This was caused by Hollywood's particular business attitude, but it was less accepted in Europe, where the star system was also present but never so forcibly adopted over the artistic and realistic values of the films.

In Europe lighting techniques reached a high point in that decade, especially in German film production. German films were considerably influenced by Scandinavian films, remarkable for their photography. We saw how the artistic conception of German films after the war reached a very high level that continued a long time. In German films lighting was an expression of their mature artistic possibilities of this medium and was among the best in European film centers. The light in German films was dovetailed to the style and the subjects selected and was very different from the lighting in French, British and Italian productions which were less vigorous, expressive, and more conventional. One of the principles German cinematographers adopted was the key light technique, which implied eliminating the classical light foundation used in Hollywood. Another method was the use of powerful arc light sources combined with a counterpart of shadows and high lights. The hard shadows cast over the walls were in many cases part of the style suiting the theme of the film. The search for different positioning of the sources in order to obtain new angles other than those usually adopted was also part of this style.

Location shots were in many cases recreated in the studio in all details, using powerful arc lights to reproduce sunlight, obtaining a high excellence that called the attention of cinematographers in other film centers. We must add the effectiveness of the special effects, combining miniatures, real shots and stop motion, or the vast settings built inside the studio, in many cases designed with false perspective. Carefully pre-planned light control and the ability to work with high intensity light sources was a factor that lent great prestige to German cinematographers, many of whom participated in co-productions filmed in English, Austrian and French studios.

Elsewhere on the same continent another lighting concept was adopted in several films that contrasted with the natural method used in Europe and Hollywood. This was developed in the newly born film industry of the Soviet Union and was applied by the cinematographer Eduard Tissé in the films directed by Sergei Eisenstein. It involved a startling pictorial lighting devised to obtain new aesthetic conceptions combining certain degrees of distortion and an abstract formulism within a natural and realistic treatment. Tissé's lighting was noted for an intense use of backlights, counter lights with cross beams to enhance the volumes of bodies and faces and in many cases with a small front penumbra. This method tended also to accentuate the luminous contour of the settings, it included strong chiaroscuros and was completed by framing with forced perspective and calculated angulations.

This style was adequate to the subjects of silent films, where the players with carefully selected faces gesticulated, sometimes opening the mouth to accentuate the dramatic situation, but as no words were spoken, the scene was only effective to produce a striking editing sequence. Those methods of lighting and image conception and combination were used outdoors and indoors. In the first case, sun reflectors, spots and large mirrors combined with several types of filters, and different lenses were employed for each situation with great ability. Apart from this careful experimental work there were very striking unplanned scenes, sprung from sudden inspiration, like the hazy shot of Odessa in *Battleship Potemkin* (1925) that Tissé intuitively shot and Eisenstein included, because it was of special value to the film's atmosphere.

This lighting method appearing in the second half of the decade had its followers, and struck many cinematographers in other film centers. But the coming of sound affected the technique of lighting close-ups in some degree: it was not adequate when the dialog was important and the actor had to be marked. In the following years the high standards of Tissé's cinematography were the outstanding mark of Russian films, as they influenced many others in that country.

# 14. The Silent Newsreel

After World War I the profession of the cameraman acquired particular prestige, especially the newsreel cameramen shown in action in posters in movie theaters, in the newsreels themselves and in trade magazines. This job aroused the fantasies of the young as a different way of life in a fascinating activity out of the daily routine of the common jobs, ideal for daring people. The newsreel enterprises contributed to this vision; for example, the *Universal Animated Weekly* magazine declared: "Our cameramen are all bright-eyed, quick-witted, resourceful newspaper men who know news when they see it and who are willing to risk leg or neck to get it for *Universal's Animated Weekly*."[1] Other newsreels in their advertising showed their cameramen in action in the most risky or showy situations, as another form to impress the audiences.

The work of the studio cameramen was similar to that of the newsreel colleague in certain activities but very different in others. Both operated similar instruments but they were in search of different ends. The studio cameraman aimed at obtaining an image of artistic quality, according to what was wanted for the film he had been working on for weeks. He was part of a production team organized to create a history, but he was not the story teller. He was the image specialist and thus his duty was to provide the best image suited to the subject.

On the other hand, the newsreel cameraman was primarily a newspaperman, seeking to cover an event, the news being his main target. First of all he had to be in the right place at the right moment, and tell the story of the facts in effective short takes. He was the story teller. He had to register facts accurately and work fast to "have the news in the can"; the image quality came later. He could not do retakes. He had no control over the beauty of the image and only required a good exposure and a sharp take. He needed a "nose for the news": a feeling to know how the facts would develop. He had to know how to manage the film inside the camera so as to be ready to shoot at any time. But the newsreel cameraman also had to be daring, cool headed, smart, and alert and let his intuition tell him how the events could develop. His work required certain qualities, very different from those of his colleague in the film studios.

In many cases the tools of the newsreel cameraman were not so refined as those used in the entertainment film industry. A large number of the newsreel cameramen were stringers, correspondents in the principal cities of the United States and Canada, who worked with their own equipment. Some were professionals and others semi-professional. Many used low price wooden cameras like the Universal, the Enermann, or the Box. The most popular camera for newsreel work was the Akeley, the preferred instrument for this branch of the film industry. The Akeley was so well appreciated by newsmen that for many years the manufacturer could not cope with requests. It was ideally suited for panning, and consequently was a must for all kinds of races, parades, sports and aerial exhibitions. Its compact 200 ft. internal pre-threaded magazine was very effective to reload quickly and the original two lens focusing system was very easy to use.

In 1925 the introduction of two new portable cameras produced some changes in how the newsreel world worked. They were the Bell & Howell Eyemo and the DeVry. They were called the first professional automatic cameras, because they were spring motor driven and did away with the hand crank. For the first time the cameraman was free of the crank handle and the tripod, and could now hold the camera in his hands while moving around. Both cameras had a limitation: short film capacities that enabled covering only 4'10" shooting. Later this limitation led to the common practice of winding the spring after each shot, to have the camera ready to the next take, and to shoot each take with the necessary time, according to the image and the action, before changing the angle. These cameras gave the news cameramen more freedom, and allowed them to effectively administer the raw stock.

The main requisite for this job was to have the equipment always ready to be used at any time and in any situation and to take it to cover the event in the best form. This expertise and intuition paid off when Ariel Vargues, in a room in the Adlon Hotel in Berlin, ready to place the camera in its case after a routine job, he heard shots in the street and took out the camera to shoot the most spectacular coverage of the beginning of the German revolution in 1919. From a window of the hotel he could film the police forces charging, the people running desperately and the bodies falling under gunfire.

During the twenties there was a large number of newsreel firms in the United States and other countries, with a brisk competition between them, and a considerable number of cameramen to cover sporting events. This produced conflicts in obtaining enough space which increased the costs of each company. In the United States this led to mergers of several firms, with the bigger ones buying out the smaller. Even so, many small firms survived in this constant competition. The big enterprises used their wealth to buy the exclusive rights to sports events, which audiences preferred. The small newsreel firms survived by being inventive, adopting all kind of tricks and pirating on such exclusions.

The cameramen entered into this scuffling as part of their duties. The competition was so stark that all means were valid to cover the event, or ruin the competitor's work. Some small firms sent saboteurs among the audience in sport stadiums with mirrors to reflect the sun's rays to the authorized newsreel's cameras. Signboards held on poles were pushed up suddenly to obstruct the camera field. Smoke grenades were also used for this purpose. A firm's exclusive coverage was pirated in the most diverse ways. In baseball, football or soccer stadiums, the pirate shots were taken with long focal lenses in strategic spots from nearby buildings or towers. On one occasion, a news firm installed a cameraman inside a water tower opening a hole in it to cover a sporting match because he was not allowed to film it openly. The big firms created a security corps to find pirate cameramen. But many small firms sent several cameramen, so if some were discovered others remained to obtain the coverage.

This kind of war to cover the news occurred between newsreel companies in many countries, specially in the sports field. In the preliminary soccer games held in the South American city of Montevideo, to select the participants in the Olympic games, the big newsreel firm Max Glücksmann, which simultaneously operated in Argentina and Uruguay, obtained the exclusive coverage. Strict controls were installed at the access gates to the soccer field to prevent pirate cameramen. But the small, highly competitive Argentinean Film Revista Valle newsreel company was undaunted. They sent fruit sellers with baskets in which several small Debrie Sept cameras were hidden. And though their load was only 21 ft. of film, this was enough to cover important sequences and the goals. On other occasions when gate controls were very strict, the cameramen entered without equipment, and when they were inside, they dropped cords from the top rim of the spectator stands to the bottom outside to pick up small Ika Kinamo cameras. Later on, the firm ran a rumor that they had not filmed the game in order not to put its competitor on guard. But when the newsreel was shown the pirated material appeared.[2]

The world of the newsreels adopted special techniques to cover their requirements. Some of them were adopted from feature film methods like installing the camera with its tripod on a car. This was very often used in parades to follow the main subject as well as takes of the public with travelling effect as a complement to shots from cameras fixed in strategic places. An effective substitute of the mobile cameras were pan shots made with long telephoto lenses. The frequent use of these lenses greatly influenced many optical manufacturers to increase their efforts to improve the aperture and image definition. But working with telephoto lenses demanded great mastery and a good tripod head.

Another resource used by newsreels was a high-speed camera to obtain slow motion, then unused in fiction films but effective in showing the arrival at a race finish, e.g. athletes, horses and cars. But often those shots caused trouble, since they affected the decisions of judges and originated conflicts and demands, especially in horse races where important sums of money were involved.

The news cameramen always suffered the inconvenience of the low sensitivity of the films then available, which did not register many indoor shots. Portable lights were not available then especially during the early days; moreover the equipment was cumbersome and had high electricity consumption. Tungsten light took some time to develop and was not too useful with ortho film. For this reason it was common practice to use some still photography methods such as reflective screens or mirrors to obtain complementary lighting. In some situations chemical candles were used made of magnesium, aluminium and potassium chlorate which produced a very intense short duration light but enough to allow several takes to cover wide spaces. After these special candles were extinguished people were dazzled and very few noticed that everything was covered with fine ash.

Filmed news was always a special attraction for the audiences. The possibility of a participant in an event of seeing his image on the screen made him feel close to the Hollywood stars. That was why during events many wanted to be in the field covered by the cameras and some had the opportunity to see themselves on the screen. Many small town movie theater owners, in order to draw greater audiences, took shots of local events, at their own cost, that were later shown after the weekly newsreel that arrived with the feature films. He would ask his projectionist or still photographer to take shots that were later developed and printed without titles. This was well-publicized in the theater itself. The system was used only in some countries but it was possible only during the silent days. It was so effective that many theater owners made small commercial spots showing the most important shops of the area. Thus many theater operators gave many projectionists and still photographers an opportunity to begin a new activity with profitable possibilities.

From the birth of the newsreel, it was a common practice to recreate events, as we have shown above, but the reconstruction had to be very carefully made. Just as many still photographers used to re-enact a handshake, the signing of a document or the cutting of a ribbon at an inauguration, to comply with camera requirements, the newsreel cameramen sometimes did the same thing. One of the pioneers of this method, well known for his imaginative and dynamic work, was Louis de Rochemont. As a young cameraman of sixteen, he obtained a sheriff's permission to reenact how a German saboteur, who in 1915 had demolished a bridge in Maine, was arrested.[4] De Rochemont was famous in his field and later became the producer of one of the most prestigious filmed magazines in the U.S.A., "The March of Time," where he continued using this technique. Later on he became a well-known Hollywood producer of feature films with a documentary touch.

Generally, apart from famous cameramen like De Rochemont, Ariel Varges or Jack Painter in the USA, newsreel cameramen were usually unknown by the audiences because no credits were shown. The ability, the efforts or the pains to cover trenchant scenes were not revealed to the audiences and remained only within the trade. The cameraman knew how hard and thankless his job was, but this was accepted as one of the rules of the game since he acted under a strong vocation.

In those years, the work habits of the American freelance newsreel cameramen had to include, among others, the following characteristics. He had to be acquainted with events in his area and therefore had to have contacts with the press who would advise him of any news developments. He would cover the facts with a few general and medium shots of the action and close-ups of the people involved. He had to be careful with the footage he spent because in this field an event exhibited rarely ran more than 50 ft. (two minutes) not including the titles. Generally the material sent was longer to allow for cutting, but that was the standard length used by the newsreel.

The pay of the freelancer could be about 30 cents to $1 per ft. of interesting material. On a few occasions the payment could rise to $1.50 to $2.00 per foot for material of special interest.[5] The material was sent via parcel post or express as undeveloped negative enclosed in black paper inside a very well sealed tin can. A data sheet had to be included describing each scene, its place and the names of the people involved. During the shooting the cameraman had to take care not to include publicity signs with trademarks, and consequently he had to select the framing angle carefully.

The freelancer obtained other sources of income from the material he shot for the news magazines. Newsreel weekly editions edited by the same firms or others included topical but not the latest events. The material for this type of film was of lower level and the national character was not so important. The subjects covered were curiosities, ingenious inventions, scientific novelties, travels or films on animals. The cameraman covering such stories had to be always alert to find unusual events that could be good subjects for an attractive piece, saleable to such magazines. The possibilities of the newsreel magazine were more attractive; they were generally made up by five or six pieces with more shots than the classic news event. Each one could be about 125 to 150 feet of long. Some magazines were also made with three long histories. This market was the one preferred by some cameramen. But there had to be a good and continuous relation between the stringers and the newsreel, otherwise the latter adopted the option system. This implied the risk of not recovering the expenses, since the sender was not always sure that his material would be accepted and he must shoot, develop and print it at its own expense and then send the positive with a synopsis of the theme. If the proposal was accepted he had to send the negative afterwards.

The coming of sound produced important changes in the work of newsreel cameramen. Some time after sound arrived and it became standard in film theaters, the freelancer's camera had to be turned 3 times per second, or an electric motor had to be incorporated.

The best solution for many was the use of the spring drive portable camera. The new operation speed reduced the effective duration of the raw stock in the camera. It also affected the sensibility of the film since the shutter speed was now about $\frac{1}{50}$ of a second instead of $\frac{1}{30}$ as with silent speed. Not all the freelancers were in the financial condition to renew their equipment and this change took some time. Popular cameras such as the Akeley Pancake were adapted with a motor and a Bell & Howell or Mitchell viewfinder on top. The newsreel enterprises needed to modernize their equipment. The newsreel industry was not wealthy but it was urged to follow the new developments.

New working methods appeared in this field. Some of the freedom of the past was lost. More technicians needed to be included in the camera crew. The heavy new sound-on-film camera encumbered this kind of coverage. The ambient noise conspired against sound recording. The wind was also discovered to be an inconvenience when sound shooting outdoors. A new member of the staff, the reporter, was now needed in front of the camera, to introduce an interview. But sound also provided a new attraction to the newsreel, and on many occasions the interviews gave the newsreels an unexpected success.

# 15. The Cameraman in Exotic Lands

Film production by explorers in search of exotic lands and primitive peoples was very successful during that time. Countless expeditions were made to distant points of the planet such as Central or East Africa, Australia, Borneo, the South Sea Islands, Egypt, Greenland, Tibet, the Sahara, the South American jungles, Alaska, the South and North Poles, China, the Himalayas and the desolate zone of Arabia. During previous decades many expeditions were made, and the filmed material proved to be of great interest to audiences and brought rewarding returns to the enterprises backing them. Thus in this way a new and different kind of film production was growing; consequently all expeditions included one or more experienced cameramen with the necessary equipment to film and develop it in the most adverse conditions.

Individuals of very diverse nature propelled the projects: explorers, ethnologists, naturalists, military men, adventurers, filmmakers, distinguished members of the European royalty, great enterprisers and eminent scientific institutes. Among those who left films of great interest were the famous couple Martin and Osa Johnson, the Marquis of Wavrin, Sir Alan Cobham, Cherry Kearton, M. P. Adam, W. J. Shepard, Paul Hofer, Walter Furtier, Leon Poirier, André Sauvage, Robert Flaherty, J. B. L. Noel, Ernest Schoedsack, Merian C. Cooper, Richard Byrd, H. Sydney Snow, J. Jackson, Paul Antoine, Robert Lugeon and others. Many required the services of experienced cameramen to film the high points of the expeditions. But many others did the shooting themselves and gradually became good filmmakers who later channeled their productions through specialized distributors.[1]

The experience obtained from these films was very useful. They led to learning the reaction of primitive peoples to the photographic process. Generally, very different peoples like the pygmies and the Eskimos did not recognize a photograph and turned it upside down or to a side to discover what it was. It was necessary that the photographed individual should understand putting the still close to a mirror. Immediately a big smile appeared on his face. In a film projection they looked back at the projector light beam and did not understand the screen image. But when they recognized a very known subject, like an animal, they were fascinated and gaped. They were not accustomed to seeing black and white images or shots with fragments of the human body.

In those expeditions great quantities of raw stock were carried, varying from 60,000 ft. to 180,000 ft. On many occasions the explorers had to abandon their material and shooting equipment, running from the danger of hostile groups as in 1928 in the New Hebrides Islands where they had to escape from cannibals. In other cases they found the difficulty of religious opposition, such as that of Moslems, based on the Koran, which forbids the reproduction of nature. Each people varied in their innocence or prejudices, facilitating or limiting the opportunities of being filmed. The naturally pleasant African people allowed themselves to be filmed in their life and habits, but others with severe looks in their eyes refused to be shot by cameras.

Great experience was obtained during those years on the difficulties met when filming in unfavorable zones. In time more was learned. It was known beforehand that in the tropics it was important to select adequate food and to control its purity strictly; the frequency of drinks as well as their quality had to be controlled. Physical efforts had to be restrained and sunburns, sunstroke, insect bites and infections had to be avoided to withstand nature's aggressiveness. Endemic diseases had to be prevented, and bathing in contaminated waters avoided. Such diseases, though momentarily overcome, could leave lifelong sequels. In the jungle, the eyes had to be protected, especially by cameramen, as they were frequently prone to conjunctivitis. The cameraman's work was always strenuous and carelessness or accidents in the day's work could be detrimental to the job.

High up in the mountains and in polar zones the human body also suffered, and after many expeditions experience taught the way to control some injuries with the limited resources available at that time. Here, conjunctivitis was not produced by infections, but by the dazzling effect of the snow and ice and special protectors were used such as filters or spectacles with small slots that acted as an additional iris. Mouth covers and head protectors were also very important to the nose, ears, and neck. During storms with strong wind and snowfall (blizzards) the face had to be completely covered.[2]

The cameraman's principal risk was the high sensitivity of the skin to extreme cold. When looking through the finder the skin of the eye could stick to the eyepiece. If the cheek touched the metal surface of the camera it could also stick. Herbert Pointing, the famous cameraman of Capt. Scott's South Pole expedition, told how in a rash moment, when focusing the lens and trying to keep his lips humid, his tongue briefly touched the metal of his camera and was immediately frozen, and trying to withdraw it the skin stuck at the contact point, bleeding profusely.[3] Breathing near the lenses had to be carefully avoided because immediately an ice film was formed that was difficult to remove. The diaphragm and focus rings of the lenses were stuck with the cold as the lubricant froze.

It was impossible to load the camera outdoors in those places as it was extremely difficult to do so with gloves, and without them the hands froze immediately. Many operators covered their cameras with black covers and, if possible, kept them close to their bodies to transmit some of their warmth to the instruments. It was very difficult to handle the film because it became brittle and its edges acted as a blade producing painful cuts on the fingers. The experiences of many explorers and cameramen were the subject of conferences in photographic and scientific societies, where many exposed the difficulties they found working under such hard conditions. They reported on the fragility of wooden cameras as they were altered by the extreme cold, the high humidity of the jungles, and the effects of the sea and the brine; in such circumstances the camera's dimensions were altered and their lighttight joints loosened. The leather was also affected, becoming brittle and easily breaking or cracking with the cold. Other inconveniences were static on the film, the lubricants freezing, troubles with the intermittent movement of the cameras, and the difficulty of changing the magazines.

In the tropics troubles were also very frequent. The high heat affected the raw stock and a good solution was to bury the film cans very deep and place a visible mark on the surface. But many other inconveniences were found: the high humidity made the film stick to the film gate; the formation of fungus on the film emulsion, on the lenses, and on the leather cases; and the need to immediately process the exposed negative. Some solutions were found such as covering the cameras with a white cover to radiate the intense heat that affected the metal body. Also, it was soon realized that the shooting had to be done only very early in the morning and near sundown. Those resources were transmitted by the pioneers to their colleagues or to the manufacturers of equipment or raw film.

The first step in that decade was selecting all metal cameras for this work, but not all were suited. Some cameras like the Bell & Howell Standard, with a high precision mechanical movement, had to be substituted because in many places the temperature altered the film dimensions and jams were very frequent; simple mechanisms were then preferred. The pre-threaded magazine was another important item, which was why the Akeley Pancake was preferred. But others opted for automatic cameras, specially treated, and winterized, like the Bell & Howell Eyemo, the DeVry or the British Newman Sinclair.

## Robert Flaherty

Some explorers became filmmakers and cameramen. This was the case of Robert Flaherty whose films led to the name given to this type of production and that defined their kind and style. In this field he was one of the most outstanding and best known in the world. Flaherty had been born in Iron Mountain, in 1884. From his early youth he accompanied his father on expeditions to northern Canada for the U.S. Steel Corporation. Later he was a mine prospector and worked with the large Makenzie and Mann Canadian enterprise. There it was suggested that he take a movie camera with him to record his travels. Flaherty bought a Bell & Howell Standard and also printing and processing equipment. In Rochester he went through a three-week course in shooting techniques and processing.

He used this equipment in his first journey to the Belcher islands in 1913. On returning, he lost the original negative in a fire when his hands were burned. In those years it was impossible to obtain a duplicate from the only print he had left. He studied the print and saw the several mistakes in it, so he decided to return and make the film again. He obtained financial support from the French firm Revillon Frères. He made contacts with the American Geographical Society and the Explorers Club of New York. He was advised in many aspects and with the bad experience he gained in his first film in those cold lands he decided to buy new and more adequate equipment. He purchased two Akeley cameras, a Hellberg electric generator, a film projector and included a Williamson portable printer. The processing equipment was made up of four bronze racks and four bronze tanks of 15 gallons each, and parts to build a drying cylinder on site.

In August 1920 he arrived in a schooner close to the selected base, Port Harrison near the Artic Circle, where he installed his headquarters and his film laboratory. There he searched for the required personnel to help in the work and to be placed before the camera. He knew that he must now recreate what he wanted to tell, which needed a subtle story. Twelve Eskimos were selected among whom was Nanook, a well-known hunter in the region who would be his leading character. Soon he instructed three young Eskimos in laboratory work, constructed the film drying cylinder and after seeing that the electric light fluctuated, he attached the printer to a wall and made a hole in place of the gate, deciding to use the weak constant light from outdoors, controlled by pieces of muslin. One of the problems in that place was the lack of clean water. The solution came from an underground river covered by eight feet of ice that had to be kept unfrozen.

Flaherty filmed the life of the Eskimos covering several aspects of their hard life. He traveled with them about 600 miles on the frozen sea as they stalked their prey and suffered with them the hardships and the danger of starving. He also experienced the difficulties and hardships of working as a film director and cameraman, and also in the process of developing and printing films under very difficult conditions. He repaired the mechanisms of two frozen Akeley cameras and a Graflex still camera. At last, he could not reassemble them again and then discovered that the Eskimos had by nature great skills in mechanics. He made them build an especially big size 25 ft. diameter igloo that broke with the standard 12 ft. size, and which collapsed several times before the dome could be installed, because it was out of the tradition of Eskimos' standards. Inside it he filmed the igloo family life.[4]

Finally the film was ready and was shown in the cabin. The projector was ready. The screen was a woolen Hudson Bay blanket. The bell of the base called the people roundabout to the white man's magic show. The audience was the Eskimos who worked on the film, their families and relatives and they filled the limited space. They did not understand the images they saw and looked back at the projector beam. Soon they recognized Nanook and a walrus, and they were fascinated with the images of the first film they had seen.

Flaherty took one year to shoot this film. In August 1922 he returned to the civilized world and in New York he edited it in three months; the film was called *Nanook of the North*. After many contacts and negotiations he managed to have it shown in New York's Capitol theater with great success and later in many countries in Europe, where it received the same approval both by audiences and critics. This was the beginning of a new profession for an imaginative man who had been trained to be and began working as a prospector and later became a film maker, cameraman and ethnologist.

The success of *Nanook of the North* encouraged Flaherty who saw new possibilities in such enterprises. The studio head of Paramount Pictures Corporation, Jesse L. Lasky, was also enthusiastic about this kind of film; he appreciated the box office success of this low budget film, and decided to produce something similar. Happy to find a new sponsor, Flaherty looked now to the diagonally opposite side of cold desolate lands. Paradise on earth must be in the South Sea Islands. After a contact with Frederick O'Brien, author of the book *White Shadows in South Seas*, he decided that the location should be the most glamorous of the Polynesian Islands.

Now he was the head of a truly important undertaking and decided to include his family in it. Together with his brother David as production assistant, his wife, Frances, as still photographer and script adviser, his three daughters and a maid, Robert Flaherty sailed from San Francisco in April 1923 on a long voyage over the Pacific Ocean. He carried with him the equipment he used in *Nanook*: the Akeley cameras, the laboratory equipment, light generator, and projector as well new items including a Prizma color cine camera with a lot of the new panchro film for it and 40,000 ft. of ortho negative for the projected film. All this equipment and the luggage added up to about sixteen tons.

In Samoa, in the village of Safune, Flaherty established his headquarters first in an old unused trading post. The laboratory was built inside a cave with a pool of fresh water in it; a little hut was erected at the mouth of the cave. The projecting room was under the trees. Flaherty's next step was his relations with the natives of the place, learning their habits, work, habitat, clothing, searching for locations, and the elements that would allow outlining a sketchy story because he had no script when he arrived. The place selected was spectacular in its panoramas. Any point he looked at was beautiful. The islanders were very cooperative after his initial harangue, translated by an old European settler. Flaherty selected and trained two Samoans for the laboratory work and after a long search found the characters for his new film. The story was the daily life of a people in the midst of nature that gave them all their needs: how they danced, the preparation of their food, the influence of the sea in their lives, their amusements, the joy of living, as well as the painful tattooing process made on one of the leading characters.

The shooting of the film took several months, but the results, when projected, were disappointing. The images did not adequately reflect the beauty of the natural scenery, nor of the bodies of the Polynesians. The contrast was poor and the images did not reproduce the subtleties in the greens of the foliage, the colorful flowers, and the blue hues of the sky and the sea; they were all turned into blacks, whites or dull monochrome reproduction. Flaherty was shocked and profoundly discouraged. Then, discussing the situation, a sudden idea came to his mind. Why not use the panchro raw stock he brought with him to make color shots with his Prizma camera that was out of service? He made tests and the result was amazing. The beauty of nature was perfectly reproduced, the images were well rounded and the golden-bronze of the natives also rendered an excellent gray tone and the photography was now outstanding.

He decided to shoot the entire production again with the new panchro emulsion, which Kodak had informed Flaherty was still in an experimental state and was tricky. But he had no other options. The laboratory was adapted to work in darkness, and Flaherty allayed the two Samoans' fears of the ghost of the cave. He cabled Kodak to supply more panchromatic film. Following their technical advice to use a K 3 filter in some situations, he selected the best hours of the day when the sun was low, and discovered the advantages of using telephoto lenses to cover close-ups and the outstanding effects of using panoramic shots. Step by step he was improving his filmmaking methods in search of new angles for shooting. He had the intuition for what made a visually striking film and was not wrong in his expectations.

Serious drawbacks, however, followed his enthusiastic endeavors. Technical inconveniences appeared during the processing. There were a series of jet-black rack flares, and a marked throbbing when the film was projected. Several inspections were made which brought about changes in the processing work, using a new Stinemann developing unit he had had built to include longer film footage. But the inconvenience persisted. He then remembered Kodak's advice that their new panchro film was still tricky.

A physical inconvenience followed the technical ones. During the filming he started feeling ill and weak until he could not even eat. He took opium as a cure, and a radio message was sent and Flaherty was taken to the city of Apia were he spent a month recovering. It took a long time to discover that he had been poisoned by the fresh water he drank inside the cave from an independent pool, which was affected with infiltrations of silver nitrate from the laboratory bath. This was also the origin of the troubles he found while processing the film.[5]

The last vexation he suffered was the fight between his lab assistants with other Samoans that ended with the death of one of them, and the killer's arrest. The delayed shooting and processing of *Moana* ended in December 1924 after using 240,000 ft. of film. Flaherty and his family returned to Hollywood. The film was very well received by critics all over the world and its photography was considered outstanding. One of the critics, John Grierson, coined a word to describe this type of production, calling it a documentary film. After this, Flaherty was considered the father of this genre with a 25 year long career maintaining his personal method of producing film stories.

# 16. Motion Picture Laboratories

In a previous chapter we saw the work method used in the motion picture processing and its evolution from the first years of the nineteenth century. This basic methodology continued during some years of the period under consideration, but there were some changes. About 1920, experiments made with the new panchromatic film required by various color systems showed that developing this emulsion demanded new procedures. It was different from the classic orthochromatic emulsion and demanded total darkroom work with changes in safety filters, and strict control of time and temperature instead of visual checking. In 1923 the introduction of the reversal film opened a new big domestic market. The film formats of 16mm and 9.5mm created by Eastman Kodak in the United States, and Pathé in France, demanded film processing with automatic developing machines, which required light exposure during the process with the reversal emulsion. In the United States the Spoor Thompson Co. was one of the first to build this kind of equipment for some film labs.[1]

These were the first attempts at a new methodology that would be coming, but they did not radically alter the classic working systems for some time. The use of the ortho emulsion was then a generally accepted standard. The image produced was better than this new panchro, which was slower in speed, had a comparatively too high contrast and needed a process that differed from the standard. The first panchro raw stock was also expensive and not easily available. Many laboratories then believed that the use of automatic developing machines was risky and the rack and tank method deemed safest. So, for some years classic techniques continued to be used as the best method in this field.

Towards 1927, radical innovations appeared in this field that were of fundamental importance for film labs. The appearance of optical sound recording gave rise to a series of studies to improve knowledge on sensitometry technology devised thirty years before by Ferdinand Hurter of Switzerland and Vero C. Driffield of England. The first steps showed the importance of film sensitivity and established the density of the negatives, checked the values of density and transparency and analyzed aspects such as gradation, intensification and reduction. This led later to conceive what in time became the classic H&F curves, where gamma values were plotted. As a consequence, the scientific requirement to control film processing defined the creation of a special department in film labs destined to oversee all chemical controls. These laboratories were in a short time equipped with new instruments such as sensitometers and densitometers built by the makers of sound equipment and film stock.

In 1929 Kodak also introduced a new negative developing formula based on such products as Metol and hydroquinone, that in the proper combination proved they were more effective than other products for other processing formulas. This formula, known as D-76, displaced other basic products such as pyrogallol, Paraminophenol, Adurol and glycine acid, which were then widely used. The results obtained were a great advance by the fine grain obtained, excellent contrast and effective control of the processing. The D-76 was widely adopted by the labs in the United States. The average gamma values in those years were 0.68 and the developing time of the negative was between 8 to 12 minutes. In the positive, the gamma was between 1.80 to 2.00 and for the variable density optical sound the gamma was 1.00.[2]

In 1928 Kodak introduced the Type II and later the Type III negative panchro film, the excellent quality of which was superior to the ortho emulsion. Cinematographers and studios now enthusiastically adopted the new panchro emulsion. That same year, this firm put a new duplicating negative and positive film on the market which was another important revolution and its yellow support made it possible that the negatives and positives could be duplicated with effective contrast control by using filters during printing. This was also a new item, which improved the work of the lab and made it possible to perform many special and transition effects in the lab instead of while shooting. All this implied totally adopting the method of time and temperature, and the use of scientific working procedures against the old artisan craftsmanship.

The adoption of optical sound imposed other radical changes in film processing. The new sound speed demanded large film rolls. Sound negative processing with a film that could not be cut demanded the use of automatic developing machines. Sound prints required similar treatment. Besides, release prints without splices were preferred. The adoption of automatic developing machines was then necessary and was consequently standard practice from that time on.

Transferring the wet developed negative to the new drying cupboards (*courtesy Archivo Nacional de la Imagen, Sodre*).

The design of the film developing machine was based in two separate room. Here we see the threaded rollers and the film that crosses the wall (*courtesy Archivo Nacional de la Imagen, Sodre*).

For some time the negative processing of silent shots used in newsreels and shorts was still made using the rack and tank system. The first transition between this method and the automatic system was the transference of the wet developed negative from the racks to the new drying cupboards. The continuous work of automatic developing machines and their improvements in safety devices led to their final adoption also for negative film. The processing of feature films was different: shooting takes with dialog with several cameras at the time required sound synchronization. This implied large amounts of sound and image negative to be processed and to be synchronized later. Consequently automatic processing was also a must with the negative and therefore the labs doing this job necessarily had to adopt it.

Motion picture processing with automatic machines produced an important change in many laboratories at small production centers in the United States and other countries. In places with limited film production, laboratories were installed in small premises. The use of processing machines now required new buildings and a more sophisticated installation that changed the old artisan work.[3] Laboratory work in its different steps was revised and systematized in each plant. The new equipment demanded a special system to provide the required solutions by means of pumps from central reservoir tanks. Replenishing solutions were used and recirculation methods adopted. Air conditioning and filtering devices were considered and applied.

The new processing machines were conceived to work half in a darkroom and half in open light sections. The method most widely used was with a wall separating two rooms. Different equipment makers adopted several mechanical methods. Some made the film pass through large tubes of glass or ebonite about twenty feet deep in which the developing solution circulated. Each tube had a sprocket over it. Three tubes were needed for developing. The first tube was for rinsing water and the next two for the fixing bath. The most common method was using several tanks, in which the film was propelled by means of sprockets. Two sprockets were used with the tanks. The film travelled through film rollers which at the end of the tanks counterbalanced the weight of the film. The change of the vertical distance between the upper and the lower rollers regulated the developing time synchronized with the speed of the machine. The length of the film loops was controlled from out of the machine. Other machines had a constant speed, but with a variable control of the size of the film loops. Another design by Erbograph, an American firm, had horizontal tanks installed one above the other and was one of the first applications of the spray washing principle. In many labs the floor along the processing machines had been raised to allow a better working level.

In some automatic machines, there were some sections for additional treatment baths after the tanks or tubes used for the developing, washing, or fixing baths. For the last step of drying, the air was maintained at a suitable humidity and temperature according to two methods: one was a small enclosed glass cabinet, the other was a large drying section to allow careful personal checking inside.

Many laboratories made the equipment they needed with their own mechanics. Others were built by firms created for this purpose. And some very well known film equipment firms also produced these items. In England two firms supplied such equipment: Lawley Apparatus Co., which used the tube system, and W. Vinten Ltd., which provided equipment which was later adopted by important laboratories like Denham. In France, in 1925 the Etablissement André Debrie made an efficient D.S.G.M. Model processing machine that was sold to many European firms. Later on they conceived a very compact

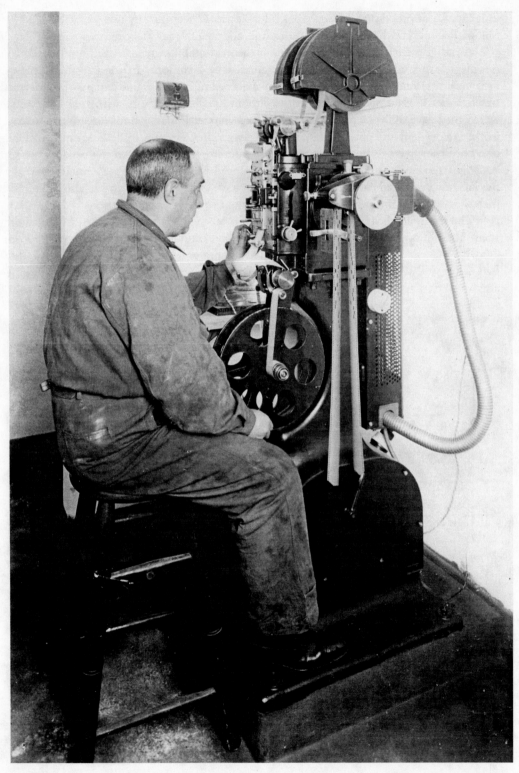

Printing the positive with automatic Debrie Matipo (courtesy *Archivo Nacional de la Imagen, Sodre*).

unit capable of processing 3,000 ft. per hour; it was 22 feet long by two feet wide. This was followed later on by the famous Multiplex line, adopted by many laboratories the world over.

Another French maker of this item was the firm Etablissements Alphonse Bourdereau, a leader in this field, after the machine created by Gaumont. In the early twenties this firm built a system that used tubes or tanks according to the requirements. Bourdereau's small model worked on the system of two-room dark-light sections with tubes and tanks, which processed 1000 feet per hour. The large model built by Bourdereau around 1923 worked in daylight and processed 2,500 ft. per hour. In Germany, in 1927 Arnold & Richter also built their own automatic, friction based developing machine in the classic two-room dark-light sections.[4] Automatic developing reduced the number of personnel required by the labs as only three persons were needed to look after each unit and it also appreciably increased the amount of processed film in comparison to the old method.

The technology changes in the film lab also reached the printing process. During the silent film period the classic use of the step and continuous printers was the adopted standard. Two classic systems were used in the United States for this work: the Duplex and the Bell & Howell. When sound appeared new equipment was needed to print the sound negative. The new sound printers now incorporated the sound printing head or attachment.

The first automatic developing machine designed by Arnold & Richter of Munich in the late twenties (*courtesy Arnold & Richter Cine Technik*).

Primarily the work required two printing steps. Later on a refined printer was developed by Oscar B. Depue to print the sound and image simultaneously in one operation. The synchronization of image and sound negatives also demanded the careful preparation of each roll before printing. The sound area affected the frame size, and in some step printers the image gate size was adapted for this process, until standard sound image sizes were adopted some time later.

Early title table with Parvo L camera (*courtesy Archivo Nacional de la Imagen, Sodre*).

The evolution of printers not only included sound printing devices but also new methods were adopted to produce automatic light changes. The old classic system of hand made light changes by the printer operator, according to visually checking on a card, was now automated according to the designs of each manufacturer. Duplex created a punched card system that allowed 18 different light intensities using an electro-magnet system. The popular continuous Bell & Howell printer used hand made light changes with sound signals to the operator. The image quality obtained with the step printer was now considered important in the production of negative and positive duplicates. The timer work selecting the light values for each shot was improved with some devices developed to provide Cinex strips with different light exposures.

New printing concepts were produced after those initial steps. After its first Debrie Matipo printer that included a punched filmstrip to obtain automatic light changes, this firm later introduced the Matipo T. This new equipment included now two automatic light change controls, one for the image and the other for the sound track. This printer also allowed printing the film in both directions enabling the rewinding of the image and sound negatives to reduce the operation time considerably. The appearance of the new duplicating film in the market induced Debrie to start work on a new optical printing method which produced specific alterations to the image. In another section of the book we will see the results obtained.

The printing carried out during those years later brought new advances in automatic operation. The French technician Leopold Lobel conceived an advanced piece of equipment: the Prestotipe, with horizontal operation and continuous high speed printing to reach the amount of about 12.000 ft. per hour.[5] Other well known printer manufacturers in Europe were Lawley Apparatus Co, Williamson Film Printing Company and W. Vinten Ltd. of the U.K. and Arnold & Richter in Germany. During this decade the laboratories showed a definite evolution of work methods that was reflected in the quality of motion picture photography. The sound imposed eliminating tinted and toned images since they affected optical sound. The new panchro film varied the image values and produced fidelity in the gray tones. This also implied changes in make-up used to correct the drawbacks of ortho film. The scientific process adopted by the labs established a standard working procedure for cinematographers while shooting. Automatic developing machines produced a considerable advance in image quality of the negative, which was now also dust free, and in clean prints. The continuous developing of long rolls of negative also allowed long take shooting, which favored the mobile camera technique and thus the use of a new film language. The new lab methods and duplicated prints were the final solution demanded by the film industry's international distribution requirements.

# 17. Trick Cinematography

The production characteristics of film comedies during the teens and twenties led to the use of multiple camera tricks required by the frequent adoption of gags as a fundamental resource. Those camera tricks followed the usual practice of changing the camera speed, using double exposure, cross-dissolve, substitution technique, masks and mirrors, the stop motion, reverted movement, mobile camera and perspective control.

However, with time, many Hollywood film productions also tended to have high budgets, dramatic films that demanded different effects connecting the photographic field with other production resources, closer to the art department facilities. Consequently, with the passing of the years, the term camera tricks began to be called camera effects or special effects.

In many situations the cinematographer was now required to work closely with the art director, who provided the required settings, backgrounds, facilities and experts to produce miniatures, painted glass and mechanical devices. Special effects combined the cinematographer's skill with those of a group of specialists in different branches, all working together. The second step in this organization was the contribution of the film laboratory to achieve such effects. The specialization in different fields of special effects gave rise to experts in this kind of work and also to independent firms engaged in such jobs.

One of the pioneers in this speciality who worked independently was Norman O. Dawn. He began as an artist in the field of photography at the beginning of last century, making glass shots for stills. Dawn travelled to France where he met Méliès and was influenced by the Frenchman's craftsmanship. After returning to America he worked in the cinematographic field where he used glass shots in the documentary *The Missions of California* (1907). In 1908 he travelled to Australia, making several films there some of which included matte shots. Afterwards he went on making films in the South Pacific, South America and Far Eastern countries. On returning to Hollywood several Studios such as MGM, Pathé and Universal retained his services to produce special effects and soon he established his own firm. His reputation was well known in the industry and he became a member in the American Society of Cinematographers.[1]

Dawn's experience with multiple exposures on painted glass was a step towards the development of this practice by other artists following this specific technique. Among them was Ferdinand Pinney Earle, who created spectacular painted glass shots for the film *Dancing in the Nile* (1923), where he reconstructed buildings and temples with extreme care. Earle also worked in other films, e.g. *Souls in Bondage* (1923), *A Lover's Oath* (1925), and the famous *Ben-Hur* (1925).[2]

One of the most striking special effects obtained in the early twenties was in the Cecil B. De Mille production *The Ten Commandments* (1923). This was one of the cases in which motion picture photography required the effective contribution of the art department and others to achieve their purpose. Paramount Studio had to build huge water tanks to create two vast "waterfalls" that at a certain moment formed a long passage. It was the scenery for the sequence in which Moses and his people, in the Exodus, cross the Red Sea, which seems to open up to afford them a long, narrow corridor.

The big scenes of the Red Sea crossing were filmed in the Guadalupe dunes near Santa Margarita, in California. There, a series of huge tanks were built, about 45 ft. high, on special platforms to form a long curved road. The cameras were conveniently placed on top, in order to shoot the perspective of this big road and thus obtain a matte shot of it. This image was later subdivided in its height to produce a black matte on which the transparent sector with the Red Sea "walls" was placed.

The natural scenes of that road representing the sea bottom, which is crossed by Moses and his people, were filmed within a third matte. The Red Sea surface was made up in small tanks of thick gelatine, filmed in stop motion. All those takes and the mattes were combined in registration to obtain the composed image, showing the multitude following Moses along the sea bottom path that ended in the background.[3]

This unusual special effect, perhaps the most complicated ever produced at that time, was made by specialists like Roy Pommeroy and Fred Moran, with the help of the several cinematographers shooting this film. Ray Rennaham took the Technicolor shots. The cinematographers Bert Glennon, Edward Curtis, Peverell Marley, A.J. Stout and J.F. Westerberg took the black and white shots. The new Technicolor Motion Picture Corporation offered to let De Mille to film this unusual effect with their system under very profitable terms, including that if he did not like the results, there would be no charge. De Mille accepted, obtaining a very important production value for this film that was a great financial success and an example of special effects. This film also brought a great honor to Technicolor, which was responsible for the complex laboratory process.[4]

As an anecdote of this toilsome, intricate strenuous and expensive process, we must point out that many of the technical staff responsible for these effects were jailed by the Los Angeles Police, because during the work a great mass of water was out of control and flooded Hollywood's center streets.[5]

The exposure control within the frame area and the use of mattes, as in the above mentioned film, had been used in the teens, but had never reached this elaborate form and had never been adopted for such expensive productions. Other trick camera techniques were also used in those years. Europeans continued using the old double exposure technique successfully. The most famous production that used this effect was the Swedish film *The Phantom Carriage* (1920) by Victor Sjöström, who afterwards made films in Hollywood. This film, photographed by the Swedish cinematographer Julius Jaenzon, used double exposure in the camera with great creativity combining the movements of the real character with his ghost.

During those years Charles Rosher, the well known cinematographer, also made a film in Hollywood with double exposures, *Little Lord Fauntleroy* (1921), where Mary Pickford played the two principal characters simultaneously as a mother and her daughter. In a scene the ghost image of the daughter must be combined with the real shot of the mother in an embrace and a kiss. For this effect Rosher used a heavy pedestal and sand bags to install the camera so as to minimize any vibration during the shooting of both takes in different positions using the respective mattes. The result was very realistic.[6]

The double exposure method was also used in classic Hollywood comedies like those produced by Mack Sennett and Buster Keaton. In *Playhouse* (1921) Keaton's face was multiplied a great number of times in a theater to show that all the singers and the theater audience had the same face. Keaton, who also was an expert in producing all kinds of effects, used a special matte with nine closed apertures that had to be opened at the right moment in each double exposure. Charlie Chaplin also made double exposures in his films. In *The Circus* (1928), shot by Rollie Totheroh, his usual cinematographer, and Jack Wilson, a ghost image of Charlie was made very perfectly. Certainly, the effect was carefully supervised by Chaplin himself as he usually controlled all details of his films.

In several cases the double exposure effect was substituted by the glass reflection method, where an image of a subject, conveniently placed behind the camera and strongly lighted, was reflected by a large glass and inserted in the same take. This system was simple and more than adequate in many situations, especially in ghost films. Very often these jobs were entrusted to experts. One of them was Milton Moore, who although he had a short career (starting in 1915 and he died in 1929), he made 17 films for Universal and was well known for his studies on double exposure techniques.

During those early days other important special effects innovations were introduced in other countries. In 1923 in Germany, the remarkable cinematographer Eugene Schüfftan developed a device patented in several countries (U.S. Patent 1,569,789 dated September 15,1923), which was known by his name. It was used in several films, including Fritz Lang's well-known *Metropolis* (1928). The Schüfftan device, adopting some principles previously used by Méliès and perfecting them, placed a precision sliding device in front of the camera. During 1924 to 1927 Schüfftan improved this device to obtain more effective results and make it easier to operate.

The Schüfftan process placed a mirror before the camera lens at 45 degrees to the optical lens axis. The silvered side of the mirror was conveniently ground in such a way to combine different subjects situated in perspective and in various planes. These images could be real subjects, miniatures, paintings, or standard settings. Some businesses were started to exploit this invention in film studios, such as British Schüfftan Ltd.

Other kinds of techniques appeared, also in Germany, to combine film images. Following experiments made after World War I by Hans Goetz, who filmed actors against colored backgrounds in order to obtain mattes by using filters, new procedures were created. Those experiences were continued by technicians in Germany and later in Hollywood, among them Max Handschiegl, L.M. Dietrich, Roy Pommeroy, Friend Baker and C. Dodge Dunning, who conceived a method that later on carried his name. It was based on the use of a bipack camera with an orange-dyed positive image in the background of the take. The negative raw stock was behind this film. During the shooting the background was lighted with blue light, while the players in front of this background were lighted with orange light. Thus a travelling matte shot was obtained since the moving players passed freely through this dyed positive and were printed on the negative, blocking the blue background behind them. This system was successfully used in *Silver King Comes Thru* (1927) and *Anna Christie* (1930). In the former the effect was very realistic and consisted in a horse jumping from a moving train. The Dunning system was soon used in other film studios before the coming of the rear projection system.[7]

In 1925, the French cinematographer Léonce-Henry Burel (who made several films with the famous Abel Gance) joined forces with Henry Debain, a technician from the Ateliers Techniques du Film, and developed a method to retouch motion picture films. The system used a special apparatus on which a print was projected on a large ground glass and after each frame was retouched, it was refilmed by a camera. The artist that did the retouching partly entered the equipment and worked on a large ground glass. After proving this system on some films it was then used in *Napoleon* (1925–27), first to change the appearance of the actor playing the role of Robespierre, and afterwards it included several projectors to produce diverse image effects required by the triptych method conceived by Gance. Later on, this image control method was used again in the Maurice Tourneur production *L'Equipage* (1928) for sketched special effects on aerial combat scenes.[8]

New experiments were made in the field of special effects with rear projection of still images. This was the base for forming experiences to better know the difficulties and needs of this method. With those practices the inconvenience of the hot spot was learned, the needs of the translucent screen density level, the intensity of the required projecting light and the situations where this method could be used. This system was adopted in a few cases but was limited in its use and the backgrounds continued to be based on large paintings or photographic paper enlargements. The development of the rear projection in moving pictures had to wait until the thirties.

In 1928 an important step was made for producing special effects in the laboratory when the motion picture duplicating film was introduced by Eastman Kodak. This allowed the production of duplicating negatives without a high contrast print, and to work with the camera in the lab to modify the reproduction of the original negative. In 1929 André Debrie conceived the idea of a special printing machine called the Truca which included all the facilities to produce image alterations. This new instrument was one of the first designs of what was later on called an optical printer, of which Linwood Dunn in Hollywood was indisputably the pioneer.[9]

# 18. Outstanding Cinematography

The films shot during the twenties with outstanding cinematography presented varied characteristics. We have selected those that deserved praise at that time and even today are selected by professionals of the trade. Some were American productions and others were made in Europe. Unfortunately the duplicate prints available today do not reflect the quality of the original version. However, a careful study of those films, which are on video or DVD or in film archives will be undoubtedly an exiting experience.

## The Four Horsemen of the Apocalypse

According to technical evolution in the twenties in the field of cinematography the achievements obtained were remarkable. In 1921 the most important film produced in Hollywood was *The Four Horsemen of the Apocalypse*, a high cost film made by Metro Studios, directed by Rex Ingram. The excellence of the cinematography in this production was difficult to achieve bearing in mind the processing techniques then used, with the rack and tank process, and the limitations of ortho film. This work was the responsibility of John F. Seitz, younger brother of George B. Seitz, a very well known film director.

John Seitz, born in Chicago on June 21, 1893, began to study cinematography, working in motion picture laboratories since he was 16 years old. In 1915 he joined Quality Picture Laboratories, a firm that was afterwards sold and renamed Horsley Laboratories. There, Seitz soon began to be responsible for quality processing, a job that provided him a lot of experience and sharpened his skills to seek excellence in his results. Then he was taken into the photographic team of the Metro Studios, where his responsibilities quickly took him to the top of his profession. There he flourished with the help of Rex Ingram, the actor, with whom he formed a long lasting team, based on similar aesthetic concepts, as Ingram was also a sculptor and painter.

According to his artistic views on this film, as in other jobs, Seitz searched for original and unusual ideas as well as dramatically effective lighting to create images according to the story. For this film he created a very strong lighting, contrasting chiaroscuros with intense cross lights, and backlights on players and the setting. He was also careful in lighting close-ups, taking into consideration Rudolph Valentino's excellent photogenic quality. After this production and the film's image treatment, Valentino was catapulted into fame.

There were countless wonderful images obtained by Seitz in this film. Among them, most of the outdoor shots filmed early in the morning and with a backlight standout, especially those of the German assault on Villeblanche, the interiors of Desnoyer castle with the occupying forces feasting and the sequence when their forced host was locked up to be executed. This film shows not only excellent photography but also elaborate art work by Joseph Calder on the castle sets and the French village, but not for the many settings of the sequence in Argentina. Ingram's direction was also of great value in the selected framing, the functional use of original World War I shots, the handling of film language, and good editing.

A large number of cameras were used to shoot this big production and nearly a million feet of negative. Seitz obtained great prestige with this film because of many war time shots in flooded trenches. The use of special effects such as when "the four horses" appeared and the beautiful long shot in the cemetery were artistic feats. After this film Seitz was considered one of the best cinematographers in Hollywood. Later on he created several devices in the special effects field.

# The Phantom Carriage

At the beginning of the decade, the two more prominent European films with excellent cinematography were made in Scandinavia. The first was *Körkarlen* (*The Phantom Carriage*), made in Sweden in 1920, and directed by the famous Victor Sjöström, who merited enthusiastic comments for his new flashback techniques.

The cinematography of the *Phantom Carriage* was also praised afterwards all over Europe for the unusual double exposure effects used throughout the film, the balanced use of the chiaroscuros, the effective image difference between the real character and the ghost and how the cinematography dovetailed with the story. Many expressed their pleasure with the film. When Charlie Chaplin saw it he said it was the best film he had ever seen. Many decades later, European directors of photography considered this production the best expression of the cinematography of that time. The well known Swedish cinematographer Julius Jaenson was the man responsible for this achievement.

Jaenson was born in Gothenburg in the mid-eighties. He started in this profession when movies took their first steps, and he learned it following the progress of this new medium. Jaenson was hired as cameraman and laboratory expert by the film company created after the French cameraman Alexandre Promio brought the new invention to Sweden. At the beginning of the new century Jaenson had already developed a good experience making his first eighty minute long feature film named *Fiskelivets Faror* (*Dangers of a Fisherman's Life*). Some time later he went to the United States and got President Theodore Roosevelt to sit for him for fifteen minutes for camera takes. In another trip to this country he filmed the first travelling scenes from a tramway with players driving in a car along Broadway, three years before Griffith made his famous travelling shots of Mary Pickford in *Home Sweet Home* (1914).

The great friendship between Jaenson and another Swedish film pioneer, Carl Magnusson, also a cinematographer, led to his work in many feature films. Over the years Magnusson became an important film producer and head of the Svenska Bio, which hired two distinguished figures of the Swedish theatre: Maurice Stiller and Victor Sjöström. Jaenson started a very close professional relationship with them that lasted many years. His first and most devoted pupil was his brother Henrik. From 1917 while Julius Jaenson was cinematographer for Sjöström's films, Erik Jaenson was the cinematographer for Stiller's films. Both brothers also worked together in the Stiller film *Sangen on den Eldroda Blomman* (*The Song of the Scarlette Flower*, 1918). Julius Jaenson was so famous in his country that he used his first name only, in the film credits. In *The Phantom Carriage* he received a great help for his difficult task from a laboratory expert named Hellman. Later on he was cinematographer for Maurice Stiller's important film *The Tale of Gösta Berling* (1924). One of his pupils was Gunnar Fisher, another great Swedish expert who become Ingmar Bergman's preferred cinematographer.

## Witchcraft Through the Ages

This Danish film, also named *Axan*, was a controversial production due to its theme. It was produced in 1921 by the Nordisk Film Company and director Benjamin Christensen completed it in three years. The subject was a combination of fiction and non-fiction describing how witchcraft developed through the ages with vivid imagination, forceful images and all kind of resources. The particular conception of this film required a first class cinematographer to create the necessary unusual compositions with high artistic sense and without losing realism and impressiveness. The man selected for this difficult task was Johan Ankerstjerne, another Scandinavian genius of cinematography.

Ankerstjerne was born in Randers, Denmark, on January 17, 1886. During his early years he started as a clockmaker. Later on he changed to motion pictures and worked on a short film for the Nordisk Co., where he continued to work as cinematographer. He began with the Danish director E. Schnedler Sorensen and soon his excellent work brought him to the attention of the renowned film director August Bloom. With Bloom he made several films of which *Atlantis* (1913) was the most outstanding. In 1915 Ankerstjerne left Bloom's studio to collaborate with Benjamin Christensen in an unusual thriller, *The Night of Revenge* (1916), where he did a successful job with excellent lighting. After some time he worked for Astra Films (a producing company owned by the film actor Olaf Fönss) where he worked on several productions. Benjamin Christensen afterwards called Ankerstjerne to film *Axan* in which he used all his experience, sensibility and inventiveness.

The cinematography of *Axan* is today considered admirable and masterly. It was a high budget production requiring character stage players, people selected for their special faces or with arthritic diseases and even taking on very old inmates of a Copenhagen asylum. The cinematography for this film included several multiple exposure techniques but also unusual combinations of shots within the frame, like a painting with fog effects, silhouettes, and mobile subjects on the screen such as witches crossing the sky mounted on brooms. This sort of plastic conception of the image such as small light touches, all made with limited technical resources and basic lighting units, had been very seldom seen on the screen. This picture gave him great renown, and afterwards Ankerstjerne shot a film in Iceland and then returned to the Nordisk Studio where he worked in its laboratory for ten years. Then he left this firm and started his own laboratory that became one of the most important ones in Denmark.

## The Hunchback of Notre Dame

This 1923 Hollywood production was praised for its cinematography and impressive production. Based on Victor Hugo's famous novel, this film was a Universal Studios super production and one of the favorite films of its head, Carl Laemmele. The presence of a new young executive, Irving Thalberg, was also felt in this important film that reached a cost of $1,200,000. The director was Wallace Worceley and the leading actor was the well-known

Lon Chaney playing the role of Quasimodo. This production demanded several sets built with the intention of using them later in other productions. The most important sets were Notre Dame Cathedral in Paris and a castle. The sets were built with great care and realism which was a great contribution to the high level cinematography by Robert Newhard.

Newhard was an experienced cinematographer, native of Pennsylvania, who had worked in New York close to famous colleagues like Arthur Miller and pioneer producers such as Thomas Ince and Fred Balshofer. He had also participated as a cinematographer in many Hollywood films and had specialized in aerial and complex cinematography. In this production he received the help of several specialists in special effects such as Tony Kornmann, Virgil Miller, Charles Stumar, Stephen Norton, Philip H. Whitman and Friend F. Baker. This large number of experts associated on one production was not frequent at that time and showed that the studio was very concerned with this complex high budget production.[1]

The result of this effort was rewarding, because the cinematography of this film proved to be remarkable, especially in the night scenes in the Court of Miracles, the interiors of the castle, the close ups of Quasimodo, the realistic scenes with the big sets and the several special effects produced. The images in the film also benefited by the use of tinted Eastman positive prints with tones ranging from blue for the night scenes, amber for interiors lighted by candelabra, magenta for the flashbacks, green for the torture scenes and melon for the love scenes. This careful use of colors was an attractive plastic complement and a new artistic value to help make this film a great success.

## The Ten Commandments

In 1923, another important film was produced which became outstanding for its special effects and the partial use of color: *The Ten Commandments*. In this De Mille production backed by the Famous Players-Lasky studio of Adolph Zukor (as seen in a previous chapter) the cinematography was by Bert Glennon with other cinematographers specialized in color and special effects. Glennon was born in Anaconda, Montana, in 1895 and entered his trade in 1912. He had had good experience as cinematographer in films like *Ramona* (1916) and *The Torrent* (1920) and was later on very much appreciated by meticulous directors such as Joseph Von Stemberg.

In this production Glennon was backed by the director, DeMille, who was very sensitive to all aspects of cinematography, especially in framing and lighting, and who demanded shooting outdoors takes at sunrise to obtain the benefit of long shadows and the relief produced in the images, notwithstanding the drawbacks of the ortho emulsion that resented red light at that time. *The Ten Commandments*, with a cost reaching the then record sum of $1,476,000, was very much appreciated by audiences for its visual spectacle, its attractive shots, and the startling color sequence of the Red Sea splitting in two. During its premiere in the United States it was applauded each time it was shown and was exhibited for sixty-three weeks, running on Broadway, and reaching the top in box-office returns.

## The Last Laugh

In 1924, *The Last Laugh* (American title of the German production *Der Letzte Mann*) was emblematic in the development of the German concept of the already mentioned unchained camera, a very intensive use of the mobile camera during the shooting. This film impressed many filmmakers the world over who then adopted the method.

The film was made in the famous UFA studios of Berlin and Karl Freund used Agfa Orthokine film stock. A Debrie Parvo camera was used in the main unit complemented with a Stachow camera. The film's cinematography benefited from Robert Herth's carefully made settings. Herth, together with Freund, planned every detail on paper, including framing and lighting, before shooting, according to German practice.

Following German techniques in film lighting, Freund made intense use of several arc lights and reflecting screens for outdoor shots of the Atlantic Hotel front and a complex lighting system controlled from a switching board to regulate the lighting units inside the windows of many huge sets with buildings representing a city. The use of miniatures of a railroad station with trains was an example of this studio department's mastery in reproducing all kinds of scenes on its back lots and with exact verity. Among the most effective shots were the city night street scenes, several hotel interiors, the bath room, the rotating pan around a room with the camera centred on Emil Jannings, and the travelling shot of the hotel's hall and rotating door.[2]

Carl Freund had been born in Königinhof, Bohemia, in January 16, 1890. He began working in still photo laboratories where he learned how to treat photographic emulsions in order to gain more speed. In 1905 he entered in the field of moving pictures and was trained in this speciality, maturing his own mode in the expressionist style. In 1913 he worked with Max Reinhart in the film *Venetianische Nacht*, filming from a gondola. In 1919 he worked as cinematographer for Emil Schunemann in the film *Die Spinnen* (*The Spiders*), an adventure film. His first film with Murnau was *Satanas* (1919) with script by Robert Wiene, and then *Der Bucklige und die Tanzerin* (*The Hunchback and the Dancer*, 1920). That year he showed his excellence as cinematographer in *The Golem*. In *The Last Laugh* he achieved a prestige in the German film industry that afforded him the opportunity to work afterwards on important productions such as *Variete* (1925), *Tartüffe* (1925), *Metropolis* (1926) with Gunter Rittau and *Berlin, Rhythm of a City* (1927). In 1935 he went to the United States where he continued with his brilliant career.

# The Battleship Potemkin

A production that was emblematic in many aspects and considered a new form of film art was made in another part of the world: in the Soviet Union. Its name was *Bronenosetz Potemkin* (*The Battleship Potemkin*, 1925), the second film of a young, extraordinarily gifted and very cultured filmmaker, Sergei Eisenstein, who had come from the stage and had training in architecture and engineering. The film was based on a real incident. Its spectacular treatment and the high level of its images made Soviet film production known internationally. It deeply influenced audiences and important filmmakers all over the world. The exceptional cinematography for this film was by Eduard Tissé, afterwards considered a great cinematographer.

Tissé had been born in 1887 in Lithuania, and studied painting. At seventeen he worked as a cameraman on several short films on nature and landscapes. At the beginning of the Russian Revolution he joined a group of newsreel cameramen where he obtained very good practice and skill defining his plastic sensibility and exceptional natural artistic perception. Thanks to a recommendations by a prominent artist he met Eisenstein with whom he immediately sympathized since both had very similar artistic ideas. After this first encounter Tissé worked in Eisenstein's first film, *Stachka* (*Strike*, 1924), and followed that with working with him on *The Battleship Potemkin*.

In *Potemkin* both applied their shared main concepts on how to carry out the job, such as the importance of framing, the careful choice of camera angles, the use of light and shade values, the placing of light sources, and the dynamics of the subjects within the film frame. Their similar ideas gave rise to a mature, artistic analysis which Tissé carefully applied in preparing and lighting each set-up using special resources such as applying oil to the seamen's naked torsos to obtain a better lighting response, as well as many other tricks.

The result was spectacular cinematography that combined with Eisenstein's carefully schemed mise en scene, producing this film's remarkable artistic level. It would be very hard to define which were the image highlights of this cinematography because the takes were extremely selected and functional. However the most memorable lighting of medium close shots were the interior of the battleship, the view of Odessa port, the seaman mourning and the impressive sequence on the Odessa Steps lighted with large mirrors. This film must be carefully analyzed to study the use of light and shadows, the placing of light sources and Tissé's careful control of each shot to turn the film into one of the most remarkable of all times.

# Faust

In 1926, once again a German production was relevant for its cinematography. The film *Faust, Eine Deutsche Volkssage* (*Faust*) was another UFA production directed again by F.W. Murnau and based on old German legends and books by Goethe and Marlowe. Hans Keyser wrote the script. Few films had had such a complete background, with engravings and paintings by the great German master painting August Von Kreling (1818–1876). This work had impressed Murnau in his youth and when this project was begun, these lithographs were the initial pictorial step on which the filmmakers and art directors Robert Herth and Walther Rohring based the film's imagery.

UFA had the practice that art directors must carefully plan all the visual aspects of a production beforehand, even the lighting, working them out in the preliminary steps with the assigned cinematographer. Other departments of the studio, such as special effects, miniatures and special constructions contributed to this end. The characteristic German attention to details and methodology and shooting control were applied during pre-production.

At this early stage when pre-production began, several important players were pre-selected for the female role of Gretchen (Margaret). Among the options was Lillian Gish, but this American star, following Hollywood standards, claimed that they should also engage her preferred cinematographer, Charles Rosher, who was in Germany. Gish was passed over and Camilla Horn was selected for the role. The responsibility of cinematography was assigned to Karl Freund, who had worked with Murnau in many films. Some time before shooting, Freund had an accident in which he broke a leg, so another famed German cinematographer, Carl Hoffmann, was then selected and worked on this film for eight months.

Hoffman had been born in 1881 and his film activity started at the beginning of German cinematography. In 1919 he was cinematographer for the renowned German actor Conrad Veidt, in a production in which Murnau also participated. Later on Hoffmann was Murnau's cinematographer for the film *Der Knabe in Blau* (1919). Hoffman and Karl Freund did the cinematography for another Murnau film, *Der Januskopf* (*The Janus Head*, 1920).

These previous films showed a good relationship and understanding. Hoffman was now a well-known cinematographer with a reputation for highly imaginative resourcefulness and experience.

In *Faust* he proved this capacity to reach the intended high artistic target. In this production he used the Agfa Orthokino film, a Debrie Parvo and a Cameraeclair combined with arc lamps and mercury vapor units. The film included toned takes that rendered many life-like scenes. Filtered light was intensively used in the most varied conditions and intense smoke was used to produce the required atmosphere. In many cases igniting nitrate film or mixing hydrochloric acid with ammonia obtained the smoke near the stage entrance. Varied resources were adopted for shooting, such as the camera on rails moving over a large miniature to show an aerial view of cities, woods, landscapes and villages in Faust's travel. Large amounts of salt were used for the snowstorm. Hoffman controlled the lighting of the scene very carefully and had built extremely high gobos to control the size of long shadows. The shots of the pact with the devil were noteworthy, as also were the interior of the church and the hemicycle scene. The cinematography for this film was a "tour de force" which German cinematography offered to international film making.[3]

# Ben-Hur

Also in 1926 a spectacular Hollywood film showed again the levels achieved by American film production and its creative and resourceful cinematography. The famous book by General Lew Wallace, *Ben-Hur*, had been written many years before. Both the book and its stage adaptation were highly successful. This new Metro production, at a cost of $4,000,000, was a complex project that took a long time to make. Fred Niblo directed it and the photography was the work of many cinematographers, the most representative of which were Karl Struss, René Guissart, Percy Hilburn, Clyde de Vinna, George Meeham, Burt Reynolds and E. Burton Steeve. German and Italian cinematographers also participated on *Ben-Hur* among which we must mention Carlo Montuori, who took important shots which made Fred Niblo want to bring him to Hollywood; Silvano Barboni, who suffered most of the conflicts on this complex production; and Alfredo Donelli who obtained interesting experience on this unusual production. The film was taken in black and white but as in *The Ten Commandments*, a color sequence was used when Jesus Christ appears, for which Technicolor's No. 2 subtractive method was used.[4]

This film was noteworthy as a large enterprise, and for several production problems at the beginning. Technical difficulties appeared in the black and white processing that required the head of Metro's laboratories to go to Rome. Rene Guissart, the French Technicolor cinematography expert, was in charge of the color sequences. Louis B. Mayer, who was in Rome at the time, decided to add his trusted cinematographer Karl Struss to the crew. Before leaving Metro for Rome, Irving Thalberg recommended that Struss never forget that his stars must always look beautiful.[5]

The film required the use of many special effects with travelling mattes and miniatures combined with natural settings. The head of the MGM art department, Cedric Gibbons, with A. Arnold Gillespie and Andrew MacDonald and a crew of designers and Italian artisans prepared very complex art work and settings that included the Circus Maximus (made twice, in both Rome and Hollywood), ships of Roman Empire times built in natural scale, the city of Jerusalem built to scale and many other constructions.

One of the most complex sequences with special effects was the collapse of the Roman senate, where natural sets were combined with miniatures using travelling mattes prepared by Frank Williams. Ben Reynolds filmed the important sequence of the sea battle between the Macedonian galleys and the Roman triremes in Livorno. In a scene in this battle one of the Macedonian ships boarded a Roman trireme, when the fire spout went out of control; the extras making up the ship's crew had to jump into the sea and several boats had to sally urgently to save them. Also the political situation in Italy provoked several fights between fascist and antifascist extras, causing important production losses.[6]

Karl Struss was in charge of shooting 65 percent of this film, including the first scenes of the chariot race, until the weather deteriorated and the sequence had to be filmed in Hollywood. He was responsible for shooting the scenes in which Ben-Hur's mother and sister were miraculously cured in the leper's hospital. The effect was obtained introducing a green filter during the take when the camera filmed the red treated make-up of the bodies.[7] The most important sequence of the film was done in Hollywood: the famous chariot race. The Circus Maximus was rebuilt in Hollywood under the direction of art director Andrew Mac Donald. This natural set was made up of several sections, which were combined with miniatures of the galleries. In some of them spectators were made up by nearly 10,000 tiny reproductions that were moved by severally devices. To shoot the mobile shots of the race, ten cameras were used installed in special designed vehicles that followed the main competitors: Ben-Hur and Messala. Fourteen chariots were used and forty-eight selected horses. More than forty cameramen were engaged to cover the scene from all possible angles with cameras hidden among the public, inside statues or in pits alongside the track.[8]

The negative used on the day when the most important scenes of this sequence were taken was the equivalent of 20 hours of projection. From this material about 12 minutes were finally seen on the screen. The total negative spent in the production was nearly a million feet. Their production costs were nearly $4 million. The Technicolor method required a print with emulsion on both sides of the film support, with a doubtful color rendering and easily damageable. However this was a small detail in a production that became a big box office success. The famous chariot race was so spectacular and well filmed that when a remake of this film was produced in 1956, the director of the film, William Wyler, and the director of the sequence, Yakima Cannut (Enos Edward Cannut) reproduced similar shots to those made thirty years before.

# Sunrise

In June 1927 in Hollywood the Academy of Motion Picture Arts and Sciences (AMPAS) was formed, an organization representing the motion picture industry of the United States and providing prizes for deserving films in several fields, including cinematography. That year the award for best cinematography was for *Sunrise*, a Fox Film Corporation production, directed by F.W. Murnau with cinematography by Charles Rosher and Karl Struss. It was the third time that a film by this famed director was distinguished for its outstanding cinematography. The Academy also rewarded this film's production. From this occasion onward the Academy Awards signified a worldwide acknowledgment of merits, and the Oscar statue (designed by art director Cedric Gibbons) meant, to professionals in this activity, renown in their field and a target to be reached.

Murnau, now in the United States, used the same methodology adopted when he was in UFA. He brought with him some close collaborators, such as his scriptwriter, Carl Mayer; his art director, Rochus Gliese; and his assistant director, Hermann Bing. The first two had secured the artistic quality of his previous films although, according to American standards, it was not common that a scriptwriter could be connected with the art design. But Carl Mayer always was a decisive contributor to the plastic values of Murnau's productions in his search for perfection, high aesthetic sensibility and valuable ideas. Rochus Gliese was also fundamental for his vast competence, his scrupulous and imaginative sketches and his care for details, including even the best lighting for each situation.

Nothing similar had ever occurred in production design in Hollywood studios, and it was not repeated until many years later. Following the methods of the time and the procedures used in UFA, the film was shot with set constructions built to production requirements. The biggest one was The City, in Fox Hill Studio, a 150 acre site in Westwood, recently built and designed for location shooting. A city was built there, a mile long and half a mile wide, at a cost of $200,000, that called for 400 workers over several months, and consisting of the center section of a city with its large and high buildings where 200 cars circulated, as well as two tramways, three two-story buses, trucks, carriages drawn by one and two horses, cycles and 2000 extras acting as pedestrians.[9]

Gliese's experience was extremely effective in designing and building seven storey buildings that were only 25 ft. high sets since everything was based on the use of false perspective. Using the same technique, this art director combined a complex miniature of a railroad station with moving trains. The German methodology of meticulous planning and sketching was a great help, even with the high standards adopted in Hollywood, because when shooting was about to begin everything had been previously organized. This film was also noted for including other innovations: one of them was the first use of the new panchro negative called Eastman Panchro in a long feature film. But this new negative was only used in the outdoors takes and the ortho negative continued to be used in indoors. This panchro film required several tests, especially to know how this emulsion responded to different filters. The film was developed in the Aller Film Laboratories instead of Fox Laboratories.

Four cameras were used simultaneously to shoot this film, but two were often the main cameras, one for the domestic negative and the other for the foreign release prints. The basic cameras were a Bell & Howell operated by Struss and a Mitchell operated by Rosher. The Struss camera was crank-handle driven but Rosher's Mitchell was electric motor driven.[10] The standard speed was 16 f.p.s. Lighting for indoor takes was effected with Mole & Richardson spots with National White Flame carbons, and while shooting outdoors with the new panchro film, the new National panchromatic carbons were adopted to provide a better light in red-orange and yellow-green rays required with this emulsion.

Several mobile takes were made in this production using special vehicles with medium size pneumatic wheels and tubes around the car that was installed on tracks. A special rolling column was also used, hanging from rails in the ceiling, brought by Rosher from the UFA studios. Struss used this unusual device in Hollywood in a circular shot following O'Brien when going through a marsh to find the women from the city. Many of the shots in the city sets were difficult and some required special effects, such as the scene in which Janet Gaynor, the female lead, crossed the street after getting down from a tram and is almost run down by a car; this required the use of a matte shot effect made by Frank Williams.

The sequence in the restaurant required several wide-angle shots and mobile miniatures in the background seen through the window. A large part of the set was a miniature and required the background extras to be smaller than in the close shots. For this, several dwarves and children dressed as men and women were used. Murnau had a good knowledge of how to use different focal lenses and adopted focals from 35 to 55mm and small telephoto lenses for close-ups, a technique not widely used then.[11]

The night shots in the city required nearly 300 lighting units, some of which were borrowed from other Hollywood studios; 160 electricians were needed while shooting on the city set to control the lighting. The Luna Park sequence also called for the use of many lamps installed on the top of the set on special platforms. This set had been carefully planned by Gliese and included mobile miniatures such as elevated trains, a giant wheel, and even large animals, e.g. an elephant. In the tram sequence a standard one was used but mounted on a car chassis covered by a wooden frame. The tram rails were installed on a mound in the studio back lot. As the space was limited, because it was taken up by sets for Tom Mix films, Gliese conceived a zig-zag tram travel to lengthen it and avoid the back side of such sets.

*Sunrise* required six months to shoot, and after its release it was an immediate success with the public and critics. It turned out to be a first rate film that achieved the proposed targets and its charm and artistic values are still valid today. Renowned Hollywood directors such as King Vidor and Charlie Chaplin made extremely favorable comments on this production. It became Hollywood's paradigm of an excellent film.

Regarding its cinematography, the work of Rosher and Struss was remarkable and a credit of great value in their careers. The sequences of the lovers under the moonlight, the fisherman returning home, the one in the barn, the town lights at night, the effective double exposures, the many shots of the city crowds, the dance sequence in the Luna Park with the elevated train and the giant wheel, the return to the lake, and the search sequence, maintain their effectiveness today, with the perspective of the time elapsed and considering the limitations of the available prints.

# Napoléon

In 1927 an emblematic film was made in Europe with, in many ways, remarkable cinematography. In France, Abel Gance completed his famous *Napoléon* that put his name alongside the great filmmakers as David W. Griffith in the U.S.A., Eisenstein in the Soviet Union and Murnau in Germany. Gance had proved his creativeness in two previous films—*J'accuse!* (1919) and *La Rue* (1921)—that showed his capacity to adopt a new, unusual and exciting technique in film editing and the use of the image as a vital tool in film language. In 1921 Gance travelled to the United States to adapt *J'acusse* to the American film market, as had been requested by Griffith himself, who wanted to release this film through United Artists.

Gance remembered that, walking in one day on Broadway with his friend Max Linder (Gabriel Leuvielle) and stimulated by the possibility of distributing his films in America, he had the inspiration of making an international quality film based on a world known historical celebrity: Napoléon Bonaparte. This idea remained in his mind and began to take form as early as 1923. He started then exhaustive research on this personality and his times, resulting in a library of 300 books and more than 3000 etchings. The primary idea was the production of a film trilogy made up of "The Youth of Bonaparte; Napoléon and the French Revolution, and the Italian Campaign." The size of this project was so vast that afterwards the first two parts were combined into a film having an 800 page script with plenty of notes and 13,000 scenes.[12]

The scenes were filmed on the banks of the Seine, in the Billancourt Studios that had been acquired with all the technical installations. But the shooting also included several locations like Brienne in Corsica, place of the Bonaparte's family home, Toulon, and many in Paris. About 1,500 extras were needed for certain scenes, e.g. the Toulon assault, and the scenes of the convention. The complex artistic direction of the film was entrusted to two distinguished experts, Alexandre Benoit and Pierre Schild, both from the stage and ballet. They based their excellent work on the vast information compiled by Gance and their own research to produce a faithful reconstruction of the epoch. Many years later the famous French art director Léon Barsac commented that this was the first time in France where the setting for an epoch film was reproduced with such scrupulous accuracy.[13]

Abel Gance always made things in a big way and did not spare the right people for this film. As personal help he demanded six assistant directors and five cinematographers, but among them the chief man was Jules Krueger. The other French cinematographers were Roger Hubert, Leónce-Henry Burel, Joseph-Louis Mundviller and Fédote Bourgassoff with the assistance of Paul Briquet, George Lucas, Emile Pierre and others. Many of them had previously worked with Gance on other productions and covered the multiple set-ups required for this production.

Jules Krueger had been born in Strasburg in 1891. He had been as press photographer before World War I and later on as news cameraman he had been a pupil of the renowned Harry Stradling during his stay in France. He began as a cinematographer in 1921 and photographed films of Emil Roussel such as *Violettes impériales* (1922) and *Les Opprimés* (1923) and obtained a good reputation for his high sense of atmosphere and careful effective framing. His previous work with Gance placed him at the head of the cinematography for this production, and he was the faithful interpreter of the several unusual innovations continuously proposed by this director. Jules Krueger was afterwards the cinematographer for well known filmmakers like Georges Bernard, Marcel L'Herbier, Julien Duvivier and Sacha Guitry.

Roger Hubert was a young cinematographer born in Montreuil-sous-Bois in 1903. Taught in the Institut Marey, he learned aesthetic culture from Jean Epstein. With Gance, Hubert found the opportunity to project his superior cinematographic capacity in this job and soon become one of the most refined French cinematographers. His technique was based on the use of a small piece of paper with a hole in front of the light to produce light touches in close-ups. Like a good painter, he used an aerograph to produce clouds on a glass in front of the camera whenever necessary.[14]

Léonce-Henry Burel, born in Indret (Loire-Atlantique) in 1892, entered this profession after studying at Ecoles des Beaux Arts and began as cinematographer in the film *Les Gaz mortels* (1916), directed by Gance. Afterwards he continued working with this filmmaker on *Mater Dolorosa* (1917), *La Dixième Symphonie* (1918), and in the last two successful Gance films, *J'accuse!* (1919) and *La Rue* (1921). His presence in *Napoléon* was, of course, unquestionable, as he was an expert in special effects, and many of the tricks made in the camera or in the laboratory were part of his work and he effected several innovations required by Gance. Burel was another reputed French cinematographer who worked later on many important films. Mundviller and Bourgassoff were members of a Russian film production group settled in Paris.

*Napoléon* was, for the cinematographers who worked on it, the best opportunity they had had in the trade, and the one that marked their professional careers. In this film they vested all their inventiveness, and exerted the maximum demand on their capacities; they broke rules, and experimented with motion picture images as never before asked. All the cinematographic technical resources of France were used in this film. Many camera makes were used such as Debrie Parvo models, JK, L, Interview, Debrie GV, Sept, Cameraeclair, Cinex Bourdereau, Guillon, Bell & Howell Standard, Eyemo, and a special underwater housing was built for submarine takes.

The use of the mobile camera was a norm with handheld shooting or mounted on many devices. The technical support of the Billancourt Studios expert Simon Feldman was extremely important. When Gance wanted the point of view of a cavalryman galloping, he created a device with a Parvo camera driven by a compressed air motor, fed from a special cylinder, mounted on the horse saddle. When travelling takes were required toward the subject with the camera moving from top to bottom, he conceived a device similar to a guillotine mounted on a sledge where a Parvo moved up and down. Feldman also built a special motor-driven tripod head to produce 360 degree uniform pans.[15]

Shooting Napoleon's birthplace in Corsica demanded a large technical staff and many actors to go there. It was found that the front of the house was difficult to cover because of the limited distance available. On this occasion a new lens was used, created by the French firm Optis, manufacturer of the Debrie camera viewfinders. This lens, named Brachyscope, produced an extremely wide-angle effect of about 20mm. This was another of Gance's visions, foreseeing the possibility of projecting this film on a wide screen, and increasing that production's magnificence.

Many technical difficulties were found while shooting this film. When filming the night scenes of the Toulon battle, the artificial rain affected the lighting units and many of them cracked, injuring several technicians and actors as well as Gance himself, who kept working on with burns on his arm. The Toulon battle took forty days to be filmed in the historic location. The scenes of the sailing boat in which Napoleon is taken by a storm had to be made in a studio tank where thousands of gallons of water poured from another tank. In many shots a special underwater camera housing was used to cover the great waves that endangered the boat. Another complex sequence was in the convention hall set. A large number of actors and extras had to be lighted requiring intense use of light units. Gance planned to produce an impressive effect in part of this sequence to suggest the ups and downs of these sessions. For this set-up Simon Feldman built a large pendulum where the camera was installed and covered a vertical high shot with a very effective vision of the crowd in the convention sessions.

A large number of double or multiple exposures were characteristic of this film. Maximum experience and skill were required. Burel was one of the experts for this kind of work. Making the well known pillow fight scene in the Brienne School dormitory between young Napoléon and his companions was very complex. Several takes included six double exposures in the camera.[14] The lighting units used in the studio varied from the most powerful arc units to mercury vapor banks including a very special unit for lighting the eyes of Napoleon for only ten frames. But there was also a profusion of light filtered through gauzes in the romantic scenes with Napoléon and Josephine. The lighting of the close-ups was always related to the situations and the dramatic effect of the sequence. Gance did not made any concession to photogenic concerns, but used large telephoto lenses in the close-ups and big close ups and was always searching for historical realism. This was brilliantly obtained by Krueger and his colleagues during the entire production.

Abel Gance wanted to include new possible developments in this production to enhance its spectacular aspects. So, he created the triptych in which the screen was made up by three images. André Debrie built a camera pedestal for him with three Parvo cameras and synchronized motors, situated to cover a very wide angle where the sides of each image continued with the others. The effect was impressive and had never before been seen. During the premiere in which this projection method was used on a giant screen, a French optician was so impressed that he applauded standing at the end of the show. The result was inspiring, and soon an optical system was developed to be installed in front of the camera lens to achieve a similar effect. The optician who devised this system was Henri Chrétien, the father of the modern anamorphic lens.

In his search for new effects, Gance filmed in color and made experiments with 3-D, but this material was never used. The final print was carefully toned or tinted to emphasize the sequences that needed such treatment. A million and a half feet of negative was used, a figure never before reached in European films and not even in big American big productions like *Ben-Hur*. Gance himself edited this film personally; he did not use the American Moviola editing machine created in 1923, but only a magnifying glass. This considerably affected his eyesight, and he recovered only after several years.

*Napoléon* impressed France and the whole world, but it did not achieve the expected financial success. The wide screen system was turned down by international distributors and Hollywood studios, fearing it would affect film standards accepted all over the world. Three decades and the appearance of the TV were needed to revive a new large screen format based on the Henri Chrétien invention he named Hypergonar.[16]

# PART III
# THE THIRTIES

# 19. Cameras

During the thirties sound technology was consolidated in many branches of filmmaking. We will see in other chapters how the changes affected film studios and reached other fields of film technology. In the theaters the variation of standards was a shock because film projection equipment required renewal or adaptation. This implied great investments at a moment when the Depression was still felt. But sound movies had now a special attraction for audiences and the profits soon overcame the difficulties on both sides of the film business.

## American studio cameras

The camera world of the film industry reflected the changes in technology. Shooting at sixteen frames per second and the use of the hand crank were definitely abandoned. The latter, however, lasted some time as a heroic resource for some newsreel stringers or short-film makers working with vintage equipment, but now turning the handle three times. But the electric motor and the small spring driven camera soon filled the gap and the crank handle was later an accessory useful only to help thread the film or to be used on special occasions.

Hollywood studios now needed new equipment suited to their new requirements. The two American studio camera manufacturers continued battling to impose their products. In the three years after the coming of sound, Bell & Howell had lost their preference among cinematographers. Many improvements had been added to the Mitchell Standard and High Speed cameras that appealed to their users. One was its easy rack-over system for framing and focusing without rotating the lens turret or moving the sunshade and filter holder, which took too much time. Adjusting the shutter angle while shooting by means of a handle was also appreciated. The refinements of the internal iris and four-way mattes were other advantages to make camera tricks easy. Cinematographers soon realized that this was the most practical and dependable camera in the industry and that it was also easily adaptable to the requirements of sound.

This condition was fundamental to win the battle for preferences. In 1932 the Mitchell Camera Company took an important step forward. George Mitchell designed a new intermittent mechanism known as NC that eliminated gear meshing and employed eccentrics and sliding surfaces (U.S. Patent 1930723). This was an ingenious way to avoid some of the noise from the mechanism. The construction of this movement demanded extreme

The Mitchell NC camera (*courtesy Mitchell Camera Corp.*).

tolerances of the parts, which were machined and lapped to 0.0001 in. and polished to a 0.0005 in. tolerance in the register pins. From 1932 to 1935 the Mitchell NC movements were made in six models named D, E, F, G, H and I, with differences according to the type of shutter used, long or short dissolve mechanism, the last being the regular one used after 1935.[1]

The new model of the Mitchell camera that appeared in 1932 was also named NC (meaning News Camera). The new camera included the noiseless movement, a hand dissolve (instead of the automatic shutter), a miniature reference shutter, a buckle trip and the improved monitoring viewfinder conceived at the end of the twenties with upright image and built-in mattes. The NC model differed from previous models in not including the floating iris system, very little used after the end of the silent films. But its most valued feature was its silent operation at 35 dB, an impressive figure for a camera without a blimp. After this, the Bell & Howell Standard finally lost its small chance to be a studio production camera and ended up being used in the newsreel field, in titles, animation, special effects or laboratory work.

The Mitchell NC was soon totally accepted by all Hollywood studios, newsreel and short film companies and film producers in many cities of the Union. Many orders came also from their long list of clients abroad such as studios and high level producers in London, Berlin, Calcutta, Bombay, Tokyo, Buenos Aires, Mexico City, Manila and Moscow. Mitchell cameras were more expensive than many other brands on the world market, but the particular design features of this instrument and its outstanding workmanship made this new model the best solution for an exacting selection.

The NC model required the use of a blimp in the film stage. As in the past, many camera departments of the Hollywood studios made their own blimps. Soon Raby Manufacturing Co. of Hollywood manufactured a practical and easy to use blimp; it included a follow focus control and an automatic parallax corrected monitoring viewfinder. A magnifier and pilot light was built in to simplify control of the lens focus and diaphragm settings. The top of the blimp was spring driven and was counterbalanced to allow easy access to the camera interior. This blimp was a standard item with Mitchell NC cameras for many years in Hollywood and abroad. Only one big studio still used its own blimp during this decade: Metro Goldwyn Mayer.

The use of a blimp required methodical work. Framing and focus checking, the change of lenses, footage control and adjusting the shutter demanded continuously opening the blimp doors. This was a limitation and a time-consuming operation for the camera crew. George Mitchell and his engineers decided to overcome this and conceived a truly silent studio camera. Renowned cinematographers like Gregg Toland were consulted in reference to the many practical details of the new item of equipment.[2]

The development of a prototype took several months. New concepts in camera design had to be adopted. It had to be a camera with the NC features but completely silent for operating on film stages where the microphone was often very near the shooting unit. The lens turret had to be eliminated since was one of the sources through which the sound of the shutter was filtered. Consequently the camera required only one lens at the front with the focus ring controlled from both sides and the back. All camera controls had to be easily accessible without opening the camera door.

The magazine had to be silenced by means of a special cover adapted to the focusing and shooting positions. The automatic dissolve controls were installed again as a useful feature. All camera controls were available at the back of the unit. The new camera box had to be small in size, relatively light in weight and conceived to damp the still audible 35 dB noise of the NC model. The new model also had to be very compact in relation to the best camera blimp available on world markets while maintaining a functional and streamlined appearance.

In 1934, after several trials, the new Mitchell BNC model was launched onto the market using the unsold Serial No.3 camera inside it.[3] This model totally covered the expectations of Hollywood cinematographers. For experts in Hollywood and the world's other film studios this was the finest camera ever designed: some called it the Rolls Royce of cameras. They felt that it was a fully dependable item of equipment and everything they wanted for easy work on a film stage, achieved without awkward changes. The new camera was lighter than an NC model with a blimp: 120 lbs. instead of 173 lbs. The running noise dropped to a value of only 21 dB.

Ironically, after this outstanding work, George Mitchell, the creator of this mechanical jewel, resigned from this firm. The new camera caught the attention of many Hollywood studios. The first two units, serial numbers BNC 1 & 2, were sold on August 17, 1934, to the Samuel Goldwyn Studios, as recommended by Gregg Toland. A BNC camera rented to the United Artists Studio was used for shooting *Stella Dallas* in 1937. Later on Gregg Toland used it during 1938 for *Wuthering Heights* in the Goldwyn Studios. The Serial No.2 BNC

Mitchell BNC studio camera (*courtesy Mitchell Camera Corp.*).

was rented in 1940 to RKO where Toland filmed *Citizen Kane* (1941). The second big purchase was ten units delivered to Warner Bros. Studios in 1938. Another BNC camera was sent to the Soviet Union during the war and used for shooting *Ivan the Terrible* (1942–1946). Later on the firm stopped the production of this model when important priorities demanded other items. In the postwar period the Mitchell BNC started a famous trajectory, maintained for nearly three decades.[4]

## French studio cameras

European camera makers were aware of the importance of sound requirements and the new techniques demanded by shooting on a film stage. In France, the Etablissements André Debrie offered first-rate motion picture equipment. After the provisional solution of covering their Parvo Model T with an ingenious blimp, they designed a new silenced studio camera which, like the Mitchell NC, was launched onto the world market during 1932. The new model was named Super Parvo and it was an enlarged version of the old Parvo L with all the additional facilities that a silent studio camera now required.

André Debrie knew very well the preferences of the vast international market they had patiently penetrated for over twenty years, covering most of the European countries, Japan, South America, India and Arabia and other Asian countries. In this decade they sold many more units than Mitchell, mainly because of the lower exchange rate of the French franc against the US dollar and that the operators felt safer working with equipment they already knew well. Another factor was that European cinematographers used different methods from those of American camera operators. This firm's products were of excellent quality and reputation, and for many years the film studios of the above areas were used to this well known brand.

The new Super Parvo followed the same design principles of the Parvo series: two independent 1000 ft. magazines placed inside the camera in parallel position, three camera doors, one at each side of the unit and the third one at the front with the shutter system, the lens and the sunshade filter holder. The motor was situated between the two magazines and was of the synchronous type 110 or 220 or 24-volt DC variable speed. The main difference of this studio camera compared with the previous silent movie version was in the construction design, with a less noisy mechanism and the noise dampening of the camera box and its three camera doors. The viewing system was based as in the Model L with the possibility of swinging the film channel and aperture plate to one side in order to see the image produced by the lens through the film or through a ground glass. This movement was controlled from the back of the camera. Also in the rear of the unit there were other controls to adjust the lens focus and iris, to turn the motor shaft, operate the camera, the viewer eyepiece, the meter and the frames counters. The intermittent drive used pilot pins and a pressure device in the film channel. The control for the automatic fade system and the shutter aperture (from 25 degrees to 180 degrees) and the window to read the focus values of the lens was placed at a side of the camera. The camera maintained this firm's classic parallelepiped shape sized about 20 × 10 × 11in (50 × 25 × 27 cm). Debrie built its classic rolling pedestal, ideally suited for stage work, which was standard in many studios, for this new camera.

For years French studios adopted the Super Parvo in large numbers. Several units were available in Paramount-Saint Maurice, Pathé-Cinéma in Joinville-le-Pont and Billancourt, Boulogne, Francoeur, Marcel Pagnol or Victorine. In other European countries the Super Parvo was standard in the new Cinecittà Studios of Rome and in Sevilla Estudios of Madrid. Georges

**Debrie Super Parvo studio camera** (*courtesy André Debrie Matériel Cinématographique*).

Périnal, the well known French cinematographer for Alexander Korda, promoted the use of the Super Parvo in the new Denham Studios in England. In South America, many studios in Argentina such as San Miguel, Lumiton, Side and Baires were equipped with this camera.

Another French studio camera manufacturer was the well-known Société Éclair, which build its first model towards the end of this decade. Their Cameréclair Studio had a four-lens turret at the front protected by a sound cover with a window for checking focus values. This front cover was very easily opened. Framing and focusing was made by a finder through the film. The intermittent drive used pilot pins. The shutter was of the adjustable type from 0 to 180 degrees. The body of the camera was self-blimped. The motor installed at rear was interchangeable for DC or AC electric supply. The 1000 ft. film magazines were installed at the top of the camera, and this design changed the classic European method of placing the film holders inside the camera body.

## British studio cameras

In 1931–32 a new studio camera was designed and built by Vinten Limited. The unit was known as Vinten Model I and it had a good reception by the British film industry. The camera had a large sound-insulated body, 1000 ft. top-mounted magazines, and several refinements such as two focus controls on each side of its front. The design of this camera was based on the Vinten Model H field camera which adopted one plane film travel and similar principles of the Mitchell Standard camera An elaborated Vinten dolly was conceived for this instrument. This new silent camera was ideal for shooting indoors with double system sound recording.

## German studio cameras

The only studio camera built in Germany was made about 1938 by the old firm Askania Werke of Berlin. This camera, known as Atelier-Kamera, followed the method of including the two 1,000 ft. magazines inside the camera body adopted by André Debrie in 1908 with their first Parvo. But the mechanical design employing the three-plane film travel had some differences from the Debrie patents also employed by earlier Askania models. The continuous drive included two 32-tooth sprockets. The viewing system was the classical method through the film with a binocular eyepiece. Only one lens was used in the front with external focus control and a bellows sunshade assembly. The camera body was sound insulated and had two access doors: one for threading the film, and another on the other side, to check the mechanical system and its lubrication. Different camera controls were situated on the back of the camera. The use of the Askania Atelier Kamera was very limited outside Germany and Austria, but it was an example of the excellent workmanship of this firm's products.

## Czechoslovakian studio cameras

During the mid-thirties the two important camera manufactures of that country, Josef Slechta and Vaclav Rysan of the Cinephon Company, joined forces to design and build some studio cameras that later arrived at studios in Prague, Berlin, Vienna, Finland and India. The cameras adopted a blimped parallelepiped body with an external double compartment

Cinephon field camera (*courtesy Filmovy Prumsyl Praha-Barrandov*).

magazine. The mechanical conception used Slechta solutions such as a special prism viewing system for checking the scene through the film while shooting, automatic and hand controlled shutter, special noise elimination in the camera body, one main continuous drive film sprocket and a four lens turret with common focussing control. After this association Slechta later produced other cameras using his name and according to the requirements of many cinematographers.[5]

## Italian studio cameras

The pioneer in constructing a studio camera in Italy was Gaetano Ventimiglia, a cinematographer. With an active participation in silent films in Italy, France, England and

Germany, Ventimiglia was also the cinematographer on an Alfred Hitchcock film, *The Lodger* (1926). In the early twenties he patented for the first time in his country a reflex viewing system using the image reflected by the shutter blades. He continued developing several film techniques while in England. After returning to his country, Ventimiglia worked intensely adapting cameras and building camera blimps. As professor of optics and motion picture camera technology in the Centro Sperimentale di Cinematografia of Rome, he developed a prototype of a studio camera known as O.G. 300, which was submitted to Benito Mussolini during the inauguration of that state film school in January 16, 1940. Only three of these cameras were built afterwards by the Officine Galileo of Milano.

The camera, known as Galileo, adopted the method of two side by side 1000 ft. magazines inside the camera body with three plane film travel, using three film sprockets and a curved film channel. The camera body silenced the mechanical drive. The camera controls were at the back and on a side. The framing and focusing were by various systems: one by means of a prism, another made use of an auxiliary parallax corrected finder, another through the film and with a special device for the focus control while shooting. The camera had two film counters for exposed film and raw stock, a frame counter and a tachometer. A bellows sunshade and filter holder were fitted in front of the camera. The shutter allowed for automatic fades. The unit also worked in reverse.[6]

## Other cameras of the decade

### SOUND-ON-FILM CAMERAS

Shooting feature films soon determined that the image negative must be recorded separately from the sound negative in this sort of production. The most obvious system, born at the beginning, was known as the double system. This process required many technicalities, due to the different kinds of film emulsions used for image negatives and sound negatives and their subsequent processing. However, the newsreel film industry soon demanded the possibility of recording image and sound on the same film to cover events with synchronous sound realism and without post-editing. A sound-on-film camera was then needed. At the beginning silent cameras were adapted for this task. The Bell & Howell Standard and the Mitchell were first used with an optical film recorder attachment. One of the pioneers in building an adequate instrument for this specific job was the Akeley Camera Company. This firm had lost the industry's preference for its silent Pancake camera and urgently need a new line of products in this field. Consequently, Carl Akeley then designed a single system sound camera that filled the gap for sound news in the late twenties and early thirties and was widely used, first by Paramount News, which installed them in their twelve newsreel sound trucks.

The Akeley sound camera had a cast aluminum body of about 10 × 10 × 21 inches (25 × 25 × 54 cm) internally lined with corduroy and with a black external finish. A Bell & Howell 1000 ft. magazine was installed on the top. Only one camera door afforded the operator access to the interior of the unit for threading the film. The mechanism was based on fiber gear drives and was composed of a large 32 tooth sprocket, a smaller one, and an intermittent movement with pilot pin and constant pressure film channel. The finder was attached to the camera door in a form similar to the silent Akeley model. The unit used the standard lens and a matched one in a sliding plate in front of the unit. The shutter had two

Akeley sound-on-film camera (*courtesy Archivo Nacional de la Imagen, Sodre*).

blades with an aperture of 225 degrees or 280 degrees. The 12-volt camera motor and the sound recording unit were installed on the other side of the camera body. The amplifier was in a special case and the operator had to use headphones while shooting. This camera adopted the famous Akeley Gyro tripod developed by this firm at that time, and specially suited to pan with long focal lenses.

Around 1934, another 35mm sound-on-film camera was launched on the American newsreel market. It was also of the single sound system but with a very refined design, following the principles of the Mitchell, with a rack over system. The manufacturer was John M. Wall, of Syracuse, New York. Many newsreel firms the world over purchased several units of this instrument. The camera body was made of aluminum alloy and some sections of its inside lined with black corduroy, which was effective for acoustic resonance and a good finish. The heart of the camera was an excellent, newly developed intermittent mechanism, which was also improved through the years.

That movement was smooth, noiseless and easily removable and replaced without tools. The working parts were made of hardened special alloy steel, ground and lapped to precision fits. There were two types of movements: double claw with 190 degree shutter opening and single claw with 170 degree shutter opening. The aperture plate was an integral part of the intermittent unit. The intermittent used claws and later on also register pins. It was based on a main 32 tooth sprocket with upper and lower pressure rollers and a flywheel where the galvanometer sound register light beam acted. A buckle switch situated over the stripper stopped the camera when any loop trouble occurred. Two film guides were included, one on the top of the film channel and the other near the buckle switch roller.

The camera shutter angle was variable from 20 to 190 degrees, depending on the type of intermittent mechanism included. If the single claw type was used, the maximum opening was 170 degrees. The shutter control was inside a door on the right side of the camera. The turret carried four Bausch & Lomb lenses in five focal ranges from 25mm to 152mm which did not rotate to focus, but moved straight in and out.

The camera used a combination-focusing viewfinder attached to the left side of the unit, on the camera door, with a focusing tube allowing considerable image amplification when racked over to the focusing position behind the shooting lens. A Mitchell monitoring viewfinder could be installed beside the regular Wall viewfinder, which had a standard viewing field of 25mm and parallax correction with a lever in the front of the finder. Other camera controls were at the back of the unit: tachometer, footage counter, speed motor

Wall sound-on-film camera (*courtesy Archivo Nacional de la Imagen, Sodre*).

rheostat (1.440 rpm for 24 f.p.s) for a 12 or 24 volt DC motor, handle for rack over, adjustable finder eyepiece and the motor spin knob. The optical sound head was installed also in the back of the camera and had a robust connection with the amplifier. A sunshade and matte box was available to be installed in front of the camera.

Since it came out on the market and for many years this camera kept these basic principles with small changes in its general appearance and features. The Wall was the most refined sound-on-film camera used by important newsreel firms in the United States and other countries. Many of the direct sound-recorded films for the renowned *The March of Time* series were filmed with Wall cameras. During the thirties and forties those cameras were often seen on the top of sound vans in several American cities and in London streets, especially in Soho Square, which was the center of many newsreel and short film companies. British Movietone News, which had its headquarters nearby, was one of its frequent users.

In 1935 the well known DeVry Company of Chicago also introduced a special sound-on-film camera to the market to be used as single and double sound unit. The change from one system to the other was made using either a standard double compartment magazine or a big size magazine, which included both image and sound negatives. This camera was know as the DeVry Professional Sound and was also compatible with the requirements of the bipack color system. The camera characteristics were: three lens turrets, two-sprocket drive, shift over framing and focusing method, and a finder with parallax control. The camera controls, with tachometer, speed control and footage counter, were placed at the back of the camera body.

The same year DeVry also launched a 16mm sound-on-film camera with only one lens and a compact film magazine, which was very handy. This showed how filming in the 16mm gauge was gaining popularity for information and teaching purposes. This was part of that firm's expanding production plans specializing in 35mm and 16mm sound projectors to cover the growing needs of this field in the USA and abroad.

During that decade some manufacturers produced improvements to optical sound recording units as attachments to standard cameras. Well known camera brands used these attachments, manufactured by firms such as Reeves Equipment Corp., or made to order for some newsreel firms. Some well-known camera manufacturers prepared their standard cameras to be transformed into sound-on-film cameras. In the United States the best known were Mitchell and Bell & Howell. In France, André Debrie produced their Parvo Model LS with its body made of Ebonite to dampen the sound of its mechanism and with the purpose of being attached to an optical sound recording unit fitted between the camera and the tripod. In many places, such Australia and South American countries, local mechanics and electronics experts included the new glow lamp and developed amplifiers and mechanical film transporting systems to cover the requirements of small newsreel firms that needed direct sound shooting. In Europe several sound-on-film cameras were made by Vinten in England, Tobis in Germany and Czechoslovakia and Éclair in France.

The French Cameraéclair-son had interesting design features. It was a double system camera. The left hand side was for recording the image with the film magazine on the top of the body. The right hand side of the camera was for recording direct sound, driven by the same 32 tooth sprocket shaft. An independent two-compartment magazine for the sound negative was installed also on top. A four-lens turret had a bellows sunshade and filter holder in its front. A finder was installed on the image sector camera door. The controls were placed at the back of the camera, which allowed reverse drive, and making fades by hand

DeVry sound-on-film camera (*courtesy Archivo Nacional de la Imagen, Sodre*).

or automatically. Newsreel firms in France and certain countries used this camera (e.g. as Spain), but it had a limited acceptance in other areas.

## Field cameras

### Bell & Howell Eyemo

Field camera was the nomenclature adopted for equipment devised for general use in the industry not requiring noiseless operation for sound shooting. Those cameras were units

**Bell & Howell Eyemo Model Z field camera** (*courtesy Bell & Howell*).

of small or medium size used away from a film stage, in documentary or short film production. During the thirties there was a considerable number of this type of cameras and about a dozen makers the world over.

The Bell & Howell Company realized that their Standard Model camera had lost its preference in the Hollywood studios and was destined for newsreel, laboratory and title work. Consequently they revised the capacity of their Eyemo portable camera designated as 71A to fill the gap in another growing film market: the short film and newsreel industry. Around 1931 the manufacturers designed new features for this camera to widen its possible demand.

The changes included the use of a 400 foot film magazine and an electric motor, new film speeds, new shutter housing shape, compact spider three lens turret, new wide spring housing, and square base.

The modifications started with the 71, followed by letters such as AA, AB, B, BA, BB, C and CA. At the end of the decade the identification of each model changed to the following designations: K (with only one lens), L and M (with compact turret, drum type viewfinder and different speeds range). Models N and O had a three-arm lens turret, a prismatic focusing magnifier, and a large ratchet-winding crank. Models P and Q adopted an electric motor (12 volt DC or 110 volt 60 cycles AC) but did not eliminate the use of the standard spring drive of the other models. Both were designed to use a 400 ft. double compartment film magazine, which included motor bracket receptacles and a lid at the back. As a complementary device for the users of Models N, O, P and Q, the firm included an accessory known as the Eyemo Focusing Alignment Gauge which permitted accurate compensation of the different positions of the taking lens and the prismatic focusing magnifier.

The versatility of the Eyemo cameras and their sturdy construction were recognized the world over. In a few years they were standard cameras adopted by most of the newsreel companies. Hollywood studios had several units, used in limited space situations or awkward conditions. Some independent filmmakers made long feature films using only these cameras. The excellent design of the Eyemo movement, without a register pin, produced very good image stability. At Republic Studios in Hollywood an Eyemo camera was used to produce background plates. The Eyemo was the preferred camera for handheld shooting from moving vehicles or airplanes. It was also the ideal camera for shorts in the jungle or in the mountains. Soon it was recognized as the ideal camera for combat shooting and proved its value in the Spanish civil war and in China. For many years Bell & Howell publicized the Eyemo as "Mr. Outside" against the Bell & Howell Standard (also known as design 2709) which was called "Mr. Inside." The Bell & Howell, standard provider of motion picture equipment to the U.S. Signal Corps and other military organizations, soon found an important market in this particular field. A few years later, in the Soviet Union, the Eyemo "Q" was duplicated as the KC-50.

## Newman Sinclair Autokine

At that time in Europe there were more field 35mm cameras available than in America. There had been camera manufacturers in many European countries since the beginning of the film industry. In England there was a firm in the heart of London, in Whitehall, the James A. Sinclair & Co. Ltd., an old and long established firm in the professional photographic field, that produced a well-known automatic movie camera named Autokine. Experts from many parts of the British Empire came in search of this camera because it was the ideal instrument for news, exploring, documentaries, scientific use and similar short films. A great part of the famous British documentary film productions were filmed with the Autokine.[7]

The Autokine was hand made unit by unit by artisans. The camera body was constructed entirely from duralumin plates, which were milled out of the solid, and no castings were used. Each piece was combined with the other by means of special small black screws in a skilled workmanship job. The duralumin was a trademark alloy produced by James Booth & Company of Birmingham. This material was chosen because it was light and strong, and did not rust, even in the dampest conditions. The camera body had a striking appearance. The camera had capacity for an internal 200 ft. film magazine, which was pre-threaded in a darkroom or film bag. The intermittent movement used a pilot pin at the gate and produced very steady images.

A clockwork motor with two springs drove the unit at speeds from 10 to 24 frames per second. Two winding handles at a side of the camera provided the necessary transport of 180 ft. of film each time the spring was wound. The lenses supplied with the camera were mounted on their own panel to fit in the camera front. Each lens had its own filter and sunshade, as well as a matching finder lens to fit on the front of the parallax corrected finder placed in the right sector inside the camera. From the back of the camera the focusing lens was controlled by means of a large lever.

Newman & Sinclair autokine camera showing the 200 ft. magazine (*courtesy Newman & Sinclair Ltd.*).

Focusing through the lens and exact framing was done with a unit installed on the camera door using a prism behind the film gate.

Several models of the Autokine were made over many years. The most popular one was called the Studio Model, but the manufacturer also provided a slow motion model and towards the end of the decade other models were made such as the "C" with a time recording unit, the "D" with a four lens turret and two reflex focusing devices (one for seeing the image in the back of the film through the gate and the other for focusing the lenses before being revolved into position) and the "E" with a through-the-film finder with a focusing tube. The standard weight of those cameras was about 17 lbs. and their size 9.5 × 4.75 × 9.5 in. (24 × 12 × 24 cm.). The Autokine was the ideal camera for the short-filmmaker. It was the standard camera used by the British War Department, the Royal Geographic Society, the Royal Air Force, the New Zealand government, the Metropolitan Museum of Art of New York, the Empire Marketing Board Film Unit, the Colonial Film Unit, the General Post Office, Gaumont-British Picture Corporation Ltd., and short-film producers in countries of the British Commonwealth. Institutions in other countries like the New York Zoological Society used them and they were also the preferred camera of wildlife naturalists and explorers like Cherry Kearton, Major Radclyffe Dugmore, and Herbert Pointing. Moreover, they were the classic cameras used by the British newsreel companies.

Robert Flaherty discovered this camera in 1931 when he first arrived in London from Berlin to work with the Empire Marketing Board Film Unit. He was as delighted as a child when colleagues there proudly showed this unique British camera ideal for the job at hand. He inspected its compact shape, the built-in spring motor, the small size magazines and its very light weight.[8] He remembered his vexations with the Bell & Howell Standard on *Nanook of the North* and with the Akeley Pancake while shooting *Tabu* (1931). With this camera he soon photographed the famous *Industrial Britain* (1931), *Man of Aran* (1932–34) and *Elephant Boy* (1935–37). Many famous British documentary filmmakers of those years, such as Paul Rotha, Harry Watt, John Taylor, Basil Wright, Humphrey Jennings and others, declared that this piece of craftsmanship had contributed to British documentary film making during more than two decades.

Newman & Sinclair also produced the Standard No. 4 Model, similar to the Autokine in construction concepts but bigger in size, more appropriate for feature films and with internal 400 ft. magazines. This unit, which came from the World War I days, had several features: a dissolving unit, focus and iris control at the back, single frame handle, brilliant finder, reversing action, and a very small electric motor. This model was not favored by the British studios but was used in laboratories and for short and scientific films.

## DEBRIE PARVO "L"

In continental Europe Debrie's Parvo model "L" camera was the preference of cinematographers in several countries. It was the standard field camera for diverse types of films from long features to shorts. Most of the French studios and film producers were equipped with several of these cameras. It was also used in many French colonies in Africa and was also a classic camera in several South American countries as well as in the Soviet Union. The Parvo Model "L" had a classic box shaped aluminum body and included the new form of viewing: on the film through the taking lens, or on a ground glass moving the film channel to one side by using an ingenious device. The drive unit was a compact 12 or 24 DC motor. Other features were automatic dissolve, external focus and iris controls, variable shutter, collapsible Newton finder, magnetic speed indicator and compact sunshade and filter holder. Probably this was the best-sold camera of this kind the world over. André Debrie sold more than 8000 Parvos.

## CAMERÉCLAIR "6"

Éclair was the classic French competitor of André Debrie in the professional camera market. Éclair products were not so widely in demand in the national and international market, because they were more expensive, due to their particular and exceptional design. During the thirties Éclair manufactured the Cameréclair "6" for the field camera sphere, a complex and beautifully made instrument ideally suited to all kinds of film tricks while shooting, and was a triumph of the inventive of its designer, M. Méry, an engineer. This camera took its numeral designation because it was provided with a six-lens turret: three were the standard lenses and the others were the finder lenses. The camera had a very elaborate mechanism built into the unit that allowed all kinds of image alterations during the take. At the back and on the left side of the camera were all kinds of controls to activate or to indicate such aspects as shutter aperture, exposed footage, exposed frames, handle turns, backwards turns, automatic dissolves, miniature shutter, frame counter, speed motor control, lens focus indicator, film meter totalizer, etc.

The Cameréclair "6" had four ways to control focus and framing: a) using a Newton finder on top of the unit; b) framing and focusing through the film and the taking lens; c) viewing through a lateral finder with a parallax corrected auxiliary lens and d) using a ground glass with the camera in stop position. The camera used 400 ft. internal separate magazines. The shutter had an aperture of 170 degrees adjustable while operating or in stop position. The movement used two film claws and pilot pins with automatic pressure film channel during exposure. The motor ran at 32 V DC or 220 V 50 c/s AC with speeds regulated. Other features were a filmpunch, a device to adjust the optical axes of the lens, bellows sunshade and filter holder, internal insertion of mattes, a finder with magnification, and two types of handles for driving at film speed or frame by frame.

This unusual camera was a jewel in its finish and a dream for the dedicated cinematographer. It was very expensive and consequently few filmmakers could afford it. It was like a Bugatti of the film industry and those who owned one treasured it dearly. The Cameraéclair "6" was used mainly in French studios such as the Groupe Éclair, Paris-Studios-Cinema , Pathé-Cinema, Côte D'Argent in Bordeaux, etc. This instrument was also a must in many French and European film laboratories for many decades. Very few units reached the United States.

## VINTEN MODEL H

W. Vinten Limited of England produced a field camera with very similar design characteristics to the Mitchell Standard. This camera used a Vinten intermittent mechanism with pilot pin and constant pressure. The viewing was effected by racking over the direct viewfinder and displacing the film instead of the camera body. Four lenses were mounted on a lens turret. A side viewfinder provided a complementary large image. The variable shutter allowed up to 170 degree aperture. The camera used top mounted 1000 ft. double compartment magazines. Several refinements were also included in the camera body.

## European portable cameras

During those years the French film market, mainly the newsreels, used various portable cameras. One named Morigraf was built by the C.T.M. firm, a subsidiary of Cinema Tirage Maurice in Gennevilliers. Later this firm was very well known for its editing table named Moritone that was widely used in French film studios.

The Morigraf was a compact camera with a three-lens turret, 100 ft. spools, spring drive or electric motor for 200 ft. magazine load and three types of viewing: by top clear finder, through the film, or using a side finder for focusing. It was the widely used portable camera adopted at that time by newsreels and the French armed forces. Some stringers for newsreel firms, such as those shooting for *The March of Time*, also used them for general shooting. The Morigraf was one of the portable cameras adopted by students of the famed Institut des Hautes Etudes Cinematographiques, created in Paris during World War II.

Another very compact French camera built for the 35mm gauge was named Le Blay. By its very small size and its body shape it resembled a typical 16mm camera, but it incorporated a 100 ft. film spool, a film lens, a through the lens finder and spring drive. It was ideally suited for limited space situations and adopted in many feature films for difficult shooting set ups; it was used in France for many years.

In Italy some compact cameras were built when the widely used Parvo L and the Prevost were not suitable for some newsreel jobs. Alfredo Donelli and Edmundo Orlandi designed the Avia for this purpose, which was built by Cinemecanicca S.A. of Milano.

Alfredo Donelli was a very well known cinematographer that worked on *Quo Vadis?* (1924) and *Ben-Hur* (1926–1927) and photographed several famous feature films such as *The Last Days of Pompey* (1926). Towards the end of the twenties his passion for movie cameras led to the design of this instrument.[9]

The Avia was a carefully conceived camera with internal 400 ft. magazines side by side, a small size internal electric motor, two types of viewing: direct through the film or using a compact monitoring viewfinder with amplified image. Another characteristic of this camera was its modern and compact body design with two handles on the sides for easy hand held takes, very much welcomed by the Italian armed forces.[10]

We have seen that European camera manufacturers were very prolific during the thirties. In Germany, the Askania "Z" field camera, with very similar characteristics to the Debrie's Parvo but with some sophistication in certain details, e.g. its improved sunshade-filter holder and limitations in others (focusing only trough the film), was then the standard unit. But the Askania Company of Berlin also conceived a portable camera named Askania Schulter designed by their engineer Dr. P. Heinisch. He started studying the pulse stability of the cameramen after running while holding a movie camera. He soon concluded that the forearms were inadequate for holding a hand camera after a short run. A new method must be adopted. So, he created an L shaped camera conceived to rest on the shoulder. His Askania Shulter was the revolutionary result, but other manufacturers only adopted this radical change in camera holding only after many years.[11] Today it is universally adopted in this type of equipment.

Askania "Schulter" camera (*courtesy Archivo Nacional de la Imagen, Sodre*).

The Askania Shulter was a very compact camera with internal 200 ft. magazines and right angle body so the heavy film sector was easily seated on the shoulder. The other sector covered the right side of the operator's face and brought the viewfinder in position on the right eye. The three-lens turret was turned by means of a push button. The focus and diaphragm were set automatically in the three lenses. An interchangeable 12 volt DC electric motor was the complementary support of the unit, with the operator's left hand. The shutter aperture was variable from 20 to 190 degrees. A direct finder allowed for viewing with a distance meter, which also permitted viewing through the film. Speed control was by a tachometer, which could be seen from the shooting position. In the first model the camera door included three shafts to install a handle for hand driving at one, eight or twelve frames per turn. This excellently finished camera was conceived for the great event of those years: the XI Olympic Games in Berlin, in August 1936. The Deutschen Wochenschau (German State Newsreel) was one of the principal users and later on the German armed forces. The Askania Schulter was exported to Austria and Italy but soon another very competitive instrument appeared, taking up part of its market.

In Munich, Arnold & Richter was a growing firm in the manufacture of diverse equipment for the film industry. In 1931 they patented the reflex system by means of a shutter with mirror blades to divert the camera lens image. This method was adopted in a new prototype camera they built in 1936 and was carefully proved by its chief engineer, Erich Kästner. The result was outstanding in its revolutionary design, especially its viewing through the taking lens without parallax problems and easy focusing. But the general conception of the camera, its easy holding design and its pre-threaded compact magazines were factors contributing to its adoption by the German armed forces. The first model used a square sunshade shaft, 12 V. motor without rheostat (which was in the battery) and a short viewfinder. A small mirror in the sunshade (later discontinued) allowed seeing the taking lens iris graduations from the

Arriflex Model I, first reflex viewing camera (*courtesy Arnold & Richter Cine Technik*).

back. This was the beginning of an instrument that maintained its basic original design and was used the world over for forty years.

During the mid-thirties the Czech Cinephon Company produced a hand held 35mm camera conceived for newsreel work. The camera used internal 200 ft. magazines. A built-in 6 Volt motor ran forward and reverse at several speeds. The viewing system was through the film by using a prism and a 7 × viewfinder with double eyepiece. The shutter was of variable type with outside visual indicator. The three-lens turret changed positions at the touch of a button. The camera included several controls and facilities, e.g. two cranks, footage meter, built-in tachometer, dissolving device, compact sunshade and matte box. This camera was used also during the German Olympic Games and in World War II.

# 20. New Film Studios

## American Studios

New shooting methods produced in the motion picture industry during the late twenties caused a commotion in the studios during the thirties. Moreover, the effects of the 1929 economic crisis gave rise to new production methods that were perfected in the following years.

The coming of sound changed the old practice in the studios where the cinematographer provided his own camera, because the new technologies demanded the standardization of equipment. Those standards were set by the studios, not by the equipment manufacturers who were forced to comply to their customer's demands. Likewise, it became evident that modernizing equipment and accessories needed investments that only large studios could afford.

Shooting with several cameras at the same time, imposed by the new sound-recording shooting methods, made ample use of cameras available at the studio. Not only new standards were agreed upon by the studios, they also selected camera manufacturers that fulfilled their own requirements. The noisier Bell & Howell Standard camera, so popular during the twenties, was slowly replaced by the noiseless Mitchell. The camera departments of many studios asked for more control devices. They also took up manufacturing accessories not provided by the industry, and kept up with strict daily maintenance guidelines on their equipment.

In many large Hollywood studios, the camera department grew from a place of limited space to a building with several sections and specialists in various fields. One variation of shooting methods with several cameras was that the blimp replaced the old camera booth. The multiple camera system was kept for some films such as musicals, where that technique was necessary to cover the scene from many angles with fixed or mobile cameras. Consequently the technical means afforded to the camera crew became more numerous and diversified.

As the number of cameras grew, the studio payroll included more people and the camera crew and its composition also varied dramatically during the first three years of the new decade. The lonely cinematographer of silent films, who had an assistant later on, was now the head of a group of technicians, and began to be known as director of photography. The use of several cameramen to cover the scene from several set-ups, adopted with the coming of sound, returned to a single camera set-up in standard dialogued scenes. The camera crew was also completed by the new job of operative cameraman and, generally, with more than one camera assistant.

The increase of film production in the studios, reaching up to fifty productions per year, demanded more technicians not only in this field of camera handling but in many other specialities. It brought about the construction of more buildings to locate previously nonexistent departments, imposed by the much increased output. More film stages were also needed. The primitive silent film stages with their precarious isolated external surfaces were replaced by new modern film stages. In one of the major Hollywood studios, Metro Goldwyn Mayer, up to 31 film stages were built on the premises. The Hollywood film studios were transformed into complex organizations with up to 5,000 employees on the payrolls.

The new technologies demanded the construction of numerous special buildings. Many were designed as sound recording and mixing auditoriums. Sound also brought its requisites to sound recording on the stage, such as isolation from the outside and acoustic control. Projection rooms also required the same acoustic conversion. The editing booths were provided with sound editing machines. That department became the noisiest place at the studio, because the vertical editing machines manufactured by Moviola produced a working noise similar to a film projector or a sewing machine, which noise was multiplied by the number of instruments being operated at the same time.

Special effects had also its space in departments such as special process works or composite photography. In some studios they were connected to the film laboratory. In others they were under the art department or the camera department. But as time went by and with the amount of work to be done, the tendency was towards total independence. In those years some studios built special sound stages specifically conceived for the new rear-projection technique; those stages were also used for the process plate that was being developed. Many studios created their own film laboratory in an independent building on the main premises.

In the mid-thirties Technicolor rapidly and increasingly imposed its system in Hollywood, altering standard shooting methods as different from black and white. The arc light, used for silent operation, returned to the film stages when Technicolor was used. Color shooting demanded a very high amount of light, which required good air conditioning to achieve minimum comfort on the stage. When a production used the Technicolor system, the camera department had to take care of that cumbersome item of equipment that was supplied and looked after by that firm, which also demanded special lighting and adequate grip equipment.

Outdoor shooting was made on the back lot of the studios or at the studio's ranch to have total control of everything needed to make use of their outdoor sets. Those permanent sets generally were Old West towns, Mexican towns, New York streets, New England streets, European streets or the special sets used in many films. As a logical tradition the outdoor sets were preserved and maintained to be re-used in future productions.

At Metro Goldwyn Mayer studios in Culver City, on Lot I, the film stages and installations contained nearly 200 buildings. The main offices were later in the administration building dedicated to the memory of Irving G. Thalberg. Lot II just across the street contained the jungle and lake used in the "Tarzan" films, many city streets, medieval castles, etc., and on Lot III, a mile and half south of the triangular main lot, was a lake with a steamboat and a waterfront with a vessel moored at the dock. Also, among other sets, there was a typical American street with the sets for the popular *Andy Hardy* film series. In total at that time there were nearly fifty permanent blocks of sets on the two back lots.

Hollywood studios operated like big film production factories, and many people and vehicles converged through the gates and were distributed along internal circulation roads. Different buildings and stages were placed facing the roads. They were identified according to their importance by letters or were numbered. In large studios such as Warner Brothers the elevated roadways added up to a total of 12 miles. Some studios were situated in the city center with stiff and severe line buildings. Others maintained the California bungalow style with tiled roofs and stucco walls or wood bungalows like MGM had near the main entrance. Some studios made up for the unseemly buildings with green spaces between them at the crossroads of internal streets and in parking areas.

The big studios were situated at different Hollywood places: MGM in Culver City, Warner Bros. in Burbank and Twentieth Century Fox on the outskirts of Beverly Hills. The small ones such as Republic on the highway to San Francisco, Columbia, Paramount, RKO, Samuel Goldwyn, Eagle Lion, etc., were close to Hollywood's center and Universal Studios in Universal City, in the San Fernando Valley.

There were many buildings at Warner Bros. studios, built in the thirties, which with time reached twenty-four stages; they enlarged their technical facilities at that time and expanded the sets on their back lot. That studio's difference from the others was its attractive background provided by the imposing Mt. Warner and other mountains, and its large terrain was crossed by the Los Angeles River.

Twentieth Century–Fox was the other studio with a big several hundred acres lot divided in two parts: the main studio lot and the Western Avenue lot. On both lots, the studio built more than thirty film stages and two filming pools through the years. A great number of permanent film sets used in their famous large-scale films were placed on those lots.

From the high cost productions to the B type pictures, the Hollywood studios were unique in that they produced their own films in contrast with most European studios where the films were made by several production companies. This California movie city had also small studios to be rented to independent producers. Hollywood was the largest film production center in the United States and in the world. It really was the Mecca of the Seventh Art for producers, artists, technicians and film makers, but was also the international reference place regarding film facilities and where the best technologies available in this industry could be found.

## European studios

In European countries, in the first three and half decades of the twentieth Century, many important film studios were built to compete directly with Hollywood production firms. Most often they were not reformed old studios, but newly designed film premises placed away from the capitals. They included the latest construction technologies after careful research in this field and with beautiful surroundings in order to have the most pleasant conditions for their particular activity.

Britain carried out very interesting examples of this kind of premises that we shall see further on. Others were built in small countries such as Czechoslovakia and Hungary, with interesting building concepts. The purpose was to promote this industry in each nation, to attract foreign producers with low production costs, and to provide up-to-date facilities in competition with other film studios in Europe.

A particular variation of this concept emerged in France, where an old studio was specially adapted to develop an experiment with different language versions. Finally we shall describe the new important film producing studio erected in Italy which is famous up to the present day.

It is interesting to analyze the technology used in each of those experiences and the way they conceived those constructions, in order to appreciate how the principal filmmaker's workshop was transformed in those days. The prevalent concept then was to work in the best controlled conditions, preferably under a roof, to reproduce the locations on the stage and to be free from weather conditions.

## DENHAM

In 1936 the London Film Productions studios were built in Denham, the most modern film production studio in England. The soul behind this project was the well known international producer Mr. (later Sir) Alexander Korda. This enterprise, with a cost of one million pounds sterling, was financed with the help of the Prudential Assurance Co. Ltd., the major stockholder. The combination of London Film Productions and Korda's investments in United Artists was the adequate mixture required to produce and release the films made by this enterprise.

In the story of British film production, Denham was the studio that produced the most memorable films in those years. They were noted not only for their high budget and spectacular use of color, but also for their artistic quality, such as many films directed later on by David Lean.

The Denham studios were situated half an hour northwest from the center of London in the picturesque landscapes of Buckinghamshire. In a lot of 165 acres crossed by the River Colne were small villages, ideal for lodging artists and technicians. Several strategically placed buildings made up Denham. The principal building was developed longitudinally on the route named North Orbital Road; in it were the reception area, general offices, production offices, technical departments, central offices block, dressing rooms for men and women, several film theaters of different sizes, the male crowd and female crowd dressing rooms, art direction, work rooms, wardrobe and lavatories and make-up rooms.

This building was outstanding for its functional design surrounding four big courts with carefully well kept lawns and plants. There was a big open area in front of many windows of personnel dressing rooms, suites and offices. In the center of the big court was a covered gallery that connected the main building with the stages.

The American architect Jack Okey made the first design of the Denham studios continued afterwards by the Joseph architects firm.[1] They searched for the best way to combine several buildings in the most rational way, according to the different activities in each. Following the experience of Hollywood studios, the several stages built at that time were parallel to each other, and at right angles to the main building, in order to provide space for future developments without changing the original plan. This was continued afterwards.

Initially there were three stages, which were gradually increased to seven, turning this studio into one of the most complete in the U.K., with a useful area of 108,700 sq. ft. Of the seven stages, two were 250 × 125 ft, two others were smaller at 115 × 110 ft, and there were three of 112 × 75 ft. The maximum height up to the upper bridges was 46 ft. The roofs of each stage were of double couple-close type and covered with sheeting. The roof skeletons were supported on independent foundations for each building. The acoustic insulation of the walls was a thick layer of mineral wool.

The main access to the stages was by big sliding doors, 30 ft. wide by 25 ft. high, insulated with Celotex plates. Those doors were vertically moved by an electric control, and they easily allowed bringing large parts of previously assembled sets onto the stage. The outside signal system conceived for the personnel consisted of colored lights, with a code where yellow gave free access, green allowed entering noiselessly, and red for no entrance.

All the stages had air conditioning in which the air inlet was situated on one of the side walls, six feet from the floor, and the air exit under the ceiling. The stages had the characteristic of not including the classical swimming pools under the floor. For shooting in open water surfaces, a big pool of 200 × 100 ft. with a depth of 3 to 12 ft. was available, although the water could not be warmed.

Some time after the construction of the Denham Studios, a new large three-stage building was erected to house the Denham laboratories, which acquired great prestige in the film industry and survived the studio.

At a right angle to the long side of the film stages, several shops were situated for set construction, metal work, painting, and also buildings for stage material storage, props, etc. Not far from there was the workers' canteen. Behind the stages was the electric station with six generators driven by Diesel motors, each generating 240V at 3.2K Amp. The lines connecting the stages were controlled by thermoelectric switches, button activated for safety. The lines to the stages supplied 120V with a capacity of 14,000 amps per stage. For outdoor shooting the Denham studios ordered four portable generators of 1,000 amps each from the Rolls Royce Company, which at that time was the most prestigious in England.

Behind the group of studio buildings was a very large back lot adequate for erecting large size sets. The River Colne crossed this field for about two kilometers in a picturesque wooded landscape that included a bridge. This was an ideal place for outdoor shooting including small islands in the river which were used in several films. Also, a cemented 330 square ft. surface near the stages offered a good place for erecting big settings such as a city street.

An old mansion very close to the river allowed beautiful views of the river banks through its windows. Sir Alexander Korda's main office was in this large and comfortable red brick building. It displayed luxury with pictures of famous painters and a large reception room. This residence had large facilities and was frequently visited by many of Korda's friends and sometimes some of them even stayed there. This was why in the first years of the Denham complex the Colne river was called the Danube in reference to the strong presence of a Magyar colony.[2]

The Denham studios were provided with first class equipment, including sound recording, grip, lighting and cameras such as the Mitchell NC. These cameras later made use of an English built blimp with a distinctive round DP (Denham & Pinewood Productions) sign. French cameras, such as the Super Parvo, were also used. Field cameras, including the Debrie Parvo L, Newman Sinclair and Vinten, were available.

The rear projection system had the characteristic that it was not installed in a stage, but was moved about to the required stage, so that it could be adapted to the already erected sets. Special projectors meant this system was housed in soundproof cabins with six cellulose screens, the biggest of them 30 × 24 ft.

The stages had a very complete lighting system with about 100 units each. Many of them were the latest Mole & Richardson Fresnel spots. Arc lighting was also of the latest generation, complemented by English built lights by General Electric. The sound recording cabins designed and built at the beginning to be incorporated with the stages were later replaced by very compact and functional mobile units.

The Denham Studios worked for a while inside the orbit of London Film Productions Ltd., until they were later integrated into the powerful group of Arthur Rank with the name of D&P, which adapted and expanded its facilities. Among the most memorable films made in this studio were *Things to Come* (1936), *Rembrandt* (1937), *The Four Feathers* (1939), *Thief of Bagdad* (1940), *In Which We Serve* (1942), *The Life and Death of Colonel Blimp* (1943), *This Happy Breed* (1944), *Brief Encounter* (1945), and *Great Expectations* (1946). All those films became emblematic in the history of British cinematography, either by their spectacular production and the use of color, the high level of their black and white cinematography, or the artistry of the settings and wardrobe. In its short life, Denham was a studio that set a particular mark in the history of the British film.

## SHEPPERTON

Other important studios were also available in England in those days. One of them was the Sound City Studios at Shepperton. It was situated about thirteen kilometers from London. It had begun in the early years of that decade with small stages. Around 1935 its facilities were renewed with the construction of new stages reaching seven units. The designers, the architects Ward & Lucas, adopted new construction concepts for the stages which are interesting to note. They applied a different way to make use of limited space by adopting a system of blocks that unified a large stage with a small one.

The separation of those areas was made by means of a building whose form was an inverted T. This building was designed so that it also incorporated the spaces for the air conditioning system and personnel facilities. The two stages were connected by means of a big silent sliding door. Both stages were isolated from each other and both had their own walls, roof, water pools and small silent sliding doors.

The other new aspect of this construction was the total absence of bridges and catwalks hanging from the top as were used in many continental studios, providing only piping scaffolds. This method was chosen because that system offered better safety and made work easier for the electricians. The Sound City Studios had five Diesel generators to provide 12,000 amps, with a maximum of 8,000 amps for a single stage when necessary, in a line of 240V feeding the 80 lighting units of each stage.

Like other studios, they had all the facilities required in this type of organization, such as production offices, workshops, warehouses, sound departments, projection rooms, editing rooms, make-up departments, canteen, restaurant, etc. The film studios at Shepperton with the passage of time became another important film production studio in England. It had become frequent in Britain to set the studios in the midst of the attractive Middlesex countryside and near a river. Years later, their facilities and the number of films produced were considerable.

## PINEWOOD

The Pinewood Studios, the other big enterprise Britain needed for its booming film business, was begun in 1935 and the first part of its construction finished about 1936. Its birth was the result of a series of curious circumstances.

The film industry was having a great success in Europe during the thirties. The prestige and high revenues of films coming from Hollywood fascinated many businessmen like Alexander Korda. This well known entrepreneur, producer and filmmaker, with experience in his native Hungary, Paris, Berlin and Hollywood, had already established his headquarters in London around 1930, and had obtained great success with his film *The Private Life of Henry VIII* (1932). This big achievement gave rise to his dream of an English Hollywood that materialized with the construction of the Denham studios.

Another important English businessman, but not from the film industry, Mr. Charles Boot, chairman and managing director of the important construction firm Charles Boot & Sons, was allured by the possibilities of the film industry. He wanted to create an important film production studio, and acquired an extraordinary country state in Bucks, a few miles from Denham, for a fraction of its cost. It had belonged to a former military millionaire who had died bankrupt, the Canadian financier Lt. Col. Grant Morden. His extensive property included a very large mansion called Heathern Hall in a picturesque setting. Mr. Boot was carrying out this purchase when this was learned by Mr. Arthur Rank, a magnate in the mills business, who had recently tried a hand in religious film production. Rank, with the habit of doing things in a big way, was unhappy with the limitations of the British film studios, and had his own ideas already about building a big film studio. Inevitably this brought a contact between the two who had the same purpose and thus the new firm Pinewood Studios Limited was born.[3]

Mr. Boot enthusiastically travelled to Hollywood to study how film studios were constructed. Arthur Rank had an expert in this field on his staff, James Sloan, with vast experience in Hollywood, continental Europe and England as well as production manager and advisor to Rex Ingram in his studio in Nice, France. Sloan was commissioned by Rank to study the design and organization of the European studios, especially the German UFA at Neubabelsberg, Berlin, famous for its well developed facilities.

The basic concepts obtained in this search defined the Pinewood project that was assigned to A.F.B. Anderson, architects, who took charge of the construction. The lessons learned at Denham were also taken into account, especially regarding the particular English climate, the way the buildings were arranged and how to landscape the natural setting.

In Pinewood they effectively took advantage of the lavish mansion that had belonged to the late Lt. Col. Morden. The results reached a maximum level of excellence and they became leaders in film facilities of this kind in Great Britain.

The foremost attraction at Pinewood Studios was that its premises included an authentic English Club, for producers, artists, creators and technicians, at the most refined level imaginable. It was situated in a luxurious and vast mansion and boasted a long line of columns. It was outstanding for the exceptional comfort of its rooms, its several bathrooms with marble walls, a Turkish bath, a luxurious ballroom, a music room, a large library, a gymnasium, a covered swimming pool, a television room (a novelty at that time), and a carefully maintained garden. All this was totally unusual in other film studios in the world and gave this place a touch of distinction.

The Pinewood studios grew very quickly and its outdoor facilities included extensive meadows, woods and a big lake. At that time they had six stages situated very conveniently near the service building which housed the production offices, the technical departments, the quarters for actors, the make-up rooms, warehouses, shops, a restaurant, etc.

The two big stages at Pinewood measured 180 × 110 ft. with a height of 40 ft. under the scaffolds. The small stages were 110 × 85 ft. Each stage had a big gate of 20 ft. high that opened vertically by electric control. Each stage had individual foundations, building skeleton and air conditioning system which removed the air five to six times per hour with two turbines, one for intake and the other for outlet at a time when the high intensity lighting generated considerable heat. The big stages included a swimming pool of $74 \times 30 \times 7$ ft. with water temperature control. The pools had special covers to protect the stage from sound resonance, thus allowing the installation of sets above them.

The signalling system for entrances and exits from the stages and sound recording auditoriums was similar to those of other studios. But here they were conceived to include a particular method of contacting the personnel, showing coded information on display signs situated in many places, such as stages, passages, offices and even in the restaurant, in order to call the wanted person everywhere for immediate telephone contacts.

The electric station was initially provided with three Diesel generators delivering 25,000 amps. The power reached the stages at the upper section of the building in order to avoid accidents and the connections were made in the scaffolding to limit the use of cables on the floor. The maximum electric current was available for the big stages which needed from 18,000 (for color productions) to 14,000 amps. The small stages needed 7,000 amps. Light units available on each stage were almost 100 units.

As at Denham studios, Pinewood was equipped with American film equipment and followed Hollywood methods. The 25 editing booths used vertical type editing machines like Moviola, and later Acmiola. British projectors were used in the two 60-seat film theaters. Mitchell NC cameras with British made blimps were the standard cameras. Some years later the Rank film industry monopoly provided its own British made equipment to this and other studios. Through the years Pinewood grew constantly and became the most important and up-to-date film studio in Britain.[4]

# HUNNIA

Hungary is a small country and consequently its film production was reduced in comparison with the big film studios of Europe. Its rich tradition in this field, the prestige of their businessmen, producers, filmmakers and technicians who found a place in Hollywood, Berlin, London and other film capitals, was a key factor in the decision to develop a small but adequate film studio in Budapest, to expand the international production of this country. The design and construction of this studio was assigned to the architect J. Padanyi-Gulyas. New construction techniques were found to develop compact and efficient film studios. The central concept was to surround the main stage with the utility buildings that supported film production.

The Hunnia Filmgyar film studio was a one stage building measuring $130 \times 80$ ft. with a height of 40 ft. under the scaffolds. That stage had the possibility of being divided in two halves lengthwise according to production requirements. Surrounding 60 percent of the perimeter of that double stage a partial three stage block construction was erected to house production offices, a technical department, different services, actors' lodgings, an electric station, air conditioning systems, sound recording and editing departments plus an auditorium.

The main stage had a couple-close type roof under which was installed a high bridge system to control the scaffolds and the catwalks over the sets. One of the two half-stages had a covered swimming pool 56 ft. long and 7 ft. deep under the floor. Two big gates allowed the access of already assembled sets to one of the stages. The other one had only one big gate. The studio had no external land facilities.

The interesting solution applied in the design of a small film studio with space limitations was unifying all complementary facilities around a big divisible space. The Hunnia Filmgyar studios in Budapest were an example of how film productions could be developed on a small scale at a time when the film industry was going through a period of expansion.[5]

## BARRANDOW

The well-known Barrandow studios in Prague were another example of the rational use of a double stage system. This film studio developed in Czechoslovakia by the architect Max Urban was notable for its modern design and elegant lines and was very appreciated for its technical facilities and the outstanding films made there.

Following the same principle we saw in Hunnia, a four stage building was built that surrounded the perimeter of a $165 \times 130$ foot film stage almost completely. This film stage was designed to be divided in two halves if needed. With a very modern design, on a major scale and with the availability of 50 hectares of land, the main studio building was erected with all the facilities required for producing more than one film at a time.

The Barrandow studios was a film studio complex which covered all the requirements of the film industry of that country and included locally produced technical equipment and also an important film laboratory. Through the years this studio was constantly developed and included a large number of new film stages and other buildings, plus the manufacture of film equipment.[6]

The Barrandov studios in Prague (*courtesy Archivo Nacional de la Imagen, Sodre*).

## PARAMOUNT SAINT-MAURICE

While the above described studios were being constructed at the beginning of the decade, an experiment was carried out in France for the production of B class motion pictures. The purpose was to take advantage of the changes in film distribution in the United States that enforced showing a double feature in film theaters to gain larger audiences.

Although Paramount of Hollywood was among the five major studios that bought cheaper films from small Hollywood film studios, they decided to experiment with producing low budget films in Europe. The idea was to develop a multi-language technique in the new sound films they produced. Thus, Paramount-Hollywood took charge of the Saint-Maurice studios in Joinville, Paris, which became Studios Paramount.

The Paramount Saint-Maurice had a long-standing record of service in the French film industry and were not far from the center of Paris, having excellent connections by train and subway (Chateau of Vincennes) and by bus. They had a property of almost 1½ acres, limited by Rue des Reservoires, Avenue des Canadiens and Rue des Presles.

As usual with French film studios, Paramount Saint-Maurice had several buildings grouped around a field in the center of which were five stages. The stages were of different sizes with varied heights between the scaffolds and the floor. The "A" was about $56 \times 41 \times 21$ ft.; "B": $120 \times 55 \times 20$ ft.; "C": $106 \times 56 \times 30$ ft.; "D": $106 \times 60 \times 33$ ft.; and "E": $81 \times 62 \times 31$ ft. A film theater was located near several small projection rooms. Close to them were the editing and synchronizing departments. The studio restaurant was in another building.

The electric power station was behind the film theater. The small outdoor back lots with some film settings were on a free space towards the Avenue des Canadiens. A big interior square with a fountain and a small round place with a group of trees softened the severity of the many surrounding buildings. In front of this place was the crucial work center of the studio, a building with several stages, where the sound postproduction work was made in five languages and recorded with the new Western Electric variable density system. The film laboratories were close by.

The films made in this studio were shot with Super Parvo Debrie and Parvo L cameras preferred by French cinematographers. American film directors resented those cameras that they found strange to work with, but ended accepting them thanks to the orthoviseur, similar to the Mitchell viewfinder. The lighting units known as plafonniers hanging from the ceiling and many lights installed on the floor were very popular at that time. During the day the shooting was done in the English language. During the night and with other film players the same scenes were filmed with dialogue in French, German, Italian, Spanish and Portuguese.

The film directors varied according to the sound versions and were American, French or from other European nations. Many film directors did not allow their names to appear as participating in this experiment. But those jobs gave to many filmmakers an opportunity. The later great film director Alberto Cavalcanti, a Brazilian, was in charge of the Portuguese versions of several films. The French cinematographer Rene Guissart made his debut there directing the French versions of several films. Other well known directors who worked there were Tristan Bernard, A. Korda and Marcel Pagnol.

This new Babel did not live long. That experiment allowed many French sound technicians to learn their new trade and was the petrie dish on which the use of dubbing techniques was developed as well as the effective control of sound on film. At the beginning the use of dialogue was abusively intense, specially in comedies. But with time and experience, moderation produced artistic results. The Paramount-Saint Maurice studios gained a place in the French film industry as a step forward in the technology of sound recording. This form of making films was a strange experience that was never repeated, although it left its mark on the film industry.

## CINECITTÀ

To end this review of new studios in Europe during the golden years of the film business, let us see now one of the most famous studios of the continent, in Italy. As seen above from the beginning of the film industry in Italy, an important number of film studios appeared in Rome, Milan, Turin, Livorno, Palermo and Venice. The development of Italian cinema was noted not only for the scale and level of their films, but also by the refined techniques used and the facilities available. In that decade the most important film producer was the Produzione Pittaluga Cines with an important film studio near St. John's Basilica, in the Rome's Via Veio.

In 1935 a fire destroyed those studios. Mr. Carlo Roncoroni, one of the firm's executives, obtained bank loans, putting his shares in the firm as collateral. To rebuild the lost studio he chose a large field of 600,000 square meters in Via Tuscolana, 9 kilometers from the Campidoglio. The project was given to the architect Gino Peresutti who developed an excellent design based on Hollywood experiences, taking in account the Italian climate and the requirement of order, symmetry, and good circulation, which included wide avenues with trees for softening the surroundings. That was very important for those who worked hard inside the film stages and needed a good and natural surrounding with lots of fresh air.

The fundamental construction work demanded 455 days, making use of 140,000 sq. mt. of the available space; 73 buildings were built that included two well elaborated big film stages with numerous gangways under the ceiling; those were later on followed by two other stages. The complex housed an electric station (that complemented the power lines coming from Rome), the direction offices, the production offices, technical departments, workshops for building the sets, scenic art, painting, decoration, stores for costumes, and set dressing. Other facilities included projection rooms, camera department, and editing rooms. Many other services such as a thermic station, fire stations, a tower with a water tank, a restaurant, etc., completed the first big step of this filming complex.[7]

The technical facilities were an opportunity for the Italian film industry to complement their technical supplies with the imported ones, as in the field of editing (with horizontal editing tables and accessories from Prevost and Microtecnica); lighting units from Rispoli and Marcucci, but also from Mole & Richardson; sound recording from Western Electric; or grip equipment from Rispoli. The cameras used in the studio were mainly of French origin but also from other sources, such as Super Parvo Debrie, Mitchell NC, Cinephon, Debrie L, Novado, Arriflex and many years later, completed with Mitchell BNC and Vinten Everest II.

After Mr. Roncoroni's death his heirs could not agree on the property. Cinecittà was taken over by the Italian government. It formed a big state trio of film organizations erected nearby, composed of the Centro Sperimentale di Cinematografia, a film school, and the Istituto Nazionale Luce, a newsreel and documentary production center. This was an unusual film organization created by the government that covered all fields of this industry for the first time in Europe.

*Top:* Aerial view of Cinecittà studios (*courtesy Unitalia Film*). *Bottom:* Cinecittà direction offices (*courtesy Unitalia Film*).

Cinecittà internal circulation roads (*courtesy Unitalia Film*).

Cinecittà road to the stages (*courtesy Unitalia Film*).

On April 28, 1937, when four feature films were in production, Benito Mussolini inaugurated Cinecittà. Mussolini arrived with a retinue of uniformed corps. Many people hailed his presence, including school students, making the fascist salute. Entering with his usual brisk step, he swung his arms vigorously as if he was rowing. He visited the installations and also climbed up to the roof of one of the buildings to admire the great complex. He did not know then that the political actions he was taking would, a few years later, bring serious difficulties to this outstanding new state film enterprise that he so proudly presented officially to his country.

Film production in Cinecittà grew rapidly, important colossal titles such as *Scipion l'Africano* (1937) and *Giuseppe Verdi* (1938), both directed by Carmine Gallone, demanded big sets on the back lot, with the reconstruction of sea battle scenes in the studio tank and the presence of a great number of extras that flooded the gates of the new installations. Other films such as *Abuna Messias* (1939) by Goffredo Alessandrini and *La Corona di Ferro* (1940) by Alessandro Blasetti were examples of the new kind of showmanship in which Italian films recreated their glorious past. The last years of the decade were of constant growth in Italian film production, going from 31 titles in 1937 to 59 in 1938, 87 in 1939, 81 in 1940, 89 in 1941 and 121 in 1942. Cinecittà was a place very much in demand for shooting a large number of films, thanks to its varied and growing space and facilities, plus stores in many fields, where producers and directors could find all they needed for their productions.

With the war came disaster. Cinecittà, being close to the Centocelle Airport, was bombed and three film stages were hit. Later during the German occupation it was ravaged, converted into an armored car factory, ending as a refugee camp where Jew and Slav refugees found lodgings in the ruins that once were sophisticated places where films had been made.

That huge state film organization that made Italians so proud vanished during the Second World War. Filmmakers made their films in the city streets and gave birth to a new kind of film that was called neorealismo. But the Italian film industry needed this important studio and in 1947 the decision to rebuild it was made. It was a considerable task and it took three years to return Cinecittà to its former splendor as the most important film studio in continental Europe.

# 21. All Talking Newsreels

When the revolution of sound came to the newsreel, audiences all over the world welcomed it enthusiastically as it allowed them to enjoy all variations of the new sound cinema. But many companies were unable to adopt the new technology as it increased their production costs and required added investments in equipment and personnel.

Older firms formed during the World War I such as Kinograms in the U.S.A., well known for the quality of their material and their correspondents all over the world, were forced to close down in 1931 when they failed at trying to add sound to their newsreels with disks. Other newsreel companies joined forces to face the new challenge. The change was important because it entailed not only acquiring new sound cameras, but also adopting a different work organization in their firms.

They were forced to incorporate new sound editing and projecting equipment to install a complex sound studio with expensive optical sound recorders, film phonographs for rerecording, several loop machines, disk recorders and playback equipment, recording consoles with amplifiers and mixers, plus the organization of a complete sound library. The staff needed for handling these new studios included many specialized technicians and top-level film narrators and commentators. Newsreels had never demanded such complex and expensive postproduction chores to bring out a weekly edition.

The new technical demands affected the shooting of images incorporating sound; they required the acquisition of one or more sound vans specially prepared to house the sound cameras with enough space to store long rolls of cables, plus a special roof platform on each van. Each of these units had an average cost of $25,000, too high at that time for an activity that was not too profitable. The new sound vans became conspicuous at public gatherings, official ceremonies and events deemed of interest to record. Since at first it was easier to operate outdoors than at indoors locations, it was quite common at that time to see several of these units parked in squares, parks or streets, shooting interviews of politicians or any other well known subjects. This was not an easy task then, due to ambient sound pollution around the location that could not always be controlled properly and that tended to mar the clearness of recorded voices.

Some times those vans could be seen lined up together for a parade or game or any other important outdoor event where cameramen of different newsreel companies covered it from the roofs of their vans, while on the ground the sound men with their earphones worried about the quality of the sound recording. Each camera had a painted logo on its magazine identifying the company it belonged to, and each vehicle had the same logo painted on its side to distinguish it from its competing neighbor. It was not unusual to see seven or eight firms covering the same event.

It also became quite common to erect high platforms for the cameras, where the cameramen framed close views of their subjects by resorting to the use of telephoto lenses. As during the previous decade of the silent era, these lenses were of vital importance to obtain close shots or close-ups of relatively distant subjects. They were then staple tools for the camera crews, and large sums were invested to buy the more luminous ones and those with greater focal lengths.

In that ceaseless competition, a newsreel firm entrusted the English lens manufacturer Taylor, Taylor & Hobson Ltd. to build for them a special 1,400mm telephoto lens to cover an event in which the king of England would participate. When the resultant film was projected on the screen, the image was very unstable as it was greatly magnified, increasing the vibrations of the camera platform much more than had been foreseen.[1]

The longest lens of that era was known as "The Big Bertha," just like the famous German gun during World War I shelled Paris. This extraordinary long lens weighed as much as the camera itself and demanded two tripods: one for the camera and one for the lens.

Newsreel cameraman with the heavy Wall camera (courtesy Archivo Nacional de la Imagen, Sodre).

At that time, working on newsreels had become a much more demanding and heavier task. The new cameras were extremely heavy and personnel to help the cameramen were more scarce than when producing fiction films. The Wall camera, one of the most sophisticated, was so heavy that its manufacturer added four short legs to its base so that the personnel moving it from one place to another could place their hands below and thus raise it. This instrument, with its Akeley tripod provided with a gyroscopic head and a film magazine, weighed more than 300 pounds without the battery, in all, fifteen times more than today's professional video camera together with tripod and battery.

Cameramen at that time had to be very strong and sturdy types to work a full day in this new form of the job. The weight of sound filming equipment encumbered the cameraman and added a new technician to the team, the sound man. He was responsible for sound recording and where to place the microphone. Although the cameraman had headphones to listen to the sound recording , the sound man was responsible for its quality and for controlling the recorded volume, surveying the vumeter and other amplifying controls, standing at the foot of the platform or of the van.

At that time direct sound shooting was a complex task; microphones were very primitive and they had to be carefully oriented towards the subject so that the camera noise would not affect the recording (it had to be placed beyond seven feet from the camera so as not to pick up the hum of the motor or the sprocket noise inside the camera). Loud ambient sounds and the wind were the sound man's greatest worries. During the first years, the microphone had its own amplifier and was always placed on a tripod with a special mount that prevented transmitting vibrations to the microphone.

In closed rooms sound recording became harder to obtain due to acoustic problems and the need to place additional equipment to light the area being covered. At the beginning of that decade all the equipment needed to film a scene indoors weighed more than half a ton. Harry Lawrenson, foreign editor of Movietone News, recalled that at the beginning of the sound era in cinema, when his firm wanted to shoot a typical marriage in a French village, his technicians saw the sour face of the priest as they unloaded their implements. Finally the priest told them that it would be better to shoot the ceremony outside the church, since the installation of all the equipment needed indoors would prevent half his parishioners from entering the church.[2] Compare this with today's compact video cameras that include their own light source.

In that decade the equipment used became gradually simpler, but it continued to be heavy and complex to operate. Direct sound shooting took its time to install the camera, adjust the focus, correct the parallax viewfinder, regulate the motor speed, make equal the values of focus and diaphragm for the different turret lenses (just in case a different framing on the same axis was needed without stopping the camera), and carefully frame in advance the different lenses, before turning on the camera motor.

The sound men also had to see to the exposure of the negative in the optical sound track, according to the sensibility of the film emulsion, the correct placing of the microphone, control the sound level with the vumeter and the quality of the sound through the headphones. The process was not simple because at that time the automation on today's equipment was not available, and the only defense the technicians had was their experience and to operate systematically. The men who operated that equipment were experts with a long background in the job and therefore had acquired excellent work methods and a knack in their trade to overcome technical inconveniences that might crop up.

Most of these technicians were mature men since in this trade there was a pyramid with its base formed by the assistants; it went up to the operators of silent cameras and reached the top with the sound camera man. The high cost of equipment, the speed and ability to operate them correctly and the accumulated experience were the parameters to determine each man's pay and for companies to defend themselves from tempting offers from competitors.

If the twenties was an era of transition and peacetime changes after a hard war, the thirties were much more convulsive when people lived through the effects of economic depressions, disasters, shocking crimes, commotions among European royalty, international political troubles, special sporting events and numerous hostilities that came to a head with the Second World War.

It was a time when the newsreel companies faced great challenges of new shooting possibilities with their equipment and the constant demand for special news coverage. And this industry adapted itself and the organizations technically to these challenges. The novelty of direct sound, with the years, wisely combined with more elaboration of the sound track in postproduction, to alternating the direct sound take, the background commentator and functional music and ambient sounds more harmoniously than during previous years.

Following the New York Stock Exchange crash, the Depression lasted several years, bringing hard times causing social and racial unrest. Many of these events affected the safety of the cameramen and they found that their presence was violently rejected by those being covered with their cameras. For example, a Paramount sound truck was thrown into a river by a frenzied mob in Salisbury, Maryland. A similar attack took place on another sound truck of the same firm in West Virginia. And there were instances when cameramen ended up in the hospital and their equipment was severely damaged (for example, when they tried to shoot a miner's strike), or even behind bars when the police in certain regions did not want a filmed record of how to they acted in such circumstances.[3]

During the New Deal years the figure that took over the newsreel screens was the United States president, Franklin Delano Roosevelt. His distinguished and pleasant appearance was covered on countless occasions, in his many speeches, recorded with close-ups and big close-ups, capturing his voice and expressive face often without the necessary establishing shots, but framing his body movement was carefully avoided, due to his physical handicap.

This was the case in the United States and in Europe; high government leaders, especially kings, were the people most commonly seen on the screens in those countries. Some like the king of Sweden thought it was not dignified to speak for a newsreel, though he allowed himself to be filmed without looking at the camera.

But dictators were becoming stars in those years in Germany, Italy and Spain, and they became the attraction on the screens of world newsreels, and in some instances their star. Hitler was the best covered of them all, not only for the quality of the takes but also for the selection of camera angles, the framing and even, during the speeches, by the lighting that the UFA cameramen prepared for him. The gestures and pauses in his speeches (which Hitler precisely rehearsed in private) enthused and exited his followers and made his opponents fear. Mussolini, on the other hand, produced enthusiasm in his followers, but usually amused his opponents.

World events during the thirties had an international weight as never before, and newsreels were hard pressed to cover them all. The assassination in 1932 of the French president Paul Doumier, who always had a foreboding of his tragic end, initiated a series of hot news.

In the same year Charles Lindbergh's son was kidnapped and for many months the story captured public attention in the U.S.A. In 1933 the series of dramatic events against the Jews in Germany ended with the Reichstag fire.

The year 1934 shook France. In January the Stavisky Affair broke out which affected all the French people and involved high government leaders. On February 6, after a huge demonstration, a crowd clashed with police forces in Paris, as thousands of leftist sympathizers advanced with the intention of seizing Parliament in the Palais-Bourbon. The Place de la Concorde became a battleground, the mounted police charged against the crowd and a bus burned fiercely under the obelisk. The clash went on for several hours. From the nearby American Embassy and the Hotel Crillon the cameramen covered the events full of fear because a women standing quite near them fell dead with a stray bullet in her head. The day after this violence it was officially reported that 16 people had died and several hundreds were wounded. Veteran cameramen confessed they had never before covered such savagery.[4]

Months later the news brought the notorious case of Violette Nozieres, who at 18 poisoned her parents in order to continue with her dissolute life. On October 1934, a visit of King Alexander I of Yugoslavia ended with his murder and that of the French prime minister, Jean Louis Barthou, in Marseilles, at the hands of a Croat terrorist, who climbed on the limousine's running board during the parade, and shot them. The French cameraman Georges Mejat who with his brother Raymond had been sent by Fox Movietone, together with a brand new sound van, to cover the event, heard the first shots and was able to film with a silent camera when the police killed the assassin with their sabers, the details of the weapon used for the royal murder, the assassin's hat and the dying victims. From afar his brother filmed the events with the sound camera from a long shot with the impressive ambient sound of the shootings, cries and commotion. Complementary shots were also made by cameraman Robert Batton who was 15 ft. from the car. Never before had a royal killing had been covered with image and sound. The result was so effective that the whole event became a long film that was distributed all over the world.[5]

Important events continued to occur. During the final months of 1934 and in the beginning of 1935, the trial of Bruno Richard Hauptmann, accused of the murder of Charles Lindbergh's baby, was one of the events that got more coverage from the sound cameras of American newsreels. Then a succession of war events began. The invasion of Ethiopia and the conquest of Addis Ababa by the Italian forces under the command of Marshal Badoglio was filmed from a truck that preceded the troops. The man operating the camera was Renato Cartoni, from the Istituto Nazionale Luce, with an Arriflex camera mounted on a tripod head called Vittoria, a prototype of a new design built by the cameraman himself that years later would make his name famous in the trade.[6]

In 1936 the Spanish Civil War began and was massively covered with film cameras by both fighting sides and by international newsreels, especially American and British. To cover it the Soviet Union sent, among others, cameraman Roman Karmen with a Bell & Howell. Karmen joined the independent Dutch cameraman Joris Ivens, and his colleague John Ferno, who with a similar camera and with the help of the famous writer Ernest Hemingway provided the shots for their famous documentary film *The Spanish Earth* (1937). Hemingway wrote the commentary and spoke the narration.

The long civil war was covered by independent teams and by the cameramen of the Departamento Nacional de Cinematografia, the FEN, the JONS, and the C.N.T. and loyal military brigades. Among them were figures such as Enrique Guerner, Antonio Solano,

Andrés Pérez Cubero, Seguismundo Pérez, Pablo Ripio, Emilio Foriscot and Mariano Ruiz who later became well known directors of photography in the Spanish cinema.[7]

In 1936 a sporting event of international interest made a remarkable presence in the news. It was the X Olympic Games in Berlin. They had strong political connotations, since Hitler wanted to show the world the outstanding characteristics of his regime. Although newsreel firms from all over the world participated in the coverage, the German government made a film for which no technical resources, efforts and expenses were spared to obtain perfect coverage.

The outstanding German filmmaker Leni Riefenstahl was assigned. She had already shown her remarkable talent in the long documentary *Triumph des Willens* (*The Triumph of the Will*, 1934). For this film covering the Olympic games, she captured the principal events with great artistic insight using a vast array of resources never employed before. In spite of a strike carried out by cameramen protesting against a woman being assigned to direct the film, sixty cameramen covered the inaugural ceremony and shot the marathon with standard and high speed cameras. Later thirty cameramen continued covering the event in several places in Germany. The most varied brands of instruments available in Germany were used: Askania Z and Schulter; Debrie Parvo, GV and Sept; Newman Sinclair Autokine; Bell & Howell Eyemo; Slechta; Cinephon, and many others.

Long traveling rails were placed in a trench dug alongside the running track to follow the athletes with two cameras mounted on an electric operated car. Aerial shots were obtained from a balloon. Many cameras were so close to the competitors that they had to be protected with special covers to avoid bothering them. For the first time submarine casings were used to house cameras during swimming competitions to obtain underwater shots. One of the first mirror telephoto lenses was used, and from 50,000 to 65,000 ft. of film were exposed daily. Well known film negatives, such as Agfa (which also made a special high speed emulsion) and Kodak were used as well as the little known Perutz film negative, whose good performance was then discovered. The total amount of exposed film reached the 1,300,000 ft. The pictorial quality of this documentary was impressive.[8]

One of the most grievous aerial disasters of those times occurred in May 1937. The Zeppelin airship *Hindenburg* caught fire as it prepared to land at Lakehurst airport, in New Jersey, and exploded, killing 36 of its 97 passengers and crew. By routine, several teams and sound trucks had gone to the airport from the most important newsreels and newspapers. The regular trips of the Zeppelin airship were a common event and nothing special was expected; not even outstanding passengers were coming. NBC equipment also went with its sound van to register sounds on disks for their special effects collection. It was raining and getting dark. Far away lightning announced that a storm was coming. The airship approached the mast and threw down its mooring lines. Suddenly the unexpected happened. A flash, an explosion and a gigantic fire with flames 200 ft. high covered the sky. In a few seconds the flames consumed the airship while its airframe plummeted to earth.

Cameramen Al Mingalone from Paramount News, Larry Kennedy and Deon De Titta from Fox Movietone News, James J. Seeley from News of the Day and Bill Deekes from Pathé News, bewildered, shot the bizarre spectacle, hardly believing what they were seeing. From his sound truck NBC narrator Herbert Morrison with suppressed cries and sobbing voice described, in short and precise sentences the disaster as it took place. Thus the world was able to see one of the most horrifying recordings produced by sound newsreels.[9]

In that decade cameramen began the routine of spending long hours searching for opportunities to cover events they knew would be saleable news. Such was the case with the famous and romantic couple formed by the Duke of Windsor, who had abdicated the British crown, and his wife, Duchess Wallis Simpson, as they moved through France after their marriage in Château de Candé. Under a special permit the marriage had been filmed by Paramount, but the couple had been surreptitiously caught by French cameraman Jean Manzon while they dined in that place, in spite of the extreme vigilance by the French police who controlled the surroundings and of Scotland Yard, who controlled the access doors. But film reporters did not accept their systematic shunning of the press.

On one occasion they discovered the lady in her Rolls Royce and chased her up to a nearby hotel in the Riviera where her husband was waiting for her. The cameramen saw the car in a parking lot of the hotel, blocked the exit with their own cars and went to sleep. On the next day they discovered that the cunning lady had hired the services of several mechanics from the garages in town to liberate her car of obstacles during the night and drive away unnoticed by the cameramen. Finally French cameraman Henri Cabrières managed to obtain a shot of her through the foliage of a plant, until in his effort to improve his shot, the Duchess became aware of what was going on and pointed an accusing finger towards the camera signaling to the operator that he had been discovered.[10]

The drama of war finally arrived at the end of 1937. It was now China's turn to suffer the relentless bombing of Shanghai by Japanese aircraft, covered by cameramen from Universal and The March of Time. Soon enough this war affected American interests, when the Panay, a U.S. Navy warship anchored in the Yangtze River, was sunk. As luck would have it, the cameramen from two newsreel firms, Eric Mayel from Fox Movietone and Norman Alley of Universal News, were aboard the ship at that moment. They filmed the bombing with a DeVry camera and saved their lives and their exposed material. Immediately an efficient and swift operation was mounted, in which a destroyer, commercial airplanes and security forces participated so that the exposed film crossed the seas and continents quickly and arrived in the United States to be processed, and immediately shown on all the screens in the USA. There, an alerted audience waited anxiously for the material. But the image that shook the world from that war was obtained at the beginning, by Chinese cameraman Wong Hai Sheng (Newsreel Wong) from the Hearst Company, showing a desolate baby crying desperately, covered with ashes, amid the ruins of what had been the South Railway Station in Shanghai.

By the end of the thirties, the international film press faced a convulsive world that made their task more difficult. Fascism in Italy, the Third Reich in Germany, Communism in the Soviet Union, Franco in Spain, the military regime in Japan, Chiang Kai-shek in China, censored their free film recordings of the chiefs of state, and made it impossible to get close to them and capture their personal intimacy. The Spanish Civil War and the Sino-Japanese War, as well the Anschluss by which Germany seized Austria, and afterwards penetrated Czechoslovakia and Poland, proved that these political regimes resisted the free recording of events; in all those cases such recordings were made by government services only.

At that time, in Germany, the Universum Film Aktien Gesellschaft (UFA) had been taken over by the government, under the command of Dr. Joseph Goebbels. In Italy, the Istituto Nazionale Luce established in 1925 performed a similar task for the Mussolini regime, and in Spain, the Departamento Nacional de Cinematografía, a bureau of the Ministry of the Interior, born in Burgos in 1938, began the production of local documentaries and newsreels. In 1942, a self-governing institution, NO-DO (Noticieros y documentales) was born covering a long period during the regime of Generalissimo Francisco Franco. The same as Hitler and Mussolini who had reliable cameramen to cover their close shots, Francisco Franco trusted Ramon Saiz de la Hoya, a cameraman from No-Do, to frame him from below to enhance his figure and disguise his short height.

At that time, the obstruction of free access to international cameras to zones where important political changes were taking place, affected the film press considerably. In the United States, an independent cameraman's dream was to worm into Nazi Germany and record material uncensored. One who achieved this goal was the renowned cameraman and documentary maker Julien Bryan, when he obtained a special permit to film the daily life in that country under Hitler's regime.

Bryan obtained material of a very good level, but logically he could not register the negative aspects of the repression carried out by the Nazi regime: the persecution of the Jews and the country's rearmament. On his returning to America, he sold about four hours of film to *The March of Time* and this firm, with cunning resourcefulness, recreated in the United States the shots they needed and inserted them into the real material, applying an old tactic that was commonly used by that famous film magazine. Thus the famous edition *Inside Nazi Regime* came to light.[11]

Julien Bryan was a distinguished freelance photographer and cameraman who, from the beginning of that decade, had long experience in this field, traveling through Russia, Siberia, China, Finland, Japan, Mexico, and several European countries. His work was always of excellent technical quality and the material he produced was also very good, following the norm not only to cover the whole story but also worrying about capturing numerous close shots with details that underlined his sequences. Many of today's films and documents about that time are based on his material.

Cameramen working in the documentary field recorded those events with a critical professional viewpoint and filmed military conflicts taking place in the world during those years. They were not capturing images for subsequent editing by private or official censors, according to criteria they did not know, but were shooting "their film" that reflected their particular point of view on the events they covered.

In those circumstances, it was coming out that in their profession, the filmmaking cameramen who went to war wanted to narrate the events their own way. This had been achieved during the Spanish Civil War by Joris Ivens and John Ferno. Also by Herbert Kline, in Spain too, and in 1937 together with Alexander Ammid in the southern region of Czechoslovakia with the documentary film *Crisis* (1938), covering the disintegration of that country after the Munich Treaty, and then *Lights Out in Europe* (1939).

In 1938 Joris Ivens, John Ferno and Robert Capa began their coverage of the Chinese War. They had flown from the United States on a China Clipper air route with stops in Honolulu and Hong Kong. They had the support of friends in New York like Luise Rainer, and Chinese patriots in the USA, that seconded their project. The group had taken two Eyemo cameras and a larger French one together with sound equipment. They had enough film stock to work on a seven to one ratio. They had arranged for a Hollywood laboratory to process the film and send it to Helen Van Dogen for editing. They had supplemented their budget by Robert Capa's agreement to supply still photos to *Life Magazine*. They prepared in advance against all contingences, including a coded system in telegrams they would send: if, for example, they said, "John is very sick," it meant "pull out of there as fast as you can." They obtained the support of Generalissimo Chiang Kai-shek's government, and that of his wife. But shooting the film they had to accept the annoying controls and the "protection" of the censors who did not allow them to take many of the shots they wanted. The

Chinese fear of foreign filmmakers was so great that each shot was simultaneously filmed in 16mm, processed, viewed and then approved or not. Once the content of each shot was accepted, the material was allowed to be sent to the United States to be processed. In spite of all this, the shots they obtained were of great human value and showed the hardships and disastrous nature of that war. The documentary was called *The 400 Million*, the music was by Hanns Eisler, and Duddley Nichols wrote the narration. Today it is a classic, but at that time it was not grasped, neither in the United States nor in the United Kingdom, what this war implied, and in France the film was not shown because the French had recently signed a trade treaty with Japan.[12]

In 1939, seven days after the German invasion of Poland and its notorious Blitzkrieg, Julien Bryan rushed into another fearless job by himself: covering the Germans seizing Warsaw. He entered Poland through Romania, taking two Eyemo cameras, a film tripod, two Leicas, raw stock in black and white for his film and still cameras, plus some color rolls for his Leicas. When he arrived in Warsaw the city was being bombed, by a dozen daily air raids, killing thousands. He recorded the faces of the inhabitants full of panic and fatigue. He heard on the local radio, that if he was found on the street he would be arrested and possibly shot. But his luck held and soon he found official support for his work. He knew that what he was recording would be an invaluable eyewitness document for the world and went on with his job. He filmed the bombed bridges over the Vistula and the people in the streets carrying the most diverse objects. He recorded the bomb craters and the raging fires. He went to the hospitals full of evacuees. He filmed the families of refugees and their neighbors and he shot details of interest, such as the dogs, cats and clothes on the beds. He had to load the cameras many times with smoke inflamed eyes, with ashes penetrating his equipment until it broke down and he had to take it to the Kodak laboratories to have it repaired, and also developed his raw stock. Bryan went out to cover more of what was going on and when he returned he found that the laboratory had been bombed; a wall had fallen over but fortunately the film was still intact.

He continued shooting until he ran out of film and decided to return to the laboratory with his film treasure. He had the film developed and made two copies of it. He buried these copies in secret and separate places to preserve them for posterity. With incredible courage and good luck he managed to elude the pincers throttling Poland, arrived in Germany and traveled to the United States with 5,000 feet of 35mm film to show the world, his remarkable documentary *Siege* (1939–40), the result of his odyssey.[13]

As the war storm advanced over Europe, the coverage of news and the war was done by the occupying nation. The international firms began to limit their operation areas as Germany advanced. The contents were more and more partial to the views of whatever country did the film reporting, and the nations that were away from the conflict had the opportunity to compare the different versions of a same event. And all the filmed material that went out of the area of each belligerent became strategic: it had to comply with the increasing requirements that were developing: the information and propaganda war.

# 22. New Lighting Techniques

As with many other aspects of filmmaking, the coming of sound produced important changes in set lighting procedures. But there were also during that time other factors that created considerable modifications in the design and placement of such equipment. The introduction of new fast speed film emulsions greatly reduced the amount of light required. The return to the system of only one camera unit to cover each set-up eliminated the need for the scene to be lighted to be taken simultaneously from many points of view. The new way of shooting with a mobile camera demanded a set floor free from lighting units and cables, and reduced the floor space for this use. This change pointed the way to reduce the number of lights over the set and the way to install and make use of them.

## New concepts of lighting

The first attempt to control light from above came with the introduction of a new lighting bank. This was the result of studies made by Mr. John Capstaff of the Eastman laboratories in Rochester. The fixture unified three polyhedral reflectors with a 2 kW lamp each and 16 heat resistant plane mirrors. Two chains hanging from the ceiling supported the whole unit in two positions: parallel to the floor or at 45 degrees. The body of the bank was also of a polyhedral shape, of about 28 × 11 × 4.5 in. and encased in a grid with a chassis that covered the whole unit. The three lighting reflectors had their own fan system and controls for centering the lamps. The convergence of the three reflectors was regulated by tensors. The amount of light provided by this bank was of 48,000 lux from a distance of 12 feet. The units were turned on in two positions: with a low voltage for rehearsals and full light conditions with normal voltage. This system was conceived to cover a scene with several of those bank units with a lens aperture of f/3.5 from a distance of 20 feet without the hazard of excessive heat. The system was very easy to install but was not favored by American film studios because the general light foundation concept changed.[1]

In Europe the German UFA Film Studios of Berlin and the French Tobis Film Studios at Epinay, Paris, adopted and elaborated a grill system to transport the cables to hang lightings units over the sets, which was known in France as plafonniers. The grills were spaced at about 3 inches. A small electric powered trolley over them worked the two wound cables from which the lighting unit hung. The up and down and side to side movements of each plafonnier were button controlled.[2] This system was the first step towards a procedure adopted for TV studios some forty years later.

## Hollywood lighting practice

In Hollywood, the old practice of installing the lamps in the upper part of the stage around the perimeter of the set was improved upon with a permanent platform system for easy installation of the spots. Those platforms were hung from the ceiling by means of chains. The structures of the platforms were joists of 2 × 4 inches forming units called bays or chairs. Each bay had two or three lighting units. Each unit was numbered for easy identification. The bays had a space called a catwalk behind the spots where the electricians, called juicers, moved to adjust each lighting unit. Sometimes the bays were installed as a bridge over the set and in that case the catwalks had several spots on both sides of the bays. On many occasions the bays also crossed over the open side of the set.

A guardrail installed towards the inside of the set unified the bays and protected the electricians from accidents. The lighting units selected were spots in order to cast the beam as far as possible from one set wall to the other. Each juicer was responsible for the spots in his bay. The juicers controlled the angle of the light beams of each spot, adjusted the flood of the light, inserted filters when necessary, window patterns, etc. When the barn doors were later introduced, their duty was also to adjust the doors to cut undesirable light beams.

The new lights installed on top of the set were conceived for modelling lights. Consequently they were spots with mirrored glass. The reflecting section of those spots was a 140 degree parabolic silvered glass mirror behind the lamp with a beam variation from 8 degrees to 12 degrees or 24 degrees to 40 degrees according to the unit. Some spots made in England

Overhead lighting units used in the sets during the thirties, many of them without Fresnel lenses (courtesy Archivo Nacional de la Imagen, Sodre).

by General Electric included interchangeable parabolic mirrors made up of 60 multisided pieces. The uniformity of the spot beam was obtained by means of a Solite wire glass in front of the lamp. The most commonly used lamps were of 2 kW or 3 kW. The standard units in the studio had a minimum of 8 degrees and a maximum of 40 degrees. Also some spots were used with condensing plane-convex lenses for special effects.

The great improvement in spot lamps arrived in 1935 when Mole & Richardson included their Studio No. 25 spot lamp with a small Fresnel lens that covered the front lamp surface. This new lens eliminated the black spot of the lamp filament and perfected the quality of the beam. The Fresnel lens had been known since the eighteenth century, when the French physicist Augustin-Jean Fresnel conceived it to improve the beam of lighthouses. It was a plane-convex lens surrounded by concentric rings. Placed in front of a spot, the Fresnel lens produced a beam of parallel rays that faded at the borders. Moving the lamp with the mirror over the lens allowed controlling the beam totally and combining many beams. The Fresnel lens later on also covered the front area of the spot. Spots were made so that their front could be opened. The beam angle was controlled by means of a helicoidal screw. This lens standardized the application of this light unit in many fields and discarded the use of plane-convex lenses with diffusers in other lighting units. Its use was finally incorporated into the new arc spots.

The lights from above were then the method generally adopted. The accepted principle was that in natural outdoor takes the light came from the sky. For indoor shots with daylight, the sunlight also came from that source through the apertures and the lighting units generally were above eye level. The best light comes from above at 45 degrees and produces natural shadows. A set was lighted by means of several beams of different intensity, flood, diffusion and directions.

The construction of lighting patterns now required many modelling sources to cover the different positions of the actors. The new film emulsions did not require a general light to achieve a safe exposure level. The amount of light needed then for black and white photography was 250 to 400 foot-candles. The general foundation light was eliminated. Some light units such as banks, scoops and strips were of more limited use with black and white. The lighting of the set was conceived independently of the lighting on the players. The multiple shadows produced by the old method were no longer accepted. The shadows were controlled by means of other beams from above. The new concept of key lighting started to be adopted; it established the natural source of light in the set and the dominant direction of highlights. This was a big step towards a realistic concept of lighting in motion pictures and most cinematographers adopted it as a basic standard. The key light was later combined with fill light to control contrast together with the wise use of back light and the background lighting for the actors' close-ups.

The set lighting techniques required also the adoption of complementary methods to cover different situations. The experience of the masters was adopted to improve the beauty of the image. A three-dimensional effect in the image was the target of many cinematographers. The new techniques were the result of research made by many tests while shooting. The knowledge acquired was that the binocular effect was the result of depth and roundness. The first was obtained by contrasting the lighting on several planes of the scene. The roundness was achieved by highlighting curved surfaces with small lighting touches. The careful use of light beams on curved surfaces, broken shadows on flat surfaces and the backlighting of scene components were some of the techniques that produced the best results.[3]

Mole & Richardson dimmer (*courtesy Archivo Nacional de la Imagen, Sodre*).

This important improvement in studio light control was followed in that decade with the creation of new devices. Bob Brant, the ingenious owner of Hollywood Scene Dock, born with the beginnings of the film industry, introduced the barn door. It was conceived to cut part of the extreme light beams of the spots. Then came the trombone that allowed putting the spot over the wall of a set. The first circular screen, the soft snoot and the bazooka, a device to install lights easily in the bays, completed those light accessories. Brant was also the originator of improvements on the old sun reflector with soft and hard reflecting screens and a firm stand. With the years many others light implements arrived at the studios, such as the cukaloris to produce broken shadows over a flat wall. This series of lighting devices was introduced as standard items in the Hollywood studios and carried to the European studios when American producers made films there, because the Hollywood technicians required the best elements they were used to.

The dimmer was another important studio lighting implement, the use of which had expanded in those years. The dimmer was a variable resistance device which allowed the adjusting of the light intensity by the electricians. Cinematographers found that its wise use could be a great help to achieve the light balance while shooting. It was most often used when the actors moved in and out on the set. It was also applied in certain circumstances when an actor was silhouetted against a bright window with his back to the camera and he then turned around and faced it, requiring the corresponding light balance to realize his features. The light control by means of the dimmer was a very appreciated ability of the electricians. It had to be carefully planned in order to synchronize the light intensity with the actor's movements. In many cases the dimmer changes were about from ten to a dozen dimmer movements. Certain scenes required the use of four or five dimmers coupled to more than one lighting unit.

The dimmer was also used on the lights installed on the moving camera. The intensity of a small light unit at the front of the camera known as a handy lamp or loupe was best controlled in its intensity by this device, maintaining the light balance while being displaced. Other lighting units used in the front of the camera had a U-shaped device housing several frosted lamps around the camera lens to produce light without shadows during a close up on a player.

## Technicolor influences

The production of several Technicolor films in Hollywood had consequences in the motion picture lighting technology in that decade. That's firm's new three-strip process required a minimum 500 foot-candles for indoor shooting. The incandescent Mazda lights were not suitable due to their limited amount of light and spectrum values. The solution was arc lights that combined with a special straw-colored filter (Y-1) which rendered a light source similar to daylight.

In 1933, the Technicolor Corporation contacted the most important Hollywood manufacturer of motion picture lighting equipment, Mole & Richardson, to investigate and build a series of arc lighting units based on five basic specifications: 1) silent operation for sound shooting with the best sound recording equipment; 2) 200 foot-candles minimum light output measured with a Weston photometer at fifteen feet; 3) a mechanical system to move the lamp carbons in order to provide a uniform level of light intensity and constant values of the spectrum during the period of operation; 4) it must have a comparatively flat distribution curve over a projection angle of sixty degrees and be free from any hot spot; and 5) the light unit should be easy to install and handle and be economical in operation and maintenance.[4]

Mole & Richardson accepted the challenge, coordinating their experiments with the National Carbon Company. Each firm separately and then together arrived at successful results. Mole & Richardson developed arc spots and double arc broads of advanced design. They incorporated an advanced arc-rotating element, a method to combine the carbons and place them at an angle of 127 degrees to obtain a maximum light intensity with the rotation of one of them at more than 10 r.p.m. The unit was provided with a heat resistant mirror and the use of the Fresnel lens on the spot and special diffuser glasses on the broads.

The National Carbon Company produced a high intensity carbon known as White Flame which was the result of a rare earth combination including cerium that obtained the required color temperature demanded by Technicolor. The research of these two firms produced the High Intensity Arc Spot Lamps of Mole & Richardson, made up of the M-R 90, which operates at 120 amps, the M-R 170, that operates at 150 amps and later the M-R 450 at 250 amps in a lamp called the Molarc. For diffused-light arc units, the firm produced the

Mole & Richardson large spot arc unit (*courtesy Archivo Nacional de la Imagen, Sodre*).

series known as Duarc Broadsides Type 27, Type 29 and Type 40. The Morlarc and the Duarc series were soon the standard lighting units used in Hollywood and abroad to shoot Technicolor system films.

When the new three-strip Technicolor system arrived at Hollywood studios, the set lighting changes being made for black and white contrasted with the requirements of color shooting. Color film production demanded again a general base lighting due to the low speed of the color process. The use of the arc light returned to the stages with a few new improved lights. This new equipment was used on the floor again and the lighting of the sets combined the tungsten lamps with blue filters from above with arc spots and arc broads from a lower level. The number of floor lighting units was considerable. Ray Rennaham, chief cinematographer of the film *Becky Sharp* (1934, RKO), established that shooting that first Technicolor feature film by the three-strip method demanded 229 arc lamps and 160 diverse tungsten lighting units.

The artistic qualities of lighting in that early period were very limited, because the first goal was to achieve the necessary technical requirements. The intense shadows were practically prohibited and the ratio between key light and fill light was no more than 1.5 to 1. The light units covered the floor of the set to provide the 1000 foot-candles that the Technicolor camera demanded. In those years the only new arc lighting units available were the broadside M-R 29, a 40 amp floodlighting unit with carbons fed by solenoids, and the M-R 27 scoop, a twin vertical trim also of 40 amps, both conceived for basic lighting. The other lighting units were the standard lights used in black and white productions as the 80 ampere rotary arc spots and the 36-in. Sun spot, a 10-kW incandescent tungsten lamp light for effect lighting.

The evolution of incandescent lighting brought the introduction of the CP (color photography) lamps with a color temperature of 3,380 degrees K and the manufacture of the blue Macbeth glass daylight filter. Lighting improvements were continued with the introduction in about 1937 of the M &R Arc lamp No. 5 Type 90 which delivered more than three times more light and 40 degrees of beam spread and substituted the 80-ampere rotary spot. The MR 150 was the new arc spot that replaced the old 24-inch Sun arcs. The radical change in Technicolor lighting came around 1939 when this firm introduced its last improved three-strip system with negatives with a very fast emulsion similar to those used in black and white (three times faster for interior shooting and four for daylight). The film *Gone with the Wind* was its cinematographer's opportunity to show how this system was able to reproduce its maximum lighting values.

The introduction of color in motion pictures was an important contribution towards scientific standardization of lighting techniques. The Technicolor Corporation was a leading promulgator of technological advances in this field. This firm

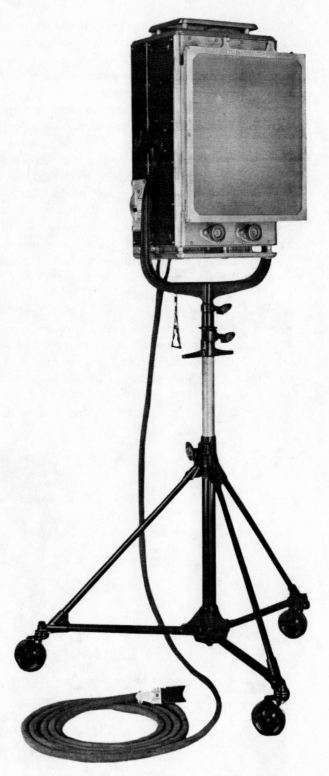

Mole & Richardson arc broad unit (**courtesy Archivo Nacional de la Imagen, Sodre**).

brought about the development of new and refined equipment, special tungsten lamps, and gelatin and glass filters that changed lighting techniques in a few years. But this firm's particular requisites in all technical aspects of the process induced cinematographers to obtain precise light readings during exposure of the film. This was possible only by means of an adequate instrument: the photometer.

The coming of sound in motion pictures prepared the industry for the development and use of certain light sensitive materials such as cesium or selenium. They made possible the recording and reproduction of optical sound. From early times, since the experiments of the French optician Jean Baptiste François Soleil in 1840, with the first actiometer to measure the light intensity, and the use of selenium by Alexander Graham Bell and also by Dr. Edward Weston during the end of the nineteenth century, a solution was sought to measure light by a scientific method. This was finally achieved in the twenties connecting a selenium plate with a galvanometer. In the early thirties the research concluded with the introduction of a practical professional photometer.

In 1931 the Weston Instrument Corp. of Newark, New Jersey, produced an instrument known as Weston Light Exposure Meter (U.S. Patent No. 2016469) that fulfilled this requirement and was used by Technicolor. This meter was a fundamental reference for film exposure and for reading light values of each light unit and establishing the amount of foot-candles in each zone of the set. The personal estimates of cinematographers was shown to be wrong on large sets with great amounts of light or after long working sessions. This was the beginning of a new and more precise working method that was later adopted as standard also for black and white films, which was combined with the use of the viewing glass.

During the early days of three-strip Technicolor system an experimental light meter

First exposure meter used with the Technicolor process (*courtesy Archivo Nacional de la Imagen, Sodre*).

was used. Its shape was cylindrical, about 5 in. long by 2.5 in. diameter with a Newton viewer on top in order to frame the covered field, and reading on the back. Technicolor later developed its own photometer to standardize the readings. It was of rugged construction with a rotary round upper unit to collect the incident light and a square base with a large galvanometer window for easy reading. For black and white films the exposure meters used in the studios were Weston and General Electric, two reflected type instruments that preceded Capt. Don Norwood's innovation with his professional incident light meter, developed during the last days of that decade.

Nearing the end of the thirties Mole & Richardson and Bardwell McAllister produced motion picture lighting equipment in Hollywood. In the United Kingdom it was the M&R subsidiary and the General Electric Co. In France Lebarden and the recently established Cremer were the most used. In Germany Arnold & Richter, Wiennert and Efa-Jupiter were the best-known makes. Italy had a preference for the lighting equipment manufactured by Ing. Marcucci and the well designed lighting units of Dante Rispoli. But when it was necessary anywhere to use the Technicolor system, this firm demanded the Mole & Richardson instruments that were the only ones that complied with their requirements.

## The classic Hollywood lighting

Consequently, one may conclude that during this period the basic principles were defined as what was later called "the classic Hollywood lighting." And this was also adopted by other important production studios all over the world. It made the image more attractive, it gave an embossed sensation and better definition, separating the image from the screen. The adopted methods were considered the principles of the chiaroscuro system which directors of photography had learned from the great classic painters.

The robust Weston exposure meter of the thirties (courtesy *Museo de la Fotografía y el Cine Oscar Mendoza*).

Color meters were also used in motion picture color photography. Here we see the advanced German Gossen temperature meter and filter indicator (*courtesy P. Gossen & Co.*).

As seen above, the basic scheme was the use of light sources formed with Fresnel lens spots placed above the sets with barn doors to control the beams and diffusers to adjust the light quality; an intense directional source called key light was adopted to determine the natural origin and direction of the main light. A secondary light called fill light with an open beam was resorted to for softening the shadows and adjusting contrast. A back light, i.e., a light from behind the subject, was also applied to separate the players from the background and make other outlines stand out. Also a light source was used close to the camera to control lighting on the faces without producing shadows, for use with a mobile camera and controlling the intensity according to the actors' movements on the set.

As in the past, lighting the actors independently from the lighting on the set was continued. For the latter, artifacts were devised to produce light patterns on flat surfaces, seeking a tangent light to produce effects on arches, columns, curved surfaces and basrelief. There was a tendency to create sfumato penumbras on the upper parts of walls to contrast close-ups of the players against them. The players were lighted very carefully so that they should always look their best, but allowing the light to play on them in intensely dramatic situations. If we examine films such as *It Happened One Night* (1934), photographed by Joseph Walker, or other similar comedies of that period, we see how scrupulously some cinematographers used lighting with these methods, both on actors and settings. During those years these techniques were standard, applied to black and white, and with small variations, to color cinematography.

## The German influence

At the same time as this trend towards perfection in photography, a series of "black" thriller films appeared in Hollywood in which needed an adequate photographic treatment to create the necessary atmosphere. In search of dramatic and realistic effects, a trenchant photography was applied, using low-key lighting intensely, as well as crosslights and backlights, using hard arc lights, applying broken light-and-shadows beams, and reducing (or even doing without) fill lights. Thus, many photography directors took inspiration from the impressionist techniques which had brought fame to German cinematography.

Towards the end of the decade, German lighting techniques were influencing cinematography in nearby European countries, such as Hungary, Austria and Czechoslovakia. But they were also strongly influencing British cinematographers since the end of the twenties, when renowned directors of photography from UFA such as Werner Brandes, Gunther Krapf, Carl Freund, Curt Courant, Mutz Greenbaum, Eugen Schüfftan, Fritz Arno Warner or qualified technicians such us Erwing Hillier, were engaged for good level productions in Britain.

British filmmaking was also reinforced by other continental Europeans who had been taught in that style: Jan Stallich, Franz Planer, Otto Heller and Otto Kanturek from Czechoslovakia, and the Austrian Wolfgang Suschitzky, who embarked in documentary filmmaking. Some were transitory while others were permanent. They were not all generous with teaching their knowhow to their British colleagues supporting them, but their trade techniques and secrets were absorbed by that keen generation of British cinematographers; in few years this was evinced with a series of British films the photography of which reached its splendor; we shall analyze some such productions further below.

Although the influence of German filmmakers also reached France (e.g., Eugene Schüfftan, with whom we shall deal later) the lighting style with dramatic contrasts was not taken up so definitely, because the French school was more clearly defined and the prevailing taste preferred filtered hard beams and attenuating intense shadows.

On the other hand, in Spain the photographic school was being formed and they also received the German impressionist influence. During that decade Hans Scheib, Wilhem Goldberger, Ted Pahle, and specially the Austrian Heinrich Gaertner (who afterwards "Spanishified" his name to Enrique Guerner) came to Spain and worked there, leaving their mark on Spanish directors of photography who applied the work methods and techniques of these masters, and who afterwards became well known in the trade.[5]

# 23. Advances in Special Effects

Film production with special effects showed improved characteristics during this period. Technologic developments were a great help and images were treated in the laboratory or in special effects department more frequently than with previous production methods. The experience gained with the use and treatment of material to obtain duplicates began to bear fruit.

## The optical printer

The optical printer, born during the last years of the twenties, allowed an extended range of possibilities in a primitive form; they were better controlled and cheaper than having to do the tricks with the camera while shooting. In the United States the studios themselves built the equipment for this purpose during those years, usually in their own special effects departments. Most of the time they were built on lathe beds supporting a projector with a special intermittent mechanism with pilot pins and a Mitchell camera facing it. Camera and projector were mechanically interconnected and aligned on a common axis, with the possibility of obtaining lateral or up-and-down off-center positions for both instruments.

The projector had a variable-intensity adjustable light source. The camera had an optical unit on its front that allowed inserting filters, masks or mattes, prisms or devices to obtain different effects. The whole arrangement was six feet long and its controls were distributed everywhere, both on the left and the right side and at each end of the instrument. Designs varied according to the mechanic that built them, and to the technicians that conceived and operated them. One of the most sophisticated optical printers, remarkable for the abilities that it provided, was the instrument built by the camera effects department of RKO, where the specialist Vernon Walker, head of the department, worked with Linwood G. Dunn, an outstanding expert in this field.

While that was going on in the United States, special effects in Europe were made in the laboratory using the Truca, an ingenious and pioneering item of equipment built by the André Debrie firm, designed to cover the needs of studios and laboratories in their world wide market. This instrument was built on similar principles, but was much larger than those built in Hollywood. Its body occupied a large part of the room and was eleven feet long. Its base was a unique piece with a cast worm gear that allowed the unit to be moved forward or backwards longitudinally. It comprised the following:

a. base for longitudinal displacement and another for cross-wise motion;

b. a mobile step printer with guides and film gate with the possibility of passing one or two films at the same time, as well as closed compartment for rolls of up to 1,200 ft.;

c. a mobile lamp unit with a micrometric filament-centering device;

d. an automatic light changing device;

e. a step printer to be used as a motion picture camera;

f. a shutter with an automatic mechanism for obtaining fades and dissolves;

g. a unit with all lenses required and with adjustable or automatic focus and a device for holding mattes;

h. a 250mm basic cine lens, and;

i. a device to print the sound track.

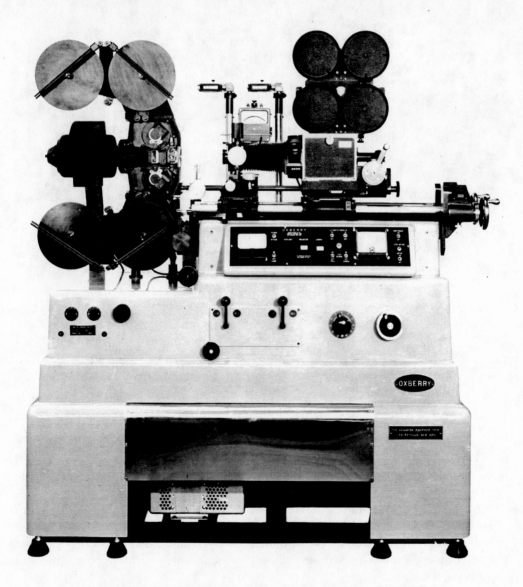

**Optical printer of American design (*courtesy Berkey Technical*).**

Truca: French optical printer made by André Debrie (*courtesy André Debrie Matériel Cinématographique*).

The Debrie Truca had most of its controls placed as a single unit on one end of the unit. Its simplest use was to act as a printer and make the transitional effects that some time before were made in the camera or by chemical methods in the laboratory.[1]

As the technicians acquired confidence in the use of the equipment, they realized that other possible uses could be applied for different purposes. But they were not the only ones to become aware of that; directors and producers also did, and they gave those departments the task of solving problems that were difficult or impossible to achieve during the actual shooting of the film.

Linwood Dunn was one of the most famous specialists in this field. He was born in

New York and had been taught his craft in the camera crews of the Pathé Studios. He went to California with that firm, working in Hollywood in serials for them, and in 13 full-length feature films in different specialities until he reached the position of director of photography. In 1928 the RKO studios called him to be part of the special effects team, where he initially made matte paintings until he became a master in handling the optical printer. With this instrument he learned how to overcome difficulties unsolved during the actual shooting, and began to experiment with a doctoring process. Thus he began to learn the intricacies of duplicating emulsions, the adequate form to print and process them, the way of getting even results with different materials, densities, contrasts, grain level of the emulsions, etc.

His first work began with a short film named *This Is Harris*, followed by *Melody Cruise* (1933) and *Flying Down to Rio* (1933), where he added many effects that gave new life to the form of presenting images or of combining them. The opportunity came almost immediately to make more complex effects such as the ones he achieved for the film *Ace of Aces* (1933), where he applied a rapid dissolve to hasten the fire bursting in a crashed plane, eliminating the part where the pilot is seen bailing out; thus dramatizing the scene, making it unnecessary to repeat the take, and eliminating the risk.

In *Flaming Gold* (1934), Dunn eliminated a sign on a tank truck crossing a scene that should have been taken out before shooting. To achieve this, he retouched the scene placing a crayon mark on a glass that he positioned in front of the printer gate to make the text illegible. Among his most remarkable achievements at that time were the combination of takes he made with the optical printer, that were shot independently in the studio or with an animation process, for the film *King Kong* (1933). In order to overcome the problems for the film *Bringing Up Baby* (1937) where Katherine Hepburn and Cary Grant had to act with a leopard, to eliminate risk and make the shooting easier, Dunn used the split screen and travelling matte techniques to combine the animal with the human figures. The solutions he applied for filming *The Hunchback of Notre Dame* (1939) were also important, combining rear projection takes, stop motion and scale models.[2]

## Rear projection

Another technical resource used at that time was the rear projection. It began with the silent cinema itself, but without adequate results because the technical implements were not then fully developed. Rear projection required a projector with a high intensity light and a movement with claw and register pins and a translucent screen of very special characteristics. It had to be provided with a camera with register pins and shutter synchronized with those of the projector in order to operate simultaneously.

As with the optical printer the studios themselves built these items of equipment, based on the designs by special effects technicians. One of the pioneer studios in developing a specific unit for this type of work was Paramount; it had created its transparency department, headed by Farciot Edouart, a Californian who had joined the industry in 1915 as an assistant cameraman in a producing unit that later on merged into the Paramount group. After an active career during World War I as a cameraman in the Red Cross Motion Picture Service, Edouart returned to Paramount to work in trick cinematography, especially in glass shots and composite scenes, which led naturally at the beginning of the thirties towards the new rear projection technique when the technical means became available.[3]

The possibilities of the rear projection process appealed to the studios when a high speed negative became available, adequate to print an image projected on a translucent screen, satisfactorily and with proper latitude. Using Mitchell or Bell & Howell movements the problems of image stability in the projector had to be solved; this demanded perfect synchronization between camera and projector, as well as a high intensity light. Solutions also had to be found to several problems: the quality of the translucent screen so that it would not lose definition in the projected image, the various methods to overcome the hot spot problem produced in the center of the screen, the elimination of grain in the projected images, and the need to widen the rear projection to suit shooting demands.

One by one all these problems were solved, at first individually, and later on with the participation of the Academy of Motion Picture Arts and Sciences Research Council in

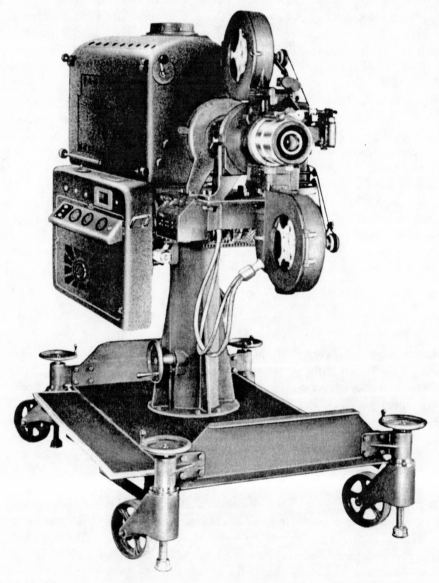

Mitchell background projector (*courtesy Mitchell Camera Corp.*).

Hollywood. This originated unified criteria, and firms such as Mitchell, Technicolor, Mole & Richardson, Bausch & Lomb, National Carbon Company, Bell & Howell, etc., were to develop adequate techniques for this process, which the studios wanted to keep concealed as it was economically very important for their productions.[4]

The requirements to use intermittent film drive in the projectors of the two most famous camera brands led to the use of the same film transport mechanism in both items of equipment. The standard camera for shooting films was the Mitchell, used in most of the studios; the exception was Twentieth Century Fox, which as seen above developed their own studio camera with devices to control rear projection effects and their own transparency projector using the same film transport movement as their camera.

Technicolor participated in solving the problem arising from the low speed of color film. They developed an efficient system involving three projectors with a beam combiner to increase light intensity considerably in special situations, or when the screen dimensions were larger. Bausch & Lomb participated in perfecting the projection lens. National Carbon Company and Mole & Richardson collaborated in the design of more efficient arc sources in the lighting equipment for Technicolor. Different materials were experimented with for translucent screens, using ground glass, cellulose, cellulose acetate, ethyl cellulose, as well as different screen thicknesses so that the center would be thicker than the edges, to even the brightness of the image and overcome the hot spot problem. For this last difficulty other methods were tried such as including a filter made from the photograph of the screen that it reproduced.

The grain in the projected image was minimized by selecting the adequate fine grain raw stock negatives such as Eastman Background Panchromatic Negative 1213, used on the plates, or by processing it, or using screens with vibrators at 60 r.p.m.[5] Many of these investigations obtained good results, such as the Mitchell projectors, and special screens with very low internal reflection.

The rear projection method had an extraordinary influence on cinematography and was widely used in Hollywood in most of the films and soon became standard in many European studios. After it was introduced, its application doubled every year; some studios used this method with mobile equipment taken to the set where the film was shot; in other studios there was a special stage to achieve this type of shooting.

The most common use was for backgrounds to be seen through windows in cars or other vehicles, and therefore it was quite common to have available mock-ups of the interiors of those vehicles with apertures allowing a comfortable placement of the camera, a moving base to install them so as to simulate their motion, and a remote control on the driving wheel handled from out of the camera's range, since the player could not see the projected background in order to move the driving wheel according to the road he was supposedly following.

The lighting of these scenes was placed in the hands of an effects specialist who, acting as a second unit, carefully supervised the execution of the effect, taking care to obtain the correct lighting continuity of the background plates consistent with the light applied on the set, the appropriate lighting on the players to enhance the realism of the scene as well as eliminating any unwanted light source that could mar the cleanliness of the effect.

## Dunning process

Although special effects systems making use of the optical printer or the rear projection system were the most often used, some systems from the past such as the Dunning process continued to be used too. For example, in *Trader Horn* (1931) scenes with images really obtained in the jungle were masterfully combined with takes shot in the studio. This process was also used in the RKO film *The Most Dangerous Game* (1932), as well as in *Tarzan the Ape Man* (1932), the first of a series that MGM studios would make, in circumstances in which the rear projection method was not good enough; in this latter film the Williams travelling mate was also applied, an old but still effective resource.[6]

In Europe the Dunning process was adopted for the first time in France for the film *La Chance Pourtante* (1931) and in Germany in *Das Testament das Doktor Mabuse* (*The Testament of Doctor Mabuse*, 1934). In spite of not using the whole method, some variations of the Dunning process were applied in the first American sound version of *Dr. Jekyll and Mr. Hyde* (1932), in which the star, Fredric March, photographed under blue light, was the noble Dr. Jekyll, and when he was lighted with a red source his face was transformed and the special make-up appeared turning him into the terrible Mr. Hyde. The film's cinematographer Karl Struss, repeated here the effect he had used in the film *Ben-Hur* for the miraculous recovery of the leading actor's mother and sister.

The Dunning process was also used by MGM in 1934 while shooting *Mutiny on the Bounty* (1935). In one scene it was necessary to show a wild storm crashing the ship against the rocks. A small boat was seen hanging from its mooring over the side. It was first decided to shoot the scene during a real storm and everybody waited for one to arrive. The result was catastrophic since the desired result was not obtained and a life was lost. The solution was obtained afterwards recreating the effect in the studio by means of a large hydraulic crane and gimbals shaking the boat that displaced and smashed the scale model of the *Pandora* ship that suffered the disaster. All this was done under an amber light that covered the whole scene while a large screen was placed in the background lighted with a blue source. Charles Laughton, who played the *Bounty*'s martinet captain, remembered the contrast between the first attempt at shooting the scene with the last one when he did not even get wet, and his surprise on seeing the film that he could not recall which scenes had been shot at the studio and which were filmed at sea.

## Other special effects

An important landmark in the history of special effects was *King Kong* (1933), a film made in Hollywood by the famous Ernest B. Shoedsack and Merian C. Cooper, producers who had previously made the documentary *Grass* (1925). This new film made for RKO included a varied galley of cinematographic effects such as the travelling matte, using a version improved by Williams himself, that used a double matting system and colored backings, sets lying flat on the ground with forced perspective, to represent King Kong climbing the Empire State Building and novel sound effects such as recording a lion's roar at half speed and reproducing it backwards to obtain the cries of the great gorilla. These varied tricks were cleanly assembled and combined by the imaginative contribution of its directors, and fundamentally of an outstanding specialist named Willis Harold O'Brien.

O'Brien was born in Oakland, California, in 1886. In his youth he worked as cowboy, draftsman, sculptor, cameraman, director and soon became an expert in animation. He began making several films on his own with animated figures; these he quickly sold bringing him into the industry at the head of a firm specializing in this field. In 1925 he made a film that brought him great prestige, *The Lost World*. His capacity in this field made RKO summon him for *King Kong,* together with Marcel Delgado, an eminent sculptor with whom he had experimented with different techniques for building scale models. Sidney Saunders, who developed a new translucent screen for rear projection, joined the team, as well as Linwood Dunn for the work on the optical printer.[7]

O'Brien applied on his patented method on the Saunders screen to eliminate grain from the emulsion by vibrating the screen. With these innovations, these various experiments, the imaginative flight and drive of the film makers, this production received the support of outstanding artists such as Mario Larrinaga and the work of numerous cinematographers such as Edwing G. Linden, Vernon L. Walker, J.O. Taylor, Bert Willis, Clarence Slifer, Kenneth Peach, Harold Wellman, William Clothier and Bill Reinhold. Thus *King Kong* became a successful technical and commercial effort that left a mark on filmmaking for many years; such was its success that it prompted a sequel: *The Son of King Kong* (1933), in which this vast technical staff repeated their refined techniques, but the resulting film was not as commercially successful as the original.

Besides the special effects we have mentioned so far (optical printing, rear projection, Dunning system and Williams travelling mate) other processes were also added in Europe at that time. Some, like the Schüfftan, were based on gadgets to be placed in front of the camera so as to combine different shots while shooting a take. Thus, in 1938, in France, director Abel Gance together with the manufacturer of optical products Pierre Angenieux, patented a system to "perfect optical devices for photography"; they called it Pictographe. That device allowed, without any adjustments, a simultaneous focus on a subject from the infinite, advancing towards the camera, up to a large close up. In fact, the principle of this device was the same one that allowed an effect known as panfocus, by interposing a subdivided lens halfway in front of another lens focused on infinity.

This would not merit a special mention when dealing with special effects if it were not that Achille Dufour and Henri Mahé, also in France, developed the Simplifilm based on the principles of the Pictographe. It was an oblong metallic coffer shaped unit, measuring $4 \times 1\frac{1}{2} \times 1$ ft. and weighing 120 pounds, with a large opening on one side, another at the rear and another in front. An internal optical system formed by several compensating lenses allowed combining a photograph measuring $18 \times 24$ cm, conveniently cut, and inserted with living subjects and sets placed in the needed perspective. The photograph should be adequately illuminated.

The system made it possible to integrate subjects in motion with photographs of building, landscapes, etc. and also allowed camera displacement in travelling takes or with a panoramic effect from a moving platform, unifying both items. A special viewfinder built into the body allowed regulating the camera, the photo and the live subjects. The instrument was usually placed in front of the camera supported by a rolling tripod or a special support. Internal lights illuminated the photograph.

Although it was not internationally adopted, the Simplifilm was an interesting variation applied during several years to reduce costs in low budget productions and provided a rapid solution, as the Schüfftan process had in its time. Although its application in France was limited, it lasted for more than three decades, being used even by television.

Film productions with special effects were very frequent at that time and by several means. In the horror film line, Universal studios had already been very successful with *Dracula* (1931), a film photographed by the famous Karl Freund, with amazing images and photographic effects by Frank J. Booth. The latter was an expert who had obtained realistic effects for Universal Studios with a large scale model of New York covering a whole stage, which was shot in Technicolor for the film *Broadway* (1929). He had also produced excellent effects for the film *All Quiet on the Western Front* (1930), with shots that included optical work and matte shots. In *Dracula*, the initial takes of the film with the car moving along the gloomy road towards Count Dracula's castle and the view of that stronghold on the top of the hill, as well as several glass shots inside the castle, were part of his contribution.

After *Dracula*, Universal continued to produce horror films, bringing out their famous *Frankenstein* (1931), directed with great care by James Whales and photographed by Arthur Edeson. In this film the special effects were by John P. Fulton, a specialist in this field who had recently been brought to Universal as head of the special effects department.

Fulton, the son of a painter, had graduated as an electrical engineer and worked for the Edison Company. At the beginning of the previous decade he had worked with Hollywood camera teams climbing step by step on the pyramid. But he specialized in special effects with Frank Williams in the latter's independent firm where Williams applied his well known process. For Universal, Fulton had already participated in *The Michigan Kid* (1929) and in *She Goes to War* (1929). In *Frankenstein* Fulton did an excellent job with the scenes at the mill, using a set at real scale combined with a scale model, and using the Williams travelling mate to insert the two leading players on top of the wooden mill at the film's climax.[8]

Another variation in special effects was a fantasy carried to its utmost. Such was the case of another Universal production, *The Invisible Man* (1933) also directed by James Whales and photographed by Arthur Edeson. Once more John Fulton was in charge of special effects that were extremely complex and demanded a large number of retakes, thousands of feet of film in different shots to achieve the wanted effects, and 64.000 frames that had to be retouched by hand. Here ingenuity was combined with mastery in special effects and imagination to solve the problems one by one as they appeared. The Dunning system and the Williams process were applied to the gun held by the invisible man and the audience sees the weapon hovering through the room seemingly unsupported. To shoot this scene the player, wholly dressed in black velvet, had to walk in a room fully covered with black velvet from ceiling to floor.

Of the many special effects used in the production, multiple exposure takes were made, objects were handled from afar, such as, for example, a bicycle held by invisible wires to make it roll down the street on a stage, and reversing the film drive in the camera. Another was registering the invisible man's footsteps on the snow and his body's print when he falls down; this demanded that the terrain where the action would take place had to be prepared beforehand and adequately; the necessary holes were dug for the footsteps deeper than normal, to compensate for the snow that would fall in them. Lids covered with snow had to be placed over each hole and then, each lid was slid off, one by one, from afar, so that the snow covering it would fall down the hole, thus simulating each footstep.

Shooting the scene in which the invisible man, standing in front of a the mirror, looks at his bandaged face and begins to remove the bandage became more complex. This shot meant making several separate takes to be joined by a travelling matte. But it involved hard work with extreme accuracy in the details and in general, and in the many repetitions up to 20 retakes of each shot were needed.

The most spectacular shot of the film was undoubtedly the invisible man's death. First we see the bed with depressions of the body on the pillow and the white sheet, an as the effects of the invisibility drug disappear, we see the skeleton beginning to show up, then the flesh covering it and finally the full body. Fulton achieved the effect directly on camera: a plaster pillow, the sheets and covers made of papier maché using several slow lap-dissolves between which he inserted a real skeleton and dolls that showed the materialization of the actor until finally the real player is placed on scene where he says his last lines, and the camera tracks back.[9]

In this film and others of this series of invisible men, Fulton showed his determination to obtain perfect results and proved his capacity to achieve it, besides a high imagination to find the best solutions for each case. In this series each new title brought new challenges that Fulton overcame efficiently, greatly striking the audiences of that time.

Other films with many special effects were those in which ghosts were the subject and were mostly comedies, such as *Topper* (1937) and its follow-ups, undertaken by Fulton in the field of special effects by using the black backing travelling mattes and the imaginative use of wires.

In the subject of aviation, Fulton himself applied special effects early in that decade for Universal studios for the film *Air Mail* (1932). He took the background plates himself with the advantage that flying was his hobby and using his own airplane. Fulton took care also in designing and moving scale models that were shot at a speed close to 200 frames per second. John Ford, who later became famous, directed this film. Fulton and Ford enjoyed making this film and were delighted that the film was recognized for the high quality achieved, especially for the perfect job done with the scale models.[10]

In the fantastic field, a production that called attention was *The Cyclops* (1940), another film by Ernest Schoedsack where many different special effects were combined such as multiple exposures, glass shots, split screen, rear projection and several sets and props in grand scale as well as the artificial reproduction of human parts in large dimensions (a hand made of latex), all this done with great care and attention to detail to accentuate realism. In shooting this film, a technique was used that until then had been used only in animated cartoons and war training films, that is, a script with a careful storyboard drawn shot by shot, a method that is routine today in commercials and complex productions.

The films with special effects became favorites in Hollywood, where many of the above described systems were born, but they also became favorites in several European countries during that time. Alexander Korda, the famous British producer, with great showmanship took the spectacular films concept to his adopted country; the productions he would make needed many of the new technologies of this field. For this he brought several specialists from Hollywood and took advantage of outstanding English actors. He applied glass shots in his films, increasing the production values of several outstanding films. He even retained the best technicians from Germany and France. For this reason the British film industry, with its new studios and its technical renewal, had an unusual impulse in this specialized field that showed off in films such as *Things to Come* (1936), *The Ghost Goes West* (1936) or in great films like *The Four Feathers* (1939). From that moment on Britain became the spearhead in high technology in this field, followed by Germany, which was losing ground in this field due to the emigration of their experts, as a result of the Nazi regime and the war, and by France which was also affected by the political events at that time.

# 24. New Color Systems

During the thirties color cinematography continued advancing and improving. One reason was development in this area by two of the most important manufacturers of raw stock film: Kodak and Agfa. Their contributions were very important to produce an adequate color film to their own requirements and to provide the required raw stock material to other color systems. On the other hand companies founded to develop color methods for motion pictures invested large amounts in research and equipment and at least one of them saw their method adopted as the standard for color pictures by Hollywood big studios and in the U.K. In the same way, small firms or independent inventors also cropped up who strove to develop their methods, though many of them were not successful in being adopted by the industry or applied in any long feature film. However, it can be said that during that period the number of color films produced was larger than in the previous decade. Let us review the most outstanding characteristics of each color system.

## Agfacolor

The principles of the Agfacolor system started with research done in Germany by B. Homolka in 1907, continued later by Rudolph Fischer, and followed by Wilhelm Schneider of Agfa, in 1932. All three were concerned with the discovery of dyes, their application in photographic emulsions and how to develop them. This research defined concepts of color couples and their improvements as procedures for primary color development and secondary color development. It was a vast and complex research work that took a long time and required patenting methods and techniques, reaching procedures to be applied to sensitive emulsions, developing systems and printing and control procedures. This arduous work resulted in a method of three-color couples incorporated in each one of the sensitive layers of the film, and also as a correct developer that would simultaneously form the correspondent dye.[1]

In 1936 the Agfa organization introduced the Agfacolor Reversal film, in 1939 the Agfacolor negative film, and finally in 1940 the Agfacolor New negative film, with a sensibility four times that of the former. The Agfacolor reversal was designed for domestic use in the 16mm and 8mm film gauges. The Agfa color negative manufactured in the 35mm gauge was the first important option that professional cinematography had to rely on: an adequate, good level material to shoot all kinds of films without the need for high investments or special camera rental and also affording a large number of prints to facilitate its distribution.

Unfortunately, the war limited the use only to Germany. It was only after the Allied occupation of Germany that this system was better known outside Germany.

The first Agfacolor long feature film was an UFA studios production: *Frauen Sind Doch bessere Diplomatten* (1940) directed by Georg Jacoby.[2] All studios were under the control of German Propaganda Ministry; the minister was the Nazi Dr. Josef Goebbels who wanted all new feature films produced in Germany to be in color. But the Agfa organization was doubtful that this system had reached the desired level.

The Agfacolor system was based on a three-layer emulsion negative with a filter. The film support was nitrate cellulose, 130–140 microns thick. The 2–3 microns thick antihalation back coating was applied to the outer face of the support and was a green dyed synthetic resin. A 6-micron emulsion to print the red and produce the cyan was layered over the inner support face. A 6-micron green layer to form magenta followed this. Finally a 2-micron thin colloidal layer acted as a yellow filter to absorb the blue light of the emulsion of the outer layer emulsion for producing yellow. The positive and the negative raw stock of the Agfacolor had similarly thick base, but the positive was manufactured in cellulose acetate. The negative was available with two kinds of emulsions: B and G. The first had a speed of about 8 Weston and was destined for shooting outdoors. The G emulsion, with a 12 Weston speed, was conceived for studio shooting with tungsten lighting.[3]

The Agfacolor was developed in standard continuous processing machines, but adopted to the requirements of the several bath solutions demanded by this system, and with certain devices to produce a long washing bath by adopting spray nozzles and a spray curtain, because very efficient washing and complete sulphite removal were essential. The steps of negative developing were: a) color development, b) spray wash, c) bleaching, d) spray wash, e) fixing and f) spray wash. The developing of the positive was more complex: with seven steps to the dye sound track and ten to the silver track. Each bath required a constant 18 degree temperature and continuous control of all solutions. The printing was made with Debrie printers using light controls through holes and correcting filters on a paper strip.

Agfacolor was the first improvement towards a professional monopack motion picture color system conceived by a manufacturer of raw stock film and not a method devised to be rented by a producer, with a complex structure, requiring the use of special cameras. The war limited its expansion outside Germany and occupied countries but after its end, the monopack method was adopted by some manufacturers. Agfacolor arrived in the United States during the war with the UFA production *Die Frau meiner Traume* (1943–44), directed by Georg Jacoby and cinematography by Tschet, where it was studied by Hollywood and SMPE experts to control its quality.

The opinion was that the image quality was good according to grain and sharpness but the color level was inferior to the Technicolor system in tint and saturation. Another Afgacolor production to reach the USA was *Baron Münchausen* (1942–43), directed by Josef von Báky and cinematography by Krien, a film that included several special effects and was a good example of the adaptability of this color system for such purposes.

## Bassani process

This was a French color system conceived in 1933 and promoted by the Société Chromofilm de Paris. It was based on a three color additive method with three images obtained by means of a special camera provided with an ingenious mechanical device that allowed moving the film gate behind the lens so as to obtain three exposures inside a standard frame. The frame speed was of 72 f.p.s. The projection method was very complex and required three unified lenses. The result was good but this method was not easily standardized and the sizes of the images obtained were similar to those of 16mm, consequently this color system did not prosper.[4]

## Cinecolor

In the thirties two firms came out with similar names but using different motion picture color systems. One was established in England and was named Cinecolor Ltd. The other was an American company called Cinecolor Corporation. Let us see the characteristics of each.

Cinecolor Ltd. of London used an additive system of color cinematography based on a series of patents by pioneers and optical experts on this field; among them were Samuel Cox, D. Daponte, Adam Hilger Ltd., and J.H. Dowell. The firm began about 1929, went through several ups and downs and was taken over by Dufay Chromex Ltd., an important English company directed by Jack Coote FRPS, a world authority in this field. The basic patents dated from 1930 and 1932 and were connected with the works of the above mentioned experts regarding the optical devices to make the images useful and make their projection possible.

This system used a camera with two lenses and a complex prism system so that the two images, 8 × 12mm in size, were laterally rotated sideways and placed in a standard 35mm film frame. In a later improvement the two images were included in a centered position of the frame. The shooting was made with a Vinten camera with an optical unit with two lenses and an optical device in its front. For projection, it was necessary to adapt another optical unit in front of the projector lens; the unit comprised two lenses combined with prisms and color filters and also a mobile device to unify both images on the screen. This device could be adapted also for a black and white projection, which was standard in those years. This color system was adopted in some experimental films but it was not commercially successful because there were limited possibilities for standardizing the additive method.[5]

The system of the American Cinecolor Corp. of Burbank, California, was completely different from the British method and had good acceptance. It was a subtractive two-color method but also three-color prints were made. Its fundamental principle was the well known Pritzma color but it also used many other procedures; it adopted the bipack technique in the camera, thanks to the help of the Dupont firm which provided a special positive raw stock, later named Dupack.

This enterprise started in 1932 encouraged by William Crespinel, an American cine color pioneer who had participated in the Multicolor system. This latter firm was transformed into Cinecolor and reorganized. The bipack system was easy to use and required a camera with an adapted film gate and a special magazine. Two negatives passed through the film channel with the emulsion side of each facing each other. Consequently the lens focus had to be adjusted. The negative close to the lens was orthochromatic (Eastman bipack type 1236) and registered the blue-green images. Its film support was red dyed to act as a red filter 23 A. The negative behind the orthochromatic was of the panchromatic type (Eastman bipack type 1235 pan) and registered the other spectrum colors of the image.

The bipack cameras were Mitchell NC, to which Cinecolor incorporated a patented four roller pressure plate with an adjusting screw, and eliminated the breathing effect of the two films in close contact. A double magazine was also required where the two films were in contact. During the processing both negatives were printed on a double emulsion positive film (Eastman type 5509 Duplitized) to produce a Prussian blue on one face. Cinecolor was characterized by its simple working system, and was not limited to only one firm for film processing because several laboratories could process it. It was only 25 percent more expensive than the black and white, and the dailies were available 24 hours after the shooting. In 1940 the first long feature film was made with this color method and later on there were many film productions in Hollywood until 1955.[6]

In 1939 the Cinecolor Corp. developed Cinecolor 16 to produce prints in this format by this method using a special machine by which two 16mm strips were obtained by the double sixteen procedure. Mr. M.Gundelfinger and Mr. J. Smith conceived this new development which included several steps, such as printing by optical reduction, sound strip application and special perforating process. Kodachrome film was required for these prints.

## Cosmocolor

It was developed by the American Cosmocolor Corporation around 1937, based on an invention conceived by Otto C. Gilmore. It consisted of a two-color system and used a camera equipped with a complex device of a beam splitter prism with two images uppermost. Optical prints with a double coated dyed positive were obtained from the negative. The RKO studios participated in research for this system, but it did not succeed.

## Chemicolor

This French color system started in Paris in 1931 and was a three-color subtractive method. It was developed by the Syndicat de la Cinématographie des Coulers on the basis of M. Leon Diddier's Pinatype procedure and contributions of other French specialists like Mr. Ploquin, Mr. Thiengard and Mr. R. Valete. A three strip advanced camera was made and also a special optical printer that included a pilot pin to be used with positive double coated bichromatized gelatine raw stock. Other methods were experimented with such as three successive takes with the same film and the adoption of a three-layer negative or the use of subtractive methods as Kodachrome and Kodacolor. During this decade the search was slow without satisfactory results and the work ended in shooting film cartoons. After France was invaded in 1940 no financial resources were found and research was halted.

## Francita process

Around 1934, the French Société des Films en Couleurs Naturelles Francita developed a three-color additive system conceived by M. Maurice Velle. The method required using a special camera with two lenses; behind them two mirrors were placed at 45 degrees; sending two 8 × 12mm images, above and below the film frame center. The film was then displaced by a half frame to place a third image in the empty space. A filter disc rotated synchronized so that in the first operation the images were affected, one by the red filter and the other by the green filter; in the second operation a blue filter affected the image. The operation speed was 48 f.p.s.

The projecting method used three lenses to unify the three images cast through their corresponding filters to be superimposed on the screen afterwards. This complex system was later improved by changing the disposition of the images inside the film frame, suppressing the mirror optical system that produced inconvenient parallax. Later on, when this firm used M. Gutmann and Pierre Angenieux patents, important changes were added to this color system. In 1935 a long feature was shown in Paris with the Francita process that allowed analyzing the possibilities and limitations of this system against the increasing development of the subtractive method. In Britain this color system was named Opticolor, but there was no relation with the lenticular process created in Germany.[7]

## Dufaychrome process

Dufaychrome was a color method developed by Mr. Jack Coote through Dufay-Chromex Ltd., London. The system used a three-strip camera with a beam splitter prism of very similar characteristics with the design of the Technicolor camera. The processing was identical to Agfacolor positive. The printing required a complex treatment with several printing stages and two resensitized steps.[8]

## Dufaycolor process

During the thirties the Dufaycolor process increasingly evolved and remained as the only micro-color screen of practical use. In 1934 this process was developed for the 16mm market by Ilford Ltd. It had a satisfactory acceptance in several European countries and in the Commonwealth. That year the film *Radio Parade of 1935* included a sequence filmed in Dufaycolor. Arthur Woods directed the film produced by British International and the cinematographer was Claude Friese-Greene. This production was shot with reversible raw stock and the prints were also in reversible film.

In 1935 several short films were also made in England with this system, produced by the British Movietone News. One year later it was possible to use the negative-positive system after the creation of a new developing process by Dr. D.A. Spencer that overcame the difficulties of the mosaic system. Other films followed these productions that showed the advances attained, including that of the crowning of King George VI, produced by Dufay Chromex Ltd., and processed by Ilford Ltd. This film was an example of the color image quality of this system. Several other shorts were made, and processing laboratories were established in Surrey, England, and in other European cities like Paris, Geneva, Barcelona, and Rome, as well as Johannesburg and Bombay.

In 1937 another important improvement was made by changing the reseau or mosaic that affected the performance of the color hue and the capacity of the emulsion for using with tungsten light. Adequate printing equipment was specially made for this system by Vinten Ltd. and Lawley Apparatus Company in England and André Debrie in France. But this color system was not successful in the United States. The film *L'Ebbrezza del cielo* was produced in Italy; it was a black and white and color production using Dufaycolor, directed by

Georgio Ferroni and cinematography by Vincenzo Seratrice. The Dufaycolor process being a reticular process had particularly technical characteristics that had to be taken into account in many aspects while shooting. The image was formed in the camera after passing through the mosaic, which required recessing the focus plane of the film gate. Likewise the film emulsion characteristics demanded some adjustments in cameras like the Vinten, the Mitchell and the Bell & Howell Eyemo, to avoid scratching the emulsion surface. During the projection it was necessary to increase the projector light source because the mosaic of the print absorbed a considerable portion of the light. During the thirties Dufaycolor was a widely known process that left its mark and had many enthusiasts, especially in substandard gauges.[9]

## Gasparcolor

During the early thirties the Hungarian technician Bela Gaspar developed a subtractive color system based on three-layer film that incorporated dyes to be bleached during development. It was a considerable advance that came out before Kodachrome and Agfacolor appeared. In 1934 a company was formed in England with the name of Gasparcolor Ltd. with a laboratory directed by the expert Adrian Cornwell-Clyne to further the commercial expansion of this process. The difference between Gasparcolor and other systems that appeared later was that the dyes were destroyed after developing and were not formed during this process, as in other color methods.

The Gasparcolor used Gevaert positive film and this manufacture created an important research department. During World War II the firm went to the United States under the name of Gasparcolor Inc. Some time later the Gevaert research department closed down and the raw stock was produced in the USA. The Gasparcolor negative was available for two or three colors. The first had an emulsion on each face of the support. It was a reversible emulsion, adding blue dyes on one face and a combination of red and yellow dyes on the other. A pink layer sensitive to blue light made up the three color raw stock. On the other face of the support there was a sensitive blue emulsion. The developing was done in automatic machines with eleven processing steps. The printing was made by step printers and required pilot pins because it was a double coated film. The result obtained was excellent, but the powerful Hollywood competition in this field overcame the commercial capacities of this process.[10]

## Gualtierotti process

This Italian color system was developed by an engineer with this name and was a two-color additive process. It used a 64mm negative with two images with standard perforation on both sides and also in the center. After obtaining the negative in the laboratory process, an optical reduction print was obtained on a 35mm positive print with two images. During the projection an optical device was interposed in the projector facilities including two filters. Each one of the images was superimposed on the screen by this optical device. In an improved version, the filters were eliminated from the optical device and the print was toned in green and red. The result obtained was acceptable but the superimposition of the two images suffered with changes of the film support due to temperature and humidity.[11]

## Kodachrome

In 1935 the Eastman Color Co. introduced a color film on the market with this name, having excellent quality and chromatic values. It was a tripack film conceived as a subtractive reversal process. The new film was designed for 16 and 8mm use and was the result of experiments made in the Kodak Laboratories in Rochester, N.Y., by Leopold Godowsky and Leopold Mannes. The developing was complex and had to be done in those laboratories. The film support was made of cellulose butyrate covered by three emulsion layers. The first layer was sensitive to blue. Under the same was an interlayer with a green filter to stop the blue light. The second layer sensitive to green with another interlayer of gelatine. Finally there was the layer sensitive to red. The exposed face of the support was covered with an antihalation backing.

Kodachrome was based on the principle developed by the German professor Rudolf Fischer about the properties of the coupling developer that allowed dyestuffs to form images, obtained by oxidizing products in the developer. Consequently Kodachrome did not include color couples as other emulsions, but they came out in the primary and secondary color development. In 1940 Kodak adopted a new developing procedure that included an independent treatment of each layer, and consisted of eleven developing steps, during which the layers were processed to form a negative, and then they received a pre-exposure with red and white light and then treated in a magenta coupler developer.

The Kodachrome film was available in two types: Daylight, to be used with 6,100 degree K, or Type A designed for shooting indoors with tungsten light, 3,400 degrees K. The speed of the outdoor film was of 10 ASA outdoors and 4 ASA indoors, requiring a special filter and photoflood lights. The speed of the Kodachrome type A was of 16 ASA under tungsten light without filters, or 10 ASA if used outdoors with a correcting filter.

Kodachrome film had wide acceptance on world domestic markets and was also used for commercial productions using Kodachrome Duplicating Film to obtain the required prints. Likewise, it was used in long features as camera original in the 35mm format to obtain the release prints afterwards by the Technicolor imbibition process. The image quality of the 16mm format also allowed blowing up to 35mm. This color system was one of the great steps in the progress of color motion pictures and frequently used later for important Hollywood film productions.[12]

## Magnacolor

This was a color system based on the patents for Prizma Color that William Van Doren Kelly developed around 1932 for the Consolidated Film Laboratories of Hollywood. It was a bipack subtractive method that used a standard bipack camera and two layer printing stock with blue-toned and red-toned film faces. This system was abandoned when this important laboratory adopted the Trucolor process.

## Morgana

This was the name adopted in 1934 by the Bell & Howell Co. for its color system in the 16mm format. It used a two color additive method based on the principle of exposing

the panchromatic reversible film through a red and green-blue filter by means of an oscil-
lating device situated behind the camera lens. During the projection the film displacement
was made so that 72 film frames alternated in the projector gate because each film frame
was projected three times on the screen while a filter disc rotated behind the projecting lens
at the speed of 2,160 r.p.s.

## Roncarolo process

This color process was created by the Italian Emilio Roncarolo and used a subtractive
two or three color method. The camera was provided with an optical unit behind a device
with three taking lenses. The processing used the imbibition printing method. In 1935 the
film *Il Museo del Amore* was made with the Roncarolo color system. It was directed by Mario
Baffico with cinematography by G. Marchi.

## Spectracolor

This is the English name of the German UFA color system used in the U.K. in 1931.
It was a two color subtractive method. The shooting was with a bipack Vinten camera using
ortho and panchro negatives specially made by Agfa for this purpose. The printing was on
a double-coated negative toned red-orange on one film face and blue-green on the other.

## Technicolor

The world's most renowned color enterprise had a considerable growth during those
years where the "number four" system was adopted. Improvements were achieved after the
Depression when only 230 employees remained in this firm, from the original 1,200 when
the crisis started. During this period the first tripack camera was conceived and built between
1932–33, and the complex three color imbibition process system was adopted. This was possible thanks to the organization devised by Dr. Herbert Kalmus, to important investments
obtained, and to a vast body of high level researchers including L.T. Troland, E.A. Weaver,
B.S. Tuttle and J. F. Kienninger. The number 4 system was the adoption of the subtractive
method, the use of a three-strip camera, and the application of the three film imbibition
process.

The three strip Technicolor camera was designed by J A. Ball and built by the Mitchell
Camera Corporation at a cost of $25,000 per unit. It was one of the most refined and com-
plex camera units ever made in this field. The first unit was made in the above mentioned
years, and by 1936 twenty-three units had been made of the nearly thirty that were built, in
all. Four of them were designed for the British subsidiary, established in 1936, with processing machines also built in the United States.

The new Technicolor camera was conceived to take three 1000 ft. negative film rolls,
which passed through two film gates, placed at right angles to each other, one of which was
of the bipack type. Between them a beam splitter prism was placed, consisting of two half
prisms cemented at 45 degrees. This cemented surface was sprayed with gold to form a semi
reflecting mirror. The camera lens image was then divided in two, one which was reflected

at a right angle to the film gate which had a red filter in front, while the other went through the prism to the film gate behind the camera lens, with a green filter in front. The bipack gate was the one at right angle. By this method three black and white images were obtained with the print of the three primary colors which constituted the principle to later produce the basic gelatine relief positives to be used for printing.[13]

The particular design requirements of this camera were very difficult to achieve in practice due to the extreme precision of some parts and the necessity to include several optical devices. The prism and the camera lenses were the most complex and both were specially designed by Taylor, Taylor and Hobson of Leicester. Horace William Lee designed the required inverse telephoto lenses with different characteristics from the standard ones (especially those of short focal distance) in order to allow sufficient clearance so as to include an adequately sized prism between the back of the lens and the plane where image was formed. As this camera worked on the principles of color rays, the color had to be corrected on all optics; consequently the concepts of apochromatism were defined. This needed research of adequate optical components to produce a correct color light diffraction when passing through the different color filters in front of the film gates. Parsons Optical Glass Co., also of England, specially built those optical elements.

The intermittent movement of each of the two film gates required extreme precision, including register pins. The movement selected as well as the pressure plate of the bipack gate were those created by Mitchell for their NC cameras. The use of three films in the camera demanded that access to its body should be by means of two camera doors, to facilitate the complex threading of the film in the drive mechanism and clean the gates. The left hand side door to the gate where only one film was installed and also allowed access to the beam splitting prism. The right door was for threading the bipack gate. The prism was removable, and demanded a very firm and high precision installation, since the required image quality should not be altered by temperature changes or camera vibrations. The prism was one of the most valuable pieces of the camera.

The camera technicians at Technicolor were specially trained by the firm to work with this refined instrument and cover any eventuality. Every three days they had to load the camera with a specially marked brass film to ensure, through the viewfinder, that the prism position and registration was maintained. The prism could be removed from its position during the cleaning operation, and the camera assistant knew the methods for handling it precisely from long practice with a wooden prism of identical characteristics. However, he even knew how to react instinctively with his foot in the proper position, if the piece should slip from his hands. The camera threading with the three negatives was complex, but the technicians were to carry it out in three minutes, according to instructions issued by the firm.[14]

Other technical characteristics of this camera were its focusing and precise framing through the taking lens by means of a rack-over device complemented with a side monitoring viewfinder specially conceived for this instrument. The magazine was a big and heavy unit installed at the top. The initial model of this magazine was later improved. Only one interchangeable taking lens was installed; these were items of a series built by Taylor, Taylor & Hobson in the focal lengths of 25, 35, 40, 50, 70, 100 and 140mm with an aperture of f/2 and with a special mount. A sunshade, filter holder and matte holder were mounted at the front assembly also including the front sector of the side viewfinder. The camera drive was by means of interchangeable motors for different speeds or diverse supply requirements and also for reverse. The camera controls were situated on a side and on the back. As the camera was very noisy working with three films and two mechanisms, a big blimp was built which required special mounting heads, like the gear head built by Mole & Richardson for this end. With this blimp the Technicolor was the biggest camera used in the industry, weighing 200 lbs.

The excellent design of this camera in all its details and its modern and attractive looks with a light blue finish led to it being known as the Rolls Royce of professional cameras.[15] This piece of equipment later included several abilities, such as remote focus control operated by two Selsyn motors, which was very useful when the unit was on top of a crane. The tripack Technicolor cameras were built in several models (types C, D, E and F) to cover all kinds of requirements, for example, high speed and submarine cinematography. They were extremely well looked after by the technicians who were responsible for them, who had precise instructions to travel very close to them, keeping the unit in their own hotel rooms. These precautions were not only for the expensive cost of the unit, but to prevent industrial espionage, which the firm feared. However one of these cameras accidentally fell into a Pinewood water tank during World War II when shooting the documentary film *Western Approaches* (1944). When the tripack system was abandoned in the fifties, these cameras were adapted to the Vistavision and Technirama wide screen process. When Dr. Kalmus announced in 1938 that the life of the tripack shooting method would be short, he foresaw this change. However this expensive item of equipment reached a useful life of more than twenty, allowing the firm to recover the investment.

Technicolor laboratory processing was an extremely complex work that was also kept secret during that time of great competition in this field. It was only made in the two plants the firm had in Hollywood and London, using specially designed equipment. The camera negatives were developed with 0.65 gamma in a D-76 developer, but before this step, they were treated with a bleaching bath to remove the red film coating that was on the emulsion surface.

The process continued with a printing step of each of the three negatives, to obtain from them three films, later called matrixes. The processing conditions of the matrixes in hot water produced a relief in the emulsion images, which was hardened to actuate during the printing process, as a cliché, with a film called blank, obtaining the release print which included a completed silver image sound track. This supposed that this blank was previously prepared and synchronized in another laboratory section.

Once the matrix was obtained it entered a laboratory section where it went onto the dye transfer machines; initially there were four banks to produce one gray printing and the printing in the three basic colors. In 1939 this gray step with a silver low contrast image to accentuate the subject's contour was eliminated and only the three basic colors remained. The blank passed into the banks from one side through a pre-wetting washing bath. After passing through a yellow dye tank and a place called a cascade, which regulated the color ratio, the matrix entered the other side. Basically, then the blank and the matrix were reunited and were married by means of a 160 ft. monel pin belt with register pins. There, both films were transported together with the effect of rubber rollers and weight pressing to keep the film in very close contact to eliminate bubbles and keep perfect registration with the belt pins.

The image contrast regulated by temperature control was made in the machine sections called hot tables on top and below several stripper wheels that drove the belt. Several steps continued the process afterwards when the matrix and the blank were separated to be washed and dried. The blank continued later to be printed passing to cyan and magenta banks with a gangway of 6 ft. between each bank. This complex imbibition printing machine of Technicolor was built in the United States following the designs of the company's engineers: B. Sugden; B.S. Tuttle, G.F. Rackett, D.F. Comstock, L.T. Trolan, W.S. Eaton and J. H. Whitnet. The manufacturer was the I. B. Corporation and the designer was Mr. Mack Ames of the Technicolor Corporation. It was an outstanding piece of machinery that required a very accurate and continuous human control.[16]

In successive years several Technicolor procedures were improved, and monopack systems such as Kodachrome were used to comply with requirements of cartoon films and some long features. The imbibition printing also reached the 16mm format. The imbibition Technicolor process produced excellent release prints with high image quality but its costs were feasible only if there was a large number of prints, with minimal quantities stipulated by contract and adequate to large scale distribution.

The first films made in Technicolor tripack were Walt Disney's *Flowers and Trees* (1933), followed by sequences of *The House of Rothschild* (1934); *La Cucaracha* (1934), with cinematography by Ray Renaham; sequences of *Kid Millions* (1934); *Legong: Dance of the Virgins* (1935) directed by Henri de la Falaise with cinematography by William H. Geene and *Becky Sharp* (1935) directed by Rouben Mamoulian, with cinematography by Ray Renaham. The preference in Hollywood and London for the new Technicolor system for long feature films was gradually increasing from 5 productions in 1936, to 8 in 1937 and 11 in 1938 but the war lowered these figures to 9 in 1939 and 6 in 1940.[17]

# 25. Progress and New Technology

## Cameras

Evaluating the improvements that came out during the period, various elements evidence the great forward steps achieved. We have already seen many cameras that appeared and how their technology improved each time. The reflex viewing system adopted by Arnold & Richter in 1937 was one of the greatest achievements of that era. In American equipment based on monitoring viewfinders, the invention made that same year by John Arnold of MGM (and that won him an Academy Award) included semiautomatic focusing and viewfinder parallax control. The gadget was of fundamental importance for using a mobile camera, when the operator could no longer rely on the ability of the first camera assistant to adjust the focus ring; now he could see in the viewfinder the resulting projected image of what was happening. The Mitchell Camera Corporation later added this innovation to their equipment based on the principle of the cam and roller linkage. It was very curious that these two very different methods of viewing an exact image rendered by a camera, the reflex and the automatic corrected viewfinder, appeared the same year, the former persisting to the present day and the latter lasting 23 years of useful life.

Analyzing camera viewfinders, we must not forget that at that time Czech camera manufacturers such as Slechta and Cinephon and the German Ernemann and Askania improved a comfortable viewing method for the operator, by means of a double eyepiece, one for each eye, so that the operating cameraman had the ability to close the left eye. Although this contrivance was maintained on the products they manufactured other camera makers did not adopt it. Another important improvement was the eccentric NC 35mm movement with registration pins, developed, as seen above, by the Mitchell Camera Corporation in 1932, with six variations (defined as Models D, E, F, G, H and I), this last one incorporated in this firm camera's manufactured from 1935 onwards, and including the BNC studio model. This refined mechanical gadget, outstanding for noiseless operation, had a long life and was later on adopted in Panavision equipment and an improved version is used even today.

Other interesting landmarks followed in motion picture camera design aimed at semiautomatic operation to facilitate the work of the newsreel cameramen. Among them, the automatic lens turret introduced by the Cinephon Newsreel Camera, that rotated by only pressing a button, and permitted changing the lens with the camera still running, without stopping it, as was usual at that time. Askania, in their Schulter Kamera, improved this lens turret by adding their own system which allowed adjusting the focus and iris lens rings while the other two lenses in the turret were automatically regulated at the same time. This same

**Cinephon camera with double eyepiece finder** (*courtesy Filmovy Prumsyl Praha-Barrandov*).

camera also incorporated the automatic magazine with its pre-threaded film traveling with a single sprocket wheel, applying the same method introduced 20 years earlier by Karl L. Akeley in his Akeley Pancake camera. This magazine system was adopted in several home cameras in the 16mm gauge, and also used by Arnold & Richter in their first 35 and 16mm Kinarri cameras, around 1925. Finally this latter firm used it (with two sprockets inside the magazine) in their first reflex camera. Portable cameras using a pre-threaded magazine have become classic equipment over several decades.

Ending this review of development in camera making we must not forget that the 16mm gauge began to be increasingly applied to semiprofessional cameras, since their characteristics and abilities were very well suited for making industrial and educational films; such cameras included the Victor Sound and the Bert-Bach Auricon, the first 16mm sound-on-film cameras on the American market, as well the Cine Kodak Special.

## Camera supports

In the range of implements for installing the camera, significant progress was made, such as the tripod head introduced by Karl Akeley for his sound camera. This head included for the first time a geared ball bearing, gyro type mechanism with a flywheel, and quick releases for movement in any direction, put in motion when the command stick was moved. Thus very smooth pans without jerks were obtained, ideally suited for long focus lenses. This head also had automatic devices to keep the camera balanced, preventing it from falling or backwards during tilt motion. Three rotation speeds and fixing systems for the horizontal or vertical displacements could be obtained with this head. The new head also included a system to obtain head levels quickly, in relation to the tripod legs, by releasing a knurled knob at the bottom of the tripod head bowl. This advanced design was in time applied to most professional tripods nowadays. Tripod heads also had other technical variations provided by different manufacturers. We have already mentioned the one conceived in Italy by Renato Cartoni with the name of Vittoria. It was the prototype of a compact head with a flywheel, designed for portable cameras such as the Parvo L, the Askania Schulter, Arriflex 35 or Novado, equipment usually employed at Istituto Nazionale Luce where Cartoni was a cameraman. Years later, his son Guido Cartoni would continue in this specific field, constructing a variation that would become a classic tripod head in Europe.

German manufacturers also worked in those years on complex heads for tripods using the half cylinder unit process to achieve the tilt motion, and using a female dovetail for mounting the camera with a complex mechanism system to make panning easy, but paying the price that the unit became too large and considerable heavy. Meanwhile in Hollywood, the friction head specially developed by the Mitchell Company was as standard adopted and cameramen daily trained their reflexes with it following a cable snaking on the studio floor. Towards the end of the decade the Fox studios developed together with their new T.C. Fox camera, an original hydraulic tripod head for their exclusive use, that provided very smooth motions. The same as the camera, this improved head was hardly used beyond the productions of that studio.[1]

From the beginning of that decade a gear head existed at MGM for a rolling tripod built with tubes, to move the camera with its blimp. A certain time elapsed till camera operators were convinced of its advantages and the maneuvering systems were improved with panning handles fitted with speed gearboxes. What made this change acceptable was when the head was applied on the supporting structure of the heavy Technicolor camera with its bulky blimp. Its construction was pioneered by Mole & Richardson and it was later on adopted by Raby Mfg. Co. of Hollywood and many others.

The mobile camera was extensively used in Europe and Hollywood. Directors such as Max Ophüls, Douglas Sirk, Karl Harltl, and Erik Charrel in Germany; Jean Renoir, René Clair, and Marcel L'Herbier in France; Kenji Mizoguchi of Japan and King Vidor, George Cukor, Fritz Lang, and Ernst Lubitsch in Hollywood extensively applied the technique of moving the camera about for which they had to use adequate equipment. We have already seen how it was used in the previous decade. In the thirties this practice continued, but the tools were improved. In 1932 Bell & Howell developed a dolly they called Rotambulator. Soon afterwards Fearless built a unit with a central column that could rise and rotate 90 degrees by means of a rack and steering mechanism in a body with four pneumatic tires that could be locked, also was very adequate for rolling in rails. The Raby company also built the Perambulator, another compact dolly of similar characteristics. Towards 1939, John Arnold, Chief of the Camera Department of MGM conceived and built an unusual dolly on which the central column had a boom with a curved end that held the camera from above in a special setting; it allowed shooting from floor level up to 16 feet as well as swiveling the boom and camera 360 degrees with a seat for the operator.[2]

European production centers also tackled this specific field. In Italy the Carrello built by Rispoli with its adjustable four wheels and telescopic column was a great contribution to camera mobility, especially for the traveling effect. In England, Vinten Ltd. was also facing these problems and developed equipment to solve them. How the traveling effect was achieved varied according to Hollywood, Britain or continental Europe, where different methods were employed. While in the first two places pneumatic tires on a flat rail with one flange was in common use, even for the displacements of certain types of cranes, on the European continent, especially in Germany, the technique applied was assembling piping tracks with elaborated grooved steel and rubber tires to absorb vibrations. During the Berlin Olympic Games, in 1936, this method used by the German studios was seen and appreciated by cameramen from Italy and France who covered the event and who later adopted this process which became standard as the years went by.

## Lenses

Several important advances were also made in the optical field. We have already seen how the Technicolor Co. had to trust Taylor, Taylor & Hobson Ltd. with the problem of designing the lenses for their film cameras. This optical firm was faced with the design and construction of apochromatic cine lenses to carry the three colors to a common focus, with the added difficulty of obtaining a relative aperture f/2 and that the different focal distances of the series kept the same chromatic correction. The diffusion of color systems in subsequent years showed the need for manufacturing apochromatic lenses for all shooting not in black in white.

This British firm not only achieved this exacting demand, but also surpassed the technical requisite of the Technicolor camera that needed sufficient clearance to locate the prism in front of the film plane. This was not only a solution for this specific problem, but it also allowed solving reflex viewing with the mirror shutter blade at 45 degrees, between the lens and the film plane.

Another important step in manufacturing lenses was the development of the coating of optical glass. As far back as 1892 Harold Taylor had discovered that a bloomed glass transmitted more light that a clear glass. In 1904 he patented the use of some chemicals to reduce reflectivity. In 1916, F. Kollmorgen experimented with optical films to obtain the bloomed glass effect. For this purpose he used fluorohydric acid vapors to leave a silicate coating on the surface of the lens. He thus obtained a 96 percent transmission of light against 89 percent for untreated lenses. But this method had marked practical limitations, among them that this treatment could not be applied on all glasses. In 1935 Dr. John Strong defined which were the non-metallic substances that could be evaporated and deposited in very thin coatings, over glass surfaces. In 1936 A. Smakula of the German firm Zeiss began to apply those principles on their lenses using a vacuum evaporated layer of calcium fluoride.

In 1938 another specialist, K. Blodgett, developed a paste for this purpose, but it was too soft and was affected by sunrays. Finally it was established that the most appropriate baths to obtain an efficient and lasting antireflection coating were sodium, lithium, calcium and magnesium fluorides. Sodium fluoride was the most appropriate at an optical level and magnesium fluoride was the one that rendered the thickest coating. The Eastman Kodak Co. coated their photo camera lenses, but only the interior faces since the process used did not last on external surfaces. Two years later that goal was achieved using magnesium fluoride. Treating the elements of a lens was a considerable step forward to obtaining improved images. The increase in contrast and luminosity, and in reproduction of shadow details, exceeded what had previously been achieved and brought a considerable advance in the field of still photo and motion picture recording.

During the last years of the decade, T.W. Clark of the Fox studios, and others, also did exhaustive research about the light transmission of the camera lenses in order to calibrate the stop of lenses of their newly developed Twentieth Century–Fox camera. The new method was based on the effective light transmitted and the light lost by reflection and absorption. A special light source, a photoresponsive tube of the voltaic type and an ultrasensitive RCA meter were used and this work was one of the first steps towards the future method of T/stop lens calibration.[3]

In 1931 several experiments were carried out with a varifocal lens, the Douglas Zoom lens, which used a bellows extension to be readjusted.[4] In 1932, Taylor, Taylor & Hobson joined efforts with Bell & Howell to produce the Cooke/B&H Varo Lens, based on the work of A. Warmisham, with an aperture of f/4.5 and a focal variation of 3 to 1, from 40 to 120mm. The unit had a parallelepiped shape and focusing was obtained with diopter lenses. Very few units were sold outside the newsreel field and they were not popular in the feature film industry. In 1936 the German firm Astro brought out the Transfocator, a lens with a focal relationship of 2 to 1. In 1938, Siemens produced a 16mm camera with the variable focal Busch-Vario-Glaukar of f/2.8 with a 4 to 1 relationship, from 25 to 80mm. Important telephoto lenses were also manufactured, incorporating technical novelties, such as the one brought out by Askania Werke based on the Smith system, that used a concave spherical mirror with a hole in its center to gain luminosity, it had a short body but a larger diameter and obtained a focal length of 600mm with an aperture of f/4.5.

## Laboratory equipment

Film processing was another field in which considerable advances were achieved. Since the appearance of continuous processing machines, improvements occurred one by one with mechanical solutions demanded by the many different inconveniences that cropped. New material were found that were more resistant to the corrosion produced by the acid baths employed. New manufacturers become experts in this field, such as the Fonda Machinery Company Inc. and H.W. Houston & Company in the United States. These items of equipment become more efficient, with automatic temperature controls for each bath, compensating mechanisms for film travel through rollers and the tanks, and throughout the whole machinery, more efficient methods to renew the chemical solutions when they became spent, etc.

The popularity of the 16mm gauge grew from year to year, increasing the production of cameras in this gauge, improving the equipment to process those films, some of which allowed developing 16 or 35mm, with controls to vary the operation speed at will in order to regulate it to the requirements of each format: 16mm required a special treatment and slower speed to reduce grain. The use of reversal emulsions and color treatment demanded more tanks with processing solutions, which made equipment longer. There were also several compact systems made that allowed processing the film in daylight.

In this field there were many noteworthy specialists who developed the required film processing techniques and among them we must mention the following: J. I. Crabtree, G.E. Matthews, J.F. Ross, E.I. Ives, J.A. Jones, and C. Tuttle, in the United States; C. Emmermann and B. Golberg in Germany and Leopold Lobel in France, among others. During those years different methods were investigated in the spray system for washing the film in certain types of color processing, such as Agfa, which process was later on taken up by some in the industry. The different problems that arose from processing techniques with continuous machines were also perfected one by one, e.g., directional effects, image highlights, aerial fog, water and abrading marks. Air conditioning began to be used in the laboratories.

Many different kinds of specialized equipment were manufactured to control processing, such as densitometers and sensitometers designed and manufactured by Eastman Kodak and Weston, and equipment such as light testing instruments from Art Reeves. Other equipment arising in this field included the photometric contrasting instrument conceived by Crabtree and Foryce, as well as the Enofilm equipment, built by the French technician Leopold Lobel, that traced the characteristic curve of an emulsion on a sheet of reticulated paper to obtain the gamma value with precision. The principles for recovering silver from the developing baths were published in specialized magazines and special instruments for that purpose were built, such as the Argentometer, to measure the level of silver in the baths, as well as equipment to achieve this recovery yielding a considerable economy.

Another variation of this was that manufacturers of raw stock conceived processing products for profitably substituting sodium carbonate and borax such as Kodalk of Eastman Kodak, an alkali with special characteristics, besides their special material for processing black and white emulsions more adequately for making duplicates and for treating sound recordings.[5] The progressive use of color in cinematography, was bound to call the attention of laboratory equipment manufacturers specializing in printing machines for this purpose to incorporate not only light sources with increased light, but also gadgets to vary the intensity of the light beam without decreasing their spectral values and allowing the insertion of different color filters. The automation for light regulation was in several cases affected by war events in Europe, deferring successful experiments that were eventually carried out in equipment built after the war.

Moreover, the war in Europe urged the transfer of German film laboratories to the already invaded Czech laboratories, to process the new Agfacolor film in a region free of enemy bombing. Firms in Hollywood and London holding color film patents, e.g., Technicolor, had to take careful precautions regarding their industrial processing secrets to avoid their theft by actual or possible competitors.

## Raw stock

The fundamental element in cinematography work, the raw stock, underwent a marked progress in the variety of emulsions offered by different manufacturers. Firms that were leaders in this field, such as the Eastman Kodak Company, with a definite research policy, placed new products on the market adequate for the specific needs of the industry. This encouraged other firms that followed those developments closely and improved their products. New firms in Europe and Asia entered the market and even those who had concentrated in producing only photo material burst into the field of cinema raw stock. At first they began with material for the growing home cinematography market and then went on to the production of negative and positive stock for the professional cinema. This took place especially in countries with a considerable internal market and a growing film industry, such as the United Kingdom with the renowned Ilford Limited Company, Ferrania Ltd. in Italy, Perutz in Germany, and Fuji and the Sakura brand from Konishiroku in Japan.[6]

At the beginning of the decade, Kodak Rochester discontinued its production of orthochromatic negative and introduced the Super Sensitive Panchromatic, identified with the number 1217, with a slightly faster sensitivity in daylight shots than the former Eastman Negative 1201, but twice as sensitive in shots taken with tungsten light, which earned the company an Oscar award together with Dupont. In 1931, Kodak introduced its new graybase film with a substance that absorbed the light on the support, eliminating the halation of the bright points of the subject, that prevented the reflection of light and the absorption of the reflections in the emulsion. This was an important step in raw stock manufacturing and in improving the photographic image, which other firms adopted later on.

In 1935 this firm brought on the market the new Eastman Super X Panchromatic 1227 negative, a material 50 percent more sensitive than the 1217 negative, with reduced contrast, gray or clear base and the same grain. Immediately afterwards other important negatives appeared such as the Eastman Background Panchromatic 1213, with an exceptionally fine grain that made this material ideal for shooting backgrounds to be projected.

Towards 1938 the Plus X negative appeared, numbered 1231, that substituted the Super X negative and had an outstanding sensibility (later rated as 64–80 ASA), and finally the ultra Speed Super XX (later rated as 100–125 ASA), a fundamental achievement, for shooting indoors requiring a great depth of field.

For laboratory work, Kodak had manufactured in 1937 the Eastman Fine Grain Duplicating 1365, that was far superior in results to those obtained by the Duplicating 1365 film and the Fine Grain Panchromatic Duplicating film 1203. This duplicating film earned another Academy Award for the company, for its contribution to the improved duplicating work and its application in special effects with the optical printer. These advances in the negative material designed for laboratory work were a stimulus to other firms in this field to make the effort of reaching these high standards in the industry. Another well-known American firm, Dupont Manufacturing Corp., had at that time two types of negative for the professional cinematographer: the Regular Special and the Superior.

In Europe the leader in cinematographic material was the German Agfa (I.G. Farbenindustrie Akt, Ges) which offered two types of panchromatic negatives: the Pankine Type H that appeared in 1935, with an anti-halation layer, high sensitivity, most adequate for interiors; and the Pankine type G that went back to 1931 and was apt for outdoor and indoor shots. In 1938 this firm added the Super Pan and the Ultrarapid for working with very low light levels. In the same country, Perutz of Munich offered the Peromnia 705, double coated, panchromatic medium speed material and the Peromnia 704, panchromatic high speed negative that was greatly appreciated by Leni Riefensthal when shooting the Berlin Olympic Games. In Belgium, Gevaert Limited manufactured the Pancromosa film, a panchromatic negative of acceptable speed, adequate for all types of work, while in Italy the Ferrania Type C 5 negative appeared some time later.[6] In England, Ilford offered the Selso negative with a good sensibility and high latitude emulsion for the substandard 16mm gauge.

## Exposure meters and filters

The exposure meter achieved another important advancement in its design when Capt. Don Norwood invented the method of incidental light reading applying a photosphere light collector (hemispherical dome of translucent celluloid) for an adequate three-dimensional light beam reading. As the new decade began, this invention became the tried and accepted professional gadget for use in Hollywood studios.

The production of filters for cinematography rose dramatically with the appearance of panchromatic emulsions and the yield of the different types of negatives available at that time. These afforded new possibilities when shooting outdoors under sunlight, and cinematographers applied them extensively to their benefit. Many film productions that left their mark for the quality of their images did so often due to the inspired use of the adequate filter for each occasion. As for 1935 a new possibility was added to the use of filters when Kodak developed the Eastman Pola Screen, that brought them a Class II Oscar for the high value of their achievement. It was promptly adopted to obtain the night for day effect together with a red filter, regulating the contrast effect of the image in the camera and the possibility of controlling light reflections on water or glass while shooting. For the already increasing the use of color in cinema, the Pola Screen was another valuable resource to darken skies.

## The camera crew

Finally the titles and composition of the camera crew for producing feature films was established first in Hollywood and at a slower pace in other countries. As seen above, during silent cinematography the cinematographer acted with an assistant, then gradually he started heading a team of technicians when the cameramen for the export negative appeared and the several camera operators required for direct sound shooting around 1928–30. Thus the cinematographer became used to heading a team, delegating different tasks. That was how the camera crew was made up with the first cameraman or cinematographer, while the camera operator was the second cameraman and the other technicians became assistants. We shall see in the next chapter who was the promoter of this hierarchy in Hollywood. In the United Kingdom, the first cameraman was also called the lighting cameraman. By the end of the '30s the man called cinematographer was credited with the title of director of photography in Hollywood.

The formation of different institutions was vital for this process, such as the American Society of Cinematographers (ASC) in Hollywood, the oldest and most important in the world, and the German Cameramen Club (CDK) that Guido Seeber tried to create in Germany before World War II, but he could not make it last due to the political regime at that time there. In 1947 the British Society of Cinematographers (BSC) was founded and in 1950 the Associazione Italiana Cineoperatori (AIC). The new name of director of photography was adopted in Hollywood and England but for some years the old name of operateur, coined at the end of the previous century by Louis Lumière for those who operated his cameras, was kept in several countries such as France, Italy, Spain, the Soviet Union, etc., with the variations of "first" and "second" to differentiate the one who was the head and lighted the scene from the other who operated the camera and controlled the assistant's work.[7] Only in Germany and Scandinavia did the director of photography continue to operate the camera, a tradition that continues to the present day.

# 26. Cinematographers

The thirties were exiting years in the development of new techniques in cinematography and the evolution of this profession. At that time new working methods were also gradually appearing in the practice of this craft, and they were being organized, as also were their aesthetic theories. Several cinematographers left important legacies in this field, achieving a well deserved prestige in world cinematography. Here are some of those who blazed trails by outstanding mastery of their profession.

## Sol Polito

An evaluation of great cinematographers of Hollywood's golden age must include the valuable contribution of Sol Polito. This outstanding American cinematographer was born in Palermo, Italy, in 1892, and was very young when he came to America. He worked first on the East Coast as a laboratory developing assistant and then as a camera assistant. His dedication and conditions pushed him to the top of this trade when in 1917 he was the cinematographer of *Queen X* produced by Mutual. He photographed many films for different producers and moved on to Hollywood, working in several studios until he finally settled with Warner Bros. There he photographed films in which he defined that studio's lighting style for "black" thrillers, where he applied a realistic style suitable to the dramatic levels of this subject. Among them are: *Five Star Final* (1931), *I Am a Fugitive from a Chain Gang* (1932) and *G-Men* (1935), together with other dramatic and action films, like *Petrified Forest* and *The Charge of the Light Brigade* (1936). All these show out Polito's abilities in lighting and his use of the low key, as well as his control of chiaroscuro, the use of hard lights and his trails projecting shadows to elaborate an image, making up a refined technique applied on black and white. In one of his most accomplished works at that time, *The Sea Hawk* (1940), Polito draws the audience's attention by projecting the shadows of the actors, at times even omitting their direct images. The images in the films he photographed show his elaborate lighting technique. He died in 1960 with more than 60 films to his credits including some in Technicolor. Hollywood regards Sol Polito as the artisan who created the title "director of photography," which gradually replaced "cinematographer," since he was the first to suggest to the heads of Warner studios the need to reorganize the photography team of a film to make it conform to the new sound techniques.

At the beginning of the sound period (which first started in this studio, as seen in a previous chapter) shooting was carried out with several cameras installed in soundproof booths; the cinematographer responsible for the images was not operating one of the instruments, but now was an expert estimating exposure, defining lighting and controlling laboratory work. It was a radical change from procedures used up to then. The position of "director of photography" proposed by Polito was accepted with the above duties, as well as the terms "operative cameraman" and "first assistant." The many cameras needed at the beginning of sound filming were later replaced again by a single one, when blimps were used on synch cameras, and the new duplicating films eliminated the need of the "foreign" negative cameraman, but the new camera crew structure was maintained and adopted by many studios, save some in Europe.

## Gaetano Antonio Gaudio

Born in Rome in 1885, he was one of Hollywood's pioneers in this trade. He started in the Vitagraph laboratories as a developing expert, continuing what he had learned in the family photography business, and becoming a cameraman. Towards the end of the first decade of the 20th century he was first cameraman on many films for various producers and studios. From the beginning he filmed for renowned directors like Fred Niblo on *The Mark of Zorro* (1920), who induced him to be always very meticulous in high budget productions with an imaginative director.

When the Mitchell Camera Corp. launched its first camera onto the market, he joined the long list of prospective buyers and managed to purchase unit No. 10 in 1921. Working with it he profited from its many advantages, but also noticed its main shortcoming: its spyglass finder which rendered a small, inverted image. He therefore devised a viewfinder with a projected image, and with the help of Bausch & Lomb, the opticians, he incorporated a prism which rendered a large, bright and upright image. He sold the patent on this

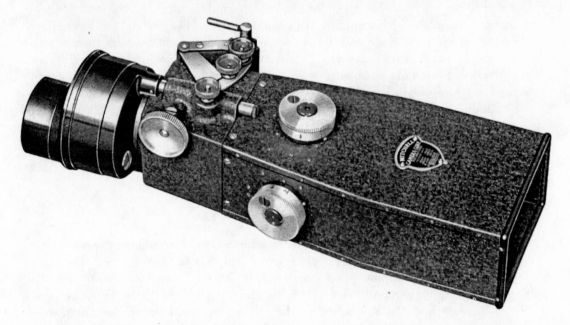

The Mitchell erect image viewfinder designed by Gaetano Antonio Gaudio and Bausch & Lomb opticians (*courtesy Mitchell Camera Corp.*).

device to the Mitchell Co. and it contributed to improving the characteristics of their instrument.

Being a restless, imaginative and precise person, he studied the best working methods, together with colleagues with whom he had founded the Static Club of America, which would later on become the American Society of Cinematographers. During his years at Warner Brothers he experimented with the effects of shooting techniques brought about by sound, making him gradually conceive the need to adapt the lighting methods used until then. Thus, he applied his best artistic sensibility by adopting a dramatic and realistic lighting for shooting films for that studio's "black" series, like *Little Caesar* (1930), but he also adapted his artistic creativeness to varying styles required by the different subjects of other productions he filmed.

His work was well noted in several biographic films he shot: *The Story of Louis Pasteur* (1935), *The Life of Emile Zola* (1937) and *Juárez* (1939). He filmed mainly in black and white, but also in color, and among the latter, the most outstanding was the first film photographed with Sol Polito in Technicolor: *The Adventures of Robin Hood* (1938). Gaudio was awarded an Oscar by the Academy for his photography of *Antony Adverse* (1937), and five other films he photographed were nominated for that award: *Hell's Angels* (1929–30), *Juárez* (1939) *The Letter* (1940), *Korvette K-225* (1943), and *A Song to Remember* (color, 1945). Some of these films were emblems of excellent photography, such as *The Letter*, directed by William Wyler.

But another important contribution to this profession was Gaudio's continuous search for efficient, combined procedures to light up a set. His method of applying light, which he called precision lighting, was a methodical use of the technical means available in Hollywood towards the end of the thirties. His methods were based on lighting from above, the application of many spotlight beams for more effective control, the use of the dimmer to regulate light intensity according to the actor's movements, establishing an intense key light to ensure the required field depth, a controlled use of fill light to regulate the ratio, the use of the exposure meter as a basic tool for tonal control and the viewing glass as an adequate complement to establish chiaroscuros. His interest in this field began ten years before when the Madza lamps came about and the problems of lighting for cinematography were studied by the Motion Picture Producers Association, the Academy of Arts and Sciences, and the American Society of Cinematographers. He improved his practice as he gained experience, which he applied when shooting *The Life of Emile Zola* and *Antony Adverse*.[1]

Gaudio's precision lighting system was spread out over Hollywood and was also applied abroad as the most natural and efficient method, as seen above in chapter four. This important cinematographer died in 1951 with almost one hundred films to his credit, two of which he also directed.

## Georges Périnal

It has been considered that British cinema achieved its industrial maturity towards the end of the thirties, when entrepreneurs like Alexander Korda and J. Arthur Rank furthered the development of this industry on a large scale, producing important films for distribution abroad, building technically planned studios, and using color by the Technicolor process. For such enterprises, Alex Korda realized the need of renowned cinematographers, so he brought to Britain one of the best French directors of photography, Georges Périnal.

Périnal, born in Paris in 1897, entered this profession as a projectionist when he was sixteen. After some time he took part in several shorts by Jean Gremillon, and towards the coming of sound he had reached the position of chef operateur. As such, his first job was for the great French director Jacques Feyder in *Les Nouveaux messieurs* (1929), and afterwards worked for another director who would become famous later on, Jean Cocteau, on his pioneering film *Le Sang d'un poète* (1930). He become René Clair's favorite cinematographer, filming for him *Le Million* (1931) and *A Nous la liberté* (1931). These films made him France's best-paid cinematographer, so Alexander Korda called him for a British film to be shot in France, *The Girl from Maxim* (1932). After filming *Le Quatorze Juillet* (1933) with Clair, Korda retained him again to photograph the film that would launch British cinema onto world markets, and would open the doors of the U.S.A.: *The Private Life of Henry VIII* (1933).

The splendor of this film was enhanced by Périnal's elaborate lighting, thus increasing his prestige. From then he continued working in other London Film Productions, making the modern Denham studios his second home and the center for experiments. There he took part in outstanding productions, which showed his craftsmanship, such as *Things to Come* (1935), directed by William Cameron Menzies, and *Rembrandt* (1936) by Alexander Korda, in which the photography reproduces masterly the great painter's style. Then came spectacular films in Technicolor produced by Alexander Korda, like *The Drum* (1938) and *Four Feathers* (1939), directed by Zoltan Korda, and especially *The Thief of Bagdad* (1940), by Ludwig Berger, Michael Powell and Tim Wheland; this film brought him and his adopted country their first Hollywood Academy Oscars for its color cinematography.

As a director of photography, Périnal improved the level of cinematography in British filmmaking and greatly influenced others to join this craft in that country who would afterwards become well known photography directors, e.g., Geoffrey Unsworth and Robert Krasker; he also inspired many of the technical staff supporting him. He was the creator of images for films by famous British and American directors, e.g., Michael Powell, Carol Reed, William Cameron Menzies and Charlie Chaplin. Michael Powell considered him the best cinematographer of the times.[2] Périnal died in 1965, leaving a varied list of almost fifty films, which make us admire, even now, his fine craftsmanship.

## Anatoli Golovnia

Soviet cinema greatly impressed the entire world with the strength and the quality of its images. As seen above, Eisenstein's films were outstanding, not only his mise-en-scene, but also because he had a top level cinematographer: Edouard Tissé, both in the silent as well in the sound periods. Other excellent Soviet cinematographers became well known, such as Andrei Moskvin, Mikhail Kaufman, I. Feldman, B.I. Volcek, V. Gardonov and especially Anatoli Golovnia.

Golovnia was born in 1900 and during the twenties he gained experience working with veteran directors like Jacob Prozanov or keen youngsters emerging from Leon Kulechov's courses in the State Film School, like Leonid Obolesky, for whom he shot *Kirpiciki* (1925). In 1926 he was graduated from the Faculty of Photography of the Motion Picture School. His career would develop mainly as a lighting cameraman for Vsevolod Pudovkin, the renowned Soviet director, with whom he worked closely, both aesthetically and artistically, as Eisenstein and Tissé had done. With Tissé and Moskvin, Golovnia founded later the new Soviet Cinematographer School.

Golovnia filmed about ten productions for Pudovkin, among which the following were outstanding: *Mat* (*The Mother*, 1926), *Konek Sankt-Peterbursga* (*The End of Saint Petersburg*, 1927), *Potomok Cingis-Chana* (*Storm over Asia*, 1928), *Dezertir* (*The Deserter*, 1933) and *Suvorov* (1941). Pudovkin had scientific education as a chemist, which probably influenced Golovnia's professional regard, but inversely, the latter very likely influenced the director regarding the images in their films, the exact framing, the search for the correct angle, the choice of adequate lenses, and fundamentally the lighting and the use of shadows, all of which gave his images a special artistic appeal.

Both were in love with their professions, becoming theorists in the specialty of each, whose ideas became known through publications. Pudovkin had written *The Film Scenario* and *Film Direction and Material* while shooting *The Mother*. This inspired his friend and closest collaborator to expose his ideas and experiences in his first book, *Composing the Image* (1938) and some time later *Motion Picture Lighting*. Both works set forth for the first time the artistic aspects and the techniques of the photography director and analyzed in detail his lighting theories. He later wrote other books about this trade.[3]

## SOVIET IDEOLOGY IN CINEMATOGRAPHY

After these texts, another well-known cameraman, Vladimir Nilsen, who had been Tissé's assistant, wrote *The Cinema as a Graphic Art*, dedicated to " Sergei Mikhalovitch Eisenstein, teacher and friend," thus completing the trilogy on the artistic aspects of the cinematographer, written while the author was professor of the State Film School and including an appreciation by the same.[4] But behind an interesting text with detailed aesthetic expositions, there was a latent ideology, politically dominant at that time, criticizing old lighting practices and working methods of the already abandoned star system in Hollywood studios, as characteristics of bourgeois cinema; such criticism was probably the outcome of a purge the author had undergone previously. These were some of the many different concepts on motion picture photography, and they reached some studios and film schools several years later.

# 27. Outstanding Cinematography

## Shanghai Express

This Paramount Studios film received two Academy awards in 1931-32 for the sound recording of Broken Lullaby and the cinematography of Lee Garmes. The film director was Joseph von Sternberg and the two starring roles were played by Marlene Dietrich and Clive Brook. It was a thriller filmed entirely in Hollywood in which the action takes place in a train traveling from Peking to Shanghai. Here, once more, von Sternberg's presence as director was the catalyst to obtain extremely plastic high quality images. Once again also, the Dietrich–von Sternberg combination reached an outstanding motion picture as achieved in *Der blaue Engel* (*The Blue Angel*, 1931). *Shanghai Express* is the story of a woman of doubtful reputation called "Shanghai Lily" who is given to a Chinese war lord to save her ex-lover (Clive Brook) The film's attraction, more than its story, is the high image quality that helped the storytelling as well as an effective work of the art director Hans Dreier. The interior settings in the train and its passengers and the night outdoor shots of the running train along the supposed Chinese landscapes were extremely realistic and imposing. The particularly angular face of Marlene Dietrich was wisely lighted with broken beams and strategic ambient shadows. This merited the Award as a tribute to Lee Garmes's cinematographic expertise.

Garmes was a reputed American cinematographer born in Peoria, Illinois, in 1898. In his youth he lived in Denver, Colorado, in his grandmother's care. As a boy he pretended to make movies where he was the cameraman. He was educated at North Denver High School and at eighteen he went into the film industry as camera assistant in New York, where he learned his trade. Some time later he went to Hollywood and worked in the Thomas H. Ince Studios where he participated in shooting numerous slapstick comedies, popular at that time. There, he met David W. Griffith, who was a producer. During this period many Hollywood cinematographers and others that came from Europe influenced him. In 1924, at Warner Bros., he started as first cameraman in a film directed by Malcolm St. Clair. During the silent period he participated in an important number of films, obtaining experience and mastering his trade. He was one of the first to use tungsten lighting around 1926 and became an expert in lighting close-ups.[1]

He worked with a varied and selected number of directors: Rex Ingram, Alexander Korda, George Fitzmaurice, Michael Curtiz, Rouben Mamoulian, Howard Hawks, Joseph von Sternberg, Ben Hecht, Victor Fleming, Julien Duvivier, Alfred Hitchcock, William Wyler, Rene Clair, King Vidor and Max Ophüls, a sign of his high reputation through the years. In 1930 he worked for the first time with von Sternberg in *Morocco* with Marlene Dietrich, whom he lighted for the first time. He adopted the side light method based on what he saw in the film *The Blue Angel*, but as he considered he was duplicating the lighting used by William Daniels on Greta Garbo, he then adopted his preferred north light system following the technique of the great painter Rembrandt.

*Shanghai Express* was Lee Garmes's 33rd film and according to his comments, the one he preferred in his long career. He was then an accomplished artist who could create mood with light and in this film he worked with a filmmaker that knew this technique very well. He knew how to exploit the photogenic quality of Dietrich's face so he had to give heed to the realism of the settings. The train used was placed on an unused railway line available in Chatswood, San Fernando Valley. The train station used for the arrival was San Bernardino and was conveniently adapted to these shots and was painted white. The town was the only set built by Hans Dreier for this sequence according to von Sternberg's instructions and had to be situated very close to the railway.

After this film Lee Garmes continued his prolific career working from thrillers such as *Scarface* (1932), *Brute Force* (1947), *The Naked City* (1948) to realistic themes like *City Streets* (1931), *Detective Story* (1951) and *Desperate Hours* (1955). He was a renowned specialist in black and white films, and in lighting famous stars like Loretta Young, Norma Shearer, Rita Hayworth, Jennifer Jones and many others. He also worked on big color productions such as *Gone with the Wind* (1939) and *The Big Fisherman* (1959). His career was long and varied because he also was a film director and producer; he took part in 112 films.[2]

# M

The first European film that was relevant for its cinematography in this decade was the German Nero film production *M–Eine Stadt sucht einen Mörder* (1932). It was directed by the now well known Fritz Lang, with cinematography by the renowned Fritz Arno Wagner. The story was inspired by a series of criminal deeds, which had happened some time before in Germany, such as the case of the Vampire of Dusseldorf, when the victims were little children like the Fehse sisters of Breslau, Hilde Kopernick and the Auffmann case. The film tells the story of a sadistic murder in an unknown city where the police pursue the criminal to the point that all the underground world is affected. The underworld decides to carry out the investigation itself and the criminal is found. But when the sadist is judged by his peers and sentenced to death, the police break in and everybody is captured. This was Fritz Lang's penultimate film before leaving his country (the last one was *Das Testament des Dr. Mabuse*, 1934). His wife, the well known writer Thea von Harbou, participated actively in this film, as in others he had previously made. But when the Nazis took over and declared him a non–Aryan, he divorced her and fled to France and thence to the U.S.A.

In the last two films Lang made in Germany, he resorted to one of his favorite cinematographers, Fritz Arno Wagner, with whom he had made four films running, and with whom he had aesthetic affinities. As a consequence of his training in architecture, Lang was very imbued in the visual aspects of his films, but in this case he left aside his tendency toward impressionism and wanted to show the life and the crude reality of those times. To this end he found the best help in this cinematographer.

Fritz Arno Warner was born in Schmiedefeld, Thuringia, Germany, in 1889 and started in the film industry at eleven working for the French firm Pathé. As a newsreel cameraman he covered the Mexican Revolution. During World War I he continued in the profession, shooting for the newsreels, and after the war he was one of the young cameramen in the movement to renew German filmmaking. His debut as cinematographer was in Fritz Lang's film *Der Müde Tod* (1921), making up a crew headed by Erich Nietzschmann and which also included Herman Salfrank.

His refined sensibility and professional know-how soon came out in film lighting in an era in which impressionism was preferred and his ability to work with light and large shadows was very well spoken of. He was also lucky to work with great directors, like Murnau and Pabst, with whom his aesthetic imagination shone and he applied it in famous scenes for these filmmakers. For example: the well known shot in Murnau's film showing the long shadow of Nosferatu on the staircase wall advancing on his victim. His cinematography for the same director's film *Schloss Vögelod* (1921) was also remarkable with excellent lighting of a castle. The lighting used on the close-ups of the miners was outstanding when he worked with Pabst in *Kameradschaft* (1931) and also in *Die Dreigroschenoper* (*The Threepenny Opera*, 1931).

In M Wagner turned all his expressive force with light and image composition to enforce the drama of the theme, even though it was a realistic film. These effects were notable in the scene when the shadow of the sadist falls on the innocent child, like fate marking its victim, or the reflection of many pocket knives reflected on a shop window around the killer's face. Wagner's brilliant cinematography was also present in the light treatment in night city scenes, the lighting and compositions of staircases, and the indoor scenes where the underworld gets together to judge the surprised psychopath. At present European directors of photography consider this film as the "evolution of German expressionism towards a soft UFA style." Fritz Arno Wagner, a cinematographer with nearly 200 films to his credit during four decades, was a creator of style standards which were later adopted by colleagues in several studios in other countries. This film was then an important landmark in the cinematography of those years.

## Ekstase

In 1933 an European film impressed the cinema world with its remarkable cinematography: the Czech production *Ekstase* (*Ecstasy*), directed by Gustav Machaty with cinematography by Jan Stallich. This film was acclaimed and achieved good box office results, but both subject and images were a very early venture in the erotic field. Because of this it was easily sold in ten countries before the film was finished. The leading star was a Viennese actress called Hedy Kiesler who afterwards went to Hollywood named Hedy Lamarr.

The film received an award at the Venice Film festival and critics' approval everywhere, even though its theme was not acceptable to all audiences. It was also a film severely censored in several countries not only for including a nude female, but also because the story was about sexual attraction and excitement. The story closely resembled a previous film by the same director called *Satiricon* (1929), that was also very successful. It was based on the story of a young, recently married, unsatisfied woman that deserts her husband on her wedding night and returns to her father's home. One day in the countryside, she bathes nude in a river, is discovered by a stranger, and circumstances lead them to make love. Her husband commits suicide and she abandons her lover. The narrative was based entirely on very poetic images, and dialogs of no more that one hundred words in all the film. But the beauty and symbolism of the country and the indoor scenes, and the quality of the images, reveals the mastery of the director and his cinematographer.

Gustav Machaty was born in 1901 in Prague and joined the film industry working as a clerk in the Praga Film production firm. He afterwards acted in foreign productions where he learned the trade from several filmmakers and where he also participated as film writer and finally he became a film director. In 1927 he directed the production *Kreutzerova Sonáta* and then *Satiricon* (1929), from which he obtained great prestige. Later on he was invited by Mussolini to Italy where he made the film *Ballerine* (1936). Afterwards he obtained a contract with MGM to help in the production of *The Good Earth* (1937).

Jan Stallich was a cinematographer who was also born in Prague in 1907. He entered the film industry in 1921 and later trained at the School of Fine Arts (in 1924). He also worked at the A.B. laboratories. In 1924 he began to work with documentary films, stepping up to become a cinematographer in 1931. *Ekstase* made him famous due to the high technical quality and artistic sensibility of the images. Like many of his colleagues, he participated in productions in other European countries such as Austria (1934), Britain (1935), Italy (1939), and Germany and France (1947). He also worked with Laterna Magika. From 1949, he lectured for FAMU (Film and Television Faculty) in Prague. Jan Stallich died in June 14, 1973. In the course of his activity in Czech cinematography he filmed 98 feature films.[3]

The cinematography of *Ekstase* was remarkable for the light of several outdoor sequences, for the close-ups of the actors, and the country scenes in the summer where the use of filters created a remarkable plastic sensation. Analyzing this film we appreciate his refined technique with the use of unconventional methods to produce very radiant light touches.

# The Good Earth

*The Good Earth* was an MGM Hollywood production that won the Academy award for that studio for its cinematography in 1937. The cinematographer was the famous Carl Freund who had recently joined MGM after his trials as film director and with the credits of several previous Hollywood films. *The Good Earth* was the posthumous production of the MGM wonder boy Irving Thalberg, and was a merited memorial. But it also was a worthy film to remember.

The standards achieved by this famous producer were outstanding for its careful filmmaking in all fields, the excellent acting of the leading roles, Paul Muni and Luise Rainer (who also received an Academy award for this film) and the faithfulness to Pearl Buck's well known book. This was a very difficult period for Thalberg at MGM, however he managed to finish the production at a time when events in China attracted world attention. But Thalberg did not learn of his last production's success as he died before the premiere.

Since his return from Europe in 1933, Thalberg had included this book in his projects and four experienced scriptwriters wrote the screenplay. The Metro production unit was under the skilled director George Hill, who travelled to China in 1934 to cover some outdoors shots, and to bring with him some native animals, clothes and props to be used during the Hollywood shooting. A search was made in Los Angeles for an adequate place to recreate the atmosphere. The principal star roles were assigned to Paul Muni and Louise Rainer to play the humble Chinese peasant and self denying wife. The script took nearly 18 months of hard work to satisfy Thalberg's and George Hill's requirements; the latter was to be the director, but a short time before the shooting, Hill committed suicide for other reasons.[4]

Victor Fleming was chosen as the new director but this filmmaker fell ill. It looked like the fates were against this project. Finally the film was assigned to Sidney Franklin, a director that had a dozen previous films and who showed good sensibility and craftsmanship to assume a high cost production. The story of *The Good Earth* is that of a couple of poor Chinese peasants, showing their progression from poverty to prosperity, after suffering distress, hunger, injustice and the turbulent Chinese society at that time with their stern traditions and in a process of change. The story shows how this simple man loses his head when suddenly he becomes rich and the dignity and hardships of his wife under the servitude of archaic traditions. Finally the solution to the crisis arrives when egotism is put aside to face the disaster of a plague.

This production was made entirely in Hollywood, but was carefully controlled even by Chinese personnel sent by Chiang Kai-shek's government, who were astonished by the accurate way their world was reproduced. Carl Freund delivered a superb photography with images of great beauty, thanks to a very studied lighting technique in which the actors were silhouetted by high backlights and the help of realistic settings under the responsibility of Cedric Gibbons, Harry Oliver and Edwin B. Willies. Many indoor and outdoor shots were memorable and were specially prepared on back lot II of MGM and in Los Angeles suburbs. In this film Freund used the blimps provided by the MGM camera department for this studio. His ability was to create an imposing monochrome cinematography with the light situated at the appropriate angle, and with the right intensity and the effective beam hardness control. All this provided extremely artistic photography.

In this film the work of special effects specialists such as A. Arnold Gillespie was also very effective. After weeks of experimenting, he reproduced very exactly a cloud of locusts coming from the sky on cultivated land and leaving when the wind changed. These shots were produced with coffee grounds conveniently overset in the right angle and later overprinted on the landscape shots by means of an optical printer. The close ups of the locusts were made with some insects that had been kept in alcohol and were carefully handled. The realism of those images was so great that few people realized that it was an efficiently made special effect.[5] With this film Freund took another step forward in his career, and was later requested by other Hollywood film studios, experimenting in shooting for the new TV media at Desilu studios, and developing the professional use of the Spectra film exposure meter for his firm, Photo Research Corp.

## La Grande Illusion

This production was considered the best cinematography of European films in 1937. Jean Renoir was the director and the cinematography was by Christian Matras. This film was based on Renoir's experiences as a flyer who was captured by the Germans during World War I as well as those of his comrades in arms as told to him. It was a truelife story that happened in a German P.O.W. camp in 1916-17, in which two prisoners escape to Switzerland, while a third one is killed by the camp commander himself with whom he had become friends. The film won a Venice Film Festival award but was prohibited in Italy and Germany and later also in occupied France. It was also a big success in Britain and the United

States. It was included among the twelve best films of the world in a selection made later on in Belgium. It was a pacifist film that exalted brotherhood among men and the understanding between individuals.

Christian Matras was one the great French cinematographers of that time who left his mark on important film productions of his country. Born in Valence (Drôme) in 1903, he began working in the movies in 1928 as newsreel and short-subject cameraman. Then he turned to long feature films with Jean Epstein as director in *L'Or des mers* (1932). He remained busy, later working with the famous Eugene Schüfftan to acquire his own naturalist style and high technical thoroughness. When he had been the cinematographer of six long feature films he found in Renoir the director with a sensibility adequate to his style. His cinematography in this film was outstanding for the naturalism required by the script, written by Renoir himself and Charles Spaak, which made credible the many indoors settings supposed to be in Germany. The images of this film contributed to the realism of the story and the close-ups and big close-ups are admirable for their lighting. In a French film industry where many cinematographers could choose the brand of camera they wanted, either domestic or foreign, Matras preferred the Debrie Super Parvo. In the Billancourt studios, where this film was made, Matras found the technical media he preferred and obtained with them the kind of images he wanted, to create the adequate humanist feeling with first class actors like Jean Gabin, Pierre Fresnay, Erich von Stroheim and Marcel Dalio.

# The Great Waltz

In 1937 the well-known French director Julien Duvivier went to Hollywood, hired by MGM to direct an American remake of his own film *Pépé le Moko*, 1936. Duvivier was a director with more than twenty films already, and was respected for his mature know-how and the varied kinds of stories he directed. Since the appearance of sound he increased the quality of his films and their commercial success. But once he arrived in Hollywood this project was altered because MGM was afraid of the Hays Office censorship, since the main character commits suicide in the end. Then the studios resold the script to Walter Wagner, who later produced this story with the title *Argel* (1939), directed by John Cromwell and with Charles Boyer acting in the leading role.

This situation was a good opportunity for Duvivier to look for other proposals closer to his preferences. He chose a musical script that gave him the opportunity to handle a bigger budget and the use of the technical and artistic facilities of one of Hollywood's biggest studios. The subject of the new project came from another European, Gottfried Reinhart, an Austrian producer recently arrived in Hollywood, and an assistant of Walter Wagner who would be the film producer for Duvivier. *The Great Waltz* was an opportunity and a challenge to use his narrative film methods that had matured over the years, and improve those applied in *Un Carnet de bal* (1937). It afforded the possibility of using big settings, a large number of extras and a mobile mise-en-scène for the dance shots.

The story was a fiction based on the life of Johann Strauss, Jr. The film had plenty of music sequences, luxurious atmosphere and wardrobes, romantic scenes and some action in the Viennese revolution of 1845. Duvivier had the adequate background and was in the proper place to obtain the best technical and artistic results. MGM had the proper structure required for this production: from among a select group of cinematographers available, Joseph Ruttenberg was chosen, who would ensure that the film's aesthetic values should reach the top.

Joseph Ruttenberg had been working for some time at MGM where he had done the cinematography for six films in three years. He had 34 productions in his career and was a reputed Hollywood cinematographer. This new project was also an opportunity for him to improve his knowledge and to experiment in new areas. The shooting was long and not easy because Duvivier used many mobile camera shots and a crane for better covering dance scenes. The extreme care that Ruttenberg used in lighting each of the scenes was worthy of a perfectionist. All the scenes in the luxurious palace, in the theater, in the stately Strauss mansion, in the Dommayer Cafe, in the bank, in the bakery, were exquisitely lighted with a masterly management of the backgrounds, the light inlet through openings and the balance of shadows and light. It was an example of the classic and sophisticated MGM cinematography of those years.

The lighting of the night scenes shot on the studio's back lot II was also excellent. These scenes represented an area of Vienna that had been, some time before, designed by Cedric Gibbons and Olivier Messel, and were near the sets where *The Good Earth* had been filmed. There was magnificent photography of the city night scenes in which people are captivated by the waltz music coming from the Dommayer Cafe. One of the most famous scenes of this film was the drive at dawn through the Vienna woods when Strauss is inspired to create a famous waltz. This was not only Duvivier's highlight but also Ruttenberg's who recreated the inspirational mood.

One day, going to the studio early in the morning, Ruttenberg saw a group of trees on which the sun was falling through the leaves, and were outlined in the haze. He stopped his car and saw that this was what he needed for the film and studied how to reproduce the effect. When the shooting was made in the selected woods he brought several fog making machines made by Mole & Richardson and perfectly reproduced the bucolic effect he had seen. During post-production the abilities of the sound effects department completed the attractive sequence. Finally we must remark on the outstanding close-up lighting that was one of his well known abilities and which Ruttenberg used on this film.

Joseph Ruttenberg was born in St. Petersburg, Russia, in 1889. When he was four years old his parents brought him to the United States and they settled in Massachusetts. In Boston he obtained a job with a newspaper of the Hearst group as part of the photography staff. This activity fascinated him because he could cover the stories and process the plates himself in the lab. In this job he won experience and soon he was a freelancer, creating a service providing photos for several newspapers.

Around 1914 Ruttenberg obtained a contract with the Boston Opera Company and later became the portrait photographer of the opera singers. This firm took him on a tour to Europe and in Paris Ruttenberg was astonished by the movies. After his return to the States, he bought a motion picture camera in New York, started a newsreel firm and created a laboratory to develop his work. Everything was right for a while but he soon realized that Boston was not the best place for this business.

In 1917 he made contacts with the Fox studio and went to Fort Lee, New Jersey, where those film studios were. After some time he started working as camera assistant there for a year, and stepped up to second cameraman until the opportunity to work as cinematographer came up during the production of the film *The Blue Streak* (1917). With Fox he took part in the cinematography of 23 films until William Fox sold its East Coast studios and went to California. They wanted to bring him with them but he decided to stay. Later on he opened a commercial portrait studio in New York and specialized in shooting film tests for Hollywood studios like Universal, Metro and RKO. He used the Astoria Paramount studios for this work. Among his clients were many important figures of the stage, many of whom were later film stars: the Marx Brothers, Helen Hayes, Walter Huston, Fred Astaire, Paul Muni, and Claudette Colbert.

During 1931 he had the chance to work with David W. Griffith of United Artists on *The Struggle* and in 1935 decided to go to Hollywood, working for Republic, RKO, and Warner Brothers. His old friend George Fosley recommended him to MGM, which, knowing his expertise in star lighting, gave him a long contract. To repay this trust Ruttenberg obtained the third Oscar for this studio for the cinematography of *The Great Waltz*. This cinematographer's long career won him further recognition after retiring with 112 films to his credit.[6]

## Quai des Brumes

This was the most famous film produced in France in the late thirties and in 1938 European colleagues remarked on its cinematography. It was another excellent job by Eugene Schüfftan, with the help of three French second camera operators: Louis Page, Mark Fossard and Henri Alekan. The director was Marcel Carné, who had had a brilliant performance over the past few years, and who had been a pioneer of the so called poetic realism style. This filmmaker was known for the precise film structure of his stories, their high artistic level and the deep sentiment in the theme. *Quai des Brumes* was a script developed by the writer Jacques Prévert based on a play by Pierre Mac Orlan. Originally the film was conceived to be co-produced with the German UFA Studios and to be shot in the harbor of Hamburg, Kiel or Brest. But although the subject had been accepted by UFA's script department, the Nazi regime bosses, already in power, were scandalized by what they considered was an apology for a deserter. Therefore, the film was then made in France, produced by M. Rabinovich of Cine-Alliance, with whom the director had difficulties in getting his ideas accepted. The harbor location selected was in The Havre but its main street was reconstructed in the Pathé-Cinema Studio of Joinville.

In this French studio the Hungarian art director Alexander Trauner designed fourteen sets adequate to different sequences. One of them was of a recreation park with a view of the harbor in the background. The biggest one included a 35 ft. setting of two Havre streets where day and night sequences had to be shot. The street set included paving stones and tramway rails and a corner with another street. The setting incorporated several shops with windows, lighted marquees and street lights. Several stripes and spots units were used, crossing above the street. A brightly lit white background represented the sky. The sets conceived by Trauner were in forced perspective but natural scale and Schüfftan's ability in lighting made them very realistic.

We have seen above some of Eugene Schüfftan's achievements but it is interesting to study his life further. He was born in Breslau, Poland, in 1893. He was very talented in his youth and was drawn to the plastic arts; he was a painter, sculptor and architect, and in the teens he entered the film industry. In 1921 he was a first cameraman; in 1923 he took part in the special effects for *Metropolis* and later on he had the opportunity to work with well known German directors like G.W. Pabst and Robert Siodmak. In 1934 he had to flee from the Nazi regime in Germany, and found refuge in France, where he participated in nine films. He worked also in England from 1932 to 1936 in three productions. During his stay in France he taught his vast knowledge to many French cinematographers who admired him and considered him their master. His lighting style varied according to the film, but being an expert painter he mastered the chiaroscuro technique, the use of contrasted images and how to place shadows and penumbra in the right places. In those days he used to apply light on the chest or abdomen of the actors and use partial light on the faces, in contrast with the background light. He was always experimenting in search of new effects to obtain three-dimensional sensations. Another of his techniques was lighting the sets with carefully placed lighting patterns. In *Quai des Brumes* those techniques were carried to the utmost. In 1940, when the Germans invaded France, Schüfftan fled to the United States and continued his career in Hollywood. He became good friends with Gregg Toland, who was also devoted to his profession, and both exchanged experiences. After the war he filmed in Hollywood and France.[7]

This film was shot using all the resources of the Pathé-Cinéma Studios at Joinville-le Pont. This was the best studio in France, eight kilometers from Paris. It was a very complete studio, which had improved its primitive installations of the twenties. The studio had its own laboratory 300 meters from the headquarters where 800 persons worked, and a large back lot for outdoor set constructions. The different sets required were erected on several of the seven stages, while the back lot was used for the two streets reconstruction. The lighting demanded almost all of the nine 300 amp arcs available, 150 amp automatic arcs units and a great number of tungsten lamps, taking advantage of the 40,000 amp electric station. Many plafonier units were also used. The film was shot with Debrie Super Parvo cameras for sound scenes and Parvo L and Cameraeclair in silent takes, many of which were used with travelling devices as the one in which Jean Gabin enters Michel Simon's shop at the end of the film.

*Quai des Brumes* was an exemplary film from the point of view of cinematography. The following were remarkable scenes: the first outdoors night sequence with the truck on the road, night indoor and outdoor takes of Panama House, the arrival of the gang early in the morning at The Havre harbor location filmed by Louis Page, the interior of the Michel Simon shop, various close-ups of Jean Gabin and Michèlle Morgan with expressive lighting and the shots of the amusement park, and especially the night scenes in the reconstructed main street, very realistic in those days. The film, a highlight of French film production in the thirties, showed a paradigmatic working style of European master in this profession.

## Wuthering Heights

The Oscar for the best black and white cinematography in 1939 was awarded to Gregg Toland for *Wuthering Heights*. It was the first time the Academy decided to grant one award for black and white and another for color cinematography. The continued use of color had improved so much that it merited its own qualification. That year an award was established for special effects both in photography and sound. That was another example of new forms of film evaluation, due to developments in the film industry.

*Wuthering Heights* was Gregg Toland's first Oscar. The renowned Samuel Goldwyn, creator of big American film stars and of refined productions, produced this film. The film director was another first rank figure in this field, William Wyler, who had been in this field since 1925 and with whom Toland had worked on *Dead End* (1937), which had been highly celebrated. With that film and now with *Wuthering Heights*, Toland began a rising career with other directors, halted only by his sudden death in 1948. All his productions were also great films, admired as examples of top-level cinematography.

Gregg Toland had been born in Charleston, South Carolina, on May 29, 1904. He studied electrical engineering until he was fascinated by the first motion picture camera he chanced to see during a shooting sequence and it pulled him into this profession. At fifteen he joined Fox studios on a vacation opportunity. He soon was integrated into the camera crew and in 1924 joined the Goldwyn Studios as camera assistant and after seven years reached the position of first cameraman on the film *Palmy Days* (1931), with Eddie Cantor. In his career he had the opportunity to work with famed Hollywood cinematographers such as Arthur Edeson and George Barnes, always with a attitude of learning and a search for excellence. He studied the work and techniques of German and French cinematographers and their realistic and surrealistic styles and the use of arc lighting.[8]

Samuel Goldwyn, who was Toland's friend and knew well his excellence, had an experimental shop built for him inside his studio where Toland carried out research work and where he obtained interesting results which he gladly shared with his colleagues, even phoning them early in the morning about his findings. Toland also always wanted to learn about all the fields connected with this trade, even taking make-up and hairdressing courses. He was very interested in optics, dramatic composition and film narrative. He made experiments with vanguard directors such as Slavko Vorkapich and Robert Florey, and as a lover of mechanics he designed various devices to be used on his equipment. That was why Mitchell Camera Corp. asked for his advice and suggestions when they were developing the BNC model. His research in film narrative made him experiment with depth of field of lenses and he always kept with him short strips of his tests in this field that were later used in many productions. He was eager to write articles about his ideas and experiences and expounded his professional views with passion.

Samuel Goldwyn's well-known nose for business and people helped and stimulated Toland in his research and Goldwyn gave him ample freedom, even lending him to other studios like Fox and RKO for important productions, because he knew, as Toland himself had said, that Goldwyn Studios would always be his home. Toland's fame was the result not only of his high artistic and technical talents, but also of his commitment to a film project, from pre-production to other aspects connected with the job, such as set design and construction, costumes, choosing locations, special effects, many of which he preferred to make with the camera while shooting, to avoid dupes, and the personal control of the release print quality. He urged his directors to select the pictorial composition of the shots and the viewing angle. He always wanted to break the Hollywood star filmmaking clichés, and persuaded the use of the lighting mood best suited to each film theme. Moreover he was the fastest Hollywood cinematographer in lighting up the sets. Those elements made him famous and explained why he was the best-paid cinematographer in the trade.[9]

*Wuthering Heights* was a sombre story by Emily Brontë based on the place where she and her sisters lived in the first half of the 1800s in Haworth, Yorkshire, England. Lawrence Olivier and Merle Oberon starred in it. The theme required an adequate sombre setting, as well as precise storytelling, which was rendered by Wyler's mastery. To produce this climate Gregg Toland created a meticulous lighting for the manor house. Practically most of the film was shot inside the studio. There were outstanding sequences in the film, e.g., the initial one of a stranger's arrival at the old mansion, the storm seen through the windows, the early morning outdoor scenes of the young couple riding in the bleak highlands, Cathy's return to their neighbors after the accident and the ball sequence. The arts of Wyler and Toland created the oppressive atmosphere of the place. Some outdoor scenes were recreated on the film stage with heavy clouds made according to the best methods of those days, which today look fake. In this film, Toland used the first Mitchell BNC cameras that Gold-wyn had bought, to which Toland added devices and lenses he preferred. This film narra-tive style and black and white cinematography remain today as a first-rate production.

## Gone with the Wind

This film was a landmark in the motion picture industry, and for decades has been an example of Hollywood's most notable productions. It merited ten Academy Awards in 1939, one of them for Ernest Haller's and Ray Rennahan's color cinematography. There was also a tribute to the Technicolor Corporation which received a special award for the quality and efficiency of their process and for their services. The film was also an example of the best in color cinematography and how it increased production values in big scale filmmaking.

The story of how the film was made is today a legend to many movie fans, but still stu-dents of this field should well remember some technical aspects. Selznick wanted to imprint his style, which meant, "do it in a big way and at the best level"; this required financial sup-port that he obtained from the Whitney family of New York. But he not could escape from the claws of his father-in-law, Louis B. Mayer, regarding the use of the irreplaceable Clark Gable, under contract with MGM. Consequently he had to give up the distribution (that he wanted to be done through United Artists) to that studio's distributor, Lowe's Inc., for half of the revenues.[10] Moreover, he had to postpone the shooting almost two years when this star would be available. During this time, Selznick organized his production team, he retained the best technicians in the trade and carried on with the special effects that would be needed.

Selznick had two specialists for this type of work: Jack Cosgrove and Clarence W. Slifer, who had worked with him on *The Garden of Allah* (1936), with experience in the Techni-color process. Work began in the summer of 1936 in the Selznick International Studios in Culver City, that had been the formerly Pathé Studios built by Thomas Ince and acquired in 1931 by RKO. The studio's front was well known for its reproduction of a classic old south-ern mansion, always shown on the standard presentation of that firm's productions. The interior of this mansion had a wall-papered hallway and a winding mahogany stairway that induced the sensation of a remarkable film that Selznick always wanted to make. The Spe-cial Effects Department was set up in this studio in the old Stage 5, designed for shooting silent material. The studio still maintained the old sets of past films and a place named 40 Acres Back Lot where many scenes of this film were made.

The first photographic special effects were a large number of matte paintings of the several backgrounds that would be required for the outdoor scenes that they realized would be of fundamental importance when reading the galley proofs of Margaret Mitchell's book. The experts also worked on other matte shots for another color production that Selznick was also producing at that time. They were also gaining experience also in aerial images with this color process and an optical printer was created using a Technicolor camera out of the firm's premises for the first time, making use of the experience that Clarence W. Slifer acquired while working with Technicolor Corp.[11]

In *GWTW* the difficulties of the first subtractive Technicolor process were overcome when they were able to use a new type of film that had a better grain structure, soft color reproduction, three times faster speed for indoor shooting, and four times in outdoor shoot-ing. Now it was not necessary to use the green and magenta filters behind the camera prism, which absorbed a lot of light. This production was a very spectacular film with a high percentage of indoor shooting, many of the shots in medium low key. The new Technicolor high speed negative was, consequently, a great help that contributed to the speed of shooting and thus reduce production costs. Now it was not necessary to use many of the M&R arc broadsides to produce the required fill light, as before. The new film emulsion allowed working with only 250 foot-candles for low keys, though the standard was 500 foot-candles with a lens aperture of f/2.8 and a negative speed of 25 ASA. It was even possible to use tungsten light in small units for light touches.

The main shooting of the film began on December 1938 with the Atlanta fire sequence, filmed on the studio back lot using the large settings of the Great Wall of Kong's Skull Island and the old sets of *King of Kings* (1927), that covered 40 acres. Those sets were prepared with a pipe system to provide fuel for the fire, and water for control and quenching. The fire control was by the Los Angeles Fire Department with 25 policemen, 50 studio firemen and 200 studio helpers. Seven Technicolor cameras were used, even one recently built that operated at 72 f.p.s. high speed which operated very noisily. It was the first time that three negatives were simultaneously driven at such speed. The most effective takes were made during the special effects process with this camera. A special process conceived for wide screen with two cameras and a mirror was also adopted.[12]

When shooting the fire scenes the cameras had to be placed in strategic places as it was important to cover the fire from the most varied angles since they would be short duration takes, specially in the most striking moments. The switch panel was operated by David O. Selznick himself. The fire began and quickly spread and in six minutes a large set, a relic of the silent film era, was turned into ashes. Stuntman Yakima Canutt doubled for Clark Gable in dangerous scenes. Many important people in the industry were present during the shooting. Among them was Laurence Olivier who was then filming *Rebecca* and who brought his new wife, Vivien Leigh, with him, recently arrived from England. Myron Selznick, her agent, introduced her to his brother, saying: "I want you to meet Scarlett O'Hara." These were the circumstances under which the producer found the star he was seeking.[13]

The complex production of this film was very well organized, but it was unusual by the industry's standards. It was entirely made in thematic continuity, excluding the Atlanta takes. In 1937 Selznick hired William Cameron Menzies as production designer (a position specially created for him) to develop the aesthetic design of the film by means of sketches and paintings he made himself or had made by other artists. This was very unusual in those days. More than three thousand color drawings were made, one for each film scene. By this method a great continuity was obtained as well as an outstanding plastic beauty. Cameron Menzies was valuable also when, together with Sam Wood, they took up the film's direction when Victor Fleming, the actual director, was ill, or when preparing special effects. This was why Cameron Menzies received a special Academy Award for his outstanding work. Many cinematographers participated in shooting *GWTW*, which took up 1,350,000 feet of film. One of the most important was Ray Rennahan, head of the camera department of Technicolor and of long standing in this firm where he took his first steps in the first color production, *The Toll of the Sea* (1922), and as cinematographer of *Winds of the Sharp* (1935). He was the official expert of this color cinematography process and worked on many Hollywood color film productions, and also in England when the firm trained several technicians there. Rennahan replaced Technicolor expert Wilfred Cline who had started the shooting with Lee Garmes for about three months.

Garmes was the other cinematographer specially contacted by Selznick who came from

England where he was working with Alexander Korda. He started making film tests of Vivien Leigh. It was Garmes who began the official shooting of the film during the Tara opening sequences. George Cukor directed those scenes. But Selznick replaced Cukor with Victor Fleming. According to Garmes, Cukor had not reached the required level because he used the script made by Selznick and not the improved script of Sydney Howard. Garmes worked on one third of the production right up to the scene when Melanie gave birth to her son. Selznick, accustomed to the old Technicolor system of bright colors, did not like the new soft colors of the improved process, and replaced Garmes with Ernest Haller.[14] A native of Los Angeles, born in 1896 and active in the industry from the early twenties, Haller worked in the Goldwyn Studios where he achieved remarkable cinematography in *Jezebel* (1938).

Shooting *GWTW* was very complex due to the large number of varied scenes in such a long film, which took more than 20 weeks to make. Some shots were made in Natchez, Mississippi, such as the cotton plantation, and a steamboat travelling on the river. Wilfred Kline took them for the James A. Fitzpatrick Traveltalks, which received this assignment. A plantation located at the end of Lot 3 of MGM studios was also used. The scenes of the first war news at the beginning of the Civil War were shot in Busch Gardens, Pasadina. One of the most shocking film sequences was the crane shot of Scarlett O'Hara when she went into the Atlanta railway station and the camera goes up to a very high shot showing the multitude of wounded soldiers along the railways.[15]

A giant construction crane was used; it had a 30 ft. long boom with a hanging platform where a Technicolor tripack camera with a Mitchell viewfinder was installed. The scene included 1,500 extras and about 1,000 dummies. Using matte painting many bodies were added later to fill the gaps, at the top right angle of the shot. Special effects were also used in the station when Melanie found her husband. There, the railroad station was retouched including smoke in the mock-up of a locomotive while a complete wagon with wounded soldiers is seen entering the station in the background. Close to one hundred matte shots were used in this production, many of which were included throughout the film and others in the opening titles. This last one was unique in the film industry because it was a long travelling take over specially prepared large size characters that composed the text. This take was later superimposed over a panoramic of a landscape view between two trees.[16]

A careful analysis of the cinematography of this film deserves several comments about its lighting techniques. However, notwithstanding the varied number of cinematographers taking part, the film shows a very coherent and functional lighting, indicating that the styles and the limitations of this color system between the highlights and low ratio were finally overcome. The scenes made by Lee Garmes evidenced his high technique and artistic refinement. This was present in the background treatments, the shadows applied on the walls, the light distribution and different shots of open spaces with many players. The lighting of Pittypat's home was also very imaginative. In that scene Scarlett is placed in the center of an image formed by shadows with a little light reaching her face; the light comes from a bedroom and it fades when the door is shut. Good lighting was also used in the scene where two big shadows of two praying women projected on a church wall were discovered, with a pan, to be Melanie and Scarlett behind the candelabrum. That was an example of the dovetailing between cinematographer and director, as well as of Menzie's hand in the pictorial composition.

There were many counterlights in this film. One of the most elaborate uses was the birth of Melanie's child, which was covered by several shots with a background of windows and the light coming filtered through Venetian blinds. Perhaps this was one of Garmes's last efforts for this production, but Haller and Rennahan maintained this level in the last three portions of this film, specially in dramatic and in night sequences. Both made good use of the excellent sets of Lyle Wheeler, particularly of the Rhett Butler mansion with its elaborate staircase which, like the one in the Tara mansion, played a fundamental part in the story and which the cinematographers lighted in excellent form with diverse small lighting units with the abilities of the new fast Technicolor three strip process used in this film.[17]

This film was one of the first in which the Mitchell background projector was used to provide production abilities in many shots. The anamorphic system was also considered a special effects resource, but finally was not used. This film should be seen in the original bright color prints to appreciate the advance of the present day color process, but the good taste and style of classic lighting methods then used still endure.

# Rebecca

At the beginning of World War II, David O. Selznick decided to bring the most noted British film director, Alfred Hitchcock, to the United States. With a generous (by European standards) contract, Selznick wanted Hitchcock to carry out a project about the *Titanic*, that was afterwards dropped due to several production drawbacks impediments. After having made seventeen films in Europe, Hitchcock started a new career in Hollywood. The new project was to adapt a romantic best seller to the screen; Daphne du Maurier, the renowned English author, had written the novel and it was turned into another Selznick top rate production called *Rebecca* (1940).

Hitchcock started to work on the film script and realized, much to his concern, that the prestige and independence he earned in Europe was of no value in Hollywood. Selznick always interfered in all details with Hitchcock's work: he did not accept Hitchcock's film script, and finally it was carried out by scriptwriters Robert E. Sherwood and Joan Harryson under Hitchcock's and Selznick's supervision. The British actors Laurence Olivier and Joan Fontaine were selected for the main roles, with Nigel Bruce, George Sanders and C. Aubrey Smith, also British, in supporting roles. Lyle Wheeler was in charge of art direction and the cinematography was in the hands of the experienced George Barnes. The combination of talents was perfect, although Hitchcock had many difficulties with Selznick during the shooting. However the film was finished and was an excellent production with good box office and it received two Academy Awards in 1940, one for the best production and the other for the best black and white cinematography.

George Barnes was a celebrated Hollywood cinematographer. He had been born in 1893 and started in the profession in 1919, in Thomas H. Ince's studios. He worked on a large number of films on which he demonstrated an elaborate lighting technique that drew the attention of important Hollywood directors like Georges Fitzmaurice, King Vidor, Ernst Lubitsch, Lloyd Bacon, Henry King and Cecil de Mille, who then invited Barnes to work in their films. Samuel Goldwyn, a talent searcher, brought him to his studio, first as second cameraman and soon as cinematographer. Gregg Toland was on his crew and learned many of his refined techniques. His private life was particularly varied. He married seven times, including the well-known actress Joan Blondell, and he was one of the few in his profession who parked his latest model Cadillac on the studio grounds. But Barnes excelled in Hollywood for the high quality of his work and not for such peculiarities. He could create oppressive moods with his lighting and use a figurative style when it was necessary. This was why Selznick and Hitchcock often wanted him.

*Rebecca* was a story developed basically in two places: Monte Carlo and Manderley on the English coast and both were built in the studio. The meeting of the two star players and their travels in Monte Carlo shows the typical false transparency effects of those times. But some of the hotel indoor shots reveal Barnes' lighting ability using suggested sources such as a bedroom, which shows plants, and chandelier shadows on the wall. Joan Fontaine's nightmare scene in her bedroom also shows excellent lighting effects. However this cinematographer's tour de force was the Manderley indoor takes, the mansion of George Fontesquieu Maximilian de Winter (played by Laurence Olivier) where, thanks to the imagination and good taste of Lyle Wheeler, Barnes had the chance to create the hallucinating mood the film needed.

Great plastic beauty was reached with the lighting of the mansion hall, the great staircase that leads to the rooms, and especially Rebecca's bedroom where the large window curtains, when opened, produced a marked light beam effect and counterlights on the players. Constructive details of the set are also carefully lighted such as bass-relief, door mouldings and shadows projecting on the walls. Other effective scenes were that of people in the fog during the shipwreck search and the Manderley fire sequence, when even some plate shots were included from the Atlanta fire sequence of *Gone with the Wind*. The lighting of the beach cottage indoors was very striking and there Hitchcock moved the camera suggestively to follow de Winter's tale of his wife's death. Barnes made many other films afterwards but this one was the most representative of his career.

# PART IV
# THE FORTIES

## 28. The Film Industry in the Forties

The Second World War that covered the first half of this decade left deep, usually inerasable scars. The motion picture industry was affected similarly by World War I, but the consequences were more intense because film industry structures were now more complex and the war reached more countries. The film industry was so developed that the new conflict affected it at several levels. The darkness that covered Europe soon influenced Hollywood with tangible effects even before the United States engaged in conflict.

Hollywood had always counted on revenues from world film markets, but now they were dwindling as the war extended over more countries. Even spectacular productions, like *Gone with the Wind*, that seemed to have a promising future, took time to recover from the domestic market what was expected from abroad. Faced with these prospects, industry investors began to restrain their investments fearing the confusing circumstances. They thought their activity could be dispensed with in such tragic moments. But motion pictures would provide other contributions that soon appeared and were promptly used.

America's sudden entry into war made evident the urgent need to organize the country to face the predicaments. Several plans had already been studied to overcome such contingencies. Among the most difficult tasks was how to instruct millions of recruits in a minimum time. Motion pictures and other audiovisual media were selected as the most effective solution to this specific need.

This resource had been tried already: during the previous decade some military experts had made tests to this end, but never before had its use been contemplated so widely or methodically in such an effective way, nor so massively applied with such urgency, and with the help of the whole film industry. Hollywood studios, important short-film producers from across the nation, and the armed forces themselves were turned to produce thousands of training films and filmstrips. They varied over the most diverse topics, such as how to interrogate prisoners, saving lives at sea, how to operate the most varied arms and equipment, survival in the jungle, detecting and sinking submarines, and hundreds of other subjects connected with the war effort.

The specialized training films for the three armed forces were carefully drawn up with very didactic and highly pedagogic techniques by university experts, animation film studios, painters and draftsmen and specialized scriptwriters. They used the most advanced audiovisual procedures aided by specially developed teaching and training equipment. With these methods the country was soon, ready to face the varied fronts of the conflict. The required personnel were thus prepared while it was being readied in an unprecedented form and speed.

Film production was soon considered a powerful weapon in important fields such as information, publicity, documentation of events, target checking, and verification of success or failure of war actions or intelligence operations. Hollywood had the mission of contributing to keep up the morale of the people and when the nation found itself at war, 25 percent of the films were connected to the war effort.[1] Likewise entertainment also reached the soldiers on the front as well as those who remained at home.

The countries involved in the war maintained, with ups and downs, their own film production. The country reaching the highest production figures from 1939 to 1945 was Japan, with 1,461 films; Germany produced 572 films; Italy 509; France 394; and Britain 370 films. The lowest production years were 1941 in Germany with 71 films, 1944 in Italy with 17 films and 27 in France, and 1945 in Britain with 28, and 38 in Japan.[2] All these films were destined for the domestic market of each, and were also exported to neutral countries or nations in the influence zone of each. Evidently film production did not collapse during the war. During nearly half a decade world film production was kept according to circumstances in each country, in film studios, laboratories and equipment manufacturing firms. But also there were studios, laboratories and factories that were bombed, pillaged or compelled to produce for the occupation forces.

American films practically did not reach continental Europe, arriving only in Great Britain, Sweden and Switzerland. In Great Britain, Hollywood producers' incomes were reduced because of limitations on money transfers. A great part of Asia was taken by the Japanese. So when Hollywood saw how some of their markets were reduced, they turned to other markets such as Latin America. Likewise Hollywood reduced the number of productions when the government imposed a 25 percent restriction on the availability of raw stock for war requirements. The American film industry was also considerably affected by the fact that one-quarter of the male personnel in the movie industry, famed film stars, film directors and technicians, were called for military service.[3]

Also in those days, audiences in America unexpectedly increased by about 20 percent, both during work days as well as weekends, maybe due to a need for more recreation in those difficult days. Despite this difficult world situation, film technology underwent a considerable development during this period. One of the main changes was the increasing use of the 16mm film format that until then had been only considered for home use and was now ideal for specific war requirements, especially in the U.S.A. The massive production of training films and shorts was to be exhibited in a new form. Instead of great film theaters in American cities, those films were destined to be shown in smaller spaces such as recruit training centers, military bases both in the rear and near the front, as well as on U.S. Navy ships. It was essential then to use a format easy to transport and to archive, handle and show, and with the added advantage of having a safety base. The 16mm format covered all those requisites; furthermore its volume and weight were about one-quarter of those of the 35mm; moreover, the projecting equipment had been improved and was then extremely compact in relation to that for the 35mm gauge.

This huge quantity of 16mm reduction prints from 35mm originals included those obtained from many Hollywood productions, especially conceived for those theaters. They were training material, films designed for information, the *Army-Navy Screen Magazine*, the so-called bubble films to prepare recruits for war and explain why they were fighting, as announced by the title of a well known series then made. Some of those films were translated and sent to friendly countries all over the world. The extended new 16mm market gave rise to a massive production of 16mm sound-film projectors. After the war, the use of the

16mm format kept growing steadily. The armed forces continued producing training films on a lower scale. Hollywood also continued using this format as another means of reaching small places without film theaters; with a cheap, portable 16mm sound projector it was now possible to rent fiction films to be shown in cultural and religious centers. Television definitively adopted this gauge for its own newsreel production. The production of 16mm films also increased in the growing market of education, instructive and sponsored films destined for many different cultural centers.

The massive use of the so-called substandard format produced important changes in the film industry. Commercial laboratories required new processing and printing equipment. Manufacturers received requests for new processing machines, not only for war requirements that used this format but also from processing laboratories that produced reduction prints. American firms that specialized in manufacturing developing equipment produced units of the most varied characteristics, according to requirements; some of these were Fonda, Houston, Cine Arts Crafts, Morse, Art Reeves, Spoor Thomson and Bridgamatic.

Among them, the unit produced by Houston Corporation, West Los Angeles, California, was remarkable for producing equipment to military requirements. This unit named by the military as K-1A Film Developing Machine, was a very compact 16mm item of processing equipment for gun and combat shooting cameras.[4] It could develop 900 ft. of reversible film in one hour, 300 ft. negative and 1,200 ft. of positive by only changing the baths. Thermostat control and refrigeration maintained a constant solution temperature. It was a very light, hermetic, easily transported instrument on wheels, weighing 1,200 lbs. It was widely used at the front at U.S. Air Force bases, flying schools and U.S. Navy ships and improved later on.[5] As training film production was in 35mm film, which was later reduced to 16mm prints, the demand increased for image and sound reduction printers which were manufactured by Busch, Depue, Schustek and Huler among others. Many films were filmed in color. Some were in Technicolor, for which this firm took charge of processing and producing reduction prints, but Eastman and Ansco color films required also new color printers from the laboratories.

During those days the working committee of the American Standards Association defined film exposures indices, which were of fundamental importance to exactly determine the sensitivity of raw stock and the readings of exposure meters, as compared to other systems such as Weston, British Standard, General Electric, Scheiner, DIN and the old British H & D.

Eastman Kodak, Dupont and Ansco manufactured large amounts of black and white raw stock in the United States during the war. In those days the fastest motion picture black and white negative was the Kodak Super XX Type 1232 and 5241 with an index of 100. The reversal material with this index was the Kodak Super XX Reversal 5261. The Ansco Ultra Speed Panchromatic Negative 256 and the Ansco Triple S Pan 2 Type had similar characteristics. Dupont had no high speed film with this index. The Kodak Plus X Panchromatic negative Type 5241, the Ansco Super Pan Supreme Type 353 and the Dupont Superior 2 Type 126 were at the medium speed level of motion picture negative (index 50). The 16mm reversible raw stock with this speed were the Kodak Super X Panchromatic Reversal Type 5256 and the Ansco Hypan Reversal Type 293. The negative low speed raw stock (index 25) were the Kodak Background Panchromatic negative type 1230, the Ansco Finopan Type 357 and the Dupont Superior 1 type 104. Kodak was the only American manufacturer of the strategic infrared film for target recognizance and defined as Infrared 1210, index 12. American color film production during the conflict was considerable, especially for covering the

Pacific War. The raw stock used was of reversible type in 35 and 16mm such as Kodachrome and Anscolor.[6]

In the second half of the forties, technology advanced to the development of products for the new TV media. The 16mm film format, which was more economic, flexible and technically reliable, was soon adopted, substituting for the 35mm format in many fields. The United States created the world's most complete infrastructure for all kinds of processing in this format. This change took longer in Europe, where at the beginning, many film professionals resisted this change calling this format spaghetti. But the economic benefit was too important, and while 35mm was standard in Hollywood for long features and TV serials, with the time, 16mm became standard for TV newsreels and low scale TV productions.

Motion picture equipment makers offered their products to TV stations and TV producers. Many automatic cameras used in the home market were built and adapted to this new media. Other camera manufacturers designed compact equipment for sound-on-film TV news recording, considerably lighter than that used in the 35mm newsreel field. Finally, refined 16mm studio cameras were made to widen the scope of this format, now a new option for cinematographers of a new age. In Hollywood, film technology also brought changes. Lenses in cameras were being replaced by new color-corrected and coated units. Mobile camera techniques used for shooting TV serials increased the number of dollies and their design; the concept of the crab dolly was then created allowing immediate direction changes; it was developed by constructors like Steve Krilanovich, and was followed up by improved instruments such as the Multidolly.[7] Finally, new compact lighting units were added to that equipment, and also in process photography and film laboratories, but without special drastic changes.

# 29. Cameras

During that time new cameras were built around the world. War made the involved countries want to cover all the different military actions by the armed forces themselves. Motion pictures were needed for information, reconnaissance, strategic and intelligence uses, documentation and evidence. The movie camera shooting war events was another very useful weapon. Camera manufacturers began to receive unprecedented orders, or were forced, in occupied countries, to build equipment for the enemy as occurred in France and Czechoslovakia short time after being occupied.

However a different situation arose in the postwar period. Motion picture makers saw that the European industry was in ruins and many film studios in occupied countries had been ransacked by the enemy or destroyed by bombing. The main entertainment industries urgently needed to recover after such long distress. Reliable foreign currency was scarcely available, so European manufacturers of motion picture equipment now had an opportunity to design modern equipment and recreate this market anew.

## European equipment

### FRENCH CAMERAS

In November 1941, during the Nazi occupation, the French firm André Debrie developed a reflex viewing system by means of a reflection on a vertical shutter blade, for their Super Parvo studio camera, (Patent: France S.G.D. 973,668). The new camera was called Model "V" and the system was known as Vision Reflexe. This was the first application of this system in a studio camera and its first use after the Munich firm Arnold & Richer had patented the method in 1931, and applied it to their handheld Arriflex camera. The new Super Parvo Reflex substituted the old design with a mobile film gate, used a top mounted ground glass and incorporated the following features:

- a vertical 45 degree-mirrored shutter system adapted to 18mm lenses;
- a variable 0 to 180 degree shutter opening;
- new film channel;
- new insulated camera housing;
- lighting unit built into camera controls;
- bipack features for special effects or color cinematography.

All these refinements plus the attraction of reflex viewing later made this model very popular in many countries, reaching a total sales record of 7,500 Super Parvos, a figure never before reached for such instruments, not even by American manufacturers.[1]

In 1940, when the German troops entered Paris, the Etablissements Éclair was promptly occupied, and the company technicians were ordered to produce a camera for the needs of the German Film Service. The heads of the firm craftily delayed fulfilling this obligation, but secretly worked on conceiving a prototype portable camera based on revolutionary concepts of two engineers of the firm with more than

The Éclair Cameflex magazine camera (*courtesy Éclair International Diffusion*).

twenty years experience in this field: André Coutant and Jacques Mathot. In 1944 they put their ideas together but they had to wait until the end of the war to bring them to light in 1946 with the name Cameflex. This piece of equipment was really an innovation of unusual design.[2]

The Cameflex was a magazine camera: the continuous drive system and the pressure plate were placed in the interchangeable magazine. The camera body housed the drive unit, the film gate, the intermittent movement, a divergent three-lens turret, a reflex viewing system and a magnetic tachometer. French mechanical ingenuity was applied in carefully designing this camera with many refinements, making it highly competitive with other similar equipment at that time. Thus this instrument was acclaimed in the 1948 Venice Biennal and in 1950 received an Academy Award in Hollywood. The most outstanding features of this camera were:

• 100, 200 or 400 ft. pre-charged magazines for instantaneous installation even with the camera running;

• spider turret allowing 18.5mm lenses;

• variable opening shutter, from 200 degrees to 40 degrees, designed so that the blades stop the light very near the focal plane, producing very high image definition;

• remarkable steady image without use of pilot pins;

• the viewing tube could be pivoted horizontally and vertically so as to allow for framing and focusing in any camera position and with the right or left eye, while simultaneously controlling the film speed in the tachometer with the other eye;

• the camera could be set on the floor to obtain a very low camera set-up;

• a filter slot in front of the aperture allowed placing gelatine filters, independent of the crystal filter in the front matte box;

• the small size electric motor, light in weight, needed only 6–8 volts; the unit could be replaced by a spring motor, or by a crank handle unit.

**Cameflex magazines for 100, 200, 400 and 400 ft. horizontal format for Aquaflex** (*courtesy Éclair International Diffusion*).

Those features were unusual in a portable camera at that time, which made this equipment attractive, especially in France. Therefore the Cameflex replaced many other makes in France like Morigraf, Le Bidru and Le Blay and, later on it competed with the Arriflex. Following the appearance of the Cameflex in 1946–47 and its later introduction to the American market with the name of Camerette, honoring an old predecessor, the manufacturers soon improved the unit to a model conceived to be used in both 35mm and 16 mm, by only changing the magazine and the film gate. Later on, it incorporated a blimp for sound shooting and an underwater shell that transformed it into the Aquaflex, the first camera specially designed for submarine shooting used in Hollywood and by the French and American navies.

## CZECH CAMERAS

The Nazi invasion forced Czech camera manufacturers to produce units for the needs of the occupying forces. The Cinephon and Slechta companies, which had been associated and were afterwards independent, were forced to build cameras for the German and Italian armies. During the war period Slechta produced double system sound cameras type BBT for the German Tobis Klang Film. Other models were BHA and BR III. Later on, Cinephon cameras were sold to UFA Studios in Berlin, Barrandow in Prague and Cinecittà in Rome. They were excellently built studio and field cameras. Slechta varied the designs according to the requirements of the buyers, but usually the camera body was molded in aluminum with a single sprocket wheel, prism viewing system, 400 ft. or 1000 ft. top mounted

The French cinematographer Christian Matras shooting with a Cameflex and using the special tripod head grip designed by Éclair (*courtesy Éclair International Diffusion*).

magazine, and included an automatic or hand dissolve device, automatic four-lens turret and external small size motor. Cinephon also built several studio cameras and continued building the handheld compact unit with internal 200 ft. cassette, built-in electric motor and through the film viewing for newsreel shooting.

In 1945, after the war the Czech film industry was nationalized and cameras were delivered mainly to the USSR, Yugoslavia and India. Slechta equipment was confiscated by the government and Joseph Slechta had to start again. He created a 16mm prototype camera and in 1948 after the changes in government policy he had to leave Prague. The firm closed and production of movie cameras did not continue. He moved to nearby Ledecko, where he had a small workshop. With the camera operator V. Novotny he assembled the last technical work team. Cinephon collapsed and afterwards camera production was resumed by the government firm Filmovy Prumisl in Barrandov, Prague.[3]

## BRITISH CAMERAS

Cameras were also made in England during and after the war. During the conflict the American Bell & Howell Eyemo and the Devry were the most used handheld cameras but there were also some new homemade models like the Newman Sinclair Autokine, with four-lens turret and other devices added according to war demands. Among field cameras, Vinten had its model H that combined with the Visatone optical recorder was useful for double system sound recording. Towards the last years of the war Vinten built a hand camera named the Vinten Normandy, with spring and electric motors, three lens turret, 200 ft. film spool, winterized features, compact rectangular body, focusing through the film gate, parallax corrected top mounted viewfinder, and pilot pin movement. It weighed 15 pounds and had a leather strap. This camera was a step-forward of a similar non-reflex previous model.

In the post war period, camera manufacture was turned toward studio and field equipment. Charles Vinten, a pioneer British film equipment maker, conceived a new studio camera with many concepts inspired by Debrie's Super Parvo Reflex but with many other new devices. The camera conceived during the war appeared about 1945–1946 and was called the Vinten Everest; it had a blimp covered parallelepiped body. Two independent 1000 ft. film magazines were placed side by side. The film gate with double side-claw and dual register pin movement was placed in front. The drive allowed running in forward and reverse. It returned to the old European concept of the film moving in three planes of travel instead of only one as in the American cameras.

This camera's reflex viewing was made up by a shutter in two 85 degree segments opposite one another, and with a lower speed rotation to reduce noise. The front surface of each shutter segment reflected and projected the image. The total shutter aperture was 180 degrees, and it could be varied to a minimum 30 degrees. Viewing was effected through a large 3 × 2 inch ground glass protected by a bellows sunshade and an eyepiece. A panchro filter could be inserted in the viewing system to control scene lighting. A rangefinder was placed on a side of the camera body and a handle to operate the lens focus ring. A three-lens turret allowed lenses from 28mm (wide angle) to 100 mm. The camera included automatic lubrication, an internal 220-volt 3-phase motor, and controls behind the unit.[4]

Soon after the appearance of the Vinten Everest the improved version came out, the Vinten Everest II, a redesigned model with a more elaborate and streamlined body with the following features:

- lens hood in camera body;
- new viewing screen for both eyes of 2.5 in. × 1.75 in. at rear of camera;
- a transparent margin surrounding the viewing screen to enable the operator to see objects moving out of the picture; push button motor switch;
- one lens mount;
- synchronizing device for back projection;
- new internal rangefinder with eyepiece and focus handle.[5]

This new camera was used during the fifties by some English studios and was sold to Cinecittà Studios in Italy and studios in Scandinavia and India. Later on Vinten Ltd. introduced a field camera called the Windsor Reflex to replace the old H model (which was based on a shift over viewing method). The new camera incorporated this new viewing system in a field camera. The movement operated with two pin claws and a pair of reciprocating pilot pins, forward and reverse operation, variable 170 degree double aperture shutter, adjustable in 20 degree increments from 10 degrees to wide open. Reflex viewing comprised a solid piece of mirrored steel with its surface polished to a bright mirror finish, a four lens turret, bellows sunshade and filter holder, 3-phase synchronous motor, safety trip plate, film punch and marker light.[6]

The British Vinten Everest Studio camera (*courtesy Archivo Nacional de la Imagen, Sodre*).

Vinten Windsor field camera (*courtesy Archivo Nacional de la Imagen, Sodre*).

J. Arthur Rank, the eminent British film industry entrepreneur who had built an empire including several studios, laboratories, production and distribution firms, film theaters, and factories totaling about 80 companies, also made a British camera which become a favorite. During the war, Rank made unsuccessful contacts with the Mitchell Camera Corp. to reach an arrangement for buying Mitchell cameras with pounds sterling instead of scarce dollars. During the contacts Rank's agent accidentally learned that the Mitchell NC model had not been patented in the U.K.[7] This camera was the workhorse of the British film industry, as it was in Hollywood, and consequently Rank decided to have it built in England; the assigned firm was Newall Engineering Co. of Peterborough, famous for the strict standards of their products.

The Newall (the Mitchell NC reproduction) was almost exact in all details, with a small variation: an exclusive magazine lid-locking device with an attractive external rotating boss. Optical Measuring Tools Ltd., of Berks, built certain optical pieces. The camera prototype was designed and built in ten months. The most complex piece was the intermittent movement, for which several difficulties had to be overcome due to its extreme precision. Rank soon found an immediate acceptance in the British film industry: the Newall was used not only in Rank's film studios, e.g., Denham and Pinewood, but also in other studios. Many important accessories were made such as a blimp (that later was redesigned), tripods, and a sound head for single sound shooting. The camera included Taylor, Taylor & Hobson's well-known lenses (another firm in his group) and Gaumont-Kalee Ltd. marketed this instrument. Nearly 500 units of the Newall cameras were sold according to their serial numbers, and were distributed to many studios all over the world during more than a decade.

Shooting in Rome with the Newall camera and Colortran lighting units (*courtesy Unitalia Film*).

## GERMAN CAMERAS

German camera production was based on equipment built by Arnold & Richter of Munich and Askania Werke of Berlin. The former produced the Arriflex Handkamera that was the standard working camera of the armed forces and used on all war fronts. More than 500 units of this initial model were produced. On July 13, 1944, the firm was heavily bombed and all activity ceased. On the other hand during the war Askania Werke produced the Askania Schulter in a new model and some units of the Askania Atelier as required by UFA Studios. For sound newsreel shooting Slechta cameras with Tobis sound equipment were used.

After the war, about 1948, a Super Steimi 35mm studio and newsreel camera was made.[8] Toward the end of the decade Arnold and Richter reassumed the production of the Arriflex and began to export it to foreign countries, naming it model II. It included a round matte box shaft, all stainless steel film gate, new mechanisms and an improved optical system with a louver over the ground glass. The new camera had to compete with old Arriflex models that had been "liberated" unfinished after the war and were offered at very low prices in some countries. Two of the first new Arriflex units arriving in USA were bought by Robert Flaherty to shoot his film *Louisiana Story* in 1948, laying aside a Debrie Parvo "L."

## ITALIAN CAMERAS

At the beginning of the forties, after making the Avia, Alfredo Donelli, the camera maker, continued building camera equipment. The new camera he designed and built was named Novado. It had 400 ft. independent magazines inside the body, a variable speed DC motor, viewing through the film, top mounted viewfinder, three lens turret, variable opening shutter and two handgrips. This camera came out during the war and was used to meet the requirements of the Istituto Nazionale Luce, the government newsreel production center, as well as the demands of the Italian armed forces. Production continued to the end of the decade, and some units reached France and even the United States. Two of these cameras are still exhibited in Italy, one in Cinecittà and the other in the Associazione Italiana Autore della Fotografia Cinematografica (AIC) as an example of Italian technology during those days.[9]

Cinemeccanica of Milan also built a field camera named Reporter, with a parallelepiped body of 30 × 21 × 16 cm. It had two independent 400 ft. internal magazines, a 12 volt cylindrical variable speed and forward and reverse drive motor placed at a side; viewing was effected through the film with an amplified image, and it had a variable opening shutter.

Around 1942 the Officine Galileo of Milano built some units of the O.G. 300 studio camera named Galileo, designed by Gaetano Ventimiglia. This camera was discontinued during the war and was not reissued afterwards. In the postwar period Italian studios were equipped with American, French, British and Czech studio cameras.

## American equipment

Demanded by the World War II effort, the powerful American industry started moving like a waking giant. In the motion picture field, production levels were not comparable with the demand of other items, and were also exported to allied forces. American photographic and motion picture equipment makers thrived with the high number and varied type of government orders. Many firms received more orders than they ever imagined. They also had to develop means to manufacture special equipment according to very precise specifications, demanding research and developing test prototypes in a short time. In the field of motion picture cameras new firms appeared as a result of ingenious specialists creating instruments with a high demand by the armed forces. Some manufacturers of aerial photographic equipment also built motion picture cameras combining both fields for the first time.

However the number, the amount and diversity of film equipment produced was far greater than the added production of similar equipment by enemy countries. In producing motion picture cameras and other items of equipment, Bell & Howell Co. of Chicago was in the first line. Their experience as supplier to the armed forces dated from many years before, in World War I, when they supplied equipment to the Signal Corps and other official agencies. The diversity of products they produced in this field, and their government contacts and experience were of relevant importance. In the camera manufacturing field a large number of 35mm and 16mm units were produced, including even home used equipment but now applied to a new purpose.

In the case of the U.S. Army and U.S. Air Force, equipment names were changed from those used by the manufacturer in their commercial production, but not with the U.S. Navy. In the first year of war there was a big demand for some products such as the Bell & Howell Eyemo cameras. Government agencies were directed to make massive purchases of these cameras from film studios, producers and film equipment supply firms, reaching agreements "for the duration." Later on, mass production of these items overcame the initial need.

The Eyemo cameras that were most used during the war were those named Model A-3 (corresponding to the commercial moniker Eyemo Q) and the Model A-4. The Model A-4 was similar to the Eyemo Model K, with the difference of having a collapsible spring motor handle to wind the spring drive mechanism, and a viewfinder with a device for projecting a reticule on a coated glass to align the camera with targets for bomb spotting recording. The U.S. Air Force initially had 4,376 units of this model available. In 1943 the manufacturer received orders for 490 to 600 units per month of this camera during the first half year, to be completed with 100 units per month to cover one year. And Bell & Howell also had to fulfill orders of other Eyemo camera models for the U.S. Army, the U.S. Navy and from abroad.[10]

Bell & Howell also produced a general aerial and ground motion picture camera of special warfare design; its designation was the A-6 35mm silent camera. It was a 200 ft. magazine-camera for a quick change of pre-threaded magazine, similar to loading a machine gun; it included a divergent three-lens turret, 24-volt DC motor, hand crank, and critical ground glass viewfinder.

Another camera frequently used in air operations was the Aircraft Gun camera, produced jointly by Bell & Howell Corp. and Fairchild Aviation Corp. It was built in eight models: M-1, M-2, M-4, M-5, N-1, N-2, N-4 and N-5. It was a very small and compact 16mm camera with internal 12 or 24 VDC motor (according to the model) and a 35mm f/3.5 lens; 50 ft. cassettes were introduced into it for gunnery training and combat recording. Some of these instruments had an image erector system. These units were required for use by observation squadrons, flying schools, the photography technical training school and fighter squadrons. Orders for this type of camera varied from 500 to 2,000 units

Bell & Howell aircraft gun camera (*courtesy Bell & Howell*).

per month. From 1943 to 1944 nearly 30,000 units were built to cover the needs of U.S. Air Force only.

Complementary to their manufacture of combat aircraft the Fairchild Aviation Corp. also produced several models of aerial photographic equipment and gun cameras similar to the one described above, but designed to be mounted on the top side of the airplane to a wing, in front of the pilot, or to be fitted into a structural part of the aircraft. It consequently required a streamlined cover to produce the least air resistance. This camera was conceived to fit the gun mount of the .30 caliber Browning machine gun and incorporated a clock unit to provide the hour, minute and second of exposure. The camera was tripped electrically by a solenoid, to keep running as long as the trigger was pressed. Seven hundred exposures could be obtained. This firm also produced the Aircraft Flexible Gun Camera H-2 with a camera body similar to that for the .30 cal. Browning. The camera set was completed with accessories such as a scoring and editing viewer and a screen projection device.[11]

One of the most original combat cameras built in the United States was the Cunningham Combat PH 550 PF Camera, designed by Harry Cunningham and developed around 1943 by American Camera Co. of Hollywood. It was built with a magnesium alloy body with a rifle-butt shoulder pod and pistol grip. It had a four-lens turret with shockproof lens mounting. The intermittent movement, with a two claw shuttle and register pin, as well as the continuous drive, were included inside the 200 ft. magazine. The magazines were inserted into the camera body through a hinged opening on top. A clear viewfinder also installed on top of the camera body had references of the field of each lens. The camera was operated by an electric motor working at three speeds: 16, 24, 32 f.p.s. The power supply was two "B" radio batteries. Two handgrips allowed holding the camera and seating the rifle butt on the shoulder to obtain steady shots. The four-lens focus control was close to the handgrip. The diaphragm opening was regulated with a finger. A catch rotated the turret. This camera weighed only 13 pounds or 15 with a 10 in. telephoto lens.[12]

Another specially designed silent camera was used for aerial shots. The Air Force adapted the old Akeley Pancake, which had been very useful during World War I. This camera was named Type A-1 and was a combination of the produ cts of Akeley Camera

Inc. and National Film Laboratories. The old camera design was improved with a Mitchell type viewfinder on top of the body, below the handgrip, and was driven by a variable speed electric motor with tachometer. Using its gyroscopic tripod, ideal for fast panning and tilting, this instrument was converted into an ideal field photography unit to follow the flight of aircraft, as well as landing and take off operations. This camera was much used during training by the Photographic Technical Training School and was a useful recovery of an instrument created twenty-five years before by an ingenious and prolific inventor.[13]

The camera called the A-5 Silent Motion Picture, 35mm Combat and General Purpose Camera by the U.S. Air Forces and the PH-330-K by the U.S. Army had an interesting birth and was manufactured by Cineflex Corp., later Cameraflex Corporation of New York. Toward the end of the war, a German Arriflex camera was captured by American troops and sent to Hollywood to be studied. After investigating it, director Delmer Daves used this unit to shoot subjective takes for the film *Dark Passage* (1948). But the camera design had been pre-

viously adopted in the Cineflex, later Cameraflex, the first American reflex camera, a reproduction of the German unit, now used to shoot the war on the American side. The Cineflex Corp. made 262 units of this camera in 1943 for the U.S. Air Force at a cost of $ 1,658.16 each, with four Goerz lenses. American ingenuity added later a spring driven motor to this camera as a complement to the 12–24 volt DC motor; the use of a spool in the 200- or 400-ft. magazines, and gelatin filter holder behind the taking lens.[14]

Bell & Howell and Eastman Kodak Co. also built home 16mm silent cameras for war requirements. The former made war model 141-A, and was a 50 ft. magazine camera with one lens and 12½ ft. spring drive for general-purpose photography. The latter made the Cine Kodak Special with a two-lens turret, interchangeable 100–200 ft. magazines and capable of taking masked shots, slow motion, and producing dissolves or fades. It was suitable for making instructional

Cineflex/Cameraflex combat camera (*courtesy Federal Manufacturing and Engineering Corp.*).

and training films. Other 16mm cameras made to government orders were the B-1, manufactured by Bell & Howell following the Filmo design, which included a three-lens turret,
and the Model 5, with similar characteristics built by Victor Animatograph Corp.[15]

Sixteen mm. sound-on-film cameras for ground and air combat photography were also
made for a two-man operating crew. E. M. Berdt Corp. produced the Auricon Master Record
Camera at that time, with three-lens-turret with studio or gun-sight finder. The unit had a
light parallelepiped body and included amplifier equipment. In 35mm sound-on-film cameras Mitchell produced the model A-9 similar to the NC model, of which the U.S. Air Force
ordered 58 units to be ready in seven months, delivering 11 to 13 units per month. The U.S.
Navy issued orders to this firm for a high speed model, while the Army also issued orders
for other Mitchell models. The number of units ordered by the U.S. Army must have been
considerable since they made a training film on how to operate and to maintain Mitchell
cameras.

A new studio camera was built in the early forties: the 20th Century–Fox, a unique
case in which a Hollywood studio produced its own camera, discarding the classic Mitchell
NC or BNC models which were standard in Hollywood. The Simplex company built this
new camera under the instructions and specifications of D.B. Clark, G. Laube, Robert
Stevens and Charles Miller. The designers followed the studio's specifications, requiring an
instrument that should be noiseless, relatively light in weight, with precise registration and
easy to operate. The heart of the 20th Century–Fox camera was its specially designed intermittent mechanism, running absolutely noiseless thus dispensing with blimps, and which
had the further advantage of high operating speed and light weight. It was based on the
principle of a single-claw shuttle working in combination with an eccentric pin and cam,
and two register pins.

Viewing was effected through the taking lens, or by using a monitor viewfinder. By moving a handle, the camera body was swiveled over an angle of 75 degrees on the axis of the
shutter shaft; this swiveling placed the focusing tube directly behind the lens. The image
seen through the monitor viewfinder was a reflected one, with automatic parallax correction. The shutter opening was variable from a maximum opening of 200 degrees to a minimum of 45 degrees. The magazines were attached externally, and were of the two-
compartment type holding 1000 feet of film. A motor attached to the rear of the body drove
the Fox camera, specially adapted to different types of power supply. This camera was provided with an automatic slating device, focusing control, synchronizing control for back
projection, and other features. The camera was so successful that it was, for decades, standard in Fox studios, and several units were built for their exclusive use.[16]

Another curious camera made during World War II was the 35mm Art Reeves Reflex
camera. The instrument was conceived according to military specifications and applied the
experience gained by the armed forces in this field. This camera had the characteristic of
using a new concept in reflex viewing: a very thin partially reflecting mirror, which diverted
5 percent of the light coming through the taking lens to the finder system, while 95 percent passed to the film. This design, which was much used many years later, had a device
by which 50 percent of the light passed to the viewfinder for better viewing and focusing.

The camera was compact; it used top mounted Reeves magazine that were 25 percent
lighter and smaller that conventional magazines. The intermittent mechanism was provided
with a registration pin, which could be put in an inoperative position when shooting at very
low temperatures, or when using film that had shrunk. The camera was provided with a
three-lens turret. An enclosed motor with speed control knob allowed working from 16 to

48 frames per second, with intermediate positions at 24 and 32 frames per second. The motors were interchangeable for 12, 24 and 110 volts. The film traveled inside the camera in the conventional American single plane film travel, with a main sprocket wheel and easy removal of the pressure plate in the film channel.[17]

In the postwar period new 16mm professional cameras appeared, designed to 16mm producers. The Maurer 16mm was one of them, designed by the well known sound equipment maker J.A. Maurer Inc. It was based on the classic design of the Mitchell, with 400 ft. top mounted magazines, specially designed mechanical movement with pilot pin, 235 degree opening dissolving shutter for automatic fades, rack over device, 3-lens turret with C-mounts, originally conceived monitoring viewfinder with bright image, and sunshade and filter holder. Later, an excellent camera blimp was added.

Mitchell also produced a 16mm professional camera with similar characteristics, with the features of its 35mm models, with four types of motor and a blimp. Another complete, but lower priced camera of this format was the Nord Professional, built by the Nord Company of Minneapolis, which included a shiftover system, automatic film threading, 100–200 film spool capacity, 240 degree shutter, electric motor drive, 4-lens turret with C mount, special Nord finder with parallax correction and sunshade with matte box.

Bell & Howell improved the characteristics of its Filmo camera in its H model, with a positive turret viewfinder, features including external magazines and an electric motor, following the line of some Eyemo models. The Filmo Specialist was the most refined of this series with a special front to install a new 4-lens turret, also including a shift-over system, vertical external electric motor, a monitoring viewfinder and sunshade filter holder.

The television requirements of 16mm sound-on-film shooting was the decisive factor which made Berndt-Bach Inc. of Hollywood envisage a wide market in this field, as well as for home use. Three camera models were conceived, including the Cine Voice with only one lens and optical sound recording, 100 ft. film capacity, corrected side viewfinder and a very compact blimped body with certain similarities with the 16mm R.C.A. Victor which had appeared in 1935. This camera was designed for home and semi-professional use, and had an extraordinary success, being adapted by many TV film reporters and TV stations in America and other countries.

One of the professional sound-on-film cameras designed by this firm was the Auricon Pro, with 200 ft. capacity magazines, and 4-lens turret and a specially designed monitoring viewfinder. The more complete Super 1200 Model had all the features for the TV producers and included top mounted 1200 ft. magazines, a new viewing system and many refinements. The TV newsreel was a new growing field which two decades later produced the gradual extinction of the classic 35mm newsreels shown in film theaters.

With the return of postwar production some special cameras were produced in Hollywood for special requirements. One of them was the high precision instrument made by Producers Service Company in that city: a special effects camera called Acme, conceived for both the 35mm or 16mm formats by changing parts, and with the following characteristics: one lens mount; 170 degree opening dissolving shutter, reflex viewing device with registration pins to coincide with the registrations pins of the movement, footage and frame counter, intermittent movement with positive registration pins, use of two or three films without adjustment, retractable built-in successive frame color wheel, light could be projected through film placed on register pins in reflex viewer to project images for painted matte, drive with variable speed synchronous or stop motion motor, forward or reverse drive and external Mitchell single or bi-pack magazines. This camera was the most complete item of equipment made to improve special effects in the optical printing. During the postwar years motion picture photography was facing a new era in which TV offered new opportunities in motion picture production.

# 30. The Combat Cameramen

The work of combat cameramen first began during the last conflicts of the 19th Century and the Boer War. The importance of a motion picture record of combat action was fully appreciated during World War I, but its actual coverage was limited. After that war, however the U.S. Army Signal Corps, of long existence, improved and organized this activity better.[1]

Shortly before the United States engaged in World War II, combat cameramen were trained in different ways. The armed forces had training centers in several branches of photography including motion pictures. Moreover, important private firms cooperated closely with the armed forces and the United States War Department. Before Pearl Harbor the well known film magazine *The March of Time* organized a school to train not only cameramen but also filmmakers in the production of training and information films. A large number of specialists were trained coming from the U.S. Navy and U.S. Coast Guard as well as from the Royal Canadian Air Force, Royal Canadian Engineers and even from the Royal Norwegian Air Corps.[2]

During 1942 another training center for war cameramen was created in Hollywood, sponsored by that industry's organizations. The courses were two months long for preparing Signal Corps Reserve personnel, according to the lines of that Army unit. The instructors were from Hollywood studios such as MGM, 20th Century–Fox, Paramount and Columbia. Effective help was received from the American Society of Cinematographers, the Research Council of the Academy of Motion Picture Arts and Sciences and raw stock manufacturers such as the Eastman Kodak Company, which offered their Hollywood Auditorium to carry out the practical courses there. In this way renowned industry specialists trained hundreds of recruits in a field that later on was intensely needed by the three services.

The required conditions for access to those training centers were: first, compliance with the physical requirements to be enlisted; second, be between 20 and 45 years old; third, show outstanding initiative and an alert mind; fourth, possess a high sense of responsibility; and fifth, steadfast performance under high pressure.

In those training courses, the selected students must have had some experience and had to prove their interest in cinematography. They were instructed in the operation, maintenance and how to overcome (eventually) all mechanical emergencies of the equipment they had to handle. They were prepared to work practically with four or five types of equipment used in the different services and were instructed to apply the best techniques to cover any event they were ordered to.

They were trained to shoot takes that would be easily edited, to control the use of pans, to change the shooting angle continuously, to estimate the correct time for each shot, to create an instinct for anticipating events and not to sicken with the shocking scenes they had to shoot. But also they had to know how to handle the available raw stock and to adequately identify the shots in the dope sheets for evaluation.

The coverage of war cameramen was very useful in several applications. Consequently they had to be very conscientious of the utility of what they were filming. Likewise it was very important to preserve the filmed material and send it immediately to the rear to process it at operations headquarters or on its way there. Generally the personnel trained in those courses finished with a practical thesis in which they were provided with a camera and a roll of film and a given task. After studying the work done they were given marks which together with the levels attained in the course determined their rank on completing the course (master sergeant or technical sergeant in the Army and photographic mate in the Navy).[3]

The American war organization was extremely efficient in training personnel for the new equipment and its maintenance. Very complete publications were made indicating the correct operation, repairing, and maintenance, as well as catalogs of spares with numbered parts listings of each item including photos, detailed drawings and instructions on shipment and storage. The instructions for motion picture equipment also included demolition procedures to prevent enemy use, the same as for other items. The method for motion picture cameras included the following instructions: 1) smash using sledges, pickaxes, crowbars, hammers and heavy tools; 2) burn using gasoline, oil, kerosene, flamethrowers or incendiary grenades or TNT; 3) dispose; throw in streams, scatter, bury in slit trenches or any kind of holes.[4]

In the United Kingdom, after organizing the training services for cameramen and film production units to comply with war requirements, recruits were trained at Pinewood Studios, where the new cameramen were graduated as sergeants. The AFPU (Army Film and Photographic Unit) comprised several sections, numbered according to the different war theaters: Middle East, North Africa, Continental Europe and South East Asia, where trained personnel were sent.[5] Film and photography specialists in the Royal Air Force also had their training center at Pinewood and were similarly distributed after completing their course. Photographic and motion picture techniques were very important in this service, especially air reconnaissance, bombing and fighter actions results. Some British firms, e.g., Vinten, received orders for two thousands camera units from the Air Force. Consequently the number of personnel assigned for filming missions was higher.

Before World War II, the Royal Navy originally was somewhat reticent to use their own photographic service as they usually engaged private firms to make the training and information films they needed.[6] As they had not completely organized their own combat cameramen aboard, in the early days of the war, the first important sea naval action was not filmed by the Royal Navy: the Battle of the River Plate, after which, the German battleship *Graf Spee* was scuttled (December 1939).

The United States Navy covered important naval action in the Pacific and the Normandy landings. Later on the Royal Navy Film Unit was better organized and covered action in the Mediterranean and the Pacific.

In the Soviet Union the cameramen were trained in the Moscow Film Institute and from there they went out to their specific missions according to the needs of the Soviet Signal Corps, which had several offices in various outposts. Very well known cameramen like

Roman Karmen, Igor Komarov, the brothers Alexeyev, Vladimir Frolenko, Mikhail Posel-sky and Advinar Sofryin were in the Tank Force commanded by general Kabukov.[7] The Soviet Air Force also had a large number of cameramen to cover photographic and cinematographic needs in enemy occupied area where they made sorties. As a consequence of this, there were many Soviet tank cameramen and higher marked than on other fronts, under hard conditions. Let's see a report of action from the front:

"On July 12, 1923, in the Oriol zone, following a rocket signal, the Soviet tanks were set against enemy positions. On top of the tank tower an armored camera had been secured. The camera controls were in the hands of cameraman Eugeni Lazovsky. The tank advanced firing on a German gun blowing it up in the air. Our tank ran over the gun and its four artillerymen. Stop. Our camera raw stock ran out. Suddenly a terrible shock deafened us inside the steel cabin: a direct hit. But the armor resisted. The tank was driven behind a mound. The bruised and deafened crew abandoned the tank through the hatchway. Lozovsky loaded the camera again. An instant to take breath and again in combat. A loud noise again. This time the enemy hits our tower, piercing it through; the bloody body of our gunner fell over the cameraman's shoulder. A new hit and our tower gunner died. But the tank driver lived on. He opened the front hatchway and left the vehicle with Lozovsky. Some distance from the tank both fainted; they were picked up after the battle. Lozovsky suffered 27 gun wounds. When he left the hospital after he was cured he returned to the front and filmed again in eight different tanks."[8]

There was a considerable number of combat cameramen of the Allied Forces during World War II. A large number of them were in the United States armed forces. The Soviet Union with its long front had about 300 cameramen who shot more than ten million ft. of 35mm negative. On July 12, 1942, 240 of them filmed combat simultaneously in 140 different zones of the war front, from the Arctic Sea to the Black Sea, which were edited to make a film called *24 Hours of War in the USSR*.

In the Axis forces, Germany had the largest number of cameramen, which were mostly in army, navy and air force strategic units. Each one of the planned invasions of European countries was filmed by a large number of cameramen, who carefully covered each operation. The German invasion of Norway was covered by 300 cameramen.[9] This work method was a practice applied by Dr. Goebbels' propaganda organization, which made efficient use of shots in their newsreels and propaganda films. The war was covered from different angles, and frequently using cameras on vehicles. One of the resources was to use crescendo shots, e.g. waists shots of surrendered soldiers with their hands up, and then a slow pan showing an extremely long column of them. Normally showing dead German soldiers was omitted but they included dead civilians or enemy soldiers.

The classic German exactness in detailed and exhaustive registration of all kinds of war events, even Nazi atrocities in concentration camps, turned out to be conclusive evidence at the Nuremberg Trials. Germany was also the country that lost the most combat cameramen. A large proportion of those casualties were Luftwaffe personnel lost during the Battle of Britain.

The other Axis countries did not reach the amount and quality of the material filmed by the Germans. Italy had its own technical media and obtained good war material. Japan was at war from 1931 and developed the required technical equipment. Their fronts were very dispersed and they lost many cameramen in the Pacific. Much of their war material was reconstructed in the studio, for example, the case of the Pearl Harbor attack, excellently made with miniatures for Kajiro Tamamoto's film *The Battle of Hawaii and Malaysia* (1942).

Japanese filmed material was also used in American propaganda films and also in U.S. Armed Forces training films.

Each country made use of the filming equipment they built or obtained from their Allies. In this field, the United States gave the U.K. and the Soviet Union extraordinary help, not only in the variety of items but also in the amount. In the U.K. the cameramen used the classic Bell & Howell Eyemo, DeVry and Mitchell, together with the British made Newman Sinclair and Vinten. In the Soviet Union the classic camera was the Bell & Howell model "Q" and even Mitchell Studio BNC cameras. The Soviet Union produced the CLP MG camera, made in Leningrad around 1940.

During the war Germany used the Arriflex Model I and other instruments such as the Askania Schulter, the Askania "Z" and the Askania Atelier, the Slechta Handcamera, the Cinephon and the Tobis-Klang-Slechta as well as units captured in the occupied countries. They had German raw stock factories and those taken over in France and Belgium; many films were shot in color raw stock to cover many different war film productions.

In Italy the Istituto Nazionale Luce was in charge of short film production and provided cameramen and equipment for official coverage. As we saw above, Italy manufactured their own motion picture cameras for war demands. Germany supplied them complementary equipment, and examples of the kind of propaganda films they made at the beginning. Japan was somewhat limited in manufacturing motion picture equipment, and in some cases used home film cameras, but they also produced military and training 35mm cameras such as a model with a machine gun shape. Two factories, Fuji and Konishiroku produced 35 and 16mm film stock, even in color. Japanese cameramen had a small manual with tables and information which was copied from the well known *American Cinematographer Handbook* by Jackson Rose, the Hollywood cinematographer.

As we saw above regarding the Russian front, the work of the combat cameramen was hard, dangerous and complex. Generally they worked in teams of two or more. But in many cases they had to work alone. They depended on their unit's organization which helped not only in supplying raw stock but also in receiving and passing on the results that in many cases was of great strategic value. The cameraman had precise instructions on how to cover what he saw and what was of important value to the war needs. Looking through the camera finder allowed having a clear perspective even in spite of being involved. Each cameraman had to be a witness of events and maintain a cool head to overcome the most relentless situations. Sometimes, besides carrying his equipment he also had to carry the raw stock required for his next assignment in the zone in which they were advancing, as in the Pacific islands which were taken one by one. On many occasions, important material filmed under hardships was lost when the ship transporting them was sunk, as during D-Day with the Normandy landings.

In the Air Force, one of the duties was filming bombing hits to be analyzed later. They also covered air fighting with enemy planes with cameras aligned with machine guns. At the beginning some aerial shots fluttered badly due to inadequate installation of the gun cameras. Sometimes cameras were installed on the fuselage sides, which allowed filming other aircraft in the formation, even when they were hit. Often the camera openings on the fuselage sides let in a freezing draft so the cameras needed a warmed covering, and the operator had his heated aircrew clothing. Each sortie was dangerous but carrying out their duty systematically helped to ease the tension.

Navy cameramen had a different routine. Battleships were not always in combat, and sometimes they traveled too long without interesting film takes. But when action came, filming was of great value.[10] This happened in the North Atlantic and especially in the Pacific, when filming aircraft taking off from the carrier or combat planes returning without fuel or damaged, making overpowering takes of their landing. During the war much material was shot in color. Naval combats were startling with the large guns firing, the continuous machine-gun fire on kamikaze's planes, their spin into the sea when hit. Shocking too was filming the kamikaze planes as they struck the ship on which the cameraman was serving or the sinking of other battleships of the fleet. Through submarine periscopes some impressive shots were taken of torpedoed merchant ships, but in many cases these were faked shots made in the studio for propaganda, information or training films.

The 35mm and 16mm formats were widely used by the United States forces. Much material from 16mm was blown up to 35mm, especially from gun cameras or 16mm black and white or color reversal coverage. During this period much was learned about which characteristics should be analyzed in designing combat cameras. New considerations had to be taken regarding resistance to diverse climates, hard work, camouflage, lens resistance and easy setting, problems of humidity and heat, lubrication and long storage. This was the basis of valuable experience that a few years later was applied by American camera makers for the Korean conflict.

# 31. Color in the Forties

In spite of the war, during the Forties and up to 1949, 120 feature films were produced with different color systems. Many of them were American Technicolor productions, but other color methods evolved in the States and in Europe; here is a short discussion of systems and changes appearing during this decade.

## Agfacolor

In 1945, the IG Farben premises, in Wolfen near Berlin, were withdrawn from the Allied mass bombing schedules. The manufacturers of the Agfa color monopack system had a unique method for making negative-positive color film which signified a considerable progress in this field and it was felt it should be preserved. Soon after, the Allied forces occupied the factory; they obtained the secret information on this color process, which served for ensuring development of the monopack system by several firms in various Western countries, and its direct adaptation by the Soviet Union and its allies. From 1941 to 1945 Germany had produced 15 feature films and countless shorts for war effort purposes, with the Agfacolor method. Now its principles were adopted and improved on, to be used by world cinematography, under different names.

## Anscocolor

Ansco Inc. already existed in the U.S.A. before the war as a member of the General Aniline and Film Corp. Group, which had originally been controlled by I.G. Farben in Germany. After Pearl Harbor, the American government took over the firm and occupied their Binghamton, N.Y., plant which they destined to produce, among other photographic items, 16 and 35mm reversible color raw stock (named Ansco color type 235 and Ansco Color Tungsten Type 234), based on the Agfa process. Many wartime films taken with this emulsion were enlarged to the 35mm format. New reversible emulsions appeared in 1946 as well as material for duplicating and printing. Among the feature films taken with Anscocolor we must point out *The Man on the Eiffel Tower* (1948) a USA–France co-production, directed by Burgess Meredith with cinematography by André Germain and Stanley Cortez; the prints were done by Technicolor. That same year Anscocolor was again used in a Franco-British cartoon production, *Alice in Wonderland* (1948) directed by Marc Maurette with five cinematographers: Andrè Duhamel and Walter Wottitz, seconded by Chain, Tellier and Benezech. In the '50s this firm finally turned out a negative-positive system that included duplicating material and MGM laboratories specialized in processing it.

## Cinefotocolor

This Spanish two-color system was developed in 1947 by two Catalan technicians, Daniel and Ramiro Aragonés, in the Cinefoto film laboratories in Barcelona. Initially, this method used one negative in a camera running at 48 f.p.s., alternately exposing two images through two filters (blue-green and red-orange) placed on the shutter. The copies resulted from using a positive with emulsion on both faces, through a complex process of dyeing and printing treatment. This initial method was afterwards improved using a special camera with an image dividing prism, filter and two film gates at right angles over which two black and white negatives traveled. A blue-green filter was installed on one of the film gates while a red-orange was on the other. These negatives needed a complex process, which included dyeing the positive, two-step printing of each negative through the two different filters, developing the positive, and a final dyeing bath. The first feature production filmed in Cinefotocolor was *En un ricón de España* (1948) directed by Jerónimo Mihura and cinematography by Isidoro Goldberger. After this, 26 Spanish feature productions were filmed with Cinefotocolor and many shorts. Shooting required special studio cameras with two magazines mounted on top, and built by the same laboratory. Sound was processed by conventional methods. This system was occasionally exported to France and was utilized till the mid-fifties.[1]

## Chromart

The American Colour firm in England developed a two-and three-color subtractive method in 1950 based on negative-positive processing, and named Simplex Two Color and Cromart Tricolor Methods. Both used developing techniques similar to Agfacolor, but the industry did not accept these systems.

## Eastmancolor

The appearance of Eastman Kodak Negative Safety Film Type 5247 in 1949–50 signified a great step forward by the American motion picture industry, after the whole world had access to the secret of the Agfacolor negative-positive system. The new Kodak raw stock was notable for its chemical property of correcting color automatically by means of masks, for rendering a better separation of recorded color, and for compensating undesirable absorption of cyan and magenta, formed during processing. This produced positives with better rendered greens and reds as well as neutral grays and whites. This was achieved after experiments in 1947 with color couples in Ektachrome photographic film. The original colors of these couplers were discharged proportionally during the development process. The combination of Eastmancolor negative with Eastmancolor Print Safety Film Type 5381, (or its 16mm version Type 7381) was the ideal solution to obtain good quality color copies at low cost in both formats. The negative had a 16 ASA index in daylight. American industry had achieved a long hoped for target in this field.[2]

Ferraniacolor In 1950 the Italian film manufacturer Ferrania S.p.a. developed this new negative-positive color process with a daylight negative rated 8 ASA and a tungsten negative of 20 ASA for 3,200 degrees K. The studio light level required was 3,000 lux with an f/2 stop. Negative developing required twelve processing steps. The color quality obtained fulfilled many expectations of the Italian film industry. After a short film, *Ceramiche Umbre* (1950), made with this color system, the first feature film in Ferraniacolor was *Toto a Colori* (1951), produced by Ponti-De Laurentiis, directed by Steno and photographed by Tonino Delli Colli.[3]

## Gevacolor

After World War II, the well known Belgian firm Photo-Produits Gevaert, in Antwerp, produced a color system based on the German Agfacolor, which included new, patented color couplers, but maintained a similar treatment. The sensitivity of this negative was 8–12 ASA in daylight. Printing was effected with the then new Debrie Matipo printers, specially made for color, provided with an automatic band with perforations for inserting color filters to regulate light and spectral values precisely. The first feature films in which Gevacolor was used were the French productions *La Maison du printemps* (1949), directed by Jacques Daroy and cinematography by Pierre Lebon and *Barbe-Bleue* (1951) directed by Christian Jacques with photography by Christian Matras.[4]

## Rouxcolor

This system had been evolved in France in the thirties by the brothers Armand and Lucien Roux. It was based on the principle of a special lens to be installed in front of the camera as well as in front of the projector. This lens produced four images with the basic colors, from the same point of view, through an optical system, with a four faced prism as the main element. During World War II the inventors improved their process, changing its initial concepts. In 1948 a film was produced with this system, *La Belle Meunière* (1948), directed by Marcel Pagnol and photographed by Willy Grichat and Georges Markmann.[5]

## Sovcolor

This name was applied by the former Soviet Union to their color productions processed in the Mossfilm laboratories using the German Agfacolor process. One of the first films shot this way in 1945 was a sport parade, and the first feature film was *Kamenni tsvetok* (*The Stone Flower*, 1946) directed by Alexander Ptushko and photographed by Fyodor Provorov. This film was filmed in Praga and processed in the Barrandov laboratories with the recently captured German color film stock. This production was followed by *Robinson Crusoe* (1946) directed by Andriyevsky and photographed in stereo-color photography by D. Surensky.[6]

## Thomascolor

Richard Thomas Enterprises of the USA developed this system in the early forties. It had been conceived as a single film additive process whereby four images were superimposed by means of a special lens. One lens was needed on the camera, and another on the projector. The lens was extremely complex, comprising four mini-lenses. The system seemed to be somewhat similar to other additive methods that had appeared in France, e.g.: Francita and Rouxcolor. It did not prevail in the industry and was not used in any feature film.[7]

## Trucolor

This system was developed by Consolidated Film Industries, one of the largest laboratories in the USA at that time. It adopted the two- or three-color subtractive methods, using a bipack camera with one panchromatic negative and another orthochromatic one. Printing was effected on a special two-layer monopack film made by Eastman Kodak, with color couplers, which did not cause diffusion. This method was afterwards improved on, and the name Trucolor was later on adopted by this laboratory as a trade mark for color processing. This name was also applied to the process and separating Kodachrome original negatives for positive printing on Dupont film. The large volume of film processed by this laboratory allowed Trucolor to be adopted in many productions, especially those of Republic Pictures Corp., of which this laboratory was a division. After Eastmancolor came on the market, Consolidated Laboratories processed it, applying the above name.[8]

# 32. Best Cinematography

About the end of the thirties and early in the forties, several productions from Hollywood were not only masterpieces in the art of motion pictures, but were also remarkable for their exceptional photography in black and white. Even today they are exemplary in their field denoting the caliber of a virtuoso in the art: Gregg Toland. The first of such productions, *The Grapes of Wrath* (1940), merited an Academy Award for its director, John Ford. The next one was a memorable film by the same director, *The Long Voyage Home* (1940), where Toland exhibited another example of the state of the art achieved in that period. Though neither of these films won an Academy Award for photography, the high image quality in both persist even today.

Both films were touching and dramatic. The images in them were carefully conceived to help tell the story and create the adequate atmosphere and feeling, but the results exceeded that goal. In *The Grapes of Wrath* the harsh reality of some sensitive scenes was enhanced by impressive sequences in which lighting was a factor evidencing the virtues of a master in film direction complemented by a master in working with light and shadows. Some scenes of the film are remembered for their photography, such as the low key in night indoor scenes where Henry Fonda returns home, lit only by the supposed light of a match, and several night outdoor scenes in the camps where the family was forced to dwell; here we find a skilful example of a natural with photographic art.

*Long Voyage Home* was another impressive film in which Toland showed his skill in lighting and making the most of his technical resources with depth of field (perhaps experimenting with the lens he had designed) to help the continuity of the story without cuts, as required by John Ford. Here again also we find spectacular takes like the night backlighted scenes on the wharves, the night on a Pacific Island, interiors in the ship and the night street scenes in Ireland. Again, the exact texture of the black and white images captures the beauty and dramatic force achieved at that time for this kind of film. Here we shall look into the highest achievements in the career of this director of photography obtained in the forties.

## Citizen Kane

This production was filmed in the second half of 1940 and released commercially by RKO studios on April 11, 1941. It was directed by Orson Welles, but it was also a Gregg Toland masterpiece. Many people believed it was the best film in the decade with the best black and white photography ever achieved. But it was not the opinion of the Hollywood Academy, which awarded an Oscar only to the original script by Herman Mankiewicz, big brother of Joseph L., the well-known writer and director.

*Citizen Kane* was a production that deliberately broke with classic filmmaking concepts. From the beginning, Orson Welles and Gregg Toland carefully planned this revolution to avoid interference from RKO executives. Both knew well each other's backgrounds when they first met on Toland's phone call to Welles in New York, previous to their Hollywood meeting. Toland showed he was interested in the project and explained his ideas of how to set it forth visually, catching unconventional form, since he had always wanted to change the classic Hollywood photography. At other meetings Toland told Welles the groundwork of all he knew and how to tell the story with film images and how to employ the best motion picture techniques to that end.[1]

Early in June RKO made arrangements with Samuel Goldwyn, Toland's employers, who hired out Toland and most of the camera crew (operator, assistant, gaffer and grip). The contract also included Toland's favorite camera, the Mitchell BNC No. 2 with five Astro Pantachar f/2.3 lenses of 35, 50, 75, 100 and 152 mm, a fast f/1.8, 40mm lens from the same source, and the then new wide-angle f/2.24mm lens by Cooke Taylor and Hobson, which would be intensively used during this production.[2]

This camera also included several accessories, which were not usually available, such as a special sunshade for the 24mm lens, a monitoring viewfinder with a sunshade in front and another at the back, a loupe with its dimmer, Scheibe filters, and others.[3] As in his other films, Toland used his several personally designed devices to obtain the effects he wanted.

In the preliminary stages of preparing the script Toland's presence was unusual at that time in Hollywood, where the director of photography never participated in the script meetings. There Toland expressed his opinions on script treatment, and contributed important suggestions for designing the 110 planned settings, conceived regarding the visual flow, the possibilities of the camera, and how to unfold the story dramatically, as agreed to by Orson Welles.

Welles and Toland envisaged filming this production with many techniques brought from the stage and applying classic film studio procedures in a new way. Therefore, the natural choice was long takes with moving cameras to reduce cuts to a minimum, in order to draw the audience closer to the story being told. Borrowed from the stage were long takes with a great field depth so that images in both near takes and background should be neat and clear. These loans had great possibilities in motion pictures, but required new technical solutions. The same happened with set-ups with the camera at floor level, creating escaping lines in the set décor which enhanced the dramatic value of scenes, but needed a new way of building decor elements.

Several long takes required special traveling shots and a combined choreography of actors and camera. Some takes were totally lighted from behind and with extremely low keylight in which close-ups and medium shots of the players were silhouetted against the light rays. One example was the unusual sequence in a projection room, made in one available at the RKO studios. Half of the film included trick photography, superimposed images with mattes, takes from a crane, use of miniatures, and glass paintings.

Each of these special cases in turn created other problems and demanded a search for adequate solutions. The takes from a very low (almost floor) level showed the top part of the décor; this broke away from normal practice in the industry as lighting equipment was usually installed in the top area; since this arrangement was frequent in most of the set-ups, light sources had to be placed on the floor. The ceiling had to appear below the normal height in rooms, so it was covered with black muslin in order to place the microphone above it to record dialogues. Sectors of the platforms on which the set floors were based had to be removed in order to install the cameras for floor level takes.[4]

Large size décor made lighting from the floor difficult. While preparing long shots with wide angle lenses, lighting equipment frequently appeared in the picture area so the pre-planning was extremely useful for the set design. The low key lighting in most of the scenes required increasing the lens diaphragm opening, causing a loss in field depth; the solution was the use of high sensitivity film emulsion, like the Kodak Super XX special to record with very low light levels or the Kodak Plus X negative in less extreme low key conditions, combined with the then new line of arc lamps Mole & Richardson had designed for Technicolor. These lights had a high penetration beam with considerable foot-candles of intensity in long distances which could be regulated by means of a shutter and other accessories. Toland used several noiseless M&R arc spots type 170, No. 6, adequate for situations needing intense light and density for different light effects. This type of arc spots was complemented by M&R Broadsides Duarcs and also by conventional tungsten spots, such as Seniors and Juniors. With these lighting techniques, Toland could use diaphragm openings of f/8, f/9, some at f/11 and even one at f/16. With these openings he obtained great field depth, whereby, in the case of the 24mm Cooke lens he achieved neat focusing from near two feet to infinity.[5]

Toland always wanted his images with maximum definition, for which he carefully selected the lenses he used each time; these he required to be non-glare treated with, for example, the Vard Opticoat coating used at that time. The then new coated lenses, the hardness of the arc light beams strategically directed at actors, sets or props, the use of special lenses with a fixed iris opening to reduce internal reflections, all these were part of his secret weapons to obtain such extremely high definition images.[4] To maintain such definition, he preferred making many tricks in the camera, like superimposed images, lap-dissolves, etc.

The best known field depth effect was Susan Alexander's suicide attempt, where the tumbler and the medicine vial are taken in close up, then the light in the bedroom is changed and the door is forced open by Kane and a servant. Some experts believe this was a trick made in the camera.[6] Another effective shot with focus depth was obtained inside Kane's parents home, where Kane as a child is shown through a window playing in the snow with his sled, and then the camera tracks back showing a general view of the room without changing the focus.

Many special effects were also made with the camera including previously prepared lap-dissolves. The automatic dissolve controls in the Mitchell BNC with footage counter and totalizer must have been extremely useful for such tricks that are usually made in the laboratory or in the special effects department, but rarely in the camera itself while shooting.

In this production, Welles' presence, a wizard as well as an expert stage director, created high pictorial art scenes with a few strategically placed elements, lighted against a black background, and with scant décor. A noted example was Kane's back outline in the Gothic archway of the Great Hall. Other indoor night scenes in Xanadu evidenced an imaginative use of light and shadow.

Welles, introduced there by Robert Wise, discovered the efficiency of the RKO special effects department, headed by Vernon Walker and seconded by directors of photography such as Douglas Travers as effects editor, Linwood Dunn making optical prints, and Mario

Larrinaga as matte artist. Strict budget restrictions induced resorting to the services of this department in an increasing scale. At first Toland probably was doubtful on the use of duplicated takes, but Dunn's excellent achievements annulled his doubts, and were a delight to Welles who asked for more and more effects to improve image values in many takes, to create new and original transition and montage effects, to extend the length of many takes, to add still photos in others, to add snowfall effects in order to eliminate grain, and to magnify the close-up of Kane's mouth when he whispers "Rosebud" at the beginning of the film.[7]

The fame of Citizen Kane persists over the years. It placed this film at top level among the best motion picture films. Its photography was also selected as the best in black and white in more than half a century of cinema. The film and its images was a perfect blend of art, skill, inspiration, pictorial good taste and efficiency. These images provide us the best example of the quality and ability of black and white images to captivate audience attention.

## How Green Was My Valley

The film that won the 1941 Academy Award for black and white photography was *How Green Was My Valley*, photographed by Arthur Miller. This 20th Century–Fox production earned the production award for the studio, the direction award for John Ford, the best supporting actor award for Donald Crisp, the best supporting actress award for Mary Astor, the art direction award for Richard Day and Nathan Juran, and interior decoration award for Thomas Little.

Based on the best-selling novel by Richard Llewellyn, this film tells the story of a Welsh family near the end of the nineteenth century, distressed by a disaster in the village mine. John Ford treated this story with great emotional force and his classic narrative competence. Arthur Miller's photography was typical of his realistic lighting, showing the family house interiors, the mine galleries, and the dwellings of the miners. All these buildings were raised on a hill in the 20th Century–Fox Ranch in the San Fernando Valley, following the plans of Richard Day, the scenery designer, who applied a forced perspective. Ford tells the story applying his usual narrative technique with a fixed camera and a limited number of set-ups to allow editing control. Ford and Miller had previously made two films together and understood each other perfectly; they exchanged few words during production, as often happened in Hollywood, contrary to what occurred with *Citizen Kane*, as we saw above.

Arthur Miller was a renowned director of photography in Hollywood, born in 1895 in Roslyn, Long Island. He started early in cinematography in the New York Motion Picture Live Pictures under the guidance of one of the pioneers of the first decade of the 20th century. There he learned the trade of laboratory operator and took the first steps towards his primary ambition: to become a motion picture camera operator. Later on, Miller had the chance to work under another motion picture pioneer: Edwin S. Porter. In 1912 he managed to get a job in the Pathé Company as a newsreel cameraman; there he first laid hands on a Pathé camera which would become his favorite instrument, using it for many years; with this camera he filmed the then well known serial *The Perils of Pauline* (1914), played by Pearl White and directed by Louis Gasnier.

His first venture to work in California was in 1918 when he photographed several films which earned him a reputation as a cameraman. A year later he returned to New York, called by Georges Fitzmaurice, the well known French director with whom he worked, hired by the Famous Players Lasky company. He photographed seven films with this director, finding there a constant stimulus to improve his skills. During that time he was strongly influenced by Anton Grot, the noted artist, on the use of light on paintings and drawings; Grot put him in touch with art directors such as William Cameron Menzies and Penrhyn Stanlaws.

In 1923 Miller returned to Hollywood to work with the then new Goldwyn Studios, which had produced several of the Fitzmaurice films. When the latter returned to New York, Miller was engaged to work for C. B. de Mille in Paramount, continuing his career in Hollywood with important achievements. He underwent the transition from silent movies to talkies with noted directors like Sydney Franklin, Raoul Walsh, Allan Dwan, Rouben Mamoulian and John Ford. Miller's photography was always at a high artistic and technical level on his many different productions, for which and for his profound acquaintance with the trade his colleagues referred to him as "The Master."

Arthur Miller photographed 133 feature films and advanced step by step in his trade, in step with its progress. He changed the old Pathé camera, which he had cherished so much in his youth, for the Bell & Howell Studio, and then the Mitchell. Finally he was one of the first to use the then new and exclusive Twentieth Century–Fox Studio camera. He worked for several studios in Hollywood such as Goldwyn, Paramount, Universal, Warner, and RKO, but his home was the Fox studio (afterwards 20th Century–Fox) where he photographed 57 films. There he plied his trade over 17 years during which he obtained three Academy Awards: one for *How Green Was My Valley*, one for *The Song of Bernadette* (1943), and finally one for *Anna and the King of Siam* (1946). Miller was the first director of photography to receive three Oscars. In 1950 ill health prompted him to retire, resorting to the milder activities of the American Society of Cinematographers, where he became president and then creator and curator of the ASC Museum.[8]

## The Magnificent Ambersons

One year after his memorable *Citizen Kane*, Orson Welles made another unforgettable film with beautiful black-and-white photography. This time circumstances were different from those of his first film. He could not avail himself of his cherished collaborators from *Citizen Kane*, Gregg Toland in photography and Penny Ferguson as art director, thus having to choose other specialists for such important tasks.

Art direction was assigned to Mark-Lee Kirk, an expert who did an excellent job. But replacing Toland was much more difficult, Welles preferred a new, young cinematographer, with little experience in the trade and free from the influences of Hollywood methods. In his investigations the name of Stanley Cortez was mentioned. Welles viewed his films (mostly B-type for Universal) as well as shooting tests he had done for Selznick. Moreover, Cortez had made an experimental film with Slavo Vorkapich, he had been part of camera crews with noted photography directors like George Barnes, and had made trials with the then new infrared negative. He had only six years experience as director of photography. Welles liked what he saw and what he heard about Cortez, and rang him up on the phone; fate inverted the situation when Toland rang up Welles regarding *Citizen Kane*. Welles in Hollywood negotiated retaining Cortez, who was in New York and had to return to Hollywood to start shooting this film in RKO studios on October 28, 1941, the first chance in his career to film a highly artistic motion picture.[9]

Stanley Cortez had been born in 1908 in New York and his real name was Stanley Kranz. After studying at New York University, he began working with well known photographers like Steichen, before being allured by the motion picture camera as a newsreel cinematographer. This led him to start working with Pathé News, from where he went to Hollywood as camera assistant in the de Mille crew, under the direction of Alvin Wyckoff, the noted cinematographer. It took him ten years to advance in his trade to reach the position of director of photography at Universal Studios in 1937. Six years later, working for RKO, Cortez saw the complicated décor set up for Orson Welles, that studio's new "wonder boy," and wondered who would be the poor guy who would have to light it. He little imagined what turns of destiny could place that difficult responsibility on him.[10]

Back in Hollywood and about to start shooting, Cortez personally met Orson Welles for the first time, and must have felt that man's magnetism and his overwhelming personality, as well as the weight of having to substitute for the eminent Gregg Toland. He had not had time to take photographic proofs of the actors nor to analyze the best form to make that exuberant set look its best, so full of glass as it was, and with a ceiling, and with so little room to place lights.

The first sequence he had to light to begin shooting was the family dinner which was decisive in showing his mettle in lighting to an extremely exacting and meticulous director; and Welles was delighted when he saw the dailies. Cortez then grasped that this complex décor selected by Welles would give him the chance to achieve excellent photography.

Many other situations cropped up which were difficult to solve, like the long sequence of the ball, filmed entirely with an elaborate crane displacement on the set built in the Pathé studios. The take was perfect, but the sound track had to be dubbed as the noise of the crane spoiled the original recording. The takes in the ice plant were also complex; they took ten days filming; snowfall sequences had to be recreated, and lighting had to be prepared in the freezing cold which kept the large tungsten lights continuously blowing up.[11] In this film, Cortez frequently applied his refined lighting technique with several oddly shaped patterns using gobos and flags, thus very effectively lighting the lavish décor of the Amberson mansion.

Some analysts speculate that Welles preferred Toland's techniques, rendering very high definition images obtained with arc lights, minimum diaphragm opening and few light touches. Another Toland advantage was his great speed in lighting each set-up for which he was recognized in Hollywood. Cortez was slower but his results were top level and gratified as he was to work with Welles, he furnished him some very good ideas. Several takes in this movie were filmed with the contribution of Harry Wild and Russell Metty. Nearly one hour of beautiful takes laboriously lighted by Cortez with arc lamps were unfortunately excluded when RKO shortened the length of the film without Welles' consent, when Welles had to fly to Rio for an American government production. In spite of this unhappy impairment, the film still achieves a high level and striking image attraction.[12]

## Beauty and the Beast

The rebirth of European production after World War II added a series of new films to world cinematography, which in several cases were examples of the high levels reached in motion picture photography. One of them was a French film with an unusual poetic theme, *La Belle et la Bête* (*Beauty and the Beast*, 1946), directed by Jean Cocteau, the renowned film maker.

Cocteau was an imaginative poet, painter, choreographer, writer, actor and film director. This was his first feature film based on a fairy story by Mme. Leprince de Beaumont. It was carried out in 1945 after the liberation of France, in very difficult circumstances for a production of this sort. There were extreme difficulties in obtaining elementary technical implements such as cameras, raw stock, availability of space in studios, electric power, material for building décor, etc. But these difficulties were overcome. The producer, André Paulvé, and the production director, Emile Darbon, managed to obtain facilities and credit at the St. Maurice Studios in Joinville and at the GM Film laboratories of the Gaumont Group.

Jean Cocteau had René Clément as a consultant, the latter with the prestige earned by his recent film *La Bataille du rail* (*The Battle of the Rails*, 1946). He was also counseled by Christian Bérard, a decorator, stage designer and painter who materialized Cocteau's poetic ideas, helped by Renée Moulaert and Lucien Carré. Arakelian, the great French make-up artist, conceived a beautiful mask for the role of the Beast, based on a lion's head which, when shooting, needed several hours to place on the leading actor's face (Jean Marais). Adequate outdoor scenery was extensively searched for and finally found in a manor in Rochecorbon, Tourain, to create the castle of the Beast.

The décor inside the gothic castle was reminiscent of Veermer and Rembrant paintings, with exquisite settings enhanced by surrealistic ornaments, like candelabra that lighted up held by living arms emerging from the walls and showing the way to the visitors, bas-reliefs of busts and faces whose eyes followed the visitor and who exhaled smoke, arms arising from the table and serving the visitor a cup of wine, window curtains along the corridors moved as if blown by wind while doors would open and close by themselves. All this was part of a fantastic world conceived by Cocteau and Bérard to be created into cinematographic images by Henry Alekan, the director of photography, specially chosen for this film by Cocteau and Clément.

Alekan was the artificer with the capacity and sensitivity to meet the director's challenge and give shape, in black and white images, to the unreal atmosphere he wanted for his poetic vision. Alekan had been born in Paris in 1909 and had studied in the Conservatory of Arts and Trades and at the Institute of Optics. He was still very young when he entered the motion picture trade as sound assistant first and camera assistant later to well known photography directors of the thirties, like Louis Page, Georges Périnal and Michel Kelber. In 1938 another master of this profession influenced him, Eugene Schüfftan, working with him on the famous *Quai des brumes*. After working on some films, e.g., *Les Petits du quai aux fleurs* (1943) and *Échec au roi* (1944–45), he showed his mettle in *La Bataille du rail*.

In *Beauty and the Beast* Alekan fashioned his first masterpiece reflecting faithfully the poetry and magic of the atmosphere to be created. This he achieved with a great technical control of the different décor, and using a hard light pattern formed with flags, gobos and cookaloris to produce a striking and visually strong light and shadow effect. His technical skill was also proved with many camera tricks, like the images on mirrors, the sudden change in the size of shadows, displacements in slow motion, and the effects made by the changing light from the candelabra. The lighting of scenes in the mysterious forest, those in the castle garden, and the sequences in the village tavern were also unforgettable.

Alekan always chose the type of images most adequate to the theme of the film at hand. In *La Bataille du rail* he applied documentary-like realism for a bitter war film. In *Beauty and the Beast* he resorted to all his imagination to obtain the effective light touches required by this poetic film. On this production he worked with a devoted camera crew made up by Henry Tiquet, Foucard and Jacques Letellier; the latter we see in the main titles with the clapper board in hand. In his long life (92 years) Alekan carried out a fruitful career as an excellent master of lighting in all sorts of productions. He was in love with his profession and wrote several valuable books on the subject.[13]

# Black Narcissus

British post-war film production was brilliant for several years, noted for its high quality photography. This was the result of having consolidated a very well organized substratum with large studios, such as Denham and Pinewood, powerful groups, like J. Arthur Rank's, and eminent producers, such as Alexander Korda of London Films, Filippo del Giudice of Two Cities, and Powell and Pressburger in Film Archers, among others.

Moreover, the presence in Britain of Technicolor Ltd. laboratories, headed by Kay Harryson, had stimulated the use of this color process during the war in popular films like *The Great Mr. Hendel* (1942), *The Life and Death of Colonel Blimp* (1943), *Henry V* (1944), *Western Approaches* (1944), *This Happy Breed* (1944), *Blithe Spirit* (1945), *Caesar and Cleopatra* (1945) and *A Matter of Life and Death* (1946). This had been the result of a short entitled *This Is Colour*, produced by Technicolor, directed and photographed by Jack Cardiff. It was an excellent film with splendid color effects, furthering the advantages of their process, now available to British producers, emphasizing the production values of the system in facilitating access to world markets, especially the USA, as well as technical support and budgetary considerations. This message had impressed the Powell-Pressburger team, who produced several of the films listed above, and decided to apply it again in their new project, *Black Narcissus*, which they intended to carry out in 1946.[14]

*Black Narcissus* was a well-known novel published in 1939, by Rumer Godden, a British writer who had lived in India. Powell read the book at the suggestion of Mary Morris, the actress, who hoped it might offer good possibilities for her career. Powell and his associate liked the novel very much but the war years were not adequate for this type of film. In 1946 the project was reconsidered and, as usual with both filmmakers, the script was carefully drawn up. The technical staff was selected as well as the cast: however the leading role was assigned to Deborah Kerr, supported by Sabu, David Farrar, Flora Robson, Jean Simmons and Kathleen Byron, among others. For art director they picked Alfred Junge, a German with long experience in UFA and a distinguished career in Britain since the twenties, including six other films for The Archers. The photography for this new project was committed to Jack Cardiff, a close associate of this group and part of the technical staff for some years.

Cardiff was born in Yarmouth (East England) on September 18· 1914, the child of music-hall actors who had worked with Charlie Chaplin before he went to America. In his childhood he traveled all over Britain with his parents who sometimes worked as extras in films, thus getting acquainted with the inside of studios, and where he also played child roles in Warton Films. In 1927 he started working as a camera assistant at Elstree studios. There he started gaining experience guided by Freddie Young, the chief cinematographer. Some time later he was hired to work on special effects for Denham, where he gained very good experience in this specialty which was of great value in his film career. In Denham he progressed to camera operator under well known directors of photography like Al Rosson, Lee Garmes and the reputed Georges Périnal. He also closely observed the working methods of other prodigies of the trade like James Wong Howe and Harry Stradling, who came from Hollywood to work for the British studio.[15]

When the Technicolor Co. came to Britain to install a laboratory in West Drayton, Denham studios called on Candiff to be part of a selection of young technicians to be trained in Hollywood. When his turn came he explained that his knowledge of the trade was not the scientific (physics or mathematics) side, but of the aesthetic aspects of photography for color motion pictures, based on his studies of the lighting techniques of great classic painters like Vermeer, Rembrandt, Pieter de Hooch, Turner and the impressionists. This unusually frank statement impressed the selecting board who nevertheless included him on the list of British technicians of the firm. The trip to the USA was cancelled but Cardiff was engaged as a camera operator in the first production with Technicolor, *Winds of Morning* (1937), shot at Denham and in Ireland, with Ray Rennaham as director of photography.[16]

After having participated on the camera crews of important productions in Technicolor (e.g., *Four Feathers*), Cardiff photographed "World Windows Travelogues" in Technicolor during two years in different parts of the world. In 1943, as camera operator for the production *The Life and Death of Colonel Blimp*, he lighted the studio takes for inserts, which impressed Michael Powell, the film's producer-director, for his mastery in that job, and promised him an opportunity to work as director of photography in one of his upcoming films. Also during the war he did the photography, as a Technicolor expert, for the Crown Film Unit production *Western Approaches* as well as several other war films using that color method. In 1945 he was in charge of the second unit on *Caesar & Cleopatra*, covering the outdoor takes in Egypt. Finally, Powell fulfilled his promise and engaged Cardiff as director of photography for *A Matter of Life and Death* and again for *Black Narcissus*, a production that gave him the great professional chance to show his great capacity as an expert in lighting and color.[17]

After this film Cardiff was considered one of the best British directors of photography in Technicolor, a distinction ratified by excellent jobs on *The Red Shoes* (1948), *Scott of the Antarctic* (1948), *Under Capricorn* (1949), *The Black Rose* (1950), *The African Queen* (1951), *War and Peace* (1956) and others. Cardiff's prolific career as photography director included 35 titles, and in 1958 he moved on to film direction.

*Black Narcissus* is the story of a group of missionary nuns in India in an odd palace donated by a local ruler and which had housed a harem before. This palace, on top of a 9000 ft. Himalayan mountain, had been transformed into a school and hospital. The strange atmosphere and the spiritual situations of the place, and the deficiencies due to isolation gradually and deeply affected the life of the nuns and their personal relations.

On organizing the project, Powell & Pressburger, the producers, decided to shoot the film totally in a studio in England, surprising the photography and art directors, who expected to have to travel to India. They soon saw it had been a wise decision, affording them great control over the shooting, the technical facilities available in the studio and the abilities of British experts were combined with imagination. This decision materialized when Pinewood Studios was chosen.[18]

A large part of contriving an Indian atmosphere in a studio fell on the shoulders of Alfred Junge, who created the delicate beauty of the Indian palace in a set built on the studio grounds, and surrounded by a wall formed with white surfaces placed at an angle of 35 degrees from the vertical. This arrangement allowed (using daylight for nearly ten hours a day) lighting the erected décor with paintings and other ornaments without variations in intensity. The Indian windows, with their special sun protectors on the openings, allowed Cardiff to produce dramatic and very realistic effects to induce the adequate atmosphere in several sequences. The expert Percy "Poppa" Day and his two sons prepared the matte shots, the glass shots, the background paintings and the scale models needed in some sequences, all of which were fundamental to achieve neat and realistic photography and evenness with other takes.[19]

Some backgrounds were photo enlargements of 8' × 10' negatives, which were later painted over in pastel tones. Many of the surrounding shadows were blue, while others were a soft green, as in the sequence when one of the nuns becomes insane. The film's climax sequence was shot at dawn to obtain the adequate light effect for the death of a nun. Cardiff achieved an alluring artistic lighting in many indoor takes in the palace, where the players were often backlighted at sunset. Also excellent was his lighting of close-ups of nuns' faces, without make-up, and which often included dramatic situations. The Technicolor system enhanced the red color of the lips which had to be diminished. The sequence in which the insane nun goes along the dark corridors of the palace was magnificently photographed by Cardiff. Some of the takes infringed Technicolor's standards of the time, not to use soft focus, so they signified advances in color treatment. Certain indoor takes required the use of small inkies behind furniture and seven arc lights covered with tracing paper and color gelatin. Cardiff's experience came very handy with miniatures prepared by "Poppa" Day, to be included in this film. But Cardiff always regretted that one of his favorite takes, of which he was very proud, was excluded from the film on editing.[20]

For this film Jack Cardiff earned in 1947 the Academy Oscar for the best color photography. It was the second time it was awarded to a European production, totally filmed in England by a British director of photography, opening the doors of Hollywood for him. Alfred Junge also received an Oscar for art direction. Finally, J. Arthur Rank, the eminent British film entrepreneur, went proudly to Hollywood with a copy of the film to show the studio heads what his organization had achieved in Britain. However the relentless Hays Code censored some sequences on religious considerations.[21]

## Great Expectations

1947 was another important year for British motion pictures and its cinematography. The Academy Oscar for the best black and white cinematography was awarded to *Great Expectations*, a British production photographed by Guy Green and directed by David Lean. This, added to the *Black Narcissus* awards, was an unusual event in Hollywood recognizing the high level reached in this art by Europeans and especially by the British industry. This award also helped raise David Lean's name among the foremost international film directors.

The first step in this project was when David Lean saw the *Great Expectations* stage adaptation by Alec Guinness at the Rudolf Steiner Hall in London, which excited him. He was fascinated by the visual possibilities of Dickens' stories. After completing *Brief Encounter* (1946), Cineguild, Lean's production firm, envisaged *Great Expectations* as their next project.[22]

Cineguild was a production firm formed by Anthony Havelock-Allan, an experienced producer of Quota films with 12 titles to his credit. Another partner was Ronal Neame who began a production career after having been a brilliant director of photography of 29 films, some of them for that very firm. The third associate was David Lean, a promising film director who previously had been considered the best film editor in Britain, and had gone on to direct three valuable films for Cineguild.

For this new project the production firm selected Robert Krasker as director of photography; he had photographed *Brief Encounter* for them, and made them very pleased with the quality of his work. But when the actual shooting started, Lean realized that Krasker was not achieving what he wanted. Neame agreed with him and, though they all regretted it very much as they knew Krasker's high capabilities, they decided that there had to be changes and released him. However many striking night scenes taken by Krasker were included in the film. Guy Green was chosen to replace Krasker, but Bob Huke was retained as camera operator.

Guy Green, born in November 1913, started very young as a camera assistant on several Quota type films in the Sound City studios. Afterwards he joined the Denham studios where he worked with well-known German directors of photography, like Gunther Krampf and Matz Greenbaum, from whom he learned German lighting techniques. He was the camera operator for Robert Krasker on the film *One of Our Aircraft Is Missing* (1942), photographed by Ronald Neame, who introduced him to David Lean, who was an editor at that time.

Green was captivated by Lean and his skill. Seeing his camera operator's good work, Neame included him in two more projects: *In Which We Serve* and *This Happy Breed*, both directed by Lean. Then, an opportunity came up when Lean recommended Green to work with Carol Reed in the photography of *The Way Ahead* (1944), and shortly after, Green went on as director of photography in the second unit of *The Way of the Stars* (1945) directed by the celebrated Anthony Asquith. When Green was on the look-out for a next job, Cineguild's proposal cropped up to replace Krasker. Green was told that Krasker had given up due to ill health, as he had caught malaria in Egypt when filming *The Four Feathers*. That was how the road was paved that led Green to an Oscar.

Lean had a very precise idea of the sort of photography he wanted to recreate the times and the atmosphere of Dickens's novel. He had a powerful pictorial sense, and he had exhaustively analyzed the style required for each of the sequences he had written for the script, together with Ronald Neame, Antony Havelock-Hallan, Kay Walsh and Cecil McGivern. Based on the fanciful imagination of John Bryan, the production designer, the décor was built with forced perspective, combining naturalism with unreality, including extravagant designs in some sequences to create a sensation of fear. Wilfred Singleton's contribution in decorating the sets was also fundamental to produce similar sensations.

The well-known story of *Great Expectations*, with Pip as a youth, his sister, his brother-in-law, Joe the smith, the apparently fierce convict Magwitch, the conceited Estella, Pip's first visit to the eccentric Mrs. Havisham, the imposing Mr. Jaggers, the voyage to London, the origin of the strange legacy and the tragic end of both Mrs. Havisham and Magwitch were the main ingredients of this melodrama carefully adapted by Lean and his associates to the requirements of a screenplay.

Special locations were chosen in Rochester, a town reminiscent of Dickens, an island on the Medway River, and the Thames Estuary, where Joe Gargery's home was rebuilt.[23] The church and its yard were reconstructed at Denham Studios, together with the ghostly trees resembling human faces. For the scenes on the islands and the fens, many smoke making implements were needed (like the ones used in the Navy for smoke-screens), but the changing wind had to be taken into account when it blew the smoke away and hindered the evenness of the takes. The film required many outdoor takes, but some demanded painted glass to obtain the effect of heavy clouds to enhance an oppressive atmosphere, as in the initial general take, panning Pip silhouetted on the road against the sky where two gallows appear.

Green studied the script carefully and made many trials to determine the adequate chiaroscuro range to obtain the atmosphere that Lean wanted. In the studio he used a lighting technique based in small touches of light with a strong backlight for impressive scenes, as when the fierce looking Magwitch grasps young Pip's arm in the churchyard. In many indoor scenes, Bryan's imaginative décor gave Green the chance to show his lighting intuition, as in the scene when Pip visits Mrs. Havisham and another when the latter dies in a fire. Green also controlled light on backgrounds selectively and applied cross lights to obtain a three-dimension effect on the image.

Taking advantage of Lean's considerable knowledge of lenses and how they rendered visually, 25 and 35mm wide angle lenses were used for Pip's youth, and 50mm and more for taking the adults, in order to change the field depth and accentuate the difference of a child's and an adult's point of view. The film was shot with Taylor & Hobson lenses, on a Mitchell NC camera, and it was processed in Denham's laboratories.

*Great Expectations* was a great artistic success all over the world and it induced the Hollywood Academy to bestow an Oscar also on John Bryan as art director and another on Wilfred Singleton for interior decoration. Lean became enthusiastic about the public appeal of Dickens's novels. After a trip to the USA where he studied audience response, he decided his next project would be *Oliver Twist* using the same team of collaborators. This film was another great success which also made Guy Green shine, he continued as director of photography until 1954, when he followed the trail of Neame and Cardiff to become a film director.

# Odd Man Out

When Robert Krasker regretfully retired from shooting *Great Expectations* he soon found another interesting project, when he was called by the Two Cities Films producers to photograph Carol Reed's next film: *Odd Man Out* (1946). Based on the well known novel by F.L. Green, it is the tragic story of a police chase of the head of an Irish revolutionary group, Johnny Mac Queen (played by James Mason), who in broad daylight takes part in a bank holdup and is forsaken by his mates. In his escape from the police he meets many diverse people in an unsuccessful search for a shelter.

The story happens during a twelve-hour period. It was made up by tense situations showing Johnny's flight, desperately looking for a friendly hand in the most varied places and back streets of the city; the film was shot in London and Belfast. The combination of Krasker's techniques and Reed's fluid narrative achieved a top level production with a quality similar to the famous *The Informer* by John Ford in 1935.

*Odd Man Out* was Krasker's sixth film as director of photography and the prelude to a similar production that afterwards made him eminent worldwide in his profession. Krasker, born in Perth, Australia, on August 21, 1913, was the child of Austrian and French parents. His initial schooling was in France where he decided to specialize in painting in an art school. Lured by photography he went to Germany to study optics in Dresden. Back in Paris he had the chance to work for Paramount Studios in Joinville, integrating the camera crew of Phil Tannura, an American director of photography who fostered his learning the trade.

In 1931 Krasker was hired by London Film as camera operator for the well known Georges Périnal, participating on important Alexander Korda productions, such as *Rembrandt*, *The Drum*, and *Four Feathers*. For nearly a decade he was a busy operator in Denham. His first chance as director of photography came in 1943 when he directed the photography of *The Saint Meets the Tiger*. His capabilities were soon recognized and that same year he was called by Filippe del Giudice, general head of Two Cities Films, the producers, to shoot two films produced by Leslie Howard: *The Gentle Sex* and *The Lamp Still Burns*. Still with Two Cities in 1944 he was director of photography in Technicolor for the first time for *Henry V* directed by Lawrence Olivier. A year later Ronald Neame called him to Cineguild to direct the photography of " *Brief Encounter*, David Lean's fourth film. After that, as seen above, he returned to Two Cities.

With Carol Reed directing *Odd Man Out*, Krasker found the opportunity to apply the best of black and white photography to obtain the dramatic sensation the story wanted, and to set forth in images the psychological portrait of the main character's anguish. Indoor scenes reproduced gaslight very realistically. Outdoor scenes marked the lapse of time passing, unfolding from broad daylight until night, with effective touches of light on back streets, buildings, walls and arcades, with takes from low angles and very effective composition. This film was another example of the lighting quality attained by this photography director, as well of the art level achieved by British postwar cinematography.

# The Third Man

*The Third Man* was Krasker's magnum opus, which in 1950 earned him the Hollywood Academy Oscar for black and white photography. Carol Reed directed this film for London Film achieving, at the end of the decade, a great success for Alexander Korda, the producer.

The story was a then unpublished thriller by Graham Green, located in post-war Vienna, where the American journalist Holly Martins, played by Joseph Cotton, arrives to work with a friend, Harry Lime (Orson Welles). The British occupation forces inform Martin that Lime had died in a car crash and had been suspected of complicity in trafficking adulterated penicillin. In search of the truth, Martin roves among the ruins of Vienna, meets Anna (Alida Valli), his friend's lover, and learns he had been an unscrupulous criminal evading the police in the city's dark streets. Martin's search, his belief that Lime is not dead and the police pursuit lead to the city's large sewers, where finally Martin is forced to shoot his friend, though the film does not settle the uncertainty of his death.

The story required an effective, adequate treatment of images of a half destroyed city, derelict buildings seen at night, depressing back streets, dark skies, wharves on the Danube, and desolate avenues in mid-winter. Reed and Krasker selected low camera angles and frames with tilted camera (Dutch shots); they used several wide angle lenses and they took shots with great field depth. The lighting was carefully prepared to simulate that street lights were the only light source, and as there were large spaces being covered, very sensitive emulsions had to be used, as well as many arc-lamps and other high intensity tungsten lamps.

Many scenes were filmed indoors in the real locations while others were shot on sets erected at Denham Studios. Much of the lighting technique was based on cross lights, backlights, and touches of light skillfully placed by Krasker. Many of the takes required special treatment by Denham's laboratories. The lighting of the large sewer tunnels was a difficult job which rendered very effective images in the police chase sequences near of the end of the film. Thus, once again, black and white motion picture photography achieved another of its highest peaks in efficiently and realistically reproducing the atmosphere that the filmmaker and the photography director agreed upon to tell this story. With this film Krasker recovered the opportunity that had melted in his hands with *Oliver Twist* of obtaining, with the adequate theme, the highest award in his trade.

# PART V
# THE FIFTIES

## 33. General View of the Decade

Worldwide, the fifties was a complex, but also fruitful decade in the field of motion pictures. Motion picture technology took forward steps leaving an imprint on cinema photography. Changes in economic and organizational structures, developed in the previous period, now became effective. Furthermore, the new show competitor, television, prompted variations in the classic cinema offerings.

The most drastic change in the business came in the world's main motion picture center, the U.S.A., when the Antitrust Law prevented the two ends of the trade, production and exhibition, to be in the same hands. This act broke the long tradition of supremacy of certain groups, but granted them enough time to reorganize the various successor firms, which process ended in that decade.

Those splits produced unrest in both ends, but also benefits: independent decisions, greater incentive, healthier competition and new production possibilities away from the large organizations, as well as a search for new competitive means. However these divisions, together with TV competition and increased ticket cost also caused failures: about 4000 theaters had to close down.

These changes also affected trade operations and percentages levels. Independent theaters selected the material they would show, as all bonds with the studios had been untied. Programs were changed and also the number of films shown, altering classic sequences. This forced studios to change their yearly production plans and handle unshown film reserves differently.

An indirect consequence of this disruption was the increased possibility for foreign films to bow into the "art theaters" circle. To fill up program gaps some theater exhibitors searched for new, a different material, allowing access to European films in such specialized theaters. Thus the American public became aware of another kind of motion picture with different cinematographic approach, more thought provoking and daring, satisfying some audiences' desires for deeper waters than shallow TV shows and some stereotyped Hollywood products fettered to the Hays code. This gap was not very wide but it opened another view and enabled comparisons.

This severance in the motion picture industry had another effect on the production field, as more independent producers appeared, ready to fill the gaps in the programming schedules of the theaters. Their low budget film projects were usually innovative and always competitive with output from the studios. The latter also grasped the possibilities of renting their production facilities or go into co-productions with independents, using their inactive structure and disregarding their own rigid production methods. Before, "B" class films were ordered from other minor studios; now they could co-operate in good quality productions, not risking their reputations with now unnecessary low quality complementary products. Independent filming premises also increased considerably, renting their facilities for TV productions, and new possibilities appeared also for art personnel and free-lance technical staff, including directors of photography who thus found attractive work options away from the studios.

In the film show field, there was a considerable growth in that period of a film projection expedient born late in the previous decade: the drive-in, an efficient weapon to compete with television as it combined going to the movies with America's favorite commodity, the motor car. The attraction of the large screen and the enjoyment of intimacy in a public movie show, induced its different appreciation, leading to the growth of such drive-ins to about 4,500 in less than two decades.[1]

The motion picture industry faced television competition with several responses. One was selling TV stations their films that had completed their theater show cycle and had no further possibilities there. RKO ventured steeply in that line, when deep in crisis they sold their whole film library to a TV programming syndicate. Other studios followed obtaining considerable benefits. Many productions were also leased for a determined number of showings.

During this decade television had grown to great importance: about 98 percent of American homes had a TV set. It was therefore imperative to incorporate new material for showing. First, shows were produced specifically for TV filmed on 35mm film from three or more mobile cameras, adapted to their own techniques and shot in independent studios. One way to overcome competition of these two media was to unite and co-produce. The old system of serials for movie theaters had finished some time ago and now TV became an outlet for "B" class films made specifically for it. First they were half-hour serials, then followed by those of about one hour. Television stars elbowed up to vie with movie stars and new celebrities were born, and some stars discarded by Hollywood reappeared on TV.

However, the large studios still believed their main source of income was the high budget feature production shown in theaters and consequently searched for other attractions which television could not offer. New systems appeared proposed by small firms or independent researchers, based on old photographic experiments, on devices applied during World War II for specific purposes, and on unfinished trials shelved by motion pictures two decades before, towards widening the format of negatives and prints to widen the image on the screen, as well as improving its quality.

Systems were conceived, such as 3-D, to render a three-dimensional effect. Devices were conceived to project an image on a surrounding screen such as Cinerama, but they were efficient only for the travelogue type of film. These were then simplified to make the system adequate for feature films without complex modifications in the theaters, such as Cinemascope and other patents with anamorphic methods. Research continued for flexible variations to all the methods while keeping high image quality, resulting in Vistavision, Technirama and others. The success of enterprising producers with spectacular films, including wide screen and systems such as Todd AO, encouraged studios which had already experimented in this field to make trials with wider gauges: 55mm and later on 65–70mm. Many of the experiments were short lived, while others signified a permanent improvement which greatly influenced motion picture photography, and drew greater attention to the effective use of the sound track. Moreover, productions specifically for television combined motion pictures with electronic images to facilitate shooting for TV shows, adopting methods similar to those of that medium.

Changes in motion picture production structures occurred in studios all over the world. European productions grew, but the audiences in these countries still preferred Hollywood films, which were tinged with escapism, were more entertaining and with added production values. But the economies of European countries were still war impaired and box office profits of Hollywood films could not be allowed to move out freely. Laws were passed to refrain certain percentages, freezing them in each company. Thus the best way Hollywood producers could recover such retentions was to invest them in new, locally made films, to be shown in the American market and other restriction-free world markets.

This policy was applied in Britain, France, Germany and Italy. Britain was the most often used center for this type of films, called runaway productions. Hollywood already had long experience in ties to British motion pictures, since the time of quota quickies in the twenties and thirties. Metro-Goldwyn-Mayer had studios set up in Elstree, while Warner Bros. had their ABPC studios nearby. Consequently, a considerable number of American-financed British-made films flowed to America and world markets. This confirmed the adoption in Britain of Hollywood equipment and production procedures.

Italy experienced a similar but lesser influence. Lower production costs and qualified available craftsmen attracted some Hollywood studios to film at Cinecittà studios in Rome. These had been rebuilt in 1947 and updated in 1950 and were chosen to film spectacular productions or co-productions, such as *Quo Vadis* (1950), *War and Peace* (1955), *Ben Hur* (1957) and other memorable works.

Again, as before, Hollywood technicians worked with their Italian colleagues. Cinecittà was equipped with material used in Hollywood, but this did not affect Italian cinematographic concepts. Moreover, they opened their way to other European motion picture usage with British and French equipment, since many co-productions were made with groups from those countries. European producers soon adopted the new wide screen techniques, especially those using their own anamorphic systems, e.g., Totalscope, Cinepanoramic, Agascope, Supercinescope, Dyaliscope, and others.

There were films made under Cinemascope patents, either by Vistavision or the Technirama systems since the Technicolor group had already extended their operations into Europe; they had begun in Britain in-1935, and followed in France in 1956 and finally in Italy in 1957. Some time later, Italian Technicolor would develop a new, low cost but effective wide screen system, much used in European studios, named Techniscope 2-P. Other important American firms, such as Mole & Richardson, Westrex, R.C.A., Ampex and others maintained this penetration into the European motion picture industry, contributing to its expansion.

The wide screen reached the Soviet Union in 1955 and in 1957 they created their own systems, e.g., Circama, as well as filming with their own anamorphic system and in 1960 with 70mm film gauge.[2]

Also, two new low cost shooting methods appeared during this period (one a consequence of the other) which sometimes alternated with the classic procedure used till then. The first one, named neo-realism, had been born in Italy during World War II, and was continued in the post-war period. It consisted of shooting commonplace subjects away from the studios, in the streets or in real locations; sometimes using non-professional players, but always observing the classical outlines of motion picture photography, and providing the advantage of shooting real, untouched situations and atmospheres. Thus, the strict requisites of studio shooting were overcome, as well as the difficulties arising from insufficient equipment, power and raw stock. This mode reduced costs appreciably and achieved effective realism, free from the sophisticated impression of studio products as used then.

The early attempts in this aesthetic form can be traced to such Italian films as *Four Steps to the Clouds* (1942), directed by Alessandro Blasetti, and *Ossessione* (1942), made by Luchino Visconti. But the new style was more defined in the famous Rossellini *Rome, Open City* (1945) and *Païsá* (1946), and reaching its summit with a series of famous low-budget films by the renowned actor and director Vittorio de Sica, among which were *Bicycle Thieves* (1948), *Miracle in Milan* (1950), *Umberto D* (1952), *Il Tetto* (1955), etc.[3]

Later on this tendency was continued in France by a group of intellectuals gathered round the *Cahiers du Cinema* magazine. This concept, which was named Nouvelle Vague (New Wave), propounded a breakaway from traditional shooting methods. They too wanted authentic situations and locations, a new aesthetic approach with certain improvisation. But they also wanted to change the classic studio photography techniques, using hand-held cameras, with the light available or using photoflood light sources, or bounced, against the typical studio light methods. Examples of this kind of films were *Les Quatre Cents Coups* (1959), by François Truffaut, *À Bout de Souffle* (*Breathless*, 1959), by Jean Luc Godard, or *Zazie dans le Métro* (1960), by Louis Malle.[4]

The technical equipment available at the time allowed this new filmmaking procedure, giving rise to a series of films which, though controversial, influenced and left a mark on many technicians involved in studios, including photography directors. The names of French cinematographers such as Raoul Coutard, Enri Decae and others were representative of this new lighting approach. This method was repeated in other countries, especially where emerging motion picture industries and young independent film makers emulated these modes. Later on, the widespread use of color increased costs considerably, reducing the proliferation of such films, since large investments were more difficult to recover.

The new mode was intensely applied in low cost independent productions: many young directors of photography abandoned the classic lighting methods with Fresnel spots for directional light, and adopted the easier solution with diffused light, which they believed was more realistic, especially with color film, and could be done with low power consumption equipment. Therefore, the lighting equipment industry produced smaller units placed on bars supported from floor to ceiling or from wall to wall, in order to facilitate lighting in real indoor settings or large white surfaces to bounce the light. But the most important revolution in the light techniques was the introduction around 1960 of the new halogen lamp with its powerful and actinic source and very small size and weight. The new designs produced in this kind of equipment in the following years were very useful for low budget film production.

# 34. Cameras

The fifties showed stimulating developments in the field of camera design in several countries. The growth of television and the final adoption of 16mm gauge for many of its uses also occurred in several European centers causing new equipment to be produced for this purpose. Moreover, when new film formats, e.g.: 55, 65 and70mm, cropped up new cameras were required, as well as for the new developing 3-D, Vistavision and Technirama systems, as seen above.

Magnetic sound recording synchronized with the images brought about new equipment, not only for TV requirements, but also for movie newsreels which still existed then. Television also needed a method to record broadcasts so as to transmit them again later on; motion pictures were a help here and several equipment makers designed items to record programs from a TV tube, before videotape appeared in 1956; after some time this method, named kinetoscope, was shelved as it was impractical and expensive.

Cinematography was also used to record information needed in technical aspects of industry, especially aircraft research and design, ballistics, the start up of space research, science, medicine, all scientific endeavors, as well as research by the armed forces. Consequently, companies were created for those special tasks, or diversified their production previously for motion pictures. Technology was developed increasingly and cinematography was becoming essential in fields other than entertainment.

Let us now look into the most important items appearing in the main studios. Firms renowned in the Western cinema equipment industry were offering new items and technical facilities, while other instruments were being made in countries which become politically isolated after World War II.

## The USA

Cameras used in Hollywood studios in this decade were practically unchanged those appearing after World War II, except those for special systems, like 3-D, Vistavision and Technirama. Some such systems were short lived while others lasted somewhat longer, as we saw above. We can say that American cameras used in Hollywood after the war and in the fifties, although highly developed in many aspects, were technically lagging behind their European counterparts in reference with innovations.

Neither the Mitchell BNC, the most refined camera of the American motion picture industry, nor the Mitchell NC, its classic complement for outdoor shooting, nor Fox cameras which were standard in that studio, were provided with reflex viewing while shooting. Operators had to resort to the not so bright image of the monitoring viewfinder which needed adjusting for parallax. Reflex viewing, one of the most important technical developments of motion pictures adopted by most European camera makers, was not applied to Hollywood cameras until 1960 in a model requiring a blimp, the Mitchell R-35. This camera was a marked change in that maker's models, not only for its reflex viewfinder, but also that it allowed shoulder support, with its magazines installed adequately for that purpose. Its features were those of a multipurpose camera, with the characteristics of a Mitchell instrument, allowing use as a hand-held cameras well as for studio work. Edmund DiGiulio was a pioneer in adopting this device.

The reason for the delay of American camera makers to adopt reflex viewing is believed to be the reluctance of the feature film and short film cinematographers to change their work habits. Camera crews were made up by men working in the trade for many years who were not ready to modify they safety routine. At that time there were camera crews of technicians with an average age of above fifty years. The same situation happened in other areas as the short film production.

But neither did the makers of the new 16mm cameras for television not use reflex

**The Mitchell Reflex, the first american studio camera with this viewing system, which was made during the mid sixties (*courtesy Mitchell Camera Corp.*).**

viewing in their new instruments. Professional equipment in this gauge, like the Mitchell 16 and the Maurer, maintained the old rack-over of shift-over methods. New camera makers, like Nord and Auricon, kept on the old system, and obtained reflex viewing, some time later, when they included zoom lenses with built-in partial reflex viewing, e.g., the Pan Cinor. Auricon introduced at that time their compact Pro 600 sound-on-film cameras with high fidelity Filmagnetic recording system on pre-stripped raw stock for newsreel shooting, with a compact, transistorized amplifier. Subsequent cameras for this purpose, e.g. the one by Morton, developed about 1956, for television shooting with optical sound recording on the film, 600 ft. magazines installed on top of the camera, three-lens turret, 240 degree shutter, and built-in veeder counter, but they went on using the old rack-over or shift-over device, with critical focusing through the lens only when the camera was stopped. When the camera was running the scene was viewed through a parallax corrected side viewfinder. This shows that the American technicians who were handling the new TV events worked with the same limitations used before the appearance of the reflex viewing in 1937.

The decade started with the Korean War, which brought about changes in combat camera design. The firm most concerned with this development was Bell & Howell, closely tied commercially to the armed forces since World War I. This firm's cooperation with its clients determined new building concepts which were quickly taken up. All equipment as well as the holding cases had to withstand the rough usage of modern warfare under extremely varied climates. The term "militarized" appeared as applied to equipment, signifying that internal and external finishes had to be totally modified to comply with specific needs.

Selecting the adequate finishes demanded months of research with the armed forces and taking into account varied factors. The different component parts had to be analyzed to determine the correct corrosion resistance of each metal for each part, considering the equipment would have to run accurately under very high and very low temperatures.

The militarized instruments had about thirty different types of finish in order to comply with requirements. The outsides of these cameras were finished in olive-drab, while scales and winding keys (chrome plated in the

The improved Filmo 70, TV news 16mm camera (*courtesy Bell & Howell*).

civilian version) were a smoky black, to avoid reflex ions. Lenses were treated the same, improving the mounts of theoptic components to resist harsher treatment and more extreme temperatures. Reading the calibrations on the focus and iris rings was made easier and they too were finished in smoky gray or black.

New, sturdier cases were conceived to resist harsh wear in warfare missions, humidity, extreme temperatures and unsuitable transportation. The experience obtained from the previous war led to this appreciable improvement in technology. The Bell & Howell equipment thus militarized and given a special designations were the Eyemo models K, M, Q and R cameras and the 16mm cameras previously known as Filmo and Design 200 Series for 50 ft. magazines.

At that time Bell & Howell was asked to adequate their different cameras to ballistic requirement of the armed forces, to the needs of the aeronautics industry, of the growing space industry and industrial research laboratories. This firm together with other makers of special cameras, such as Traid Corp., Neyhart Enterprises, Fairchild, Century Engineering Inc., Beckman & Whitley, Hi-Speed Equipment Inc., Wollensak Optical Co., Red Lake and others, where the suppliers of specialized equipment for high speed photography, flight testing; data recording; rocket and missile tracking; instrumentation; time and motion study; wind tunnel testing, research and development; gunnery and ballasting studies; radarscope recording, atomic effects testing and industrial machine analysis. A new and different world was appearing in motion picture photography calling for new specialists.

## Great Britain

In many aspects British motion pictures followed a trend similar to that of the USA, since there were strong ties between the two industries. The most important studio camera maker there was a member of the Rank group, G.B. Kalee who, as we saw above, had copied the Mitchell NC and developed many accessories for it (blimps, viewfinder parallax control devices, tripods, etc.) The Rank group, in association with the BBC, also produced a double system sound recording camera which included a Cameflex and a perforated film magnetic recording unit in a blimp. This organization also developed its own Vistavision camera with the film traveling horizontally.

The cameras for feature films by W. Vinten Ltd. were for some time used and appreciated for their reflex viewing, but they never managed to be wholly accepted in British studios, perhaps due to the Rank group's quasi monopoly. Therefore Vinten diversified its camera production towards scientific work, but one of them for the 16mm format was noted for its versatility. Its name was Scientific Camera Mark II and it was very compact; it was provided with a three-lens turret, reflex viewing by means of a 144 degree fixed opening shutter, 50 or 200 ft., magazines variable speeds for 8, 16 or 24f.p.s and 12 V built-in motor. This instrument was later on adapted to high speed up to 250 f.p.s.

Another well-known British firm, Newman Sinclair, conceived a new hand-held camera, about 1960, for 35mm format. It was called P/400, and was driven by a 12 V motor. It was provided with three lens offset turret, mirror shutter, register pin movement, external 400 ft. pre-thread magazines and front tachometer. This firm also made later a special blimp for this camera and a 16/35mm version of this instrument. The Acmade company made instruments for scientific research, and other firms, like Ernest Moy and Marconi, produced instruments for telerecording.

British television belatedly adopted the 16mm format as standard, and their newsreels used the then new 16mm Arriflex cameras. For such newsreels they produced a magnetic unit to record sound on pre-stripped film with a transistorized amplifier to turn the Arri S into a sound-on-film camera, as they were the representatives in Britain of the German makers, Arnold & Richter.

## Japan

Japanese manufacturers probed the professional camera market with various instruments. The Doi Ltd. company produced a 16mm professional reflex cam-

Newman Sinclair P-400 magazine camera (courtesy Newman & Sinclair Ltd.).

era similar characteristics to the Arriflex 16, but with a guillotine reflex shutter. The old, established Seiki Seisakusho, firm built 35mm cameras based on the Mitchell patents and very important for the motion picture industry of this country.

## France

In the fifties, this country was still in the van of camera equipment production in Europe. The André Debrie firm produced the new Super Parvo Color studio camera; it was adapted for use with anamorphic lenses and included a new, special, type A (anamorphic) shutter block, an improved film channel to allow steadier image registration, a special sunshade to be used with wide screen systems, and other improvements. This firm also launched the Parvo 58, new version of the Parvo "L" equipped with a new shutter traveling very near the film and allowing the use of very wide angle lenses as the new Angenieux 14.5mm anamorphic lenses, and zoom lenses such as the Pan Cinor 38–150mm with its reflex viewing finder. The camera was provided with a new viewfinder on the right side of the camera.

This firm kept on producing high speed cameras, e.g. the "G.V." (Grand Vitesse) model for photographing up to 240 f.p.s. with a long standing reputation in the trade. In 1960 they added their Debrie 16 Kinescope camera with high precision mechanism, V shaped gate to ensure absolute sharp and steady images, 25 f.p.s speed, rapid phasing adjustment, and 2,266 ft. magazines for one hour's shooting. Another special instrument at the end of the decade was the 35mm Ciné-Theodolite camera, for 24 × 36mm frames, horizontal film travel, marking device and 400 ft. film magazines.

The Éclair company, too, built in that decade special equipment for scientific research cinematography and for industrial controls, which were applied to the basic Caméflex camera, to the Caméflex 16mm television camera for kinescope recording, and to the Défilement continue (continuous running) Caméflex conceived for scientific and industrial research work.

In that period, this firm also continued building the renowned Camé 300 Reflex, acknowledged as one of the best studio cameras and used in countless productions in France, Italy, Poland and Czechoslovakia. Éclair brought about important changes when they offered new competitive equipment for the international television market.

Other French firms were also producing cameras, e.g. the Compagnie de Travaux Mécaniques, which was building items for journalism work and the renowned Cousteau-Girardot underwater camera. The well known engineer André Coutant of the Société d'Etudes et de Réalizations Industrielles developed the Camé-Twin, a special instrument for shooting traveling mattes using two films passing through two film gates at right angles and with many refinements. Lightweight and newsreel cameras were being made, like the Morigraph and the Leblay, but they were eventually discontinued in view of the popularity and conveniences of Éclair's new Cameflex which was widely accepted in the newsreel market too. Other instruments for television also appeared, like the 16mm camera built by Marcel Levillan of the Matériel Cinématographique LMC company, which showed an image on ground glass, through a 4× magnified viewfinder, it had a 4-lens turret with a

Debrie's Super Parvo color studio camera with standard matte box (courtesy André Debrie Matériel Cinématographique).

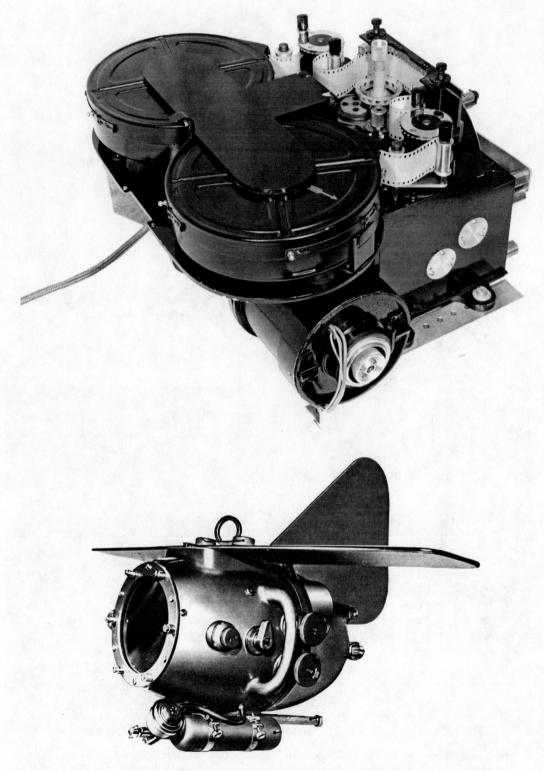

Top: Debrie Cine-Theodolite camera (courtesy André Debrie Matériel Cinématographique).
Bottom: Éclair Aquaflex underwater camera (courtesy Éclair International Diffusion).

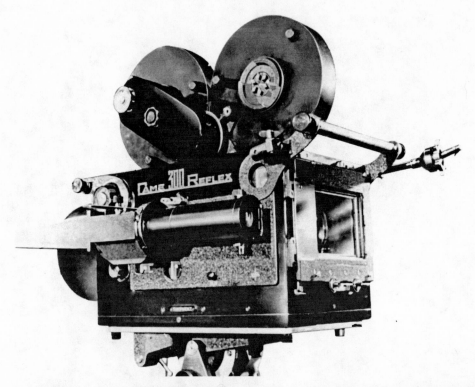

Top: Éclair Camé 300 Reflex studio camera (*courtesy Éclair International Diffusion*). Bottom: This image with five successive exposures of the French film *Le Mouton à cinq pattes* was made with the Éclair Camé 300 Reflex, specially designed for these kinds of tricks (*courtesy Éclair International Diffusion*).

sunshade in front and a top mounted magazine allowed 400 ft. rolls or 100 ft. spools. The drive motor was of the asynchronous type. Sound was recorded by the optical system with fixed density galvanometer.

But in the French TV field the favorite cameras were the Sonoflex and Sinchroflex, made by the Tolana company for direct sound recording on a magnetic track built into the film. These instruments included reflex viewing, externally controlled interchangeable lenses, bellows sunshade, almost silent running (55 db), and 200 degree opening shutter. Based on a design similar to the Auricon Pro, the Sonoflex was a compact camera allowing a film load of 200 ft. spools, while the Synchroflex was more developed, with 1000 ft. capacity double compartment magazines installed on top. With both these cameras, the then named Radio Diffusion Télévision Française carried out their filmed interviews, and TV producers had the equipment at hand for their needs.

Finally, among several 16mm amateur cameras made in France at that time, the well-known Pathé Webo stands out, with its reflex viewfinder, variable opening shutter, 3-lens turret and spring drive with reverse. But it increased its possibilities when the company added an electric motor and externally installed magazines for greater capacity, allowing it to be used as a silent camera for interviews.

## Germany

The expansion of German production of motion picture equipment became apparent in this decade, the important Arnold & Richter company vigorously re-initiated their operations which became evident when in 1950 they brought out their Arriflex Model II with a all stainless-steel film gate, cylinder matte box shaft and louvre over ground glass but without changes in film movement and shutter. In 1954 surged the model IIA with a 180 degree shutter and cardiod film movement giving registration action. The new design included a removable nose to use the camera in blimp, a new brighter, sharper optical system and a new mechanism. In 1957 the model IIB also included a stronger handgrip motor to pull the new 400 ft. color magazine

**Arriflex II B camera (courtesy Arnold & Richter Cine Technik).**

*Top:* **New Arriflex intermittent mechanism** (*courtesy Arnold & Richter Cine Technik*). *Bottom:* **Arriflex 1000ft. camera blimp** (*courtesy Arnold & Richter Cine Technik*).

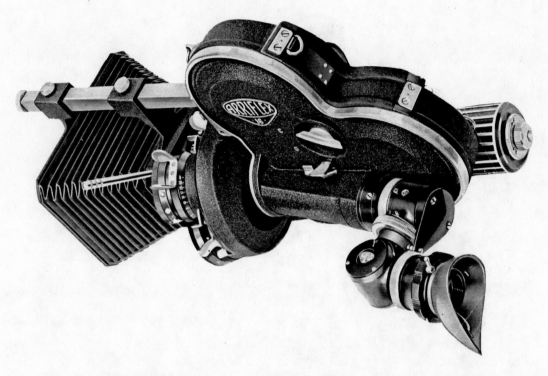

**Arriflex 16mm camera (*courtesy Arnold & Richter Cine Technik*).**

and a bellows matte box with filter holder. New implements flowed out ceaselessly, but two items were noteworthy: the Arri 35 400 ft. sound blimp with synchronous motor, and the Arri 1000 ft. sound blimp with a Newall magazine, to adapt the camera for studio work. The Arri 16 ST also appeared at that time, which was accepted world wide for its many abilities and accessories.

The last development of the Arnold & Richter Co. in that decade was the Arricord camera, which combined an Arriflex IIB with a magnetic device recording sound on 17.5mm film, included in an elaborate blimp, resulting in a double system 35mm sound camera, to meet the requirements at that time of newsreels for movie theaters.

But there were also other firms in Germany manufacturing equipment for cinematography. One of them, Askania Werke, maintained production of their Askania Model "Z"; this firm also created their Trick Camera specially designed for special effects and animation, the Rotax for high speed film recording, the RöntgenKamera for work in medical research and seven other specialized models. Another firm, Crass, also produced different special effects cameras. The ample German motion picture industry was then still using cameras as the Minicord V 16, a single system sound camera made by the Klangfilm company, and the Zwischen film 6018 bild-ton-kamera, a 35mm sound recording item built by Fernseh Gess. Other firms produced special high speed cameras and equipment for scientific work.

In East Germany the best-known camera was the Pentaflex, manufactured by ZeissIkon, a 16mm professional instrument with reflex viewing. It was provided with interchangeable 200 ft. and 400 ft. preloaded magazines, a three-lens turret with built-in diaphragm ring control, 12 V motor either used as a hand grip or installed at one side, a 0 to 189 degree variable opening shutter which allows filming frame by frame, bellows sunshade with matte

**Arriflex Arricord sound-on-film camera (*courtesy Arnold & Richter Cine Technik*).**

box, crank handle for reverse drive which allows coupling a spring drive, time-marks registering device and other abilities. It was ideal for TV shooting, as well as for educational and industrial films. The same firm made several 16 and 35mm cameras for scientific work, capable of running from medium to very high speeds, (500 to 5.000 f.p.s.).

## Italy

Camera production in Italy in that decade was only a limited number of 35mmNovado units (which were also distributed to a few European countries, as well as two models in the 16mm gauge for television. On the latter, one was the Sonoretta, with a very updated design, a non reflex viewfinder, the motor mounted beneath the camera body, with double magazine mounted on top, and provided with double system optical sound recording. The other, more widely accepted in Italy, was the Orafon, made by Microcine SRL. It was a compact camera, with double magazine, provided with two viewfinders and an access door on which its optical sound recording unit was installed; its speed was variable at 16 or 24 f.p.s. and it had a three-lens turret with bellows sunshade and matte box. At that time special 16mm cameras for scientific research were built by Carlo Ventimiglia, a cinematographer, the son of the well known expert Gaetano Ventimiglia.

## Switzerland

The Paillard S.A. firm, established in Sainte Croix and with a long reputation for their Bolex amateur cameras, saw in the growth of television and the widespread use of the 16mm format an opportunity to promote their equipment on the professional and semiprofessional markets. Through 130 agents distributed worldwide their highly finished cameras

The famous 16mm Bolex Paillard reflex camera and how it was designed (*courtesy Bolex-Paillard S.A and Archivo Nacional de la Imagen, Sodre*).

were sold very satisfactory and were being intensively used in films of diverse kinds. Television spots further opened the market to using the camera for that purpose in many countries as well as for newsreels. All this induced the makers to improve new models, like the H-16RX. On such reform was the addition of reflex viewing by means of a prism; others had a variable opening shutter, an electric motor, and several accessories (like an automatic fade unit) which, together with zoom lenses, increased the possibilities of this instrument, even in some forms of scientific research work. Thus the Paillard Bolex became a classic, medium-cost instrument, very much used in many productions and scientific film institutes all over the world.

## Czechoslovakia

After World War II, the Czechoslovakian motion picture industry changed radically as it was taken over by the government. Joseph Slechta was sent to Ledcko, near Prague, to set up a small workshop where, together with V. Novotny, a camera operator, they built a stereoscopic camera; this was one of the last instruments he worked on. The Czech government firm, Meopta-Somet, manufactured a sound recording 16mm camera with 400 ft. magazines, three-lens turret and optical sound recording system. The Cinephon company collapsed in 1948 and gradually became the Povazka Bystrica in Slovakia; some of their cameras, like the hand-held 35mm with 200 ft. capacity, were used for many years for newsreels in that country.

In 1951 the government company Filmovy Prumsyl was formed in Barrandow, Prague, which began producing several types of 35mm cameras, of which later on were noted for their high quality and refined design, like the ARK 1A, 35mm; ERK 1, 35mm and TK 4, 16/35. This company also built several items of equipment for laboratory work exported to near of 50 countries.

## Soviet Union

After the end of World War II the Soviet motion picture industry undertook camera production for that vast community of nations. One of the factories cowing this out was Mashpriborintorg, in Moscow, which made a variety of equipment for all aspects of Soviet cinema. Among the cameras one of the most noteworthy was the KC 50, a 35mm instrument for newsreel work, identical to the Bell & Howell Model Q, Eyemo. The camera design resulted in the Rodina for 35mm format, with 400 ft. internal magazines or external 1000 ft., side by side, installed in the back of the camera body; reflex viewfinder provided by a variable opening shutter from 0 to 160 degree, mounted on top, motor coupled on one side, and a bellows sunshade filter holder at the front. This camera followed the design principles of the Parvo Debrie model L.

Another studio camera was the Moska KC 32, built similarly to the Mitchell NC in some aspects (e.g. the intermittent mechanism), provided with 1000 ft. double magazines mounted on top, but independent driven, and with a monitoring viewfinder and camera controls installed on the left hand side of the camera. It was driven by a 220 V motor.

This factory also produced the Convas, a hand held 35mm camera cleverly designed somewhat similar to Éclair Caméflex and the Morigraf, regarding the pre-loaded 200 ft.

and 400 ft. magazines mounted at the rear, it was provided with a non-divergent three-lens turret, reflex viewfinder and a tachometer installed beneath it. A cylindrical shape electric motor was coupled on one side and was interchangeable with a spring drive; it was also provided with a sunshade and allowed filming with anamorphic lenses. This camera was widely accepted and was intensely used for Soviet newsreels and in the production of shorts in the many studios working in this field. It was also used by astronaut Vladimir Titov in his flight around the earth in the "Soyuz" spaceship.

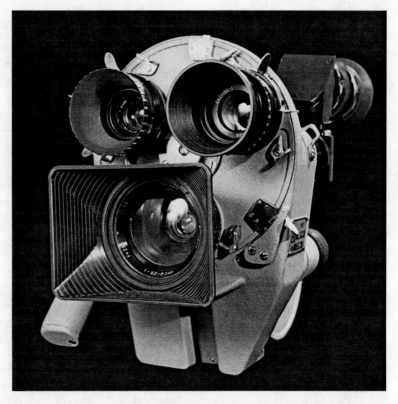

Improved version of the Soviet Convas Automatic camera (*courtesy Archivo Nacional de la Imagen, Sodre*).

# 35. New Screen Techniques

Since early in the fifties new projection methods were researched in order to recover more theater audiences from TV, as indicated by drops in box office sales. Any such attractiveness would have to be an imaginative novelty, and should be intended to improve the scenic effect that motion pictures now required. Among the first methods that were studied one that drew more attention was the three dimensional effect, defined as stereoscopic motion pictures, and commonly known as 3-D.

## Stereoscopic motion pictures

Investigating how to produce realistic images with a grand show effect, researchers looked into the past and saw that still photographers had experimented in stereoscopic vision, with cameras as well as viewing and projecting devices, and showed rich results. They went back to 1858 when J.Ch. D'Almeida had made experiments with relief projection of photographic plates by the anaglyph principle, as well as by darkening the projected image, synchronized with the vision of each eye. About 1893, William Friese-Green continued with the experiments and these principles were adopted, with variations, in the field of still photography, as well as in aerophotogrammetry (aerial survey). These experiments were extended to motion pictures in 1897 by C. Grivolas, who built an instrument to take simultaneous images for that purpose, but these attempts did not materialize until 1909 when a patented system was developed by the Société des Établissements Gaumont. About 1935 Louis Lumière continued with this research to the utmost point that the anaglyph system allowed.

The anaglyph principle worked by viewing, through two colored filters (red and green), the projection of two superimposed images taken by a stereoscopic camera and projected, each set of images, through each of two filters of such colors. A convincing relief effect was thus obtained. In 1927, Dr. Edwin Land experimented with a similar process, but instead of two colored filters, he applied transparent sheets of conveniently oriented polarized material. In this field, about 1938, J. Mahler, a Czechoslovakian scientist, produced innovations which were put in practice in the USA by Polaroid Inc. It was an important variation to achieve the same end without altering the chromatic values of the images. Other methods followed, e.g. the one known as Eclipse, in which a projected image was substituted by another, and simultaneously, a synchronized shutter operated in a viewing device before the spectator's eyes. Finally devices were created with moving grids on the screen, or lenticular surfaces which did not require viewing devices for the audience.[1]

Among the first practical consequences for 3-D motion pictures, we must note the work carried out early in the '30s by Leslie P. Dudley, a British expert on the subject, as well as that of the American J. Norling, about the same time. Norling's experiments were centered on the polarized light, developed together with J.F. Leventhal for producing shorts for MGM, printed in two colors by Technicolor, and named Audioscopiks; these were followed several years later by others, named Metroscopix.[2]

In 1937, MGM studios produced one of the first 3-D feature films taken by two Bell & Howell 2709 cameras, combined with and fronted to a special optical device. This film was *Three Dimension Murder* directed by Peter Smith. The 3-D expert was John Nickolaus and the cinematographers were B.C. Parker and Jack Smith. It was a low budget film made in a very short time on a studio back lot, and was released in 1941 as an unprecedented novelty.

In 1939, J.A. Norling used the polarized light method for some films produced by the Chrysler Motor Corp. to be shown at the 1939 New York World's Fair, where the spectators were given polarized-filter cardboard spectacles. Two synchronized projectors, each with an adequately placed polarized filter, projected superimposed images on a screen prepared to avoid the depolarization of light. The film was a documentary on totally automated motor car manufacturing and the audiences who saw it were estimated at about a million and a half. The same company made two more such films around 1940, one of which was in Technicolor.[3]

After this series of trials, the methods to be adopted were being defined about 1952–53. One was the anaglyph system with two filters in two colors, which was soon discarded; another was the use of polarized filters. Moreover, there were variations in the taking procedures, either with single film or with two films, which meant the use of one or two cameras. One of the first films was *Bwana Devil* (1952), taken with polarized filters and which was followed by others when the film-makers adopted this system.

The polarized filters method was soon standardized, generally adopting the system on one film eye. The equipment in all the studios was different, but the differences were not great. In most cases, there were Mitchell NC cameras fronted to an optical device which deviated the image 45 degree by means of two mirrors or prisms. For takes with dialog the camera was covered by a large blimp. The optical axes were 2½ in. apart.

But there were variations. RKO used a camera, specially designed by J.A. Norling, in which two films traveled in a compact, unified unit, provided with a shift-over viewfinder as well as a double direct viewer to catch each of the images; it was provided with a compact double capacity magazine. MGM applied a system with two Mitchell NC cameras placed at right angles, with only one mirror, which allowed taking extreme close-ups. Universal adopted a system with two Mitchell NC cameras fronted to an optical system, but inverted in relation to each other.

In those days, with 3-D at its acme, the Stereocine Corp. cropped up to rent its novel filming equipment made up of two Eclair Cameflex cameras fronted to an optical system with two mirrors centered precisely on the optical axes of the camera lenses. Other companies appeared which designed and rented their 3-D filming methods, e.g. Natural Vision, used by Columbia. On the other hand, Warner Bros. and Twentieth Century Fox, among other studios, created their own equipment on their premises, but did not disclose their technical characteristics. Technicolor also offered their three strip cameras at right angles to an optical unit.

Some studios gave their 3D systems distinctive names. Panavision was the trademark name for Paramount, and Stereoscopic was that of 20th Century–Fox. MGM considered the name Tri-Dee process.

3-D systems with two films caused inconveniences for their audiences: the viewers sometimes felt dizzy, had tired eyes, nausea, or there was a lack of three-dimensional effect, or bad image quality. These problems were analyzed and it was found that most of them were caused by faulty projection due to unsynchronized projectors, misadjusted centering of images, and lack of frames in one of the copies because of repaired breakages impeding synchronization. Sometimes the problem was caused by difference in light intensity in the two projectors.[4]

Finally, the Nord Company of Minneapolis developed, mainly through their expert Roy Chapp, a 3-D shooting system to overcome the inconveniences of taking the images corresponding to each eye in two different films and showing them through two synchronized projectors, each with a different filter. The two images were printed side by side vertically within the conventional dimensions of the silent movie frame. On projection with a normal projector, a special lens provided by the Nord Corp. was mounted on it, and an optical device was placed on the outside of the projection booth window. By this method the images were optically rotated 90 degree and superimposed to obtain the 3-D effect with panoramic format projection.

The Motion Picture Research Council systematized all the different offered methods, searched for standards to be adopted, offered access to investigations and obtained experiences, and stimulated research for using a single film in order to overcome the various inconveniences of double projection. Many cinematographers in different studios took part in the design of 3-D equipment; among them we must note: John Arnold and John N. Nikolaus at MGM, Sol Hapring at 20th Century–Fox, Fred Gage at Warner Bros., Farciot Edouart, Loren Ryder, Dr. Charles Daily and Ferdinand Eich at Paramount, Emil Ostes and Terry Rackett at Columbia, and Eugene E. Polito and Fred Campbell at Universal-International.

Also, several experts from various companies participated in the technical design of different systems: J. A. Norling of Loucks & Norling of New York, R.G. Wolf, Henry Ludwing and A.S. Bodrero of Stereocine Corp., Roy Clapp of Nord Systems, R.E. Schenstad who invented the 3-D projection process with a single projector for Stereocolor Inc., and Fred Baker and Dr. Julian Gunzberg of Natural Vision Corp.

The primary lessons learned in these experiments were: to avoid the use of wide angle lenses greater than 40mm, the use of 50mm lenses for medium shots and close-ups and that on taking close-ups lens spacing must not exceed 2½ in. to obtain a more realistic image reproduction. It was also important, in this kind of shooting, to pay attention to the definition of the takes and to enhance the depth of field. It also ensued that back projection could be used if it was adequate to the system, that it was advisable to plan traveling effects carefully and to emphasize perspective imaginatively, in order to make the most of the qualities of the system.

In the 1952–53 period the 3-D productions planned and most of them carried out were: *Bwana Devil, Fort-Ti, House of Wax, Renegade Canyon, Charge at Feather River, Arena, Sangaree, Inferno, It Came from Outer Space, The Moonlighter, Burning Arrow, Devil's Canyon* and *Hondo*.

In other motion picture studios there were many experiences with 3-D. Europe had a solid tradition of 3-D applied to still photography which was promptly transferred to motion pictures even before World War II. Some feature films had been produced in Germany, like *Nozze Vagabunde* (1937), *Zum Greiffen Nah* (*Nearly Touching It*, 1939), and *Sech Mädel Rollen* (*Six Girls Drive Into the Weekend*, 1939), using a camera built by the Zeiss company, with the system designed by O. Vierling, the firm's expert. Minor productions were carried out in Italy, following experiments by Ing. Gualtierotti, with an optical system he had invented based on the anaglyph method, with similar characteristics to the one developed by Louis Lumière in France. In both these countries it was usual to shoot with a single 35mm film carrying the two images: one for each eye.

The Soviet cinema also carried out experiments in 1939 at the Soviet Union Film Institute, which were continued after World War II with many films and a special SK5 stereoscopic motion picture camera was developed using only a single film. *Robinson Crusoe (Part I)* was the first 3-D and color film made in 1946 with this system, with cinematography of D. Surensky in the new Stereokino Studio.

Different systems were also conceived in several European countries using their own cameras. The system used in Britain was the one designed by Dudley made up by two Newman Sinclair cameras fronted to an optical system with two large mirrors at 45 degree. In Italy the Cristiani system used a single camera with an optical device which subdivided the image in two images with dimensions similar to those of the 16mm format.

A Dutch system named Verivision also used a single film with the image subdivided by an optical device to form two images of 13.5 × 22mm each. A French system designed by J. Juillet superimposed two images one on top of the other on a 35mm film. In Spain, Daniel Aragonés of Laboratorios Fotofilm used the bipack cameras of his Cinefotocolor system to make 3-D. In those years when 3-D was at the crest of the wave, an Argentinean engineer, Jorge Duclout, carried out experiments with these methods. Most of the above 3-D productions were shorts.

The practical carrying out of 3-D feature films lasted little more than a year; soon other processes using wide screens cornered the attention of producers and proved more efficient commercially. Another reason for the decline of 3-D was that Hollywood 3-D productions were taken with two films, which necessitated enlarging the projection rooms of movie theaters thus increasing expenses. But undoubtedly the main reason was the box-office results in movie shows produced by the greater attraction of the novel wide screen.

## Wide screen techniques

### CINERAMA

The Broadway premiere of *This Is Cinerama* on September 30, 1952, at the Broadway Theater, was one of the first wide screen achievements that called producers' attention to the possibilities of drawing audiences to movie theaters. Its inventor was Fred Waller, a special effects expert Paramount Studios who had had a bee in the bonnet for years of a highly striking and unusual movie show. In 1938 he had been consulted by an architect, Ralph Walker, on the possibilities of projecting motion pictures in a spherical building the up coming New York World's Fair. There he materialized his final projects and created what his subconscious had been yearning for.

Together with Walker and associated architects, Voorhees Foley and others, they studied, developed and invented a system for that purpose. They were sponsored by Lawrence Rockefeller, and formed the Vitarama Corporation. Practical experiments were carried out and they even took some films with eleven cameras. But World War II had started and the project had to be held in abeyance when the U.S.A. became involved.

A friend of Waller, who was present at the experiments, was an officer at the Naval Academy and an gunnery expert. He was impressed by the images he had seen and realized the possibilities of applying the system to gunnery training. Asking about it, Waller studied the problem, consulted several experts and saw its feasibility. Several tests were made for gunnery experts of the US Army Air Corps and the Marines, who procured financing to adjust Vitarama to war purposes, building what was known as the Waller Flexible Gunnery Trainer.

It consisted of five unified projectors showing special films in which aircraft images were targets, fired at by four trainees from electronically synchronized machine gun simulators, under a controller's guidance. A remarkable characteristic of this trainer was that projection windows were placed strategically and the images were projected on a large curved screen which rendered a very realistic effect.

Seventy-five of these gunnery trainers were built and they supplied a large amount of valuable information to the training staff. Five million dollars was spent in this training system and 300 million feet of film were used to feed it, fulfilling the requirements of the three armed forces. Countless rounds of ammunition were saved with this training system, and innumerable benefits were obtained, especially in the Pacific War, where it is considered that it saved 300,000 lives.

When peace returned the Cinerama Productions Company appeared, headed by Lowell Thomas, a well-known journalist, and the system was developed. This time it furnished an unprecedented film show, and it became one of the most talked about topics in the Seventh Art. The width of the screen was six times that of the largest movie theaters. The new method included the new stereophonic sound directional concepts (sound coming from all sides).

A special camera was conceived for simultaneously filming on three 35mm negatives placed side by side horizontally with a 0.997 in. × 1.116 in. image on each, equivalent to a six perforation frame. Each image was taken through a 27mm lens, in order to cover a 146 degree viewing angle. Each lens was installed in a special mount precisely adjusted to cover a third of the total field, but the two side ones with their optical axes were directed diagonally across each other; of course, the axis of the mid lens was normal. A single rotating shutter operated in front of the three lenses. Focusing and diaphragm systems were also synchronized for each lens simultaneously. The three 1000 ft. magazines were installed behind the camera, which was heavy, requiring a special support.

Three synchronized projectors were used for showing, placed so that the left hand one covered the right sector of the screen, while the middle one covered the central sector and the right hand projector covered the left sector. The screen was curved, made up by 1,200 vertical strips of perforated tape to reflect light to the audience adequately. A special device was fixed on the projectors, on both sides of each film to conceal the joints of the three films on the screen. Each projector was capable of taking 50 minute reels brought up by a motorized system. A projection operator was in charge of a synchronization system to keep the equipment from falling out of phase. Sound was recorded on and reproduced from a six-track band. The film travel speed was 26 f.p.s.

Cinerama revolutionized motion pictures, but it did not compete with Hollywood studios, as it had not been conceived for fiction feature films, but to show spectacular events in nature and similar happenings, consistent with a film show. But Hollywood studios realized in what direction they should research for novelties on the show side of the business. And that track had already been marked two decades before by Claude-Autant Lara in 1925 and Abel Gance in 1927. After Cinerama, other large screen systems were developed, such as Circama, using eleven 16mm cameras, or Thrillamara, using standard 35mm film and requiring two projectors.[5]

## Anamorphic systems

The adoption of the anamorphic system with a cylindrical lens for shooting films and showing them on a wide screen was furthered commercially early in the fifties by Twentieth Century Fox studios with Cinemascope as their brand name. Its background began late in the nineteenth century when patents in this field were granted to Ernest Abee, the founder of the Zeiss company in Germany. Ernest Zollinger was another expert who obtained patents in 1912. Several other scientists also studied this optical device to be applied experimentally in color films with the additive system.

Specialists, such as Rudolph, Parker and Phillips, also worked on different applications of the anamorphic system, e.g. recording sound on film, and others, but never in search of a wider image on the screen. In France, Henri Chrétien, professor at the Sorbonne, was one of the first in this field. On May 30, 1927, at the French Academy of Sciences, he presented a paper specifically on taking motion picture films and projecting them on a panoramic screen by means of cylindrical lenses, and using standard film. At this event Louis Lumière introduced him.

An American expert, H. Sydney Newcomer, who was studying optics in France, held a conversation with Chretien and encouraged him to develop the method which would impress American producers. On returning home, Newcomer also worked to develop a lens of this kind, achieving positive results in 1929. Shortly afterwards, in 1930, Prof. Chrétien exhibited his lens in New York, showing that their practical application was feasible. But the time was not right: the whole world was suffering the effects of the economic depression started the previous year and the motion picture industry could not afford to invest in a field that was not essential.

The circumstances in the early fifties, explained above, and the vivid impression on audiences produced by Cinerama, led Twentieth Century Fox to push this system ahead. In 1951 its president, Spyros Skouras, took an interest in Prof. Chrétien's Hypergonar lens system and went to France. They carried out several tests and applied the system on a Cameraéclair with very satisfactory results. After personally hearing Chrétiens's explanations, Skouras sent Earl Sponable, the studio expert, who returned to Hollywood with the Hypergonar lens as a prototype of the optical system that Bausch and Lomb later developed.

The Fox studios were not looking for a simple optical device. They wanted to develop a wide screen system including an anamorphic lens for their cameras, a sound recording method, and an adequate, highly reflective, surrounding screen. Moreover, the film theaters would have to be reconditioned. Sol Halprin was at the head of a group of experts to carry it out, made up of Loring Grignon, sound engineer; Grobes Lauber, camera engineer; William Weishest, chief projectionist; and Carl Faulkner from the sound department.

Experiments were carried out with the co-operation of Bausch & Lomb to produce highly luminous anamorphic lenses, and to reduce the divergence of the perpendicular. This complex operation was only partially achieved, but was improved later on. The aspect ratio, which initially had been 2.66 to 1, was improved to 2.55 to 1, in order to fulfill the required four stereophonic sound tracks. The new Bausch & Lomb optical units for coupling on were almost three times in size and weight those of Prof. Chrétien's original optical device. Fox cameras had to be adapted to them; the aperture dimensions were modified to 0.868 in. ( 0.735 in; the film travel speed was maintained at 24 f.p.s.; a reticule was added to the viewing system; the sunshade was extended horizontally; monitor viewfinders with wider images were designed. The initial difficulties were overcome one by one.

The premiere of the first Cinemascope production was on April 28, 1953. The film was *The Robe*, directed by Henry Koster, with cinematography by Leon Shamroy. It was projected on a specially designed curved screen 80 feet wide, and almost four feet deep in the center of the curve. It was a whacking success, as were the box office returns. Fox soon prepared other productions to follow up their hit in the show world. Among them were *How to Marry a Millionaire* (1953), a film with the provisional title *Twelve Mile Reef* and *Prince Valiant* (1954). In the projects to show Cinemascope productions to the general public, Fox studios made arrangements with Bausch & Lomb to have three thousand of five thousand projections lenses delivered by some time late in 1953.

The patents held by Fox limited other studios from using this system independently, except for France and its dominions. In 1953–54, important studios like MGM, Warner and RKO rented the use of Cinemascope system.[6] That same year, a French optics enterprise produced the Cinepanoramic anamorphic unit for coupling, which was used in French and Italian productions under different names. Then the Dyaliscope lens appeared, made by the Satec company in France, and several other models followed. All of them were more compact and lighter than those of Fox studios.

By 1955 the anamorphic system had been adopted in more than 32,000 movie theaters all over the world and dozens of productions were made, using more than 17 designations. Some time later besides the lens units for coupling, block units appeared which included the cylindrical and the spherical optical components unified, and soon after the anamorphic lens was complemented by the recently created zoom lens. This wide screen

**Arriflex camera with anamorphic lens (*courtesy Arnold & Richter Cine Technik*).**

method became global and standard during that decade, not only for large productions in color but also in black and white films, especially in Europe. All the industry took up the wide screen and the 2 to 1 ratio became standard the whole world over. In the Soviet Union the work of professor D.S. Volosov made possible the design and manufacture of anamorphic lenses in block units of 30, 35, 40, 50, 75, 80, 100, 150 and 200mm.[7]

## Vistavision

Similar to other Hollywood studios, Paramount searched for their own wide screen system, independent from the tracks their competitors were following. In 1953, when other wide screen methods were being established, John R. Bishop, head of Paramount's camera department, along with his experts, developed a wide screen method taking greater advantage of the 35mm format film. Its principle consisted in making the film travel horizontally from left to right in an old double frame, two-color camera, developed long before by William Fox. The new method was provisionally named Lazy-8; it was first applied for the film *White Christmas* (1954). The negative frame area was 1.472 × 0.997 in.[8]

This wide screen option endeavored to obtain greater imager definition reducing 1.63 times the horizontal image taken by the camera by optical printing, with a 90 degree rotation of such image. A standard negative was thus obtained allowing either a greater enlargement on projecting the image in movie theaters or projecting a double frame copy with a special projector. The grain was considerably reduced and a much better quality was achieved. The method was patented by Paramount with the name of Vistavision and was adopted by this studio as standard for color productions.

The characteristics of the method were exhaustively analyzed and finally a camera was designed, totally different from the others, with the raw stock and take up magazines installed at the rear of the camera body, and the monitor viewfinder on top. The Mitchell Co. made the Vistavision cameras based on Gaetano Ventimiglia's patents.[9] The new camera included the renowned Mitchell movement and was provided with all the refinements of a studio instrument, and its size was considerable, with its blimp and lenses for focal lengths from 21mm up to 152mm. Around 1955 a Vistavision hand held camera was built for 400 ft. load, with a single taking lens, a parallax corrected viewfinder with turret for several lenses mounted on top of the camera body, and a double compartment magazine installed at rear of the camera. The shutter was of fixed opening type of 170 degrees. The unit weighed 17½ lbs. and was driven by a 28 V DC electric motor.

Many movie theaters were equipped with horizontal travel projectors for the 8 lateral perforations frame as supplied by the Century company. The application of sound was studied too, finally adopting the system named Perspecta. For theaters not equipped as above, a reduced image standard copy was used which had its advantages, as it allowed a greater enlarged projection with wide angle lenses. The Vistavision system lasted quite some time, but after it was laid aside the cameras were used for filming transparency plates.

## Todd-AO

In 1955 the American producer Michael Todd and Dr. Brian O'Brien of the American Optical Co. developed a wide screen shooting system using 65mm wide negative raw

stock with 70mm wide film for projection. Initially, the filming speed was 30 f.p.s., but later on this was reduced to 24 f.p.s. The image was unsqueezed as normal spherical lenses were used to print the image in a 5 perforation frame. The aperture dimensions were 2.072 × 0.906 in. Originally the cameras used with this system had been specially conceived for it. Some time later the Todd-AO company had the Mitchell Corp. manufacture a hand held camera for this format which was named Todd-AO Ap-65.

Lenses of 28, 40, 50, 60, 75, 100 and 150mm were used with the Todd-AO system. Projection was made with 70mm film or with anamorphic prints by reduction to 35mm with six magnetic track sound recording. The first film shot with this system was the successful *Around the World in 80 Days* (1954), directed by Michael Anderson and Oscar award winning cinematography by Lionel Lindon, which induced another Hollywood studio (as we shall see below) try to adopt its own new wide negative format. In the Soviet Union the 70mm film was adopted in 1960 as the standard format for negative and positive wide screen production. Professors Volosov and Rusinov designed the camera lenses.

Todd-AO 65mm camera build by Mitchell (*courtesy Mitchell Camera Corp.*).

## Technirama

About 1955–56 another wide screen system was also developed by the renowned Technicolor Corp. It was based on the works of Gaetano Ventimiglia, with the same principles as the Vistavision in that it printed images on a horizontally traveling 35mm film on an 8 perforation frame. But improvements were achieved in image registration incorporating an anamorphic unit in front of the taking lens. Further horizontal compression was made in the printing process. Thus the film could be projected with Scope type anamorphic systems of 2.55 to 1 and 2.33 to 1. The anamorphic unit used with the Technirama camera was of the Delrama type, designed by Prof. Albert Bowers based on prisms, and manufactured by N.V. Optische Industrie, of Oude Delft, in Holland.

**Technicolor Technirama camera and Delrama anamorphic system. This camera was adapted from the three-strip model (***courtesy Technicolor Corp.***).**

For this system Technicolor used the old three-strip cameras, adequately modified to make the film travel horizontally; the magazines were attached behind the camera side to side, with 1000 or 2000 ft. capacities. The cylindrical lenses were of 50mm, 75mm, 100mm and 135mm focal lengths. A system with rack down movement allowed ground glass focusing and framing through the taking lens. Viewfinder and ground glass markings were provided for 1.302 in. × 8.37 in. Additional vertical marking were provided to keep important action within lines for unsqueezed 1.85:1 reduction prints.

Two different motors drove these cameras: synchronous 220 V., single phase AC, or 96 V. DC, multiduty. The cameras maintained their specially designed monitor viewfinder adequate to their requirements, and incorporated a lens sunshade applied in front of the anamorphic attachment. Shortly afterwards this firm brought out a hand-held camera as complementary to the heavy studio model.[10]

Technicolor Technirama camera side view (*courtesy Technicolor Corp.*).

## Fox 55 format

During this decade the studios raced intensely with wide screen methods since many were not satisfied with their achievements. So late in 1955 the Fox studios, which had very successfully launched their Cinemascope system shortly before, wanted to improve their image quality even more, applying the 55 format to the previous system. For that purpose they converted an old 70mm Fox camera applying anamorphic attachments to it.

This combined format altered the average focal lengths of standard cylindrical lenses and normal lenses, which now become 100mm and the one for close-ups 152mm. The film *Carousel* (1956) was filmed with this system. It was distributed in 35mm Cinemascope format, but image definition increased and grain was reduced, by about 50 percent respectively. This was another step on the track towards spectacular shows, which continued in the following decades.[11]

Technicolor Italiana toward the end of this decade considered developing a new low cost wide screen system. Giovanni Ventimiglia was in charge of this work with Giulio Monteleoni: he was the son of Gaetano, who created the principles of the Vistavision system and its prototype camera. The new system appeared in 1962 and was called Techniscope 2P. A large number of films were made in Europe and USA with this system. The first film in Techniscope was *Ieri, oggi, e domani* (1963), directed by Vittorio De Sica and cinematography by Giuseppe Rotunno.[12]

# 36. Mid-Century Technology

As with cameras, other aspects connected with motion picture photography underwent considerable progress during those years, since the boom of the cinema industry furthered the development of technology. Let us study these fields one by one, where significant changes are appreciated.

## Optics

We have seen above how the need for wide screen cinema induced research into and application of cylindrical lenses leading to gradual development of anamorphic systems. In 1951, the old established French opticians Société d'Optique et de Mechaniqe de Haute Precision Som-Berthiot took full advantage of their newly acquired computer for calculating optic combinations, engaging four specialists, Culviller, Rosier, Reymond and Baluteau, to develop a zoom lens, Pan-Cinor. It greatly improved on previous German and British models produced before the war, which were more expensive and mechanically more complicated.

The new French zoom lens was aimed initially at the wide and growing market of 8, 9.5 and 16mm movies as well as TV. The first model had a focal length range of 3:1 since it varied from 20 to 60mm. Its aperture was f/2.8 with diaphragm stops down to f/22. The field covered was seen through a variable viewfinder, coupled and independently adjusted and parallax corrected from 5 ft. to infinity. The unit weighed 2 lbs. and was provided with a detachable sunshade. Zooming was effected by means of a lever which rotated a lens ring.

New, more elaborate models were produced about 1954–5 with the series named 4, in which the zoom range was increased, the covered image diagonal was enlarged so as to include the 35mm format, the TV orthicon and vidicon tubes, as well as wide screen format film such as Vistavision. Image quality was also considerably improved as well as color correction and the focal variation method by means of a vertical lever. But the most important improvement was a coupled reflex viewfinder to follow the displacement of the object; this was achieved by inserting a semi reflector crystal optical unit at a 45 degree angle, also including a rangefinder to adjust the focus.[1] This item proved to be very useful to convert to reflex viewing some widely used 35 cameras like the Debrie Parvo 58 and many 16mm cameras.

The Pan-Cinor 4 models for 16 and 35mm gauge films had focal length ranges of 15.5 to 70mm, 25 to 100mm, 38.5 to 154mm, 40 to 170mm and 60 to 240mm, with apertures

**Debrie Parvo camera with the reflex Pan Cinor zoom lens** (*courtesy André Debrie Matériel Cinématographique*).

of f/2.4, f/3.4, and f/3.8, according to each model. They signified a priceless help in the work of movie and TV newsreels, and they soon became standard parts for 16mm sound-on-film cameras such as Auricon. In time, they were adapted for feature film production, when their image quality approached that of fixed focal length lenses.

The Zoomar Corp. also competed with Som-Berthiot at that time in the U.S.A., but they soon abandoned movie camera lenses to specialize on TV and scientific and industrial work. Another was Zeiss-Ikon of Dresden (formerly in the German Democratic Republic), which developed the Pentovar 16 (for their Pentaflex camera) made in three models: mod. I had a focal range from 15 to 60mm with relative aperture of f/2.8; mod. II, from 30 to 120mm with a relative aperture of f/5.6; and mod. III from 15 to 120mm which required an adaptor.

Near the end of 1957, the optics firm Pierre Angenieux in Loire, France, launched their Angenieux zoom Type L lens with a focal length range from 17 to 68mm and an aperture of f/2.2, which could be focused at a minimum distance of 3.9 ft. The innovation of this lens was its coupled reflex side-viewfinder with a beam-splitter placed within the optical unit so that it also allowed for focus control. Other Angenieux zoom models followed in 1958, like the B12, 35 to 140mm, for 35mm format, and in 1959, the LB1 with the same characteristics, except its aperture of f/2.2. Another achievement of Angenieux at that time was their extremely high speed lenses with f/0.95 aperture for 25mm, f/1.3 for the 5mm fixed focus model and f/2.5for 75mm telephoto lenses, which were adopted by Bell & Howell for their celebrated Filmo Model 70 hand-held 16mm cameras. Thus, their lenses became better known on the American market.[2] Shortly after, Angenieux became a leader in zoom lenses with long focal length range for 16 and 35mm formats, and they were widely used both in motion pictures and in TV.

Other well-known lens makers elaborated their products and the industry had a considerably improved series of lenses for 16mm and 35mm gauge cameras. Consequently there was a greater number of professional lenses available in the world.

Among them were Hollywood's favorites, the II series Cooke Speed Anchor by Taylor, Taylor & Hobson with seven designs introduced towards the end of 1958, and followed later on by the III series, marked with aperture scales in T values, which in many models were T/2 (f/1.9) and were mounted to fit onto Mitchell, Newall, Arriflex and Caméflex cameras. The Kinetal series of this firm included lenses from 9, 12.5, 17.5, 25, 37.5 and 50mm with T/2 and 75, 100, and 150mm with T/2.8, and T/4, respectively. This firm's Telepanchro series included 152mm lenses with T/3.2, 203mm with T/4.5, 318mm with T/4.5, 406mm with T/4.5, and 558mm with T/6.2. Later on this firm added their Varotal series zoom lenses to their fixed focal length ones both for movies and TV.[3]

The Kinoptic company in France also created a new group of lenses in their well known Apochromat series which were noted for their effective correction of the three primary colors with a range of focal lengths from wide angle lens of 5.7mm (f/1.8) followed by 12 different focal lengths right up to 500mm (f/5.6). Some time later this firm developed their extreme wide angle lens of 1.9mm (f/1.9) which in time became famous.

In Germany, the old established Astro-Gessellschaft in Berlin kept renewing their lenses, and in 1956 they brought out a 150mm telephoto lens with great definition and contrast, and with an unusually large aperture for this type of lens: f/1.8.[4] Two other German firms, Carl Zeiss of longstanding repute, and Jos. Schneider, had their established channels into the international motion picture market especially the latter through Arnold & Richter, the noted camera makers in Munich. Around 1960 the former opticians were marketing their 32mm and 50mm Planar lenses and 65mm Sonnar, all with f/2 aperture while Schneider was offering its Cine Xenon series for 28, 50, and 75mm, all with f/2 aperture.

The German Kilfitt company was noted for their Makro 90mm (f/2.8) lens for close-ups down to 8 in. with filter stage and for their well known telephoto lenses with seven focal lengths from 135mm to 600mm. Later they brought out a 40mm normal lens with a device for pre-setting the diaphragm beforehand, which after opening it for focusing would instantly return to the pre-set aperture.

In Switzerland, the Kern firm in Aarau complemented their variety of lenses for the Paillard cameras with their standard Ivar series of wide angle, normal and telephoto lenses with apertures of f/2.5 and f/2.8, while the Switar series had apertures of f/1.4 and f/1.8. Moreover, in the Soviet Union in 1959, they ventured into making lenses for 16mm cinematography complementing the already going production for 35mm format.

In the United States in 1955, the then new and later reputed firm Panavision Incorporated first launched printing and anamorphic projection attachment lenses, named Panatar, later Super Panatar, and five standard Auto Panatar lenses for professional cinematography with 35mm, 40mm, 50mm, 75mm, 100mm and 150mm focal lengths, mounted to fit on Mitchell NC and BNC cameras. It also included a special large aperture lens named Ultra Speed Auto Panatar for 50mm focal length and f/1.0 aperture. Robert Gottschalk, the company's president, later entered the field of manufacturing 65 and 35mm advanced motion picture cameras and lenses.[5]

Also in the U.S.A., Bausch & Lomb offered a series of eight lenses for 35mm format and three for 16mm with apertures of f/2.3 for focal lengths up to 100mm, coated with their distinctive Balcote anti-reflective coating. Another American optics firm, Century Photo Equipment Co., brought to the market their 500mm telephoto lens with f/5.6 aperture. The also American Traid Corp. introduced their 3.45mm great wide angle lens for 16mm gauge, covering a 165 degree field and with "C" type mounting and f/1.9 aperture. Wollensack Optical Co. launched three lenses for 8 and 16mm formats, with focal lengths of 6.5mm (f/1.8), 9mm (f/2.3) and 25mm (f/1.4). Finally Kodak brought out their 50mm (f/1.9) Cine Ektar lens for their high speed camera.

It was at that time, near the end of the decade, when professional cinematography started learning of the gradual progress of Japanese optics, with rare earth minerals and specialized companies, such as Canon, Kowa Optical Co., Keihan Optical, and Ichizuka Kogaku Co., which were delving into products for cinematography, the same as other important optics makers in that country were doing efficiently and successfully in photography and other optical fields. In the Soviet Union some institutes such as the Optical-Mechanical Organization of Leningrad (L.O.O.M.P.) designed and produced optical elements for motion picture photography. The lens series named Lenar was one of the best known in the field of Soviet zoom lenses.

Classic camera pedestal used in Europe. This unit made by Éclair supports a Cameblimp (*courtesy Éclair International Diffusion*).

## Dollies, camera pedestals and cranes

Though optics, by means of the zoom lens, allowed giving the sensation of a moving camera, many film directors frequently used the mobile camera as a new film language method, producing a considerable output of equipment for moving the camera about. Such production was intensified to meet the growing demand from the many television shows cropping up everywhere. The boom of TV shows filmed with several cameras from different angles required many dollies and camera pedestals for this purpose.

Dollies were also frequently used when several directors, like Alfred Hitchcock, William Wyler, Orson Welles, and Otto Preminger in the USA and many others in Europe, often applied the technique of long takes with the cameras following the moving players. Cranes were also used on such occasions, and they were essential in large scale productions with huge crowds, and ascents to considerable heights to cover extensive sceneries.

During that period the use of dollies boomed. New instruments appeared, e.g. the extremely maneuverable Houston Fearless Cinemobile with a hydraulic system to raise the camera boom. Another elaborate dolly appeared about 1956 built by National Cine Equipment named the Crab Dolly, affording quick changes in wheel positions to effect any kind of movements, controlled from a central panel. J.C. McAlister, the well-known Hollywood maker of lighting equipment, produced a Crab Dolly which merited an Academy Award. Moreover, Moviola Mfg. Co., noted editing equipment makers, also entered this field and built an elaborate dolly with many movements and control facilities which was exported to European studios.

Houston Fearless also designed two types of cranes for movies and TV following the specifications set by the Motion Picture Research Council, the first of which was adopted by several studios. At that time, Chapman Studio Equipment developed a series of cranes, from the crab crane with its optical axis at a height of 7½ ft., to models like the Small Stage Crane with 12 ft. max. optical axis, and larger size models with four and six wheels to reach heights of 16 and 25 ft. above floor level.

The making of such mobile camera supports was more limited in Europe. In Britain Vinten built equipment both for motion pictures and for TV. Debrie and Éclair manufactured rolling pedestals in France. Such equipment was built in Italy by Ianiro, which would afterwards produce the famous Elemack dolly. In 1960 the Italian firm ATC-Electricità s.r.l. developed the Gina Crab Dolly, an unusual combination of traveling car and crane to shoot continuously up and down from 0.50 m to 4 m with a rotation of 360 degrees.[6]

## Motion picture raw stock

A wide variety of raw stock was produced during the fifties. The use of materials for

**European travelling car used with piper rails (***courtesy Archivo Nacional de la Imagen, Sodre***).**

color filming increased, both for the negative-positive system and the reversible method. Towards the end of the decade there were on the world market about sixteen well known manufacturers of raw stock for cinematography in eleven countries. They were Kodak, DuPont and Ansco in the USA; Kodak-Pathé and Bauchet in France; Gevaert in Belgium; Agfa in East Germany, Perutz in West Germany, Ferrania in Italy; Kodak and Ilford in England; Fuji and Koshiroku in Japan; Svema (later) in the Soviet Union, Foton in Poland, and Valca, Negra and Mafe in Spain. In the cases of Poland and Spain, they produced material only for printing positives.

Towards the mid-fifties the most important multi-layer raw stock trade marks for color cinematography were: Agfacolor, Agfachrome, Anscocolor, Anscochrome, Eastmancolor, Ektachrome, Kodachrome, Ilford Colour, Fujicolor, Konicolor, Gevacolor, Ferraniacolor and Sovcolor. All these materials modified their characteristics as time went by, improving the image quality reproduction and increasing sensitivity.

The best known of these color films, the Eastmancolor negative, appeared in 1950, named type 5247; it was replaced in 1952 by type 5248 (25 ASA T and 16 ASA D with Wratten filter 85). The improvement of this material brought it in to type 5250 in 1959 (50ASA T and 32 ASA D with filter). Thus, European color negatives such as Gevacolor Type 653 and Ferraniacolor type 82 were "demoted" to nearly 50 percent of the sensitivity achieved by Eastman color negative in 1959–60. The exception was Agfacolor negative type B333, made in Wolfen, German Democratic Republic, which had a 40 ASA sensitivity for daylight shooting and which later was known as Orwocolor.

Regarding black and white raw stock which was still widely used, the material from Kodak was also outstanding, with the appearance in 1954 of Eastman Tri X negative Type 5233, with 320 ASA Daylight and 250 Tungsten, and in 1955 the Eastman TRI X reversal type 7218 (16mm) with 200 ASA D and 160 ASA T, which merited an Academy Award for its exceptionally high sensitivity and fine grain. That year Kodak also brought out their Plus X Reversal type 7276 (16mm) with 50 ASA D and 40 ASA T. Finally, in 1959 they put out the Eastman Double X negative type 5222 (35mm) and 7222 (16mm) with a sensitivity of 250 ASA D and 200 ASA T.

About 1960, Du Pont offered, among others, the following black and white films: "Superior 2" Type 9368 with 125 ASA, D and 100 ASA T, "Superior 4" type 9288 with 320 ASA, D, and 250 ASA, T, as well as three reversible films, the most sensitive of which was rated at 160 ASA D and 125 ASA T.

European black and white raw stock from makers such as Gevaert, Agfa, Ferrania and Ilford were easily accessible to the Western world's cinematography, with similar average sensitivity ratings for negative and reversible material. They also reached the high ratings of 250 ASA D and 200 ASA T, e.g. in the Gevaert Gevapan 36 type 191, 250 ASA D and 160 ASA, T in the Gevapan type 880. Agfa Isopan Record, with1,250 ASA was the highest sensitivity achieved. In Italy, the then new Ferrania P 30 became, in 1960, one of the home made negatives for black and white most widely used in that country.

## Antivibration devices

A very interesting novelty appeared in France in the fifties: a specially designed device to support the camera on vehicles vibrating intensely, such as a helicopter, as an answer to requests from Albert Lamorisse, the French director, when planning the shooting of his celebrated film *Le Voyage en ballon* (1960). It was realized with the co-operation of several experts, such as a French navy engineer named Fieux specializing in gyroscopes, and consisted of a column shaped like the number 7, which held the camera, compensated for vibrations and included a seat for the operator.

The column comprised a camera support based on the Cardan principle, with a combination of mechanisms and a container with viscous material, absorbing three types of vibrations. This instrument, named Helevision, allowed taking extremely steady close-ups from an Alouette II helicopter in flight 40 ft. above ground, with a Cameflex camera equipped with an Angenieux 35–140 zoom lens and a Coutant Asservisseur for automatic exposure control. This new instrument made shooting from the air very easy and led the way to similar implements from other firms.[7] Later on two new antivibration devices were also developed: a) the Danelean, a British instrument specially conceived for mobile film making to use the camera with tripod when filming from a moving vehicle and based on counterbalance weights, and b), the American Kenyon Gyroscopic Stabilizer, originally designed for use with high magnification binoculars but a good option when shooting with hand held cameras.

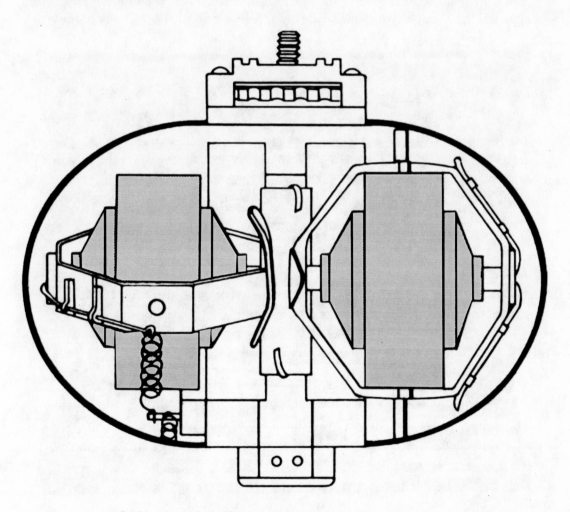

**Inside view of the Kenyon stabilizer (*author's collection*).**

## Lighting equipment

Lighting technology also improved during this decade. The complex evolution of color cinematography induced specialized firms like Mole & Richardson to design equipment especially for this purpose, for example, their series of complex voltaic arc lamps. Near the end of this period some of these were copied in the Soviet Union, especially their M&R Duarc Broadside and the Spot type 170, along with a series of incandescent spot lamps, all reproduced by Mashpriborintorg, in Moscow.

The need for using light-weight lighting equipment for TV and for documentary and industrial production determined the increased use of photoflood type mirrored lamps. Several makers designed units adequate for installing this type of lamp individually or in combinations, which led to their use even in feature films when shooting indoors. Thus, extensible bars appeared to be installed in real indoors, between wall, floor and ceiling, the lamps fitted on by means of C clamps.

Over voltage lamps were also increasingly used; they had brand names such as Colortran, Cinetron, Grover and Garnelite. The Colortran Co. was noted for its different types of packed lighting units, which included Par 38, R-40, Par 56 and Par 64 lamps to reach the

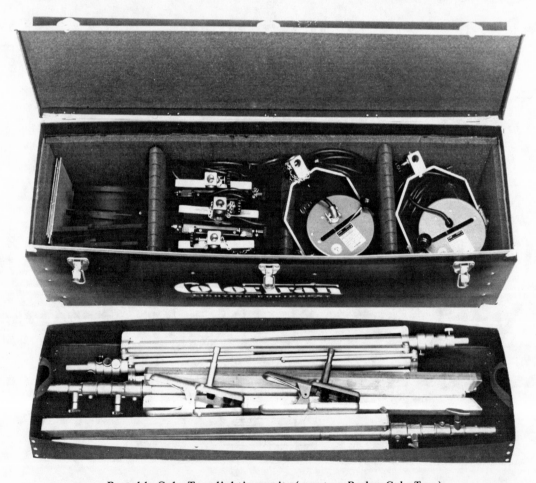

Portable ColorTran lighting units (*courtesy Berkey-ColorTran*).

needed color temperature of 3,200 or 3,400 degrees Kelvin and great light intensity, without resorting to the classic, heavy, lighting equipment nor to have generators available. Their special characteristics made it possible to attain high key levels using normal home power sources. They also produced a series of new lamps and special converters to regulate the voltage applied to them.

Thus, lamps could be fed with low voltage while installing or during rehearsals, and adequately over-voltage during effective shooting, achieving the needed light levels with low consumption. Different types of converters were made for the several portable kits that were being created. At a time when certain productions (or parts of them) called for being filmed away from the stages, and this was impractical due to the low sensitivity of emulsions and the low efficiency of conventional tungsten lamps, the above type of lighting made it possible and was very effective for industrial movies, TV and feature films.

But in Hollywood studios, classic lighting was maintained, and in certain productions high light intensity was required up to about 2.000 fc. Thus the use of high intensity units (e.g. the M&R Brute Molarc) was increased, which led to improving carbons fitted on them; the National Carbon Co. produced the Super High Intensity yellow-flame carbon, substituting the white-flame one. Mole & Richardson also improved on the units themselves and on the characteristics of the Fresnel lenses in order to resist higher temperatures. About 1955–56, an idea from the Douglas Aircraft Company led to conceiving a mobile unit for filming on location, with modifications on the necessary lighting equipment and power source, which was afterwards standardized through other specialized firms.

In Europe large tungsten lighting units were built, specially in Germany where three firms built, in 1955–56, large 20 kV Fresnel spots. In Britain, the Mole & Richardson branch designed and built its own 20 kV spot, named Conquest. In Italy at the end of the decade the Coemar company, led by S. Marcucci (an engineer), offered a 10 kV GF/10 spot, with twice the efficiency of standard items with the same consumption. In the same country Ianiro produced a series of spots named Polaris of 500/750 W, Castor of 1½ kV, Pollux of 5kV, and Vega and Alpha Centauri both of 10 kV.

In 1957 General Electric developed important improvements on their 10 kW lamps,

Powerful 200,000 W tungsten Arri spot (*courtesy Arnold & Richter Cine Technik*).

with an internal collector to reduce blackening, avoid heat cracking and lengthen their useful life to 75 hour; they also made remarkable research and development on noise-free filaments. That same year Mole & Richardson maintained their policy of renewing their range of lighting implements, including new articles, especially pedestals and grip equipment.

From 1958–59 there was an increase in the use of dimmers of different sorts, manufactured by well known firms in the field such as Century Lighting Inc., General Electric Co., Kliegl Bros., and Mole & Richardson. The model built by this latter firm was of the portable type, with two 5kW and four 2 kW circuits and ten dimmer control levers. Dimmers were frequently seen when shooting TV shows with three or more cameras simultaneously, and had a ready market in TV stations. About 1960 General Electric built a lighting item of the sealed beam tungsten-filament type, named Multi-Par, with several units mounted and centered in order to produce a convergent light beam; the remarkable feature was that it allowed for dimming control without altering color temperature.

Also in this period, the Dyn Rensa Co. of Japan manufactured 200 A arc lamps with three carbons, and for AC, since there was no DC in the studios in that country. These items were made from a German design with two carbons in a "V" and spring distance control.

These were the developments during the last period in the massive application of tungsten lamps, before the appearance, in 1959, as we saw, of an achievement that radically changed lighting equipment: the halogen lamp, of very small size and weight and high intensity, ideal for color cinematography.

## Light and color meters

Exposure control by means of exposure meters was an already accepted practice among motion picture professionals, and also the growing boom of color cinematography by diverse methods required the use of color meters. New models like the Weston Master IV–745 and the model 614 with a flat disk for incident light only were added to the already classic general use ones like the General Electric

Spectra color meter (courtesy *Archivo Nacional de la Imagen, Sodre*).

DW68 and the Weston Master II. Weston provided meticulous experts with their model 703 and 614 for general commercial lighting. Norwood's Brockway MII and M-3 Director were adopted by many cinematographers.

The Spectra company gradually increased the production of its Golden Crown PR3Due to their acceptance in studios, because of their inherent advantages for meticulous work. Spectra also made the Spectra 3 color meter for determining the exact color temperature of the light sources, it also indicated the necessary filters selected from two scales: red-blue and green-red. An attachment made by the Harrison firm, applied to Weston and General Electric exposure meters, measured color values and indicated the needed filter. The first spot meter made by Elwood also appeared at that time.

European manufacturers also produced instruments for measuring light and color. In Germany, Gossen & Co. made the TriLux Model C for incident light readings taken with a flat disk on a remote handle, and the Model Sixtomat X2 for reflected and incident light with a built-in diffusion screen. They also produced the Sixticolor, a color meter with direct reading in Kelvin degrees or Mired values. Rebikoff was another brand which produced a color meter with two photoelectric cells covered with filters, with an indicator scaled in degrees Kelvin.

In Britain, JARO-Salford, a member of the Rank group, developed a high precision professional exposure meter for incident and reflected light, with an extension cable between the two components for certain forms of reading, very much used in British studios.

In those years an incident and reflected light exposure meter with professional characteristics was built in the Soviet Union. It was sturdily built and designed with a special concept following classic norms: it was known as the 3III-4. The requirements of the Comecon market group were covered with this instrument.

Finally we must point out the remarkable advance in exposure control achieved in France by the engineer André Coutant, who conceived an innovatory device to automatically control the exposure of the image contained in the camera itself, using a degrading filter, which rotated governed by a cadmium sulphide photoelectric cell. This device, named Asserviseur Coutant, was applied onto the Cameflex camera and was an important step in exposure information in professional motion picture cameras. Cadmium sulphide cells were later extensively used in exposure meters.[8]

## Processing equipment

Motion picture laboratories were improved during that decade with important technologic innovations in developing, control,

Gossen Lunasix exposure meter (*author's collection*).

**Debrie TV film processing van (courtesy André Debrie Matériel Cinématographique).**

and printing equipment created by American as well as European manufacturers. The gradual boom of color movies induced such changes in the different processing stages. The strict organizational discipline to maintain high quality standards and maximum performance of equipment, exerted continuously day and night, moved manufacturers to thoroughly control design efficiency and product performance. The new trend of cinematography towards television prompted many makers to aim at compact and simplified 16mm processing equipment to meet the needs of TV stations and independent producers.

Several American manufacturers specializing in processing equipment brought onto the market new items for independent laboratories that were appearing due to the considerable increase of television production. In some cases the demand grew so much that the sales of some makers exceeded several hundred units per year. About 1957, firms like Houston Fearless and Filmlink developed, for large production installations, fast spray processing methods to improve and make bath action more effective. Afterwards, the Otomo company in Japan also manufactured a developing machine based on similar principles. The international industry also contrived other ways of keeping the baths agitating, e.g. with inert gas bursts from the bottom of the tank. Several firms also manufactured small compact equipment to develop negative or reversible material for newsreel processing which was offered to small television stations and producers. Work in this field was also intense in Europe, where the two most important manufacturers were André Debrie in France and Arnold & Richter in Germany.

The former won an export award in their country in view of the impressive sales of their products abroad, reaching laboratories even in the Soviet Union and its satellite countries. Their Multiplex series equipment of longstanding reputation was continued in models for black and white as well as for color, such as DPR for reversible film, and the complete Aiglone series equipment for television, which could operate at high speed in broad daylight, using processing tubes in plastic with an entirely automatic threading due to a complete new film feeding system.

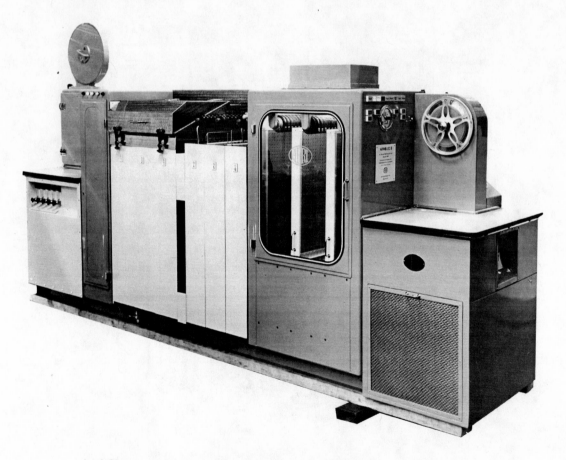

**Arri film processing machine (*courtesy Arnold & Richter Cine Technik*).**

Arnold & Richter become renowned in world markets for the high precision of their Arribloc series processing equipment which was sold to laboratories in North and South America, Italy, France, and about fifty other countries.

Developing equipment makers cropped up in many places. Mashpriborintorg in the Soviet Union started making developing equipment for 35mm, such as Model 40II-1, near the end of the decade. In Czechoslovakia, Meopta and later on Filmovyl Prumysl in Barrandov (Prague) built their own processing equipment including the spray method. This field was also covered in Britain by well known experts firms like Vinten Ltd. and Newman & Guardia. Canada was noted for the compact processing equipment made by Canadian Applied Research Ltd., which also made large scale processing equipment also using the automatic spray method. Another developing equipment maker who appeared in Europe was De Oude Delft company in Holland with a very compact 16/35mm unit.

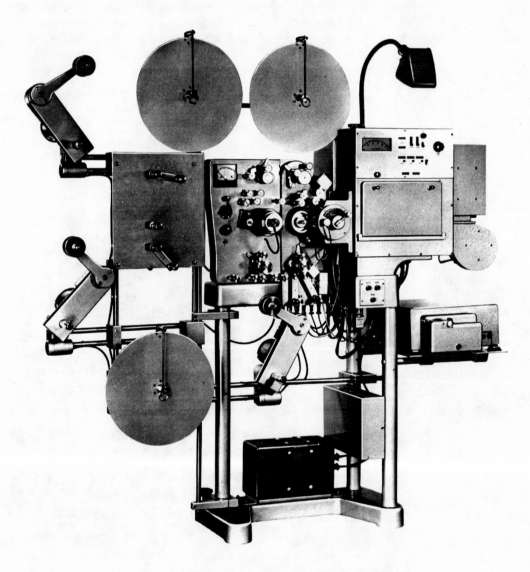

**Bell & Howell color printer (*courtesy Bell & Howell*).**

In France, the old established Bourdereaux company continued making large scale-models in conjunction with Éclair. Finally, in South America, a cinematographer and filmmaker, Francisco Tastás-Moreno, established a company to design and manufacture several types of developing machines for black and white and color, in 16 and 35mm for various laboratories in Uruguay and Argentina and also building other laboratory equipment.

Hazeltine color analyzer (*courtesy Hazeltine Corp.*).

Film printers were another item of similar increase. First, the American makers of the Peterson printers, the Motion Picture Equipment Co., created a series of accessories to attach onto Bell & Howell printers, models J and D, such as automatic fade, electronic cueing systems and sound printing heads. Soon after, Bell & Howell improved their equipment to include such devices. In 1955 the Dish-Schurman firm developed a printing head for color film, based on three light sources and with several filters for each and a dichroic beam splitter system for Bell & Howell printer Model D. As a consequence, Bell & Howell developed an automatic printer for color film by the additive system in 1958, based on dichroic mirrors to divide the white light from a 1000 W lamp into the three basic light color beams: red, green and blue; the printer was controlled by a perforated paper and a radiofrequency system. The Metro Goldwyn Mayer laboratories were among the first of many to install the model A of such equipment. Afterwards, Bell & Howell kept on with other models of color additive system printers, with color light valves and governed by perforated tape. Experiments were carried out in 1957 for applying color television to print color films. The Hazeltine Research Corporation in America devised an instrument to analyze the chromatic values of each scene by means of a TV color monitor; it provided the information needed for additive color printers when a color negative was inserted in the device. This significant contribution to color printing technology speeded up the process appreciably and reduced costs by eliminating color control strips and prints, giving the required information to the operator. The Hazeltine Color Analyzer soon became a standard item in USA. European firms also designed new equipment based on similar principles like the color film analyzer, named Etalco, developed in France by Mr. Armand Roux of the firm Somopra.[9]

Also during that period, in the field of film printers, in the USA, J.M. Developments Inc. produced a complete printer named JMD-Model II, which among its abilities included having an additive system color head, as well as magnetic and optical sound recording. Other laboratory equipment makers, such as Houston-Fearless and Depue, among others, produced various types of continuous printers as required by motion pictures and television.

Oxberry put a high precision optical printer on the market: a complex item of equipment for carrying out all sorts of special effects, including in it their special camera for this purpose. It became standard equipment in top level laboratories and was so for many years.

Printing equipment was also developed in other countries of the world. Debrie's Matipo printers were made either in color additive or subtractive models. Several printers were built in Germany by Arri and Union which were sold worldwide. In Japan, the Daichi Seiki Co. created a complex printer. Similar products were built in the Soviet Union. In Italy, Prevost built film printers and the Technostampa laboratory made its own optical printer based on the Acme special effects camera while the SPES laboratory produced several high speed printers in black and white, some of which were sold to other laboratories. In France, Samopra also conceived an optical printer called Multirex, with principles based on the American design. Finally, firms in Britain, Holland, Belgium and Czechoslovakia also built other equipment in this field, as well as the need arose in the then nascent worldwide cinema industry to complement processing motion picture photography.

# 37. Cinematographers of the Fifties

## American cinematographers

The motion picture industry in all its fields has had a greater growth in the United States of America than elsewhere in the world. There were several hundred directors of photography plying their trade in this century during this decade and there were more than 250 invited to join Hollywood's elite in the American Society of Cinematographers. Many of these image experts were under contract either per film or in medium or long terms, operating in several large production groups in Hollywood, as well as a large number of independent producers, laboratories, special effects firms, animation companies, educational and short film concerns, newsreels, etc.[1]

It was a period of intense activity in which some directors of photography participated in many films per year (Henry Freulich and Harry C. Newman had the record of shooting eleven films in 1953). The average was from three to five feature films per year. Besides, there were numerous television shows and serials. In Hollywood, work in this field was mainly by cameramen who had started late in the twenties, thirties and forties, while the senior group from the beginning of silent movies was already retiring.

Among the many directors of photography, some were noted in the industry for their work, their versatility and adaptability to changes, their style and techniques and for having been awarded or nominated for Academy Oscars. We have commented above on some of these masters of lighting and their best accomplished films; let us now consider some others who won their colleagues' recognition as being among the best lighting cameramen of their times.

## JAMES WONG HOWE

Howe, who real name was Won Tung Jim, was one of the best known. In 1955 he was awarded the Academy Oscar for his photography of *The Rose Tattoo*, where he showed his lighting ability, his artistry, and his capacity to narrate in black and white images Tennessee Williams' dramatic story. Like many colleagues, he travelled long to reach the top of his career. He had born in Canton, China, in 1899, arrived in the USA when he was five, and settled in Washington state. As a boy he was a photo fan starting with a Brownie camera. After his father's death he lived with an Irish family and later with an uncle. He tried boxing and then went to a flying school and worked in a portrait photographer's studio. One day in Chinatown he saw a team filming outdoors and was fascinated with this trade; one of the cameramen encouraged him to join as an assistant and shortly after he started cleaning camera equipment in Jesse Kasky studios. In 1917 he became a camera assistant and later on an operator on Alvin Wyckoff's team. He also worked with other well known cinematographers such as Henry Kotani and Bert Glenon. His first lighting cameraman job was shooting *Drums of Fate* (1923), and he improved his career by working with several important directors such as Erich Von Stroheim, Victor Flemming, Frank Borzage and Lewis Milestone. His reputation grew rapidly, as he was very sensitive, hardworking and skilful. MGM hired him in 1928 and advertised him as the great Chinese cameraman. The Mitchell Camera Corp. too, years later in their publicity for their then new BNC model, showed him as Hollywood's great Chinese camera man. His career continued with 96 films and his 97th won him a deserved first Academy Award.[2]

James Wong Howe worked for most of Hollywood's major studios: Paramount, United Artists, Metro Goldwyn Mayer, 20th Century–Fox, Warner Bros., RKO and Columbia. In 1955 he filmed in color the famous *Picnic*, which confirmed his capacity and sensibility with color. He also directed two feature films and a short. In all he filmed 117 films almost 55 years of practicing his profession.

## MILTON KRASNER

Another noted Hollywood director of photography, he was born in 1898 and joined the industry when he was 15 as an extra and errand boy at the old Vitagraph studios (Brooklyn, N.Y.). Drawn by motion picture techniques, he managed to join the studio's laboratory where he worked for years. In 1920 he decided to go to Hollywood, a natural goal for anyone in the industry, and worked there on a few films as camera assistant.

After a short spell back in N.Y. he settled down in Hollywood when he joined the camera team on Jackie Coogan's Banner Productions. He went through the fascinating experience of constantly learning about lighting for whomever he was a camera operator for, acquiring proficiency in the trade, techniques, methods and new means. Hal Mohr was one of his favorites for whom he was camera operator. In the early thirties he advanced to the position of director of photography, having become skilful in lighting for films regarding most diverse subjects, applying the adequate techniques and style in each case as comedies, thrillers, horror films like *Frankenstein* or special effects productions such as the *Invisible Man* series. Some of his films noted for their photography were *The Woman in the Window* (1944), *The Dark Mirror* (1946), *The Set-up* (1949) and *All About Eve* (1950). In 1954 Krasner finally achieved a deserved Academy Award for excellent color photography for *Three Coins in the Fountain*. Like many other professional men he worked for several different Hollywood studios, filming more than 140 films in a long career.[3]

## LEON SHAMROY

He was another of Hollywood's masters of lighting for motion pictures. Born in New York in 1901, he came from a family of Russian university scholars: his father was a chemist, his uncles were engineers. He received a good education including at Columbia University. After graduation he worked in the family business but he was captivated by motion pictures and joined a laboratory where he learned this trade thoroughly. He participated in many amateur film projects and documentaries, one of which he did with Robert Flaherty in

Mexico. The excellent photography of these independent films opened the possibility of working as a lighting cameraman on about a dozen productions.

About 1930 he took part in making a film in Spain and then went on travelling, enduring many hazards. He was preparing an ethnographic film on several countries of the Far East where he covered diverse regions. On returning home the War Department considered that the material had high strategic value in view of the world war menace at that time.

He continued filming in Hollywood in a productive career of three to five films a year, whereby during World War II, he took part in many of the then new Technicolor films. This specialization won for him a first Academy award for the *The Back Swan* (1942), and soon another Oscar for the color photography of *Wilson* (1944). Shamroy obtained his third Oscar with *Leave Her to Heaven* (1945). In the post-war period he continued as a color expert and lighting cameraman, and in the fifties he was chosen to shoot spectacular wide-screen productions, earning his fourth Oscar for *Cleopatra* (1963).

Shamroy worked with the most varied lot of Hollywood's best directors. His thorough knowledge of the profession, his sensitive lighting, his search for effective light touches and great skill in color took him to many of Hollywood's large productions.[4]

## HAL MOHR

Hal Mohr was undoubtedly highly respected among Hollywood's directors of photography, his production exceeding 500 films in a long career. He was versatile enough to photograph or to direct a film, to obtain the highest award in the industry and then adapt himself to the new requirements of the upstart television. He proved his quality in everything he grasped, and this took him to the presidency of the American Society of Cinematographers.

Mohr was born in San Francisco in 1894 and he was already behind a camera when he was only sixteen. First he was a film carrier for a firm who rented them to cinema theaters. He built a camera with discarded pieces from a projector. Sometime later he built another improved version. This led him to become an independent cameraman, and as such he managed to film an important official ceremony including President Taft which he immediately managed to sell. Later on he joined a small motion picture company as cameraman where he learned more. The seed of his trade was sprouting and he decided to go to Hollywood where he got a job at Universal Studios. The experience of this sphere opened doors for him to direct single reel films with the famous Harold Lloyd. This work was interrupted by World War I where he was transferred to the Signal Corps in Paris.

His return to cinematography proved difficult, but he kept on directing single reel films. There was a radical change when he began working on Charles Rosher's camera crew doing films for Mary Pickford and then for Eric von Stroheim. In 1925 he achieved a job of lighting cameraman for Dolores Costello films at Warner Bros. In1927 he took part in the first experimental sound film, *The Jazz Singer*, which broke with all previous usual shooting techniques in motion pictures. After that historic, unique experience, which he treasured in his memory, Al Mohr continued in the most varied types of films for several studios in a highly fruitful career in which he obtained his first Academy Award for *A Midsummer Night's Dream* (1935) for Warner Bros. and again but in color for *The Phantom of the Opera* (1943) for Universal along with Howard Green. He was one of the pioneers in using intensely the Garutso lens which afforded great depth of field, as evidenced by his photography in *The Four Posters* (1952). Hal Mohr was active for several decades and died at the age of eighty.[5]

## RUSSELL METTY

This director of photography was another of the Hollywood school of that time, in which the first cameramen plied a trade sprouted long before in the silent movie era. Russell Metty was born in 1906 and started in motion pictures working in a laboratory. He joined RKO in 1924 where he progressed step by step in the camera team till he reached the top position in 1935. He worked for many years in Universal Studios filming all types of productions from comedies to tragedies, some of which were renowned, such as *Miracle in the Rain* (1956) and *Man with a Thousand Faces* (1957). He became an expert in long takes when he had to shoot them for Orson Welles in two of his films, *The Stranger* (1946) and *A Touch of Evil* (1958); in the latter he took a long crane shot which is still remembered.

Metty admired the imaginative flights of Orson Welles and how he urged his assistants to search for new aesthetic perceptions. In consequence the films Metty photographed are noted for his dramatic treatment of lighting. In 1960 he was awarded an Oscar for his excellent photography for *Spartacus*, a spectacular production directed by the exacting Stanley Kubrick. On this film Metty provided his experience and refined lighting, indoors as well as in complex scenes on different locations, and often in trick shots. *Spartacus* was an example of high artistry, but also of what a complementary film director and director of photography can achieve when their aesthetic views coincide and each is an expert in his field. Metty shot 115 films. He was nominated for an Oscar for his photography of *Flower Drum Song* in 1968 and he died ten years later.[6]

There were many other worthy American directors of photography at that time, but their large number restrains us from mentioning them all. Among many others we cannot omit John Alton, born in 1901 of Hungarian origin, who settled down in Hollywood in 1924 after having made films in Germany, France (in the Paramount studio), England and, together with Alfred Gilks, was awarded an Oscar for the dazzling musical film *An American in Paris* (1951). The industry considered him tops in creating dramatic climates, and his good taste for color, as well as his readiness to share his mastery of the profession. He did this through his famous book, *Painting with Light*, where he expounded his cinematographic lighting methods, and also while shooting *Puerta Cerrada* (1939) in Argentina, he communicated his wisdom to other cinematographers and to the technical staff working with him in the Estudios Lumiton and Estudios Argentina Sono-Films of Buenos Aires. Back in Hollywood he continued displaying his great capabilities on such films as *The Teahouse of the August Moon* (1956).[7]

Boris Kauffman was representative of the noted cameramen of the American East Coast, but with a long European background. He had been born in Bialystok, Russia, in 1906, and was the brother of the reputed director Dziga Vertov and of the camera operator Mikhail Kaufman. He joined the French cinema industry in 1928 working for the well known French documentary film makers Jean Lods and Jean Vigo; for the latter he did remarkable photography for the film *L'Atalante* (1934). In 1942 he went to the USA where he showed his skill in several films; in one of them, Elia Kazan's *On the Waterfront* (1954), he portrayed the world of New York's docks very true to life, winning an Academy Award for it. He continued applying his vigorous chiaroscuro style in another Elia Kazan movie, and then in the film version of Reginald Rose's work *Twelve Angry Men* (1957), directed by Sydney Lumet.[8]

William Mellor, born in 1904, was also characteristic of the thirties generation. He showed his high professional quality with his photography for *A Place in the Sun* (1951), earning him an Academy Award; then a very well achieved work in *Giant* (1955), and winning another Oscar for his excellent lighting of *Diary of Anne Frank* (1959). Sam Leavitt, another cinematographer of the new generation, showed his evolution in the trade and his skill with black and white with his excellent photography for *The Defiant Ones* (1958), from which the industry learned of the possibilities of the rich chiaroscuro tonal range of Kodak's Plus X emulsion. Finally in this review of the well known American cinematographers of those years we must mention the name of Joseph Macdonald, born in 1906 and author of the photography of famous films like *Yellow Sky* (1948) and *Viva Zapata!* (1952), and Robert Surtees, a distinguished cinematographer who earned Academy Awards with *King Solomon's Mines* (1950), *The Bad and the Beautiful* (1952) and *Ben-Hur* (1959).

Lionel Lindon was another cinematographer who came up in the forties, with valuable experience and specialized in adventure and spectacular films; Michael Todd, the well known producer, selected him to shoot on location in several countries for his spectacular film *Around the World in Eighty Days* (1956) with his new Todd-AO system which film earned him his first Academy Award for its photography. Finally, we must not omit the meticulous Loyal Griggs, nor the mastery skill of Robert Burks (Alfred Hitchcock's favorite) in that director's film *To Catch a Thief* (1955) which obtained that year's Academy Oscar for his color photography.

## Other countries

After World War II, motion picture production was revived, increasing the number of first camera operators in several countries. Many European directors of photography showed their mettle as there had already been a tradition in this field. The older specialists who had glittered before the war shone again, but new generations came out to show they continued the level of their predecessors.

In Britain, the quality of motion picture photography had been criticized, but it had improved during the thirties with the intensive production of quota quickies, and it flourished after the war. The photographic quality of British productions soon became noteworthy because of the Oscars received. At this time there were more than sixty directors of photography in Britain and in 1957 the Academy Award was granted to *The Bridge on the River Kwai*, photographed by Jack Hildyard, which film evidenced the refined school of British lighting cameramen.

Hildyard had started in his profession in 1932 at Elstree, as second camera assistant, working with renowned masters like Harry Stradling and Robert Krasker. He started as lighting cameraman after 1946 and after his eleventh film, David Lean, the film maker, retained him for shooting *The Sound Barrier* (1952). After that he achieved dazzling black and white photography for *Hobson's Choice* (1954), which made Lean ask him to photograph *Summer Madness* (1956), and next to shoot his above mentioned first spectacular film.

Many others in Britain shone in photography for motion pictures, like the group that worked at the Ealing Studios during the effervescing period it was headed by Sir Michael Bacon, the renowned British producer. Among them there were veterans like Gordon Dines, born in 1911, who started in the trade in 1926 at Elstree, experienced on noted films like *Blackmail* (1929), also *The Blue Lamp* (1950), *Secret People* (1952) and *Cruel Sea* (1952–3), where his skill applied the studio's characteristic technical accuracy and documentary realism.[9]

Also at Ealing was Douglas Slocombe, born in 1913, the son of a journalist and educated in France where he took part in amateur moviemaking and photography. His professional career started as a war news cameraman for British United Press. He began as a camera assistant at Ealing, and later was a camera operator for Wilkie Cooper. Slocombe shot many films at Ealing on which he left the mark of his refined lighting technique, for example: *Dead of Night* (1945) and *The Captive Heart* (1946). Famous Ealing comedies like *The Lavender Hill Mob* (1951) or *The Man in the White Suit* (1951) were examples of his skill in black and white as in color with films like *The Titfield Thunderbolt* (1953). Examples of his excellent black and white photography were seen later in films like *Freud* (1963) and *The Servant* (1963).[10]

Oswald Morris was another well-known director of photography of that generation. He started in the profession early in the thirties. He learned with the intensive production of quota quickies from well known foreign directors of photography like Otto Kanturek with his German lighting style or noted British cinematographers like Ronald Neame or Wilkie Cooper with whom he worked as camera operator. Like practically everybody in Britain, his professional career was interrupted by World War II. In 1949 Neame, as film director, asked him to do the photography for *The Golden Salamander* (1950), the turning point to reach the top of his trade. The quality he showed made John Huston call him to photograph *Moulin Rouge* (1952) and later *Moby Dick* (1956), two films which evidenced his artistic gifts and how versatile Technicolor was in allowing experiments as the de-saturated color system. His career continued with diverse films with the best known British and American directors, including the meticulous Stanley Kubrick on *Lolita* (1962). He kept on working up to the eighties.[11]

Undoubtedly, Freddie Francis was also an eminent cinematographer. Born in 1917 he had started in the trade in the thirties at Elstree. He was a camera operator for Christopher Challis, and met the meticulous pictorial demands of Power & Pressburguer, the producers. He was an operator on Oswald Morris' camera team and became director of photography in the second unit for *Moby Dick*. He photographed several celebrated films of the fifties, e.g. *Room at the Top* (1958) by Jack Clayton, Charles Crichton's *The Battle of the Sexes* (1959) and Karel Reitz's *Saturday Night and Sunday Morning* (1960). An Oscar was awarded in 1960 for his black and white photography of *Sons and Lovers*, directed by Jack Cardiff, a colleague. Later on he continued as a film director.[12]

This brief review of noted British directors of photography should not omit one who in the course of a long career became a reference in his trade, both in Britain as well as abroad: Freddie Young. Born in London in 1902, he was attracted towards cinema, among other reasons, because early in his life he lived at Shepherds Bush, near the Old Gaumont studios. He managed to get a job there in the laboratory and later as camera assistant for ten years. Working free-lance and as a second cameraman, he took part in two films, *The Flag Lieutenant* (1927) and *Somme* (1928) where he prepared some trick shots. *Victory* (1929) was his starting point as director of photography, continuing as free-lance on several films for different directors, and even did a montage for Hitchcock's *Blackmail* (1930).

He took part in one of the first sound movies in Britain, *White Cargo* (1929), and personally experimented with the changing techniques for this new medium. He filmed a large number of productions for Herbert Wilcox and was one of the first in his generation to work in Hollywood studios. During the war he worked with the Army Kinematograph Unit where he was chief cinematographer, making several training films.

After the war, the British MGM, which had built modern studios at Boreham Wood, Herts., hired him to head the camera department and as director of photography. There he photographed more than thirty films for MGM with well-known Hollywood as British directors for about 15 years. He later achieved tops in the trade photography for David Lean films which deserved Hollywood Academy photography awards, e.g. *Lawrence of Arabia* (1962), *Dr. Zhivago* (1966), and *Ryan's Daughter* (1970). Young did the photography for more than 125 productions, the last of which when he was 81 years old. His career, experience, and professional touch were symbols making him a teacher and guide for several generations of noted British cinematographers.[13]

In France, as seen above, there were a number of renowned directors of photography with their own style. The French motion picture industry was firm and steady, comprising at that time 60 directors of photography, 52 camera operators, and 58 first and82 second camera assistants, besides several experts in special photographic effects. There were also two government schools for training cameramen: the well known Institut des Hautes Études Cinématographiques (IDHEC) born in 1941 during the World War II on the lines of the Italian Centro Sperimentale di Cinematografía, and the École Professionelle de Photographie et Cinématographie (Professional Photography and Cinematography School) created in 1923 and from which Louis Lumière was the first president of the council.[14]

There had been many renowned French lighting cameramen. The following generation went through the above named training centers. One of the most eminent directors of photography was Phillipe Agostini, born in 1910, a camera operator for Georges Périnal and Armand Thirard. He showed excellent lighting styles in *Les Dames du Bois de Boulogne* (1945), *Le Plaisir* (1951) and even thrillers like *Rififi chez des hommes* (1954), among others. Armand Thirard was representative of the old French photography. Born in 1899, he was a cameraman for reputed French directors, like Clair, Duvivier, Carné or Clouzot. He was the operator on famous French cinema masterpieces, e.g. *Manon* (1948). At that time he contributed his forceful and expressive images in several memorable films like *Le Salaire de la peur* (1952) and Henri Clouzot's *Les Diaboliques* (1955).[15]

Enri Decae was one of the best-paid and most versatile French cameramen. Born in 1915, he graduated from the above mentioned E.P.P.C. and started working on shorts. After World War II he did an excellent job for Jean Pierre Melville's first film, *Le Silence de la mer* (1948); then he became the favorite photography director of young film makers like Claude Chabrol and Louis Malle, adapting his work to the Nouvelle Vague style, which late in the fifties was being generally adopted, sponsored by Georges de Beauregard, the well known producer. His subsequent work was varied but within the classic conditions of filming in the studio.[16]

The work of cinematographer Raoul Coutard had similar characteristics. Born in 1914, he joined the motion picture industry in 1957, having had a long experience in photographic journalism for *Life* and *Paris-Match* magazines, from which he moved on to filming shorts. He became the typical cinematographer of the Nouvelle Vague vanguard style, using bouncing light and hand held cameras to achieve realism, fast work and low costs, as opposed to the classic lighting system. His most representative works at that time were Godard's already mentioned À *Bout de souffle* (1959), *Tirez sur le pianiste* (1960) by Truffaut, and *Une Femme est une femme* (1960) again by Godard.[17]

But there were other top ranking chief operators in the French photography school, with great skill in the classic lighting style. Among them was Christian Matras, also mentioned above, who at this time photographed films like *La Ronde* (1950), *Madame de...*, (1953), and *Lola Montes* (1955). Robert Lefèbvre, born in 1907, started in the trade in 1917, was one of the most prolific French cinematographers; his photography for *Dieu à besoin des hommes*

(1952) was remarkable and he did even better for Jacques Becker's *Casque d'or* (1953). Another reputed French cinematographer was Louis Page, the master of many professionals of the fifties. Another remarkable cinematographer was Claude Renoir, nephew of the director Jean Renoir, who showed his exquisite color palette in *Le Fleuve* (*The River*) (1950) and *Le Carrosse d'or* (1953). Finally, a great master of the French motion picture lighting was Michel Kelber, born in 1908 in Russia, with great experience and artistry skill and responsible for the excellent images of famous films like *Le Rouge et le Noir* (1954) and *French Can Can* (1954) and requested in many co-productions in Europe. Jean Burgoin, born in 1913, was a French cinematographer who during this period shot 19 films, of which the most notable were those for André Cayatte, the director, such as *Nous sommes tous des assassins* (1952), *Avant le déluge* (1953), *Le Doissier noir* (1955) as well as *Mr. Arkadin* (1955) for Orson Welles.[18]

Spanish cinema had a relative thrust in the fifties, both in film productionas well as cinematographic quality. The Instituto de Investigaciones y ExperienciasCinematográficas (I.I.E.C., Institute for Cinematographic Research and Experiences, later called Escuela de Cine (Film School), had been erected on the lines of the French IDHEC. There, new operators were trained who showed their quality in the fifties; for example, Juan Julio Baena whose images with neo-realistic influence were noted in films like *Los Golfos* (1959), directed by Carlos Saura, and *El Cochecito* (1960) directed by the Italian Marco Ferreri, who showed his expertise in all kind of films. After a successful career, Baena was later director of this film school that taught the new generation of cinematographers.[19] In the Spanish motion picture industry there were then about sixty recognized chief operators, influenced by either German or French cinematographers. We already have mentioned the German cinematographers. The French school came through Michel Kelber, Jules Krueger, Christian Matras and others.

Spanish cinematographers were faithful disciples of the respected Spanish pioneer of Europe motion picture photography Segundo de Chomón. Moreover in their sunny, varied landscape they followed the steps of their famous painters. A peculiar aspect of this trade in this land was the keeping of family traditions from father to son or to some of near kin, which was also frequently done in some European studios.

Among the best known chief operators at that time and in the next years were veterans like Alfredo Fraile, born in 1912 and who started in the trade in 1924, who achieved excellent black-and-white photography for Antonio Bardem's film *La Muerte de un Ciclista* (1955), considered the best in Europe that year, following Gregg Toland's classic pan focus techniques. Another recognized director of photography was Antonio Berenguer, born in 1913 and trained in a motion picture laboratory in Germany. His superior lighting technique was appreciated in *Bienvenido Mr. Marshall* (1952), directed by José María Berlanga, and in many others. In the following years Berenguer became the favorite cinematographer for international, large scale co-productions filmed in Spain.[20]

Among the old school cinematographers with great skill and artistic sensibility we must note the following: Cecilio Paniagua, born in 1911 and taught by Guerner, with a long career of the most varied type of films; José F. Aguayo, also born in 1911, the unique case of one who started as a bullfighter, was later still photographer and newsreel cameraman, with a long career as cinematographer, working in about three films per year, crowned by his excellent photography for Buñuel's famous film *Viridiana* (1961). Others in the list are Antonio Ballesteros, Emilio Foriscot, Francisco Sempere, Sebastian Perera, Valentin Javier and Federico Larraya.[21]

The Associazione Italiana Cineoperatori (AIC) was formed in Rome on May 13, 1950, the second European institution grouping the technicians of camera crews. Near the end of the decade, the members were 33 directors of photography who added the initials AIC to their names, and later their number rose to fifty. By 1960 the membership was supplemented by thirty camera operators and seventeen assistants. Italian professional cinematographers were well organized and were recognized the world over for their old reputation of technical and artistic skill. Several of them worked in productions in other countries, and some foreigners went to Italy to participate on local or international productions. Two of them were Vaclav Vich, born at Karlovy Vary in 1896, and the Hungarian Gabor Pogany, both famous in the Italian film industry.[22]

In that decade, the Italian films most noted in European markets for the quality of their photography were *La Strada* (1954), with black and white photography by Otello Martelli; *Senso* (1954), photographed partially in color and black and white by Aldo R. Graziati and Robert Krasker; and *Il Grido* (1957) filmed in black and white by Gianni di Venanzo. There were many other Italian productions noted for their beautiful photography, made by directors of photography of this country whose prestige went beyond local into international spheres. Some are listed below.

Carlo Mountuori was one of the most highly respected cinematographers in Italy, sometimes called "master of masters." Born in 1885, he started as a painter and then moved on to photography, working with noted artists of that time. He joined motion pictures in 1910 and in 1924 had the chance to work intensively with Fred Niblo on *Ben-Hur* (1925), thus obtaining international repute. His artistic sensibility and technical skill made him a favorite of many film directors. He photographed a long list of films for famous directors like Zampa, Germi, Blasetti and De Sica.

Piero Portalupi was another great Italian cinematographer. Born in Genoa in 1913, he graduated as an electrical engineer, but switched to motion pictures, and his perfect skill and artistic abilities led him to jump to director of photography in 1939. He was an expert in motion picture techniques and was named professor of the celebrated Centro Sperimentale di Cinematografia (CEC). He was the first one to use the Ferrania color process and earned a prize for photographing *Preludio d'Amore* (1943). He also adopted Gregg Toland's pan focus technique. In the fifties he photographed more than 15 films, among them the last version of *Ben-Hur* (1959) with Robert Surtees, which earned an Academy Oscar. Later on his recognized skill caused him to be called to integrate photography teams for international large scale productions such as *Cleopatra* (1961).

The list of famous Italian cinematographers would be too long, but it must include Aldo Graziati, usually known simply as "Aldo." Born near Venice in 1906, he was professionally taught in France with prominent film makers like Renoir and Soldatti. He photographed famous films, e.g. *Othello* (1952) for Orson Welles, as well as *Miracolo in Milano* (1952) and *Umberto D* (1953) for Vittorio De Sica. He died in 1953 leaving us his famous posthumous film, *Senso*, directed by Lucino Visconti. Other important names to list among the great are Giuseppe Rotunno, Aldo Tonti, Pasqualino de Santis, Gianni Di Venanzo, Leonida Barboni, Anchise Brizzi, Marcello Gatti, Armando Nannuzzi, and Arturo Gallea.

As we saw above, German motion picture photography suffered considerable loss when many of their valuable men migrated to other studios before and after World War II. Hollywood, Britain, Spain and France sheltered many German experts. In the fifties German cinematography was recovering its high quality and vigorous style with directors of photography like Jurt Hasse, Georg Krause, Helmut Ashley, Curt Courant (cinematographer of the famous *Le Jour se lève* (1939) with P. Agostini, Siegfried Hold, Richard Angst, Werner Krien, and many others which followed the steps of masters like Carl Hoffmann, Werner Brandes and Fritz Arno Wagner.

The cinematography of Czechoslovakia was also affected by the emigration of many of its prominent photographers like Jan Stallich, Otto Heller, and Miroslav Ondricek. But this country quickly reorganized its motion picture industry and also recovered its previous high level and technical quality. In 1960 Jan Kuric's photography for *Holibie* (*The Dove*) was recognized in European spheres. Mention must be made of well known cinematographers in those years such as Jaroslav Tuzar, Jan Stallich, who returned to his country in 1951 for the film *The Emperor's Baker*, and Jaroslav Kucera. In the next decade Mirolslav Ondricek continued the work of the great masters of cinematography in the Czech film industry.[23]

The technical standards and quality of filmmakers and cinematographers in Poland were realized abroad when its motion picture industry was rebuilt after World War II. Names like Rudolph Mate were outstanding in European cinematography in films such as *The Passion of Joan of Arc* (1926), *Vampyr* (1931), *Foreign Correspondent* (1940) and also in Hollywood with the film noir *Gilda* (1946). The Polish film *Kanal* (1956), photographed by Jerzy Lipman, was also an example of the forceful black and white photography and the quality this country achieving in this field. There were other skilled operators, e.g. Jerzy Wójcik, and other generations followed, formed at the celebrated Lodz Film School, with promising cinematographers like Jan Laskowsky, Stefan Matyjaszkiewicz and the mentioned Jerzy Lipman.

Scandinavian cinematography was an early example of excellent photography. The renowned photographers of silent movies were replaced by post-war batches where Olle Hedberg, Ake Dahlqvist, Martin Bodin and Göran Strindberg stood out. The last two were the favorites of Alf Sjoberg, a very artistic film director who was extremely scrupulous about lighting. Strindberg was distinguished for *Fröken Julia* (1950–51) and *Hon Dansade en Sommar* (1952). At that time Sven Nykvist, who would become the most remarkable photographer of modern Swedish motion pictures, came out with a film showing his elaborate craftsmanship, *Barrabas* (1952), also directed by Sjoberg. Meanwhile, another film director, Ingmar Bergman, was earning international renown with films which were excellently photographed by Gunnar Fischer, another prominent Swedish motion picture photographer, but after some time, Bergman called Nykvist for his next films.

During the fifties the foremost names in the Soviet motion pictures continued leading in their field including new ones, such as Eduard Tissé, Andrei Moskvin, Yevgeni Andrikanis, Yuri Yekelchik, Sergei Urusevsky, F. Dobronravov, M. Kirillov, Abram Kaltsati, Alexander Shelenkov, Apollinari Dudko, Wulf Dudko and many others who worked in the Mosfilm, Lenfilm, Kiev and Alma-Ata studios.

During those years, there were some directors of photography in Mexico who were gaining reputation, such as Raul Martínes Solares, Victor Herrera, Jorge Stahl and especially the veteran Alex Philips. But the most relevant figure was Gabriel Figueroa, who had earned international fame for his excellent lighting technique, indoors and outdoors, his careful image composition, and how his skies stood out. This prominent cinematographer, born in 1907, who was also a painter and musician, started in the trade in the thirties, and managed to project the plastic art of his country's great painters into his photography. Figueroa learn his craft in Hollywood with Gregg Toland. His work for *Los Olvidados* (1950), directed by Luis Buñuel, is considered his best in that decade. Other important films photographed by Figueroa were *La Perla* (1946) and *El Angel Exterminador* (1962), also directed by Luis Buñuel.[24]

The best-developed cinematography in South America at that time was in Argentina, where there were many studios and very good techniques. Lighting methods and laboratory requirements were influenced by José María Beltrán, a noted Spanish cinematographer, banished from his country by the Civil War. He helped form a batch of excellent Argentinean directors of photography. Two American cinematographers, John Alton and Bob Roberts, also helped in this task. The new wave of directors of photography included Ricardo Younis, Américo Hoss, Aníbal González Paz, Humberto Peruzzi and Ricardo Aranovich, and continued the work of such distinguished veterans as Alberto Etchebehere, Antonio Merayo, Francis Boeniger and Roque Funes. Later on Beltrán continued contributing his excellent photography for productions in Brazil and Venezuela.[25]

Finally, in Japan, the most famous cinematographer was Mitsu Miura (1902–1956) who trained many talents and was considered as the master in this field. Other important cinematographers were Asaichi Nakai *Ikiru* (*Living*, 1952), Kazuo Miyigawa *Rashomon* (1950), *Ugetsu Monogatari* (*After the Rain*, 1953) Koheo Sugiama *Jigoku-Mon* (*Gate of Hell*, 1953), etc. The work of Japanese directors of photography was outstanding with color films due to the long tradition behind them regarding their special taste, the use of complex tones and shades of colors. They used their own Konicolor system on *Karumen Kokyo ni Kaeru* (1951) with cinematography by Hiroyuki Kusuda. A special Konicolor camera was required.

In 1953 Eastman color film was imported and the Japanese laboratories obtained excellent results in the prints working with half of the foot-candles which were standard in Hollywood studios. Agfacolor and Technicolor systems were also used. In 1932 the first cinematographers society was created in Kyoto called the Japan Cameramen Association. In 1936 this society was unified in Tokyo. After the war, in 1954, the actual Japanese Society of Cinematographers was established with 389 members.

## Best Cinematography of the Fifties

| Year | Image | Title | Cinematographer | Country |
|------|-------|-------|-----------------|---------|
| 1951 | B&W | Miss Julie | Göran Strimberg | Sweden |
| 1951 | B&W | A Place in the Sun | William Mellor | USA |
| 1951 | Color | An American in Paris | A. Gilks & J. Alton | USA |
| 1952 | B&W | The Bad and the Beautiful | Robert Surtees | USA |
| 1952 | Color | The Quiet Man | W. Hoch & A. Stout | USA |
| 1953 | B&W | From Here to Eternity | Burnett Guffey | USA |
| 1953 | Color | Moulin Rouge | Freddie Francis | U.K. |
| 1953 | Color | Gate of Hell | Kôhei Sugiyama | Japan |
| 1954 | Color | Senso | A. Graziati & R. Krasker | Italy |
| 1954 | B&W | On the Waterfront | Boris Kaufman | USA |
| 1954 | Color | Three Coins in the Fountain | Milton Krasner | USA |
| 1955 | B&W | Muerte de un Ciclista | Alfredo Fraile | Spain |
| 1955 | B&W | The Rose Tattoo | James Wong Howe | USA |
| 1955 | Color | To Catch a Thief | Robert Burks | USA |
| 1956 | B&W | Kanal | Jerzy Lipman | Poland |
| 1956 | B&W | Somebody Up There Likes Me | Joseph Ruttenberg | USA |
| 1956 | Color | Around the World in 80 Days | Lionel Lindon | USA |

(continued on page 346)

## Best Cinematography of the Fifties, cont.

| Year | Image | Title | Cinematographer | Country |
|------|-------|-------|-----------------|---------|
| 1957 | B&W | *Wild Strawberries* | Gunnar Fisher | Sweden |
| 1957 | Color | *The Bridge on the River Kwai* | Jack Hildyard | UK |
| 1957 | B&W | *Il Grido* | Gianni Di Vennanzo | Italy |
| 1958 | B&W | *The Defiant Ones* | Sam Leavitt | USA |
| 1958 | Color | *Gigi* | Joseph Ruttenberg | USA |
| 1958 | B&W | *Ashes & Diamonds* | Jerzy Wójcik | Poland |
| 1959 | B&W | *Breathless* | Raoul Coutard | France |
| 1959 | B&W | *The Diary of Anne Frank* | William C. Mellor | USA |
| 1959 | Color | *Ben-Hur* | Robert L. Surtees | USA |
| 1960 | B&W | *The Dove* | Jan Kuric | Czechoslovakia |
| 1960 | B&W | *Sons and Lovers* | Freddie Francis | UK |
| 1960 | Color | *Spartacus* | Russell Metty | UK |

# Closing Words

We have come to the end of this historical review of the first sixty-nine years of motion picture photography. We saw its first wobbly steps and how it progressed both in art and technology. At the end of the first five decades of the 20th century this recording medium had reached the top of its possibilities. It was used to produce feature films to be shown in large film theaters, it was a fundamental support for television, and was intensely used in educational, publicity, informative, scientific, industrial productions, and for home movies.

Motion picture photography had never before, nor would it afterwards, have such widely varied applications. Motion pictures were the fundamental means for recording moving images. So the production of the most varied equipment as well as raw stock for this medium reached its highest point.

This peak of cinema production did not allow the industry to realize properly that towards mid century, another registration process was being born that would change this situation radically. A substitute was arising based on recording images by electronic means, which was more economic and flexible, and which would radically limit the possibilities attained. One only had to wait for its evolution, and when this happened it changed the industry's structures totally. In a short time access to the market of motion pictures would be greatly limited. In less than two decades, video stole the home movie market from cinematography, and step by step, the vast market previously conquered by 16mm.

From the sixties onwards the motion picture medium evolved constantly, but without radical changes which would totally vary established basic technologies. The quality of emulsions on raw stock was considerably improved, rendering more crisp images, fine grain, less saturated colors and making the look more natural, giving a wide exposure latitude as well as greater sensitivity than years before. Color degradation in the prints was also reduced; also the unforeseen deterioration of the old safety film obtained in the fifties was overcome with new film support.

The classic construction of cameras did not change much, but their size and weight were reduced. The blimp was done away with by improving the intermittent mechanism in order to adjust the stroke and also reduce the noise at its source. The drive motor was built into the camera, applying digital electronics to speed regulation, new synchronous systems, shutter control and other control devices. Developments in optics managed to substitute the lens turret, and the long range, automatic controlled zoom lens was adopted as a standard part.

The viewing systems of modern cameras were also improved to include a brighter reflex image, flickering free, and feasible for video recording and with electronic monitors for easy control of the outer image rim. The basic camera support, the tripod, was maintained, but improved with legs built with light, sturdy metalloids and with silicone containing heads for allow easy operation.

The size and weight of lighting equipment was considerable reduced by the appearance in the late fifties of the revolutionary halogen lamp, made with quartz, much smaller than incandescent ones and radiating more light. Heavy, complex arc projectors with high light intensity were substituted by enclosed arc lamps called HMI or variations as DC metal halide arc discharge lamps, odide lamps, and xenon lamps as well as special fluorescent light equipment.

As such equipment became smaller, lighter, consumed less power, and produced brighter light, shooting methods began to change radically in the low budget productions. Shooting began to be made away from the studios and the sets, using real locations instead, with the least lighting equipment, compact cameras and new sound recording methods. In some cases, this brought about breaking with the classic lighting systems used in the studios, as we saw above.

All sorts of mobile camera supports appeared: compact-traveling tracks with silicone wheels and easily assembled tracks, camera arms, sophisticated automatic dollies, antivibration devices for shooting from varied types of vehicles or with hand-held cameras, in order to move about in all circumstances. The sophistication of shooting media and its video control became standard in professional movie making, and, due to today's more sensitive emulsions, in many cases a decor lit for shooting differs very little in light intensity from an ordinary room.

Motion picture laboratories had to adapt their work when videos invaded the production of all sorts of shorts. Laboratory developing and printing processes were gradually improved with electronic and computer controls but without radical changes in the basic methods. The video transfer to a motion picture image will be a crucial point to the future of the motion picture photography. Changes in special effects were radical; the elaborate methods to modify and combine photographic images were displaced by electronic digital images invading this field, and computers very efficiently produced trick images with different techniques.

These drastic changes in technology occurred gradually in the last decades. At the beginning, image experts refused to accept the new competitive medium. There was a large difference in quality between the old and the new systems, as well as in work methods. Those trained in cinematography had become used to systematizing their work accurately in an expensive, not very flexible method. Video is cheaper, flexible and too automatized to accept much accuracy. So, gradually, camera operators in motion pictures started taking up video, and then directors of photography followed; they realized that the key issue in their trade was their skill in lighting and in other techniques to aesthetically control their images. The profession of director of photography expanded considerably the world over and this trade was represented in a large number of countries with its own institutions. Never before had the experts of this trade been so internationally close, like now.

The two media are now dovetailed and photography directors will switch from one to another without difficulty. But photographed images in motion pictures are still the most refined medium to impress an audience. Technology changes are now so great that it is difficult to foresee the future of motion pictures, but its rich tradition of important artistic achievements and its high techniques at present predict its continuance as feasible. This review of its brilliant past and of those who made it is intended as inspiration for present day experts in the trade to trace their future road what ever the medium.

# Notes

## Chapter 1

1. Moreno, *Curso Técnico Cinematografico*, pp. 2–4.
2. Coissac, *Histoire du Cinématographe*, pp. 101–10.
3. Macgowan, *Behind the Screen*, p. 47.
4. Ibid., p. 58.
5. Sadoul, *L'Invention du Cinéma*, pp. 159–60.
6. *Ibid.*, pp. 90–91; Spottiswoode, *Focal Encyclopedia*, p. 301.
7. Reinert and Passinetti *Filmlexicon* p. 313; Macgowan, p. 95–96; Sadoul, p. 133.
8. Macgowan, p. 73.
9. Roger Manvel, "Les Pionniers Britanniques du Cinéma," *La Technique Cinématographique*, 1955: 465–66.
10. Reinert, p. 204; Bestetti, *Cinquanta Anni di Cinema Italiano*, p. 9.
11. Sadoul, pp. 193–94; Grassman, H. Hans, "Les Pioneers des Industries Techniques du Cinéma Allemand," *La Technique Cinématographique*, No. 160 (1955): 477.
12. Sadoul, pp. 196; *L'Illustration*, Nov. 1935: p. 7.
13. Madrid, *50 Años de Cine*, pp. 40–45.
14. Vivié, *Historique et Développement*, p. 45.

## Chapter 2

1. Madrid, *50 Años de Cine*, pp. 15–16.
2. Barnouw, *Documentary*, p. 9.
3. Ibid, pp. 13–15; Villegas-López, *Cine Frances*, p. 36. Sadoul, *Historia del Cine*, p. 25.
4. After the work of Girel in 1897, the first Japanese cameraman was Shiro Asano. See: Hidenori Okada, "La Vía Japonesa," *Archivos de la Filmoteca*, No. 32 (June 1999), pp. 95–99; also Institut Lumière, *Notices Biographiques*, Lyon, France, pp. 407–15.
5. Nieto, Jorge; García, Mesa, Héctor; Douglas, M.E., González, Raúl; De los Reyes, Aurelio. *Cine LatinoAmericano 1896-1930*, pp. 121, 144–46, 191, 229–30.
6. Sadoul, *L'Invention du Cinéma*, pp. 308–10.
7. *Ibid.*, 308; Barnouw, pp. 19–20.
8. Sadoul, *Diccionario del Cine*, pp. 193, 242, 91.
9. Caneto, G.; Casinelli, M.; González Bergerot, H., Navarro, E.; Portela, M.; Smulevici, S. *Cine LatinoAmericano*, p. 19; Becquer-Casabelle and Cuarterolo, *Imágenes del Río de la Plata*, p. 65.

10. Alvarez, José, C.; *Breve Historia del Cine Uruguayo*, p. 2–10. Cinemateca Uruguaya, 1957.
11. Maria Rita Galvao, in García-Mesa, *Cine Latinoamericano*, p. 91.
12. Vivié, *Historique et Développement*, pp. 53, 64.
13. Joseph Mascelli, "Billy Bitzer," *International Photographer*, Nov. 1957, p. 5–6.
14. Joseph Mascelli,"Cinematography—Then and Now," *International Photographer*, March 1959, pp. 5–7.
15. Petrie, *British Cinematographer*, p. 8; Low, *History of the British Film*, p. 36.
16. Low, Rachel. *The History of British Film, 1914–1918* (London, 1950), pp. 72, 156–57.
17. Jean Mitry, "Les Operateur du Muet," *Cinématographe*, No. 69 (July 1981): 44.
18. Leyda, *Kino*, pp. 414–15.
19. Franco Vitrotti, "Quel Vitruttin di Casa Ambrosio," *40 Anniversario*, pp. 36–49.

## Chapter 3

1. Pathé Frères Catalog 1913, p. 67.
2. Vivié, *Historique et Développement*, p. 56.
3. Newman, Arthur, "Camera Mechanism, Ancient and Modern," *Journal of the Society of Motion Pictures and Television Engineers*, XIV, No. 5 (May 1930): 537; Orna, B. and E. "Casimierz Proszynsky (1875–1945): A Forgotten Pioneer," *British Kinematography*, June 1956, 196–7; information kindly provided by Michael Rogge, Amsterdam.
4. Laurence Roberts, "Cameras and Systems: A History of Contributions for the Bell & Howell Co, Part I," *Journal of the Society of Motion Pictures and Television Engineers* 91 (October 1982): 934.
5. *Ibid.*, p. 940; Bell & Howell Design 2709 Brochure, Form No. 7112.
6. Cocci, Franco. "Breve Storia della Akeley," *Immagine*, Nuova Serie, No. 22, pp. 10–13, 1992, Rome.
7. McKay, *Handbook of Motion Picture Photography*, pp 69–73; Lescarboura, *Cinema Handbook*, pp. 99–100; Gregory, *Motion Picture Photography*, pp. 353–356, Raimondo-Souto, *Technique of the Motion Picture Camera*, p. 124–25.
8. Kingslake, *History of the Photographic Lens*, p. 263; Rayton, W.B., "Optical science in cinematography bibliography," *A.S.C. Cinematographic Annual* 1, 1930, pp. 41–54.

# Chapter 4

1. Macwogan, *Behind the Screen*, p. 72; Barsac, *Le Décor de Film*, p. 12.
2. Barsac, *Le Décor de Film*, p. 12; Villegas López, *Cine Frances*, p. 41; Sadoul, *L'Invention du Cinéma*, pp. 376–77; Sadoul, *Historia del Cine*, p. 34–35.
3. Vivié, *Historique et Développement*, p. 65; Pathé Frères, Catalog, 1913, p. 10.
4. Low, *History of the British Film*, pp. 248–56.
5. Berriatúa, *Los Proverbios Chinos de Murnau*, p. 126.
6. "The Studios ... way back when ..." *American Cinematographer Magazine*, January 1969, p. 72.
7. Balshofer and Miller, *One Reel a Week*, pp. 54–56.
8. Macbean, *Kinematograph Studio Technique*, p. 99.


# Chapter 5

1. Vivié, *Historique et Développement*, p. 66.
2. *Ibid.*, p. xix.
3. Lescarboura, *Cinema Handbook*, pp. 210–14; "Improved Stineman System for Developing and Printing Motion Picture and Aerial Mapping Film," The Stineman System, Los Angeles, undated; Marescal, G., "Le Tirage et le Développement des Films Cinématographiques," *Bulletin de l'Association Française des Ingénieurs et Techniciens du Cinéma*, No. 17 (1958): 3–6.
4. Jones, *The Cinematograph Book*, pp. 36–44.
5. Ducom, *Le Cinématographe Scientifique et Industriel*, pp. 189–90.
6. Laurence Roberts, "Cameras and Systems: A History of Contributions for the Bell & Howell Co, Part I," *Journal of the Society of Motion Pictures and Television Engineers* 91 (October 1982): 936–7.
7. Löbel, *La Technique Cinématographique*, pp. 268–83.


# Chapter 6

1. Ducom, *Le Cinématographe Scientifique et Industriel*, p. 298.
2. "Color in the Motion Picture," *American Cinematographer* 50, No. 1 (January 1969): 120–21; Cornwell-Clyne, *Colour Cinematography*, pp. 451–455.
3. "A Pot-Pourri of Film Widths and Sprocket Holes," *American Cinematographer*, 50, No. 1 (January 1969): 98–103; Rogge, Michael, "One Hundred Years of Film Sizes," *Cinematographica* Website.


# Chapter 7

1. Smith, *Two Reels and a Crank* pp. 66–68; Fielding, *The American Newsreel*, p 5.
2. Raimondo-Souto, "Brief Historical Notes of Ten Famous Cameras," *International Photographer*, August 1968, pp. 10–11.
3. Croy, *How Motion Pictures Are Made*, p. 259; Fielding, p. 121.

4. Low, *History of the British Film*, p. 152.
5. Smither, *First World War U-Boat*, pp. 48–50; Brownlow, *War, West, and Wilderness*, pp. 28–30.
6. See: U.S. Navy film MN. 1145: Abandon ship," 32 min, b&w, sound, unclassified, 1942.


# Chapter 8

1. Angela Dunn Fox, "A Man and His Camera," *Daily Variety* Forty-Eighth Anniversary Issue, 1981.
2. Robert J. Laurence, "The Mitchell Camera: The Machine and Its Makers," *Journal of the Society of Motion Pictures and Television Engineers*, February 1982, pp. 141–52; Mitchell Camera Corporation sales brochure, circa 1920.
3. Sales brochure of C.O. Baptista, Chicago, p. 4, circa 1935.
4. McKay, *Handbook of Motion Picture Photography*, pp. 90–95; Gregory, *Motion Picture Photography* pp. 361–364; Raimondo-Souto, *Technique of the Motion Picture Camera*, pp. 126–127.
5. Lescarboura, *Cinema Handbook*, pp. 60–69.
6. Gregory, pp. 364–367.
7. Alvar, *Técnica Cinematográfica Moderna*, pp. 83–87; Joseph A. Dubray, "The Evolution of the Motion Picture Professional Camera," *Cinematographic Annual*, pp. 69–73.
8. Ducom, *Le Cinématographe Scientifique et Industriel*, pp. 179–181.
9. Information kindly provided by Mr. Adolfo L. Fabregat, Montevideo.
10. The Geyer camera built in 1921 used a very compact large capacity top mounted magazine.
11. Information kindly provided by Mr. Vaclav Simek from the National Technical Museum of the Czech Republic.
12. Mariani, *Guida Practica della Cinématografique*, pp. 308–313; Ricardo Redi, "Alcuni apparecchi famosi," *Immagine: Nota di Storia del Cinema, Nuova Serie*, No. 22, 1992: 27; Paul Allen, "Wide Film Development," *Cinematographic Annual*, 1930, pp. 183–95; Paul Raibaud, "Promoteurs et Réalizateurs du Spectacle sur Écran Large," *La Technique Cinématographique*, December 1955, pp. 393–400.


# Chapter 9

1. *Cinematographic Annual* 1, 1930, p. 557.
2. *Ibid.*, p. 567.
3. Alvar, *Técnica Cinematográfica Moderna*, pp. 95–97.
4. Harold Dennis Taylor (1862–1943) was the technical director and designer of T. Cooke & Sons, of York, England, optical instrument makers who had their lenses made by Taylor, Taylor & Hobson, of Leicester. His work was renowned the world over and his designs were adopted by several makers.
5. Horace W. Lee (1889–1976) was another important designer in optics who worked for 23 years for Taylor, Taylor & Hobson; he conceived the remarkable f/2 Speed Panchro for this firm which was intensively used in cinematography in Hollywood and the U.K. He also designed the lenses for the tripack Technicolor camera.

6. The Bausch & Lomb Company, in Rochester, New York, was founded by J.J. Bausch, and was initially devoted to making lenses for spectacles. They afterwards added optical instruments such as microscopes. In 1883 they started making camera lenses designed by the Zeiss company, and later on their own designs developed by Edward Bausch and others in the firm.

7. Walker and Walker, *The Light on Her Face*, pp. 266–67.

8. Lescarboura, *Cinema Handbook*, p. 186.

9. R.E. Farnham, "Motion Picture Studio Lighting with Incandescent Lamps," *Cinematographic Annual* 1, 1930, pp. 253–61.

10. Bordwell, Etraiger, and Thompson, "Film Style and Technology to 1930," *The Classical Hollywood Cinema*, Part 4, p. 253.

11. Scotland, *The Talkies*, p. 82–89.


## Chapter 10

1. H. Mario Raimondo-Souto, "Evolución y Tecnología del Estudio Cinematográfico," *Notas del Cine Uruguayo*, No. 2, December 1977, pp. 25–37.

2. Crowther, *The Lion's Share*, p. 147.

3. Villegas López, *Cine Francés*, p. 268.


## Chapter 11

1. Brownlow, *The Parade's Gone By ...* , p. 220.

2. Miller, *One Reel a Week*, pp. 177–78.

3. Brownlow, pp. 173–76. The twenties were the golden years of aerial cinematography. Many specialists in this field, such as Harry Perry, Elmer G. Dayer, and many others, with Paul Mantz as chief pilot, or Dick Grace as stunt pilot, were famous in the U.S. and worked in a large number of films with aerial stunt sequences or controlled crashes.

4. McKay, *Handbook of Motion Picture Photography*, pp. 125–27.


## Chapter 12

1. *Cinematographic Annual* 1, 1930, p. 573.

2. Berriatúa, *Los Proverbios Chinos de F. W. Murnau*, Vol. 1, p. 248.

3. *Ibid.*, pp. 237–58; *Mon Ciné*, No. 195, Paris, November 1925; Stefan Lorant, "Die 'Entfesselte' Kamera," *Illustrierte Film-Zeitung*, March 1927; Eisner, *F.W. Murnau*, p. 83.

4. Maltin, *Art of the Cinematographer*, p. 86.


## Chapter 13

1. Turner, *Cinema of Adventure, Romance & Terror*, p. 14.

2. De Mille, *Autobiografia*, p. 115.

3. Victor Milner, "Painting with Light," *Cinematographic Annual* 1, 1930, pp. 92–94.

4. Walker and Walker, *The Light on Her Face*, pp. 220.


## Chapter 14

1. Fielding, *The American Newsreel*, p. 117.

2. Domingo Di Nubila, "Film-Revista Valle," *Lyra*, Buenos Aires. 186–188, 1962, p. 36.

3. Fielding, pp. 149–150.

4. Lescarboura, *Cinema Handbook*, p. 367.

5. *Ibid.*


## Chapter 15

1. Leprohom, *L'Exotisme et le Cinéma*, pp. 47, 83, 92, 113.

2. Raimondo Souto, *Manual del Camara de Cine y Video*, pp. 223–234.

3. Brownlow, *War, West, and the Wilderness*, p. 430.

4. Robert J. Flaherty, "How I Filmed 'Nanook of the North,'" *Film Makers on Filmmaking* pp. 68–75; Clemente, *Robert Flaherty*, pp. 23–36; Griffith, *The World of Robert Flaherty*, pp. 40–41; Arthur Rosenheimer, Jr. "Un Maître du documentaire," *La Revue du Cinéma*, January 1947.

5. Barsam, *Nonfiction Film*, pp. 135–139; Clemente, pp. 38–46; Leprohom, pp. 136–137; Calder-Marshall, *The Innocent Eye*, pp. 112–120; Robert Flaherty, "Robert Flaherty Talking," in Manvell, *The Cinema*, pp. 25–26; Brownlow, pp. 482–484; Gromo, *Robert Flaherty*, pp. 10–11.


## Chapter 16

1. "Highlights of Lab History," *American Cinematographer*, January 1969, pp. 105.

2. Emery Huse, "Sensitometry," *Cinematographic Annual* 1, 1930, pp. 118–119.

3. Rosa Cardona Amau, "1915–1923, Consolidación y ampliación de los laboratorios industriales," in Catalina and del Arno, *Los Soportes de la Cinematografia*, pp. 62–84.

4. Scotland, *The Talkies*, pp. 98, 99, 101; Arnold & Richter, *50 Jahre*, p. 21.

5. Alvar, *Técnica Cinematográfica Moderna*, p. 435.


## Chapter 17

1. Rovin, *Movie Special Effects*, pp. 20–21.

2. Dunn and Turner, "The Evolution of Special Visual Effects," *ASC Treasury of Visual Effects*, pp. 28, 30.

3. Bessy, *Les Trucages au Cinéma*, pp. 129–131

4. De Mille, *Autobiografia*, pp. 233–236.

5. Fry and Fourzon, *The Saga of Special Effects*, p. 134.

6. Brownlow, *The Parade's Gone By...*, p. 229; Maltin, *The Art of the Cinematographer*, p. 15.

7. Dunn and Turner, p. 42; Carrick, *Designing for Films*, p. 97–99.

8. Bessy, p. 86.
9. Boussinot, "Debrie, André," *Encyclopedie du Cinéma*, Vol. 1.

10. Rippo, *Cine-Tecnica*, pp. 273–274.
11. Bury, A., "Askania Shulterkamera und Schäfentiefe" *Kinotechnik*, 23, pp. 198–201, 1941.

## Chapter 18

1. Turner, *Cinema of Adventure, Romance & Terror*, pp. 3, 17; Fry and Fourzon, *The Saga of Special Effects*, pp. 43–45; Rovin, *Movie Special Effects*, p. 33; Crowther, *The Lion's Share*, pp. 91–101.
2. Berriatúa, *Los Proverbios Chinos de F.W. Murnau*, Vol. 1, p. 237–273; *Fantastique et Réalisme dans le Cinéma Allemand*, p. 70.
3. Berriatúa, *Los Proverbios Chinos de F.W. Murnau*, Vol. 1, p. 297–357; Brochure from UFA, circa 1926.
4. *AIC 40 Anniversario*, pp. 28, 33.
5. Eyman, *Five American Cinematographers*, p. 4.
6. Crowther, pp. 96–97.
7. Higham, *Hollywood Cameramen*, p. 124.
8. Brownlow, *The Parade's Gone By ...* p. 408.
9. Motion Picture World, I-15-1927.
10. Higham, p. 125.
11. Berriatúa, pp. 408, 425, 427.
12. Coissac, *Les Coulisses du Cinéma*, p. 115.
13. Brownlow and Gill, *Cinema Europe*; Barsacq, *Le Décor de Film*, p. 41.
14. Gilles, *Les Directeurs*, p. 88
15. Coissac, p. 113; Villegas-López, *Cine Frances*, pp. 104–107. Sadoul, *Historia del Cine*, pp. 199–200.
16. Paul Raibaud, "Promoteurs et Realisateurs du Spectacle Cinématographique sur Eécran Large: Le Triple Écran de Napoléon Bonaparte," *La Technique Cinématographique*, December 1955, pp. 396–397.

## Chapter 19

1. Laurence J. Roberts, "The Mitchell Camera: The Machine and Its Makers," *Journal of the Society of Motion Pictures and Television Engineers*, February 1982, p. 143.
2. Carringer, *The Making of Citizen Kane*, p. 74.
3. Roberts, "The Mitchell Camera," p. 148.
4. Angela Dunn Fox, "A Man and His Camera," *Daily Variety* Forty-Eighth Anniversary Issue, 1981; Carringer, p. 68; Raimondo-Souto, *The Technique of the Motion Picture Camera*, p. 78.
5. Information kindly provided by Mr. Vaclav Simek of the Photo-Kino Department, National Technical Museum of Prague.
6. Baldi, Alfredo, "I Ventimiglia, Tre Generazioni in Cinema," *Cuaderni di Immagine, Colonia di Testimonianza sul Cinema*, N. II, Roma, Associazione per la Richerche di Storia del Cinema, 1993, Roma; Redi, Ricardo, "Una Machina da Pressa del 42," *Immagine*, Nuova Serie, N. 22, pp. 19–21, 1992, Roma; Redi, Ricardo, Alcuni Apparechi Famosi, *Immagine*, Nuova Serie, N. 22, pp. 23–30. 1992 Roma."
7. Arthur Newman established his business in 1903 in Haymarket, London, and in 1910 joined James A. Sinclair to set up a manufacturing division for still cameras and shutters. In 1926 the firm moved to Whitehall.
8. Rotha, *Documentary Diary*, p. 51.
9. AIC, "La Scomparsa di Alfredo Donelli," *Un Treno di Ricordi*, p. 156.

## Chapter 20

1. Powell, *Une Vie dans le Cinéma*, p. 318.
2. *Ibid.*, p. 319.
3. Wood, *Mr. Rank*, p. 78.
4. Information kindly provided by Mr. P. Américo Ilaria, architect.
5. Pierre Vago, "Studios de Cinéma," *L'Arquitecture d'Aujourd'hui*, April 1938, pp. 3–81.
6. Stanislav Brach, "Barrandov die Tschechoslowakische Filmstad," *Kinetechnische Mitteilungen*, May 1963, pp. 41–42; Jan Novák, "La Construcción de estudios y de Cinematógrafos en Checoslovaqia," *El Cine Checoslovaco*, March 1954, pp. 3–5
7. H. Mario Raimondo-Souto, "Evolución y Tecnología del Estudio Cinematográfico," *Notas del Cine Uruguayo*, No. 2 (December 1977): 25–37; Mario Guidotti, "Donde Nace el Film: Cinecittà," *Unitalia, Edicion Española, Film*, December 1957, pp. 24–29; Brochure edited by Cinecittà, Undated (circa 1961).

## Chapter 21

1. Algate, *Cinema & History*, p. 44
2. Harry Lawrenson, "The Newsreel. Its Production and Significance," *Journal of the Society of Motion Pictures and Television Engineers*, November 1946, p. 362
3. Fielding, *The American Newsreel*, pp. 206–207.
4. Shirer, *Berlin Diary*, p. 16.
5. Information provided to the author by the Spanish Fox's cameraman, Mr. Antonio Solano, February 1957; F.W. Murnau, "L'Attentat de Marseille," *Historia Hors Série* 12, 1919–1939, La France Entre Deux Guerres, January 1969, pp. 66–67.
6. Guido Cartoni, "Il 'Kinopeket' e la Testata 'Vittoria,'" *AIC 40 Anniversario*, pp. 130–132.
7. Information provided to the author by the Spanish Fox's cameraman, Mr. Antonio Solano, February 1957.
8. Riefenstahl, *Memorias*, pp. 177–181.
9. Fielding, p. 215.
10. Philippe Este, "Les Actualités," in Marion, *Le Cinema par Ceux Qui le Font*, pp. 331–332.
11. Fielding, *The March of Time*, pp. 188–195.
12. Ivens, *The Camera and I*, p. 143.
13. Julien Bryan, "War Is, Was, and Always Will Be, Hell," in Jacobs, *The Documentary Tradition*, pp. 167–174; Rotha, *Documentary Film*, pp. 325–326; Yannick Bellon, *Varsovie, quand même*, Procinex, 1954.

## Chapter 22

1. Alvar, *Técnica Cinematográfica Moderna*, pp. 178–179.
2. *Ibid.*, p. 142.

3. G. Gaudio, "A New Viewpoint on the Lighting of Motion Pictures," *Journal of the Society of Motion Pictures and Television Engineers*, August 1937, pp. 157–168; C.W. Handley, "The Advanced Technique of Technicolor Lighting," *Journal of the Society of Motion Pictures and Television Engineers*, pp. 174–176.

4. Cornwell-Clyne, *Colour Cinematography*, pp. 68–69.

5. Petrie, *The British Cinematographer*, pp. 31–32; Llinás, *Directores de Fotografía del Cine Español*, pp. 439, 538, 544.

## Chapter 23

1. Brochure from Etablissements André Debrie, circa 1935.

2. Eyman, *Five American Cinematographers*, pp. 103–118; Dunn and Turner, *ASC Treasury of Visual Effects*, p. 91; Fry and Fourzon, *The Saga of Special Effects*, p. 57.

3. Turner, p. 107.

4. Bardwell, Etraiger, and Thompson, "Film Style and Technology to 1930," Part Four, *The Classical Hollywood Cinema*, pp. 259–260.

5. Harold E. Wellman, "Composite Process Photography," in Dunn and Turner, p. 212.

6. Turner, *Cinema of Adventure, Romance & Terror*, p. 124.

7. Fry and Fourzon, p. 46.

8. Dunn and Turner, p. 117.

9. *Ibid.*, p. 120; See also: Bessy, *Les Truquages au Cinéma*, pp. 220, 226–228.

10. Fry and Fourzon, pp. 68–69.

## Chapter 24

1. Cornwell-Clyne, *Colour Cinematography*, p. 355.

2. Alfredo Castro-Navarro, "Apuntes Técnicos Para una Historia de la Cinematografía en Colores," *Nuevo Film*, Primer semestre, 1967, p. 26.

3. Cornwell-Clyne, p. 360–366; See also: Fernández-Encinas, *Técnica del Cine en Color*, pp. 118–120.

4. Uccello, *Dizionario della Tecnica Cinematografica e della Fotografia*, p. 35.

5. Cornwell-Clyne, p. 271.

6. Spottiswoode, *Film and Its Techniques*, p. 217; Rose, *American Cinematographer Handbook*, p. 81; "Color in Motion Picture," *American Cinematographer*, January 1969, p. 164–165; Spottiswoode, *Focal Encyclopedia of Film & Television*, p. 128.

7. Fernández-Encinas, p. 90–92.

8. Cornwell-Clyne, pp. 414–418.

9. Fernández-Encinas, pp. 103–108; Dufaycolor, Inc., "Color Photography with Dufaycolor Film," undated.

10. Alvin Wyckoff, "Gasparcolor Comes to Hollywood," *American Cinematographer*, November 1941, p. 141; Déribéré and Caillaud, *Enciclopédie Prisma de la Couleur*, pp. 79–80.

11. Rippo, *Cine-Tecnica*, p. 331. See also Uccello, p. 135.

12. Rose, p. 68; Castro Navarro, "Apuntes para una Historia de la Cinematografía en Colores," *Nuevo Film*, Primer Semestre, 1967, pp. 24–26; Mareschal, *Les Techniques Cinématographiques*, pp. 75–78.

13. Cornwell-Clyne, pp. 455–457.

14. Cardiff, *Magic Hour*, pp. 46–47.

15. J.A. Ball, "The Technicolor Process of Three-Color Cinematography," *Journal of the Society of Motion Pictures and Television Engineers*, August 1935, pp. 127–135; Winton Hoch, "Technicolor Cinematography," *Journal of the Society of Motion Pictures and Television Engineers*, August 1942, pp. 96–107.

16. Vivié, *Cinema e Televisione a Colori*, pp. 105–112.

17. Angel Pérez Palacios, "40 Años de Color en el Cine," *Revista Internacional del Cine*, No. 17–18 (July–August 1955): 47–50.

## Chapter 25

1. Clark and Laube, "Twentieth Century Camera and Accessories," *Journal of the Society of Motion Pictures and Television Engineers*, January 1941, p. 60.

2. William Stull, "MGM Builds Unique Camera Boom," *American Cinematographer*, December 1939, pp. 539, 572.

3. Cameron, *Sound Motion Pictures*, pp. 643–644.

4. Farciot Edouart, "The Evolution of Transparency Process Cinematography," *ASC Treasury of Visual Effects*, p. 115.

5. Eastman Kodak Company, *Motion Picture Laboratory Practice*, p. 87.

6. Ferrania Limited started in 1938, on the Ligurian Appenines, Italy, near the village of Ferrania. Manufacturing of nitrocellulose started with the firm SIPE (Italian Exploding Products Society). During 1913 an enterprise named FILM was formed which produced positive movie film. This firm was taken over by Agnelli's family with the name of Ferrania, producing negative and positive motion picture film, plates and cameras and other light sensitive products.

7. Lods, *La Formación Profesional de los Técnicos de Cine*, p. 101.

## Chapter 26

1. Gaetano Gaudio, "A New Viewpoint on the Lighting of Motion Pictures," *Journal of the Society of Motion Pictures and Television Engineers*, pp. 157–168.

2. Powell, *Une Vie dans le Cinéma*, p. 385.

3. Yuri Sókol, "Anatoli Golovnia," *Film Soviéticos* 11, 1970, pp. 15–17; The last books of Golovnia were *Siomka Tvetnovo KinoFilma* (Shooting in Color), *Masterstvo Kinooperatora* (Mastership in Cinematography) and *Eksponometriia Kinosiomky* (Exposure Meter Control).

4. Nilsen, *Cinema as a Graphic Art*, pp, 134.

## Chapter 27

1. Higham, *Hollywood Cameramen*, pp. 158; Maltin, *Art of the Cinematographer*, p. 25.

2. Maltin, pp. 40–42; Turner, *Cinema of Adventure, Romance & Terror*, p. 199. See also Lee Garmes, "La Photographie," *La Technique Photographique*, 1968, pp. 110–118.

3. Information kindly provided by Mr. Vladimír Opela from Národní Filmovy Archiv, November 1998, Prague.

4. Crowther, *The Lion's Share*, p. 235.

5. Rovin, *Movie Special Effects*, p. 35; Fry and Fourzon, *Saga of Special Effects*, p. 75.

6. "Joseph Ruttenberg," *International Photographer*, September 1962, pp. 8–19; Eyman, *Five American Cinematographers*, pp. 38–40; Joseph V. Mascelli, "Cinematography—Then and Now," *International Photographer*, March 1959, p. 7; Walter Banchard, "Aces of the Camera XXI: Joseph Ruttemberg, A.S.C.," *American Cinematographer*, September 1942, pp. 397–426.

7. Gilles, *Les Directeurs de la Photo et Leur Image*, p. 159.

8. Gregg Toland, "Using Arcs for Lighting Monochrome," *American Cinematographer*, December 1941, pp. 558–559; see also, Douglas Slocombe, "The Work of Gregg Toland," *Sequence*, Summer 1949, pp. 69–76.

9. Gregg Toland, "L'Operateur des Prie de Vues," *La Revue du Cinéma*, January 1947, pp. 16–24; Walter Strenge, letter to the author about Gregg Toland, 1965; George Mitchell, "A Great Cameraman," *Films in Review*, December 1956, pp. 504–512; Maltin, pp. 17–21; Mascelli, p. 15.

10. Crowther, pp. 261, 263.

11. Slifer in Dunn and Turner, p. 124; Rovin, p. 40.

12. Slifer in Dunn and Turner, pp. 125–126; "The Evolution of Motion Picture Lighting," *American Cinematographer*, January 1969, p. 108.

13. Crowther, p. 266.; Rovin, p. 40; Fry and Fourzon, p. 75; Gerald Gardner and Harriet Modell, *Pictorial History of Gone with the Wind*, pp. 182–184.

14. Higham, p. 46.

15. Slifer in Dunn and Turner, p. 133.

16. Dunn and Turner, p. 133.

17. "The Evolution of Motion Picture Lighting," *American Cinematographer*, January 1969, p. 108.

## Chapter 28

1. Balio, *The American Film Industry*, p. 227.

2. Sadoul, *Le Cinéma Pendant la Guerre*, p. 6.

3. Balio, p. 226.

4. "Model 1" Houston 16mm Processor, *International Photographer*, (publicity), October 1944, p. 31.

5. Several improvements were made during those years in developing equipment, such as infrared lamps built into the drying cabinet replacing 1000-watt heaters; a built-in siphon system replacing the drain valves, preventing deterioration and maintenance problems; use of photo electric devices; cartridge-type water filter instead of standard sand type filters, etc.

6. *Army Air Forces Photographic Equipment*, May 1945, p. 79. In Japan, during the war, Fujifilm produced black and white and color reversal raw stock for the armed forces. See Inedori Okada, "La Vía Japonesa: Apuntes para la historia de la fabricación de película cinematográfica en Japón," *Archivos de Filmoteca*, June 1999, p. 98.

7. Lee Garmes, "New 'All-Direction' Baby Camera-Dolly," *American Cinematographer*, September 1950, p. 19.

## Chapter 29

1. André Debrie sales brochure No. 450: Super Parvo "Vision Reflexe," circa 1950.

2. André Coutant and Jacques Mathot, "A Reflex 35mm Magazine Motion Picture Camera," *Journal of the Society of Motion Pictures and Television Engineers*, August 1950, pp. 173–179. See also undated brochure produced by Éclair Corporation of America about Éclair NPR camera, circa 1969; Raimondo-Souto, *Technique of the Motion Picture Camera*, p. 105.

3. Information kindly provided by Mr. Vaclav Simek of the National Technical Museum, Prague, May 2, 1999, and Prof. Jaroslav Boucek, October 19, 1972.

4. A.E. Jeakings, "Two New British Cameras," *The Cine Technician*, September-October 1946, pp. 136–137.

5. W. Vinten Ltd. sales brochure, circa 1952.

6. *Ibid.*

7. Petrie, *The British Cinematographer*, p. 65.

8. "Die neue Atelier—und Reportage Kamera, Super-Steimi fur 35mm Normalfilm," *Filmtecnica*, No. 2 (1948): 31–32.

9. Riccardo Redi, "Alcuni Apparecchi Famosi," *Immagine, Nuova Serie*, No. 22, 1992, p. 30.

10. *U.S. Army Air Forces Photographic Equipment*, May 1945, pp. 83–105.

11. U.S. Catalog, *Description of Air Force Cameras and Accessory Equipment*, July 1943, pp. 59–70.

12. William Stull, "The First Real Combat Camera," *American Cinematographer*, November 1942, pp. 474–490.

13. *U.S. Air Force Cameras Catalog*, July 1943, p. 60.

14. Information provided to the author in 1963 by Mr. Delmer Daves.

15. *U.S. Air Force Cameras Catalog*, July 1943. p. 64–67.

16. B. Clark and G. Laube, "Twentieth Century Camera and Accessories," *Journal of the Society of Motion Pictures and Television Engineers*, January 1941, pp. 50–64; Cameron, *Sound Motion Pictures*, pp. 636–646.

17. Art Reeves Motion Picture Equipment Co., "The Art Reeves Reflex Motion Picture Camera," *Journal of the Society of Motion Pictures and Television Engineers*, June 1945, pp. 436–442.

## Chapter 30

1. The U.S. Signal Corps was formed in 1861. The Photographic Section covered the area of still and motion picture photography and had a School of Photography at Columbia University.

2. Fielding, *The March of Time*, pp. 273–274.

3. "Uncle Sam's Cameramen Are Coming," *American Cinematographer*, September 1942, pp. 395, 418.

4. Cameraflex Corp., "Instruction Handbook of Camera Ph 330 K.," p. 38. Undated, circa 1945.

5. *Film and Video Archive Handbook*, pp. 26–27.

6. *Ibid.*, p. 32.

7. *Cinema Chronicle*, No. 10 October 1945, p. 7.

8. "El Quinto Tanque de un Camarógrafo," *Films Soviéticos*, No. 11, 1970, p. 22.

9. Raymond Fielding, " The Nazi-German Newsreel," *Journal of the University Film Producers Association*, Spring 1960, p. 4.

10. Wilton Scott, "Adventures of a Combat Cameraman," *American Cinematographer*, September 1942, p. 394.

## Chapter 31

1. Fernández-Encinas, *Técnica del Cine en Color*, pp. 233–240; Alfonso Del Amo García, "El Sistema Bypack del Cinefotocolor," *Inspeccion Tecnica de Materiales en el Archivo de una Biblioteca*, pp. 121–122; Information provided by Mr. Aragonés in letter to the author dated January 29, 1968.

2. Alfredo Castro-Navarro, "Apuntes Técnicos para una Historia de la Cinematografía en Colores," *Nuevo Film*, Primer Semestre, 1967, pp. 31–33.

3. Ferrania. Catalogo Generale Materiale cinematografico, undated, circa 1950.

4. Angel Pérez-Palacios, "40 Años de Color en el Cine," *Revista Internacional de Cine*, July–August 1955, p. 50.

5. Vivié, *Cinema e Televisione a Colori*, pp. 115–116; Pérez-Palacios, p. 44.

6. Leyda, *Kino*, pp. 338, 392, 452, 453.

7. Cornwell-Clyne, *Colour Cinematography*, pp. 282–283.

8. Cornwell-Clyne, pp. 343–345; Rose, *American Cinematographer Handbook*, p. 80.

## Chapter 32

1. Carringer, *The Making of Citizen Kane*, p. 67.

2. The camera crew was made up by Bert Shipmen, operative cameraman; Eddie Garvin, assistant cameraman; W.J. McClelland, gaffer; and Ralph Hoge, grip. (Carringer, p. 69). The Mitchell No. 2 camera was not the only camera used. In some scenes two cameras were used simultaneously, as in the long take in which Kane, in a rage, breaks up the furniture in the room. It is presumed that portable cameras were used during the shooting of the newsreel sequence. See also Mitchell Camera Corp. publicity of BNC model with Toland comments: "5,000,000 feet of film ... since I began using Mitchell Studio Camera No. 2., the most satisfactory camera I have ever used." *American Cinematographer*, February 1941.

3. Carringer, p. 68.

4. Gregg Toland, "Realism for Citizen Kane," *American Cinematographer*, February 1941, p. 54.

5. *Ibid.*, p. 55. The daylight spectrum of arc lamps allowed using the 100 ASA value of Kodak Super XX. Toland experimented with lenses provided with Waterhouse stops to increase field depth, thus obtaining better definition and contrast. His work in this field was later continued by Stephen Garutzo leading to the invention of the Garutzo lens.

6. See the explanation how this shot was made in Carringer, p. 82.

7. Dunn and Turner, "Cinemagic of the Optical Printer," ASC *Treasury of Visual Effects*, p. 237. One of the factors that contributed to the good quality of special effects made by Dunn and others in RKO was that this department had been developed further than in other Hollywood studios; another was the standard of excellence demanded by Welles.

8. Miller, *One Reel a Week*, p. 131, 132, 195, 200, 201; Higham, *Hollywood Cameramen*, p. 134; "Touring The Motion Picture Industry with Arthur Miller, the Dean of Cinematographers," *International Photographer*, January 1963, pp. 8–9, 16–17.

9. Higham, p. 106.

10. *Ibid.*, p. 104.

11. *Ibid.*, p. 107.

12. Carringer, p. 128; Higham, p. 108.

13. Among other books of Henri Alekan we must mention *Des Lumières et des Ombres*, 304 pages, Paris: Éd. Sycomore.

14. Powell, *Une Vie dans le Cinéma*, p. 576–577.

15. Petrie, *The British Cinematographer*, pp. 74–78.

16. Paladini, *Guerra e Pace*, p. 303–304.

17. Information provided to the author by Mr. John Drake, Jack Cardiff's camera operator, March 1959.

18. Cardiff, *Magic Hour*, p. 87. Powell, p. 446.

19. Powell, p. 448.

20. Cardiff, p. 90.

21. Wood, *Mr. Rank*, pp. 224–225.

22. Brownlow, *David Lean*, p. 207.

23. *Ibid.*, p. 212.

## Chapter 33

1. Balio, *The American Film Industry*, p. 366.

2. Gordichuk, *Sovietscaia Kinosiomosnaia Apparatyra*, pp. 3, 4.

3. Gian Luigi Rondi, "Cinema Italiano 1945–1951," in *Il Neorealismo Italiano*, pp. 9–26.

4. Mitry, *Dictionnaire du Cinema*, p. 194.

## Chapter 34

1. Bell & Howell Militarized Camera Equipment brochure, circa 1954.

2. Traid Corp. brochure, circa 1955.

3. Lloyd Thompson, "Progress Committee Report," *Journal of the Society of Motion Pictures and Television Engineers*, May 1960, p. 329.

4. Information kindly provided by Mr. G. Allen and L. Findjan, of James A. Sinclair & Co., Ltd., dated April 1960 and September 1964.

5. *Gaumont-Kalee Single-System Magnetic Recording Equipment*, published by the engineering division of the BBC, London, circa 1959, pp. 51–68.

6. Seiki Co. Motion Picture Equipment Catalog, Tokyo, undated.

7. Weise, *Die Kinematographische Kamera*, pp. 104, 109, 132, 392–393.

8. Information kindly provided by Mr. Jaroslav Boucek in letter of October 19, 1972.

9. Mashpriborintorg Motion Picture Equipment Catalog, circa 1956; Gordichuk, *Sovietscaia Kinosiomosnaia Apparatyra*; Convas Automatic Camera manual, Moscow, undated; MPI Bulletin, Moscow, undated.

## Chapter 35

1. Cornwell-Clyne, *3-D Kinematography*, pp. 29, 59, 62, 104, 107, 163, 164.

2. *Ibid.*, p. 51; John A. Norling, "Basic principles of 3-D Photography and Projection," in Quigley, *New Screen Techniques*, p. 46.

3. Norling in Quigley, pp. 44–45.

4. Arthur Gavin, "All Hollywood Studios Shooting 3-D Films," *American Cinematographer*, March 1953, pp. 108–110, 134–139.

5. Claude Autant Lara used the system named "triptych screen" in his film *Pour Construire un Feu*, and Abel Gance used it in *Napoleon* (1927).

After Cinerama, the Cinemiracle system was conceived with similar principles but differences in camera and projection methods. See also, Ralph Walker, "The Birth of an Idea," in Quigley, *New Screen Techniques*, pp. 117; Fred Waller, "Cinerama Goes To War," in Quigley, *New Screen Techniques*, pp. 119–126; John W. Boyle, "And Now … Cinerama," *American Cinematographer*, March 1953, pp. 480, 498, 500. See also, Cinerama brochure, 1952. See also, Cameron, *Sound Motion Pictures*, pp. 558–559.

6. Warner Bros. later used the Warner Superscope based on lenses made in Germany by Zeiss Opton. The first English production in Cinemascope was *Knights of the Round Table* (1953), made in London by MGM.

7. Cornwell-Clyne, pp. 114–28; Earl I. Sponable, "Cinemascope in the Theatre," in Quigley, *New Screen Techniques*, pp. 187–92; "Is the Cinemascope the Answer?" in Farber, *Theater Catalog*, pp. 205–209; Charles, G. Clarke, "Cinemascope Photographic Techniques," *American Cinematographer*, June 1955, pp. 337; Henri Chrétien, "Le Dispositif Hypergonar," *La Technique Cinématographique*, December 1955, p. 398.

8. John R. Bishop and Loren Ryder, as told to Arthur Gavin, "Paramount's 'Lazy' Double-Frame Camera," *American Cinematographer*, December 1953, pp. 588–607.

9. Ventimiglia conceived the principles of the Vistavision system and developed a camera in Italy which was used later on the Italian production *Il Quatro dil Getto Donante* (1956). See Alfredo Baldi, "I Ventimiglia, Tre Generazione in Cinema," *Quaderni di Immagine*, Associazione Italiana per le Ricerche di Storie del Cinema, 1993, p. 31.

10. Information kindly provided by Technicolor Corporation, Hollywood. See also Guido Marpicati, "Il Sistema Technirama-Technicolor," *Filmtecnica*, No. 6, 1960, pp. 30–32.

11. Pierre Hémardinquer, "Nouvelle Transformation de la Projection Cinématographique," *Cinéma Amateur*, July 1956, pp. 17–21.

12. Baldi, p. 31.

## Chapter 36

1. V. Chappert, "Progress de L'optique Francaise," *La Technique Cinématographique*, December 1955, pp. 423.

2. Lloyd Thompson, *Journal of the Society of Motion Pictures and Television Engineers*, May 1956, p. 254.

3. Taylor & Hobson Ltd., "Lenses for Motion Picture Photography," compilation of technical leaflets, 1956–1958.

4. Lloyd Thompson, *Journal of the Society of Motion Pictures and Television Engineers*, May 1957, p. 244.

5. Lloyd Thompson, *Journal of the Society of Motion Pictures and Television Engineers*, May 1959, p. 279.

6. *Filmtecnica*, No. 6, 1960.

7. Joseph Garrec, "Les Derniers Progrès de la Prise de Vues," *Le Technicien du Film*, No. 77 (November 1961): 6–7.

8. "L'asservisseur Coutant sera une nouveauté du Salon," *Le Technicien du Film*, No. 76 (October 1961): 20–21.

9. F.R.C. Bernard, "Un Analizzatore elettronico per film a colori," *Bolletino Tecnico A.I.C.*, No. 5, 1960, pp. 22–24; Henriette Dujarric, "Une Étalonneuse Couleurs Francaise," *Le Technicien du Film*, April 1960, pp. 4–5.

## Chapter 37

1. The most important film studios in Hollywood during those years were Allied Artists, American National, California Studios, Centaur Studios, Columbia Pictures, Walt Disney, Filmcraft Studios, Fox Western Avenue Studios, General Service, Goldwyn Studios, Key West, Kling Studios, La Brea Productions, Metro Goldwyn Mayer, Motion Picture Center, Paramount, Sunset, Republic Studios, Hal Roach Studios, RKO-Pathé, Universal International, Warner Bros., Ziv Studios and Biltmore Studios.

2. Higham, *Hollywood Cameramen*, pp. 75–97; Eyman, *Five American Cinematographers*, pp. 60–89; "James Wong Howe," *International Photographer* 35, No. 10 (October 1963): 10–16.

3. "Milton Krasner," *International Photographer* 37, No. 6 (June 1965): 12–17.

4. Higham, pp. 18–34; Maltin, *Art Of The Cinematographer*, p. 29; "Leon Shamroy," *International Photographer*, May 1963, pp. 8–17.

5. Maltin, pp. 75–94; "Al Mohr," *International Photographer*, March 1965.

6. "The Story of Russell Metty," *International Photographer*, July 1965, p. 16.

7. Alton, *Painting with Light*; Di Nubila, *Historia Del Cine Argentino*, Part 1, p. 178.

8. Sadoul, *Diccionario Del Cine*, pp. 248; Salles Gomes, *Jean Vigo*, p. 71.

9. Anderson, *Making a Film*, p. 222.

10 Petrie, *The British Cinematographer*, p. 138; Philippe Carcassonne, "Douglas Slocombe," *Cinématographe*, No. 69 (July 1981): 14–18; *Kinematograph Year Book: 1956*, p. 72. *British Film Yearbook: 1947–1948*, p. 351.

11. Petrie, p. 124, Young, *Seventy Light Years*, p 117–118; Campbell, *Practical Motion Picture Photography*, p. 188.

12. Campbell, pp. 187–188.

13. Freddie Young wrote also several technical articles and two books: *The Work of the Motion Picture Cameramen* (1972) and his autobiography, *Seventy Light Years: A Life in the Movies* (1999).

14. *Tout Le Cinéma-Annuaire: 1952*, pp. 22–23, 30–35.

15. Gilles, *Les Directeurs De La Photo Et Leur Image*, pp. 7–9.

16. Jacques Fieschi and Jérôme Tonnerre, "Henri Decae," *Cinématographe*, July 1981, pp 9–13; Mitry, *Dictionnaire du Cinéma*, p. 80; Gilles Colpart, "Henri Decae," *La Revue du Cinéma*, No. 432 (November 1987): 67–74.

17. Jérôme Tonnerre, "Raoul Coutard," *Cinématographe*, No. 69, pp. 19–22. *Dictionaire du Cinéma Seguers*, pp. 105–106.

18. Reéne Prédal, "Dictionaire des Chefs-Opérateurs Français des Années 81, *Cinéma Quatre 21* (September 1981): 35; Llinas, *Directores de Fotografía del Cine Español*, pp. 540–41.

19. H.M. Raimondo-Souto, "Docencia y Tecnología Cinematográfica en el Viejo Mundo," *Notas del Cine Uruguayo,* No. 4 (December 1978): 24–25.

20. Muñoz-Suay, "La Expresión Cinematográfica de la obra de Berenguer," *Revista Internacional de Cine,* No. 1 (August 1952): 49–50.

21. Alvaro Germán, "Antonio L. Ballesteros: La realidad del Color," *Anuario AEC 1997–8,* p. 21; *Anuario AEC 1996–7,* p. 20.

22. *Bolletino Técnico A.I.C.,* No. 3, (April-May 1960): 28–29; Mario Bernardo, "Necessitá Della Storia," *A.I.C. 40° Anniversario,* pp 12–13.

23. Information kindly provided by Mr. Vladimir Opela from the Czechoslovakia Film Archive (NFA).

24. Cristina Martin, *Anuario AEC 1997–8,* pp. 13–14.

25. Llinás, Francisco Llinás, *Directores de Fotografía del Cine Español,* pp 390; Domingo Di Nubila, *Historia del Cine Argentino,* Tomo II, pp. 178–179.

# Bibliography

## Journals

American Cinematographer (Hollywood)
Anuario AEC (Madrid)
Archivos de la Filmoteca (Valencia)
Boletín de A.U.C. (Montevideo)
Bolletino Tecnico A.I.C. (Rome)
British Kinematography (London)
Bulletin de l'Association Française des Ingénieurs et Techniciens du Cinéma (Paris)
El Cine Checoslovaco (Prague)
Cine Soviético (Moscow)
The Cine Technician (London)
Cinéma (Rome)
Cinetécnica (Buenos Aires)
Cinetecnica (Turin)
Der Deutsche Kameramann (Munich)
Ferrania (Milan)
Film and TV Technician (London)
Il Film Italiano (Rome)
Film Today Books: Screen and Audience (London)
Film, TV, AV, Video (Stockholm)
Films Soviéticos (Moscow)
Filmtecnica (Rome)
Historia Hors Série (Paris)
Image Technology (London)
Immagine (Rome)
International Photographer (Hollywood)
Journal of the Society of Motion Pictures and Television Engineers (White Plains, NY)
Journal of the University Film Association (Columbus, OH)
Kinematograph Weekly (London)
Kinetechnische Mitteilungen (Wolfen, Germany)
Kinotechnik (Berlin)
Mon Ciné
Notas del Cine Uruguayo (Montevideo)
Nuevo Film (Montevideo)
Revista Internacional del Cine (Madrid)
La Revue du Cinéma (Paris)
Studio Review (London)
Le Technicien du Film (Paris)
La Technique Cinématographique (Paris)

## Books

Abbott, L.B. Special Effects: Wire, Tape and Rubber Band Style. Hollywood, CA: ASC Press, 1984.
AIC. 40° Anniversario. Roma: Associazione Italiana Autore della Fotografia, 1997.
_____. Un Treno di Recordi. Roma: Associazione Italiana Autore della Fotografia, 1990.
Aldgate, Anthony. Cinema & History: British Newsreels and the Spanish Civil War. London: Scholar Press, 1979.
Almendros, Nestor. Las Luces de Néstor Almendros. Barcelona: Seix y Barral, 1982.
Alton, John. Painting with Light. New York: Macmillan, 1950.
Alvar, M.F. Técnica Cinematográfica Moderna. Madrid: Yagües Ed., 1934.
Alvarez, José, C. Breve Historia del Cine Uruguayo. Cinemateca Uruguaya, 1957.
Anderson, Lindsay. Making a Film: The Story of Secret People. London, George Allen and Unwin, 1951.
Arijón, Daniel. Grammar of the Film Language. Hollywood, CA: Silman-James, 1991.
Arnold & Richter Kg. 50 Jahre. Munich: n.p., 1967.
Aronovich, Ricardo. Exponer la Historia: La Fotografía Cinematográfica. Barcelona: Editorial Gedisa, 1997.
The Arts Enquiry. The Factual Film. London: Oxford University Press, 1947.
Bacher, Lutz. The Mobile Mise en Scene. New York: Arno Press, 1978.
Baechlin, Peter, and Maurice Muller-Strauss. La Presse Filmée. Paris: Unesco, 1951.
Balio, Tino, ed. The American Film Industry. Madison: University of Wisconsin Press, 1976.
Balshofer, Fred J., and Arthur C. Miller. One Reel a Week. Berkeley and Los Angeles: University of California Press, 1967.
Barnouw, Erik. Documentary: A History of Non-Fiction Film. New York: Oxford University Press, 1974.
Barsacq, Léon. Le Décor de Film. Paris: Seghers, 1970.
_____, and Elliot Stein, eds. Caligari's Cabinet and Other Grand Illusions. Boston: New York Graphic Society, 1976.

Barsam, Richard Meram. *Nonfiction Film.* New York: Dutton, 1973.

Becquer-Casaballe, Amado, and Miguel Angel Cuarterolo. *Imágenes del Río de la Plata–Crónicas de la Fotografía Rioplatense, 1840–1940,* 2nd edition. Buenos Aires: Editorial the Photographer, 1985.

Berriatúa, Luciano. *Los Proverbios Chinos de F.W.Murnau.* Madrid: Filmoteca Española, 1990.

Bessy, Maurice. *Les Truquages au Cinéma.* Paris: Prisma, 1951.

Bestetti Carlo, ed. *Cinquanta Anni di Cinema Italiano.* Roma: Edizione d'Arte, 1953.

Blakeston, Oswell, ed. *Working for the Films,* London: Focal Press, 1947.

Bluem, William, ed. *The Movie Business.* New York: Hastings House, 1972.

Bordwell, David, Janet Etraiger, and Kristian Thompson. *The Classical Hollywood Cinema.* New York: Columbia University Press, 1985.

Bossi, Dimitri. *Eterno Giorno: Vita e Cinema di Gianno di Venanzo Operatore.* Roma: Centro Sperimentale di Cinematografia, 1997.

Bouillot, René. *La Practique de l'Éclairage.* Paris: If. Dujarric, 1991.

Boussinot, Roger. *Encyclopédie du Cinéma,* Vol. I & II. Paris: Bordas, 1980.

Brard, Pierre. *Technologie des Caméras: Manuel de l'Assistant-Operateur.* Paris: Editions Techniques Européenes, 1969.

Brownlow, Kevin. *Napoléon: Gance's Classic Film.* New York: Alfred A. Knopf, 1983.

_____. *The Parade's Gone By...* London: Secker & Warburg. 1968.

_____. *The War, the West, and the Wilderness.* New York: Alfred A. Knopf, 1979.

Bustillo-Oro, Juan. *Vida Cinematográfica.* Mexico, D.F: Cineteca Nacional, 1984.

Calder-Marshall, Arthur. *The Innocent Eye.* London: W.H. Allen, 1963.

Cameron, James. *Sound Motion Pictures.* Coral Gables, FL: Cameron, 1959.

Campbell, Russell, ed. *Photographic Theory for the Motion Picture Cameraman.* New York: Barnes, 1970.

Campbell, Russell, ed. *Practical Motion Picture Photography.* New York: Barnes, 1970.

Cardiff, Jack. *Magic Hour.* London: Faber & Faber, 1996.

Carlson, Verne, and Sylvia Carlson. *Professional Cameraman's Handbook.* New York: Amphoto, 1981.

Carringer, Robert L. *The Making of Citizen Kane.* Los Angeles: University of California Press, 1985.

Catalina, Fernando, and Alfondo del Arno. *Los Soportes de la Cinematografía.* Madrid: Filmoteca Española, 1999.

Catelain, Jaque. *Jaque Catelain Présente: Marcel L'Herbier.* Paris: Vautrain, 1950.

Clairmont, Leonard. *Profesional Cine Photographer.* Hollywood: Ver Halen, 1956.

Clark, Frank P. *Special Effects in Motion Pictures.* New York: S.M.P.T.E., 1963.

Clarke, Charles G. *Professional Cinematography.* Hollywood: A.S.C., 1964.

Clemente, Jose L., *Robert Flaherty.* Madrid: Ediciones Rialp,1963.

Coissac, G.-Michel. *Histoire du Cinématographe.* Paris: Editions du Cinéopse, 1925.

_____. *Les Coulisses du Cinéma.* Paris: Les Editions Pintoresques, 1929.

Collections Seghers. *Dictionnaire du Cinéma, Suivi d'un Répertoire des Principaux Films.* Paris: Editions Seghers, 1962.

Connio-Santini, Carlos. *Introducción al Color.* Buenos Aires: Lab. Alex, 1954.

Consiglo, Stefano, and Fabio Ferzetti. *El Almacén de la Luz.* Buenos Aires: Adisica, 1985.

Cornwell-Clyne, Adrian. *Colour Cinematography.* London: Chapman & Hall, 1951.

_____. *3-D Kinematography and New Screen Techniques.* London: Hutchinsons, 1954.

Cox, Arthur. *Optica Fotográfica.* Barcelona: Omega, 1952.

Crowther, Bosley. *The Lion's Share.* New York: Garland, 1957.

Croy, Cromer. *How Motion Pictures Are Made.* New York: Harper & Bros., 1918.

Culhane, John. *Special Effects in the Movies.* New York: Ballantine Books, 1981.

Challis, Christopher. *Are They Really So Awful? A Cameraman's Chronicle.* London: Janus, 1995.

Del Amo García, Alfonso. *Inspección Técnica de Materiales en el Archivo de una Biblioteca.* Madrid: Filmoteca Espanola, 1996.

De Mille, Cecil. *Autobiografía.* Barcelona: Argos, 1960.

Déribéré, M., and L. Caillaud. *Enciclopédie Prisma de la Couleur.* Paris: Prisma. 1957.

Ducom, Jacques. *Le Cinématographe Scientifique et Industriel.* Paris: Albin Michel, 1923.

Dujarric, H. (ed.) and Erwin Huppert. *Le Technicien du Film Manuel.* Paris: Le Technicien du Film, 1973.

Dunn, G. Linwood, and George E. Turner. *The ASC Treasury of Visual Effects.* Hollywood, CA: American Society of Cinematographers, 1983.

Eastman Kodak. *Motion Picture Laboratory Practice,* Rochester: Eastman Kodak, 1936.

Eder, J.M. *Die Photographischen Objective.* Halle: Knapp, 1911.

Eisenstein, Serge, *Reflexions d'un Cinéaste.* Moscow: Editions du Progres, 1958.

Eisner, Lotte, H. F. W. Murnau, Paris: Le Terrain Vague, 1964.

Eyman, Scott. *Five American Cinematographers.* Metuchen, N.J.: Scarecrow Press, 1974.

*Fantastique et Réalisme dans le Cinéma Allemand 1912–1933.* Bruxelles: Musée du Cinéma, 1969.

Ferncase, Richard K. *Film and Video Lighting Terms and Concepts.* Boston: Butterworth, 1995.

Fernández-Encinas, José Luis. *Técnica del Cine en Color.* Madrid: Escuela Especial de Ingenieros Industriales, 1949.

_____. *Sensitometría Fotográfica Aplicada a la Cinematografía*. Madrid: Escuela Especial de Ingenieros Industriales, 1946.

Fielding, Raymond. *The American Newsreel: 1911–1967*. Norman: University of Oklahoma Press, 1972.

_____. *The March of Time: 1935–1951*. New York: Oxford University Press, 1958.

_____. *The Technique of Special Effects Cinematography*. London: Focal Press, 1974.

_____. *A Technological History of Motion Pictures and Television*. Berkeley: University of California Press, 1967.

*Film and Video Archive Handbook: A User's Guide*. London: Imperial War Museum, 1997.

Fry, Ron, and Pamela Fourzon. *The Saga of Special Effects*. Englewood Cliffs, N.J.: Prentice-Hall, 1977.

García-Mesa, Héctor, ed. *Cine Latinoaméricano: 1896–1930*. Caracas: Conac, 1992.

Gardner, G., and Harriet Modell. *The Pictorial History of Gone with the Wind*. New York: Wing Books, 1980.

Geduld, Harry M., ed. *Film Makers on Film Making: Statements on Their Art by Thirty Directors*. Harmondsworth, UK: Penguin, 1967.

Gilles, Christian. *Les Directeurs de la Photo et Leur Image*. Paris: Dujarric, 1989.

Golovnia, A. *Filmarea in Colori*. Bucarest: Energeticä de Stat, 1953.

_____. *La Luce nell'Arte dell'Operatore*. Roma: Bianco e Nero, 1951.

_____. *Masterstvo Kinooperatora*. Moscow: Iskusstvo, 1965.

Gordichuk, I. S. *Sovietscaia Kinosiomocinaia Apparatura*. Moscow: Iskusstvo,1966.

Greenhalgh, P., and A. Farber. *Theater Catalog*. Philadelphia: n.p., 1953-54.

Gregory, Carl Louis. *Motion Picture Photography*. New York: Falk, 1927.

Griffith, Richard. *The World of Robert Flaherty*. New York: Capo Press, 1953.

Hall, Hal, ed. *Cinematographic Annual*. Hollywood, CA: ASC Publishers, 1930.

Halliwell, Leslie. *The Filmgoer's Companion*. New York: Hill and Wang, 1977.

Happé, Bernard, L. *Your Film and the Lab*. London & New York: Focal Press, 1974.

Heredero, Carlos F. *El Lenguaje de la Luz*. Madrid: Alcalá de Henares, 1994.

Higham, Charles. *Hollywood Cameramen*. London: Thames and Hudson, 1970.

Hutchison, David. *Special Effects 1*. New York: Starlog Magazine, 1979.

_____. *Special Effects 2*. New York: Starlog Magazine, 1980.

_____. *Special Effects 3*. New York: Starlog Magazine, 1981.

Ivens, Joris. *The Camera and I*. New York: International Publishers, 1969.

Jacobs, Lewis, ed. *The Documentary Tradition: From Nanook to Woodstock*. New York: Hopkinson and Blake, 1971.

Jeanne, René, and Charles Ford. *Abel Gance*. Seguers, Paris, 1958.

_____ and _____. *Le Livre d'Or du Cinéma Français*. Paris: A.D.C., 1946.

Jennings, Mary-Lou, *Humphrey Jennings: Film-Maker, Painter, Poet*. London: BFI, 1982.

Jones, Bernard. *The Cinematograph Book*. London: Cassel, 1916.

*Kinematograph Year Book: 1956*. London: Odhams Press.

Kingslake, Rudolf. *A History of the Photographic Lens*. Cambridge: Academic Press, 1989.

Kobal, John, ed. *Hollywood Glamour Portraits*. New York: Dover, 1976.

Kulechov, León. *Tratado de la Realización Cinematográfica*. Buenos Aires: Editorial Futuro, 1956.

Lassally, Walter. *Itinerant Cameraman*. London: Murray, 1987.

Lega, Giuseppe. *Il Fonofilm*. Florence: Nemi, 1932.

Leprohom, Pierre. *L'Exotisme et le Cinéma*. Paris: Susse, 1945.

Lescarboura, A. C. *The Cinema Handbook*. New York: n.p., 1921.

Levin, Roy G. *Documentary Explorers*. New York: Anchor Press, 1971.

Leyda, Jay. *Kino. A History of the Russian and Soviet Film*. London: Allen & Unwin, 1960.

*El Libro de Oro del Cine*, 3rd ed. New York: Chalmers, 1927.

Llinás, Francisco. *Directores de Fotografía del Cine Español*. Madrid: Filmoteca Española, 1989.

Löbel, Leopold. *La Technique Cinématographique, Projection, Fabrication des Films*. Paris, H. Dunod et E. Pinat, 1912.

_____, and M. Dubois. *Manual de Sensitometría*. Barcelona: Omega, 1955.

Lodz, Jean. *La Formación Profesional de los Técnicos de Cine*. Paris: Unesco, 1951.

López-García, Victoriano. *Técnica del Cine Sonoro en Color y Relieve*. Madrid: Aguado,1943.

Low, Rachael. *The History of the British Film: 1914–1918*. London: Allen & Unwin, 1950.

Lutz, E.G. *The Motion Picture Cameraman*. New York: Charles Scribner's & Sons, 1927.

Macbean, L. C. *Kinematograph Studio Technique*. London: Pitman, 1922.

Macgowan, Kenneth. *Behind the Screen*. New York: Delacorte, 1965.

Madrid, Francisco. *50 Años de Cine*. Buenos Aires: Ediciones Tridente, 1946.

Malkiewicz, Kris. *Film Lighting*. New York: Fireside, 1992.

Maltin, Leonard. *The Art of the Cinematographer*. New York: Dover, 1978.

Manvell, Roger. *The Cinema 1950*. Harmondsworth, Middlesex: Penguin, 1950.

Mareschal, Georges. *Les Techniques Cinématographiques*. Paris: Idhec, 1966.

Marion, Dennis, ed. *Le Cinéma par Ceux Qui le Font*. Paris: Arthème Fayard, 1949.

Mascelli, Joseph V. *The Five C's of Cinematography.* Hollywood, CA: Cine/Graphic, 1965.

_____. *Mascelli's Cine Workbook.* Hollywood, CA: Cine/Graphic, 1973.

McKay, Herbert C. *The Handbook of Motion Picture Photography.* New York: Falk, 1927.

Mendez-Leite, Fernando. *Secretos del Cine.* Barcelona: Juventud, 1950.

Millerson, Gerald. *The Technique of Lighting for Television and Motion Pictures.* London: Focal Press, 1972.

Mitry, Jean. *Dictionnaire du Cinéma.* Paris: Larousse, 1963.

Moreno, Juan J. *Curso Técnico Cinematográfico.* Instituto Cinematográfico Argentino, circa 1940.

Nash, P. *The Color Film.* London: Oxford University Press, 1937.

Naumburg, Nancy, ed. *Silence! On Tourne.* Paris: Editions Mondiales, 1938.

*Il Neorealismo Italiano.* Venezia: Mostra Internazionale di Venezia, 1951.

Nilsen, Vladimir. *The Cinema as a Graphic Art.* New York: Hill & Wang, 1959.

Nykvist, Sven. *Culto a la Luz.* Madrid: Ediciones del Imán, AEC, 1997.

Noble, Peter, ed. *British Film Yearbook: 1947–1948.* London: Skelton-Robinson, 1948.

_____. *The Fabulous Orson Welles.* London: Hutchinson, 1956.

Noble, Ronnie. *Shoot First! Assignments of a Newsreel Camera-man.* London: Pan Books, 1955.

Offenhauser, William H., Jr. *16-mm Sound Motion Pictures.* New York: Interscience, 1949.

Paladini, Aldo. *Guerra e Pace.* N.p.: Capelli, 1956.

Pérez-Millán, Juan Antonio. *Pascualino de Santis: El Resplandor de la Penunbra.* Valladolid: Semana Internacional del Cine, 1993.

Petrie, Duncan. *The British Cinematographer.* London: British Film Institute, 1996.

Powell, Michael. *Une Vie dans le Cinéma.* Arles: Actes Sud, 1997.

*La Prise de Vues dans la Formation Professionnelle de Cinéma et de Télévision.* Paris: IDHEC, 1960.

Quigley, Martin, Jr., ed. *New Screen Techniques.* New York: Quigley, 1953.

Ríos-Enriquez, Héctor. *Técnica Fotográfica en el Cine.* Caracas: Conac, 1979.

Raimondo-Souto, H. Mario. *Manual del Cámara de Cine y Vídeo.* Madrid: Cátedra, 1997.

_____. *The Technique of the Motion Picture Camera.* London: Focal Press, 1982.

Ramelli, A. Cassi. *Edifici per gli Spettacoli.* Milano: A.Vallardi Ed., 1948.

Reinert, Charles, and Francesco Passinetti. *Filmlexicon.* Milano: Filmeuropa, 1948.

Riefenstahl, Leni. *Memorias.* Barcelona: Editorial Lumen, 1991.

Rippo, Gisouè Gino. *Cine-Tecnica.* Torino: Lavagnolo, 1940.

Ritsko, Alan J. *Lighting for Location Motion Pictures.* New York: Van Nostrand Reinhold, 1979.

Roberts, Kenneth H., and Win Sharples, Jr. *A Primer for Film-Making.* New York: Pegasus, 1971.

Rose, Jackson J. *American Cinematographer Handbook and Reference Guide.* Hollywood, CA: n.p., 1953.

Rotha, Paul. *Documentary Diary.* New York: Hill and Wang, 1973.

_____. *Documentary Film.* London: Faber, 1952.

_____, and Roger Manvell. *Movie Parade, 1888–1949: A Pictorial Survey of World Cinema.* London: The Studio, 1950.

Rovin, Jeff. *Special Effects.* New York: Barnes, 1977.

*RTNDA Television Newsfilm Standards Manual.* New York: Time-Life, 1964.

Ryan, Rod, ed. *American Cinematographer Manual.* Hollywood: ASC Press, 1993.

Sadoul, Georges. *Le Cinéma Pendant la Guerre 1939–1945.* Paris: Denoël, 1954.

_____. *Diccionario del Cine.* Madrid: Itsmo, 1977.

_____. *Dictionnaire des Filmes.* Paris: Editions du Seuil. 1965.

_____. *Historia del Cine.* Buenos Aires: Losange, 1960.

_____. *L'Invention du Cinéma:1832-1897.* Paris: Denoël, 1948.

Salles Gomes, P.E. *Jean Vigo.* London: Faber & Faber, 1999.

Samuelson, David, W. *Motion Picture Camera and Lighting Equipment.* London: Focal Press, 1977.

_____. *Motion Picture Camera Data.* London: Focal Press. 1979.

_____. *Motion Picture Camera Techniques.* London: Focal Press, 1978.

Schaefer, Dennis, and Larry Salvato. *Masters of Light.* Berkeley: University of California Press, 1985.

Scotland John. *The Talkies.* London: Crosby Lockwood and Son, 1930.

Seeber, Guido. *Der Praktische Kammeramann.* Berlin: Lichtbilbuehne, 1927.

_____, and G.V. Mendel. *Theorie und Praxis der Kinematographischen Aufnahmetechnik.* Berlin: Lichtbilbuehne, 1927.

Shirer, William. L. *Berlin Diary,* London: Hamish Hamilton, 1942.

Silver, Alain, and James Ursini. *David Lean and His Films.* Los Angeles: Silman-James Press, 1974.

Smith, Albert E. *Two Reels and a Crank.* New York: Doubleday, 1952.

Smither, Roger. *First World War U-Boat.* London: Imperial War Museum; Lloyd's Register, 2000.

_____, and Wolfgang Klaue. *Newsreels in Film Archives.* Wiltshire: Flicks Books, 1996.

SMPTE Committee. *Control Techniques in Film Processing.* New York: SMPTE, 1960.

Spottiswoode, Raymond. *Film and Its Techniques.* Berkeley and Los Angeles: University of California Press, 1951.

_____, ed. *The Focal Encyclopedia of Film and Television*

*Techniques.* London & New York: Focal Press, 1969.

Sussex, Elizabeth. *The Rise and Fall of British Documentary.* Berkeley: University of California Press, 1975.

Taylor, Deems, Marcelene Peterson, and Bryan Hale. *A Pictorial History of the Movies.* New York: Simon and Shuster, 1943.

Taylor, Theodore. *People Who Make Movies.* New York: Manor Books, 1967.

Turner, George E., ed. *The ASC Treasury of Visual Effects.* Hollywood, CA: ASC Press, 1983.

_____. *The Cinema of Adventure, Romance and Terror.* Hollywood, CA: The ASC Press, 1989.

Uccello, Paolo. *Dizionario della Tecnica Cinematografica e della Fotografia.* Roma: Edizione Cinespettacolo, 1950.

U.S. Bureau of Aeronautics. *Technical Publications.* Washington: Government Printing Office, 1942.

U.S. Bureau of Naval Personnel. *Photographer's Mate 1&C & Mate 2.* Memphis: n.p., 1962.

U.S. Navy. *Optico 3,* La Habana: n.p., 1955.

U.S. Navy Training Courses. *Photography Vol I & 2.* Washington: Government Printing Office, 1947.

Valera, Juan A. *Arte y Técnica Cinematográfica y Televisión.* Buenos Aires: Albatros, 1944.

Villegas-López, Manuel. *Cine Francés.* Buenos Aires: Nova, 1947.

Vincent, Carl. *Storia del Cinema.* Cernusco Sul Naviglio: Garzanti, 1949.

Vivié, Jean. *Cinema e Televisione a Colori.* Roma: Edizione dell Ateneo, 1956.

_____. *Historique et Développement de la Technique Cinématographique.* Paris: BPI, 1944.

Walker, Joseph, and Juanita Walker. *The Light on Her Face.* Hollywood: ASC Press, 1984.

Watts, Stephen, ed. *La Technique du Film.* Paris: Payot, 1939.

Weinstock, A. (Gérant). *Le Tout–Cinéma–1952.* Paris: Société Nouvelle des Editions Guilhamou, 1953–54.

Weise, Harald. *Die Kinematographische Kamera.* Viena: Springer, 1955.

Wheeler, Leslie J. *Principles of Cinematography.* London: Fountain Press, 1965.

White, David Manning, and Richard Averson. *El Arma del Celuloide .* Buenos Aires: Marymar, 1974.

Wood, Alan. *Mr. Rank: A Study of J. Arthur Rank and British Films.* London: Hodder and Stoughton, 1952.

Yellin, David G. *Special.* New York: Macmillan, 1972.

Young, Freddie, *Seventy Light Years.* London: Faber and Faber, 1999.

_____, and Paul Petzold. *The Work of the Motion Picture Cameraman.* London: Hastings House, 1972.

# Video Documentaries

Bellon, Yannick, *Varsovie, Quand Même,* Procinex, 1954.

Brownlow, Kevin, and David Gill, producers. *Cinema Europe–The Other Hollywood.* Image Entertainment, 1995.

# Index

365